THE JEWISH MIND

THE
JEWISH MIND

by

Gerald Abrahams

חֲבָלִים נָפְלוּ לִי בַּנְּעִמִים : אַף נַחֲלָת שָׁפְרָה עָלָי.

Psalm XVI, 6

BEACON · PRESS

CONTENTS

Contents

NOTE ON TRANSLITERATION

I HAVE, in transliterating Hebrew words, used, roughly, the Davidson technique: but I have varied it in a few particulars. The Q is not used. Also I transliterate the Komats as O not A. My reason for this, and other divergences from the scholastic orthodox, has been my desire to accommodate, not only the Hebrew of the texts, but the Hebrew that is used as part of Yiddish. Let me add that I have occasionally found the conventional modes of transliteration cramping, and have made empirical departures.

For those who are not acquainted with the abbreviation, I would mention that T.B., in a reference, stands for TALMUD BABLI.

The vocal pronunciation used is what is called the "Lithuanian".

PREFACE TO THE AMERICAN EDITION

When the barbarians of an age other than ours burned alive the saintly Chanina ben Teradion, shrouded in his Sefer Torah, the martyr bore witness from the flames: " The parchment is burning, but the letters are soaring aloft." How often, how very often, in Jewish history has the parchment, which is the people, been destroyed; and from the embers has the spirit risen and survived to inspire the scribes of other parchments, Jewish and non-Jewish, and to inspire new and fresh cultures with old, eternal aspirations.

Certainly the relatively new parchment of the Anglo-Saxon lands is heavily inscribed with the letters of the Jewish spirit. Quintessentially, so is the best tradition of the United States of America, expressing the ethos of exile; for these states originated in an exile, and their human values have continuously and repeatedly been enriched by the accession of other exiles. Understanding this, it was a Jewish poet, Emma Lazarus, who saw in the statue-borne beacon, not a gaudy symbol of triumph, but a welcoming lamp guiding to a golden door.

To the refugee from tyranny and terror every door of escape seems to be a golden door. Many of the doors open onto disillusion, even onto paths that lead to other tyrannies. But if any trust can be laid in the continuities of history; then, when allowance is made for all the cyclical changes of evolution, or — to apply modern terminology — its short-circuits and its feedbacks, the Jew has reason to believe that here is one dwelling from which some at least of the old and hideous spectres have been exorcised.

Into this utterance let no one read fulsome praise or the attribution of improbable virtues. From the detached, and to that extent unbiased, standpoint of one whose nearest approach to the U.S.A. has been along the lines of thought, it is not expected that there should flourish in that land any strong growth of the philo-Semitism that young Jews dream about, or that there should not flourish any of the anti-Semitism without which the older Jew would not recognize his world. In the United States, as elsewhere, there is, still, more acceptance by the brain than sympathy of the heart. But one thing seems to be certain: More than anywhere else in the world, except in the State of Israel, it is probable that in the United States the alien immigrant and his children, whether they assimilate or not, will never be treated as the barely tolerated recipients of a strained charity. Xenophobia is not known in the U. S. A., and the subtle class distinctions of a classless society may emphasize the social discrimination that Jews have suffered everywhere. But there is no suggestion, in the mass, and practically no political scope for the suggestion, that the Jew is unwanted in the United States. In that respect he resembles the refugees of many nations and many creeds that have found cities of refuge on the American plains. Perhaps no one person likes the newcomers, but the nation as a whole endeavours to love them. To what degree they deserve to be cherished depends on their own works and ways. This is true of individuals and of groups. Whether, then, they be regarded as five and a half million individuals, with no more unity than a common origin; or whether they be regarded, in more realistic terms, as something of a group; the Jews, in this environment, are free to prove whether or not they deserve to be highly esteemed. It is believed that Jewry, in fact and in high proportion, has made rich contributions to the happiness, progress, and welfare of this land.

It was an English Jew, Israel Zangwill, who described the United States as a melting pot. He conceived it as a syn-

thetic process in which differences are fused into uniformity. I believe, and hope, that that conception is an
exaggeration of one aspect of the truth. No land should
want uniformity, other than the denominator which is acceptance of the basic postulates of the civilisation that the
land supports. When the uniformity demanded is highly
specific, and such as can only be spread by force, we are
back in the lands of uniforms and tyranny.

The draftsmen of the American Constitution took it,
from the learning of the best Judaeo-Christian tradition,
that men were created equal. They did not say: identically
similar. Moreover, having adopted as basic this Judaeo-
Christian truth, they held no expectation that specific
religions would cease to communicate their particular and
peculiar messages; nor did they desire that particular cultures, particular literatures or particular languages should
cease to flourish in the new commonwealth. From that
time onward there has developed and flourished an individual, recognisable, American culture. Let the fact that
the hymn of the Republic is Hebraic, Biblical, be disregarded; still America has, in the spirit of that culture, protected and preserved other cultures. That, for bitter example, before World War II, German newspapers published in the 1930s in New York held greater circulations
than the *Berliner Tageblatt* was, perhaps, a condition of the
contemporary re-emergence of whatever real German culture may have survived from beneath the waves of the
flooding Teutonic barbarism.

Analogously, civilised Jewry is welcomed in the U.S., is
acclimatised there, and can on that soil express all the aspects of its trimillennial thought. One need not seek out
names from the many individual Jews who have helped to
make American history; Jews who fought alongside George
Washington, or with, or against, Abraham Lincoln. The
land of those great men is receptive of Jewry because
American culture, like the culture of Britain, owes so much
to the Scriptures; also because the best American con-

3

ceptions of work and worth are precisely the bourgeois, urbane — civilised — standards that Jews have helped so much to spread.

Individual Jews matter, of course. But in the long perspectives, there is no need for individual portraiture. That Great Britain received from the Confederate South a great jurist is one of a myriad of interesting facts. More important are the stories of masses. What is now the United States of America, on a continent discovered by a sort of refugee Jew, became, from the sixteenth century onwards, a refuge for all exiles from persecution. Inherently, then, the domestic tradition is a better one than that of tolerance. Tolerance implies that there is something to tolerate. The American conception is of right, not of sufferance. When, therefore, in the nineteenth century, Czarist Russia caused its Jews to seek refuge, America received them with no questions asked. And in the U. S. A. they multiplied as in a lighter Goshen. Nor was it very different when in the twentieth century Central Europe drove out its Jews. To America, at least, the refugee could say: In your land I can be a traditional citizen.

So an America, compact of the descendants of many different national and social groups, accepts diversity as part of its riches. Among these riches, let it be ventured, the treasures of Jewry — the inestimable, unworldly treasures of Jewry — are great accessions, more important than the achievements of individual plutocrats.

Of the Jewish contribution to American culture, let Americans write. We know that American idiom and American humour have been influenced by the Yiddish. But what I have in mind are profounder influences, harder to describe. That they obtain is a fact that justifies an attempt to tell the American public — as many writers are doing now — what the Jew has to offer to the world spirit.

In this book I do not attempt, whether in the European or in any other context, to define what exactly is the

Jewish element — " the extra soul " — that the Jew adds to his environment. The principles of Relativism, and the principles of Indeterminacy and Uncertainty that Jewish and non-Jewish scientists have found in physics, hardly compare in difficulty with the subtleties that thwart any attempt to define, or even describe, this historic entity, which is the oldest surviving function of cultural unity in space-time.

If religion in some form or degree, is, as I believe, inseparable from the analysis of Jewry and from any phase of its history, the manifestations do not lend themselves to easy classification.

But one thing I think is certain. Some ethical significance, some moral force, attaches to Jewish history and Jewish continuity, if only by reason of the fact that Jewish existence owes something to the world morality that it has helped to create. When, then, we experience, as we do now, world-waves of triumphant nihilism; when, even among the best spirits, there are manifestations of a distressing ethical neutrality; when people cannot decide firmly that the shield used by a defender of the good is not to be equated with the panoply of force that is donned by the tyrant; then the Jew, however hard he tries intellectually to betray himself, shows to the world a being whose survival is evidence of the abiding presence of an ultimate force that makes for righteousness.

Because of the strong human and ethical implications of Jewish survival, I think that those analysts are wrong who draw curves of increasing nationalism and decreasing creeds, of increasing materialism and decreasing spirituality, and draw conclusions — unhappy word — about world, or American, or Diaspora Jewry. They extrapolate, I think, ungrounded laws and wrong conceptions of continuity. Whether in the orthodox atmosphere of narrow areas, or whether in the " emancipated " atmosphere of other narrow areas, Jewish life proper dies hard. While it lives it can inspire the world with all its old impulses. For this is the group from which springs the vital belief that man, as a moral being, is to some extent the arbiter of his own fate. Of the classical conception of men trapped by the gods (as was Oedipus), a fly to wanton boys, a function of blind chance, I venture to say that not even a Jewish atheist reconciles himself to that world-view. If he does not pursue righteousness himself, every Jew is the descendant of someone who pursued righteousness. Therefore Jewry survives as ethical force — and as the protest of history against the denial of distinctions between good and bad, right and wrong, sacred and profane.

To the Western world, the Jewish contribution, conscious or unconscious, is important because the Western world is bemused in that process of materialisation which goes with the great developments and rapid acquisitions of material processes and powers. In the materialistic order there are those who have no words of religion or axiology in their basic vocabularies. But Jewish life is not like that, and American life is not yet like that.

Relevantly to the theme of this book, let it be repeated that basic American culture is a Biblical culture, in the heart of which Jewish life finds a congenial nacreous matrix. America, even with the great ethical values stated minimally, is yet a high development of the type of urban civilisation in which good Jews are citizens. America is also a land which, although it must develop long before high culture is the property of all its inhabitants, is yet devoted to that high culture; and its great *Kulturmenschen* have made their mark in history. By reason of that valuation, Americans — non-Jewish as well as Jewish — value learning and value Jewish learning. When the parchments of other lands have been destroyed, the letters may well have soared into this sector of the firmament. Acting on that thought, the writer of this book commits his study in the mental and spiritual aspects of Jewry to an audience that he believes to be, by all American traditions — including the traditions of American Jewry — receptive and sympathetic.

6

The American Gentile is closely enough associated with the history of Jewry to be interested in the spiritual, as well as the physical, vicissitudes and problems of Jewry. The American Jew, believed at this moment of time to be reacting from assimilation, is anxious to think more deeply about the inheritance that so many have neglected.

Those Jews give nothing to America who sacrifice their special pattern of life to a materialistic uniformity. The citizen of New York can be as practical, as technological, as preoccupied with the utilities, proximate and remote, as any citizen of Moscow. Indeed at those extremes of politics there is a meeting of standards, an acceptance of common tastes. Let them ask: What is to distinguish Western culture from the mass-produced utilitarianism of the modern East? The Avatars of Vishnu-land are lowering and uninspiring. From the West we seek light. Only some such colour, some such music, as derives from the ancient and tried cultures of the Occident can preserve any group from the social entropy which is always taking place, as standards give place to averages, maxima to minima.

If those trends to utter materialism develop further, it will be left to the votaries of a few forgotten sects to keep alive the memory of a world which knew more than physical comfort. When the masses average themselves out on the plane of bolshevist (that means majority) acquiescence, some unsatisfied minds will go exploring and searching for the old strongholds of intellectual and spiritual aristocracy.

If they find letters on the forgotten parchments that they disinter, those ancient symbols — Hebrew or otherwise — may well be evidences of a spirit that the Jew, the Jewish Jew, has endeavoured to conjure from his warm past and to project into the cold skies of hopelessness, where men wander hopelessly, to move creatively over the uniformity of the undifferentiated void.

7

PREFACE

THIS book may find itself described as an inquiry into the meaning of a word. Such a criticism I should not resent, for many very good books amount, in the last reckoning, to the life-work of some grammarians, and their mausolea.

I have, however, picked out a difficult word. The term "Jew" is a challenge to Semantics as well as to Semitics. Here it is not a question of stating a few facts about the way in which a word came to be used: nor of the clarification of a few ambiguities in the use of it. This is a word impossible to define or describe except in some narrow context: but when it is found in some such context only one aspect of the word will be under consideration.

This principle of uncertainty is enhanced by the fact that the concept Jew is a living, changing concept; a modern idea, yet continuous in mysterious ways with very old ideas that wonderfully survive in all their derivatives.

To the question: What is the Jew? must, therefore, be added the question: What was the Jew? or What has the Jew been? In the exploration of those aspects further questions develop. Is there, perhaps, a real Jew, distinguishable from a nominal Jew? We shall find, working from that point of view, that the question is not only, "What does the word Jew mean?" but "What should the word mean?" and, speculating, "What will it come to mean?" At that stage we discover that we are exploring complex ideals rather than simple ideas, and pursuing them through time, not isolating them with reference to some place. Here, then, is not an abstract universal, but something in the nature of that concrete universal which cannot be fully apprehended until one apprehends the whole universe.

So the word remains indefinable, "until Elijah comes", or until the end of time—whichever shall be sooner!

What we have at this moment is the privilege of participating in, enjoying, and studying a symphony; a symphony in which player and listener are part of the music: a necessarily—and happily—unfinished symphony. Evidently no writer can record this. But if I have succeeded in conveying to any reader, Jewish or non-Jewish, some appreciation of the values and experiences that suffuse the time-space of Jewry, I shall have achieved the performance of a worth-while task.

GERALD ABRAHAMS

I am greatly indebted for advice and criticisms, tendered to me at proof-stage, by Rabbi Dr. Isidore Epstein, and other learned and accomplished friends. I would mention Rabbi Nemeth, Rabbi Wolf, Dr. Marcus Goldberg, Dr. Otto Eisner, and Mr. Harold Nagley—all of Liverpool: and Miss Shula Doniach and Dr. Lionel Stoll of London. Rabbi Z. Plitnick of Liverpool has clarified many issues of Halacha for me.

To these I offer my thanks.

FOREWORD TO A JEWISH BOOK
IN ENGLISH

Dieu fit choix de Cyrus avant qu'il vît le jour. (RACINE)

THREE hundred years have now passed since, uninvited but undisguised, a remnant of Jewry entered Cromwell's England, and there initiated one of the completest processes of integration, one of the closest symbioses with Gentile life and culture, that has ever been achieved by unassimilated Israel in any arc of the Diaspora.

In the long history of Jewry the vicissitudes of the group in England are among the strangest and most interesting. Thus we may surmise that, had the printing press been earlier invented in Europe, we would not be lacking in evidence that the Hebrew speaking, Hebrew writing, Jews of pre-Expulsion England achieved standards of Jewish culture in their few centuries that were not equalled here until the Yeshivoth of Lithuania and White Russia sent their emigrants to England nearly a thousand years later. There is reason to believe that Manasseh ben Israel, who led the Jews back, stands rather lower on the ascending planes of Halacha and Drash than did the Payetan, Isaac, who perished at York, or the Tosafist, Tam,[1] who was killed at

---

[1] Jacob of Orleans (d. 1189): not Jacob ben Meir (1100–1171), who is known as Rabbenu Tam, and is the greatest of the Tosafists (*see* p. 156 *infra*). (The attribution Tam, "simple heart", is frequently and piously added to the name Jacob.) As for Manasseh ben Israel, he was not original except in some "lost Tribes of Israel" speculation. His *Vindiciae*

the coronation of the Lionheart. We know also that the Jews of Norman England were well esteemed: that their uncorroborated oaths were accepted against many: that their legal learning was absorbed into Gentile Law; that their Starroth (Documents) gave a name to an institution.[1] Yet, for all their distinction, perhaps partly because of their distinction, they suffered a life—and a death—much less happy than that of their less distinguished successors. Explanations of this are all too obvious. Was that Latin land England? Let us grant that this pioneer of the modern, erastian, republic was then at a primitive stage of its evolution—a stage only recently recapitulated by many European states. Suffice it to say that, though, in the later island of Cromwell, Manasseh ben Israel failed to realize his Messianic dreams, yet his followers found a new world: found in the Bible-conscious seventeenth-century England a nation vastly different from the feudal, Vulgate-ignorant, savage crusading aggregate of the thirteenth century. They found no ease, no obvious path to Zion. But here the subtler Providence of the Goluth was operating to provide the People of the Book with an ideal partner in a great elective affinity.

". . . who speak the tongue
That Shakespeare spake; the faith and morals hold
Which Milton held."

Few of the leaders of England in the seventeenth century can have been clearly aware that they were the custodians of a culture so sympathetic to the Jewish genius that their spiritual successors were destined to be accused of Hebraism. At the outset, even the unique Cromwell was unable to conjure in his followers any enthusiasm, or to extract from

---

Judaeorum is conventional apologetic. But very useful is *El Conciliador*, as to which *see* note on p. 16 *infra*.

[1] Star Chamber. A theory adopted by John Richard Green and other English historians.

them some formal invitation to a group that he valued shrewdly, in the material as well as in the spiritual scale. Let it be written down as a miracle that he so failed, for undoubtedly any formal promulgation of welcome to the Jews would have been revoked, with all his other works, at the Restoration. But the communication that he received (from the Judges) and transmitted, to the effect that the presence of Jews in England contravened no Common or Statute Law (their expulsion having been by executive act), this communication granted much more than its words disclose.[1] This finding unconsciously embodies all the principles that militate against discrimination: principles that may be said to constitute a Biblical-Jewish element in British Protestantism.

Externally regarded it is a statement of tolerance, and tolerance in its very nature begs a great question. Tolerance implies that there is something to be tolerated; in this case a Jewish problem, or, more accurately, a Gentile problem, the problem of curing an endemic hate. But just as many great pieties develop from ulterior motives (as, in the Hebrew phrase, one moves from LO LESHEMO to LESHEMO[2]), so out of tolerance can develop complete acceptance. The sensitive casuist recoils from expressions like "not on sufferance but as of right". That such a

[1] It is now maintained, by that considerable historian, Dr. Cecil Roth, that the Council of State gave Cromwell a formal authority to allow the presence of Jews in England: but that the page containing the minute of that authority was later torn from the record. However, by 1660 there were *faits accomplis*. Already in the Robles case (1656 et seq.) a Portuguese Jew had (implicitly) been allowed by the Privy Councis to stay in London, and there were many Jews there. Incidentally, it il known that later (1680) the Privy Council considered, *and rejected*, a proposal to create a London ghetto, with a legal organization of its own.

[2] "Not for its own sake" to "for its own sake". The Rabbis held that acts of value should be done even for ulterior motive: they would later be done for their own sakes (e.g. T. B. Pesachim 58a).

13

proposition requires statement implies its falsity. But eventually, when nothing requires to be said, then tolerance has transcended itself and become friendship. In England that friendship evolving, with the intellectual affinities that have strengthened it, has made this civilization into a soil for unique blossoms.

Such a life has rarely been vouchsafed to Jewry. Not in the supposedly higher culture of Moorish Spain (where Maimonides lived among Moslem Marranos); nor in that Germany of the *Aufklärung* (where the children of Mendelssohn were apostates), nor in Revolutionary France (where Constitution was first shown to mean less than political conscience): not in any of these cultures has Israel been successfully symbiotic. Occasional high syntheses have occurred—embodied, for example, in Lusitanian Abrabanel, secular statesman and Rabbinic homilist,[1] who ranks in Jewish culture above Disraeli, for the one adorned Israel whilst the other used Israel as an ornament.[2] But whereas Iberia and Lusitania found Jewish culture intolerable, the cultural matrix in which Disraeli was an "alien patriot" has not expelled its irritant pearls. Surprisingly, the less sensitive atmosphere has proved the better home for the exotic. Blessed are the phlegmatic. Once their hostility is conquered or forgotten, their friendship is permanent. Thus only in the Anglo-Saxon lands has Jacob of the Haggadah, seeking to live in peace, found something better than the descent into Egypt. And only those lands can reasonably be trusted never to produce a Pharaoh that knows not Joseph.

[1] Dom Isaac Abrabanel (1437–1508), Treasurer to Alfonso V of Portugal, and author of "Sources of Salvation", etc. His sons, of whom the best known is Dom Judah, also achieved great distinction in the religious and political fields.

[2] His valuation of Jewish culture did not cause him strenuously to advocate the abolition of the Christian form of oath that kept elected Jews out of the Commons until 1858. Later Jewish members, not requiring Baptism, have been equally indifferent to Jewish causes.

Of what Jews and Gentiles do for each other in the political-economic spheres others have written, or will write.[1] Here the subject is Jacob rather than Joseph. In three centuries the English of Shakespeare has been moulded to express the morals of Milton. English is a Biblical language, and, incidentally, by reason of its verbal weight and its concrete imagery, better fitted for the translation of the Old Testament than any other European tongue.[2] English thinking, traditionally, is Bible-conscious. Much English music (from the time of Handel and earlier[3]) has been inspired by Biblical thought. English poets have relived the Psalms. Thus from English sources there has sprung a literature which is "on the Bible" even if not about the Bible. Nor has English Gentile learning been unproductive in works of scholarship concerned with Jewish texts and Jewish institutions.

Because of these things, and because England has favoured the maintenance of Jewish education among Jews, the latter

[1] Suffice it here to say that the demands made by Britain on its citizens are such that every Jew is happy to comply with them. Jewish enthusiasm makes its contribution, therefore, in worthy terms. While it was possible for a Jew to give to Britain a theory of benevolent aristocracy, it has not been possible for any Jew to do for British intellect such mischief as Auerbach did in Germany with his doctrine of BLUBO (Blut und Boden) that has cost so many Jewish (and Gentile) lives. Similarly, since there have been no Junkers or Nazis in Britain, there have been no Thyssens.

[2] It is commonplace now that English idiom is indebted to the translators of the Bible for many expressions. Apart from literary ideas, such as "the pitcher going too often to the well", "wheels within wheels", "a tale that is told", "the wilderness blossomed like the rose", etc., we have conventional phrases like "a drop in the bucket", "apple of the eye", "a brand from the burning", "a lamb (or, an ox) to the slaughter"; (inaccurately) "a voice crying in the wilderness" (*see* p. 96 *infra*); also Shibboleth, and the "sparks that fly upward". This, incidentally, may be unfounded. Luther (following Rashi) renders Job V.7: "as the storm birds take wing"—a more "probable" rendering.

[3] Certainly from the times of Tallis and Dunstable.

have been able to express their thinking here, and to unfold their researches in English, without any feeling of embarrassment. Nor need it be feared that the medium is wrong. On the other hand, that the medium is right is evidenced by the presence, in excellent English translation, of many of the most important Jewish classics, including the Babylonian Talmud. Indeed the first translation of Maimonides' *Guide for the Perplexed* into English, by the hand of an immigrant scholar, is more reliable than Ibn Tibbon's rendering, into Hebrew, of the original Arabic.

In this way the Anglo-Saxon lands have become places where Jewish scholarship is normal. Let it be granted that nowhere in the world—not even in Israel—is any academy likely to recapture the abnormally high standard of Talmudic learning that was achieved in the great Yeshivoth at various periods, and especially, during recent centuries, in East Europe.[1] But, as a sorry compensation for great disasters, the West has inherited the smouldering embers of the Eastern learning and is able to revive some flames, producing in our hearths, not perhaps the intense gleam of Iluyism, but the lambent glow which emanates from scientific collation and systematic exposition.[2]

Since that study is now taking place in England and in English on a large scale, no apology is required for the

[1] Evidence of the high standard is strikingly afforded by the Rabbi of Rozhnoi, who escaped from White Russia during the war, and, arriving in England with no knowledge of English or Latin, became, in a couple of years, a master of the Roman Law, and has since written in English an interesting essay comparing the Jewish, Roman and English systems (*Three Great Systems of Jurisprudence*. Kagan).

[2] It is, perhaps, fitting that the Jews were led back into England by Manasseh ben Israel: essentially a collator, rather than an original thinker. His best work *El Conciliador*, written in Spanish, musters Jewish learning on all the apparent contradictions that can be found in Holy Writ. Translated into English over a century ago, the book has been esteemed by the English clergy.

writing in English of any work of scholarship, or scholarly work, or less ambitious essay, on topics that belong to Hebrew and Yiddish. On the other hand, because the life of the Jew is so emancipated in England, it happens that many Jews here are not, generally, so well informed as to their language, their history, and as to their own spiritual treasures, as were those to whom the world conceded nothing else. For those to whom the paths of the stars are more familiar than the ways of Nehardaa, some English studies in Hebraica are desirable and necessary. Also it it believed that among the English-speaking Gentile peoples there is abundant interest in the life and thinking of the group that has carried the Bible through two millennia. They do not seek apologia for the Jews, nor are they here offered any apologetic. They wish to know about the thought and life of those who have rejoiced and suffered as the custodians of the "lively oracles of God": to be told what the oral traditions are and how they are realized—if, indeed, they are realized—in the lives of present-day Jewry. What they are offered here is the author's appreciation of certain thoughts that he thinks are Jewish thoughts; certain standards that he holds to be Jewish standards; and a few reflections on the success, or failure, of these thoughts and these standards in penetrating and influencing the lower levels that are ordinary life.

To the Gentile and Jewish readers who are unaware of it, let it be said that Jewish learning, from which citations are made here, is of an extent considerably greater than, say, the Graeco-Roman classics. It is a deep and vast ocean which scholars have navigated according to their skill, and which some great minds have plumbed and charted. The author claims only to have bathed off some of the gentler beaches. Evidently, then, this can only be an "essay" of limited range. But, as it is said in the Ethics of the Fathers, the fact that one cannot complete an undertaking does not justify the abandonment of it.

The material has been absorbed from atmosphere of learning rather than derived from specific sources. A debt is owed by the author to many exponents of Jewish learning, including some very distinguished ones. These are not mentioned by name, because it is not desired to associate them with pronouncements and opinions which may deviate from orthodoxy, religious or scientific. A debt is owed to family traditions of learning, and to many friends and acquaintances whose utterances have stimulated movements of thought. If one may quote again the Ethics of the Fathers without being thought ignorant (a frequent Jewish fallacy this!) let it be said: "Who is wise: he who learns from all men: as it is written. From all my teachers I have gathered understanding."[1] But let none of them be suspect of heresy on this account![2]

[1] Psalm CXIX.99. Note how the Rabbinic "peshat" varies (with modesty) from the translation adopted in the Authorized Version. ("I have more understanding than all my teachers; for thy testimonies are my meditation".)

[2] As a final answer to anyone who suggests that this book is written in the wrong language, I would respectfully quote the reply given by the poet Else Lasker-Schüler, when refusing to allow her *Hebraische Balladen* to be translated into Hebrew. She said: "They *are* in Hebrew."

CHAPTER ONE

IN SEARCH OF JEWISH IDENTITY

THIS is a group that has lived in time and found no place. Nomadic in its pre-literary origins, and nomadic in a deeper, crueller, sense during most of its recorded experience, this folk is a creation of history, not of geography.

Barely four centuries, and those unhappy ones, compass a Jewish attempt—a precocious effort before the dawn of politics—to constitute a theocratic nation settled in a land. More than twenty later centuries have not exhausted the patterned and melancholy saga of a people in exile and a God in exile.

During the longer period, which is, in perspective, the substantial period of Jewish endurance, identity has been preserved without the aid of a national territory. They were called out of Egypt, and out of Babylon, and out of Persia: only to go "astray in the ways of life". They experienced reality in their exiles and oppressions. But the Jews that returned with Ezra were dwellers in a phantasm—"as those that dream". The kingdom that they eventually built was an unreality, a political schizoid, in which spirit was not in harmony with behaviour and there was no unity.

In that period the communal cohesion that had been inspired by the magnanimity of Cyrus and Darius was soon dissipated, as pagan culture elicited from the over-intelligent Jews their latent individualism. The fiery, prophetic spirit of Ezra-Nehemia, and later the Maccabi, could not burn long among the fleshpots of Jerusalem. So it had been in earlier days, when the spirit of Joshua, Gideon, Samuel and Elijah had failed to prevent a prosperous people from "settling on its lees". The ancient pattern is a tragic one. Time and again, when the people are under pressure, Jewish zealotry flames forth to prevent some ancient or modern empire from making a desert in Israel and calling it peace. The resistance succeeds. Then Jeshurun waxes fat again and kicks. Comes the invading conqueror, and the last revolt—such a rising as Bar Cochba's, *absit omen*—collapses in unrelieved catastrophe.[1]

After that the Ghetto, in many and various places and conditions, and at all times.[2] Ghetto identity is unpolitical, yet it is more substantial than the Kingdom of Herod, and more substantial than whatever political reality there was in the medieval kingdom of the Khazars, where Judaism flourished for two centuries as a national religion, like a ghost in an alien dwelling[3]. In ghetto life, which has moved

[1] Second century c.e. Revolt against Hadrian. This Emperor forbade the practice of Judaism (Rabbi Akiva was killed for refusing to accept the decree), and prevented the rebuilding of the Temple. Eventually he razed Jerusalem. Little is known of the rebel leader, Bar Cochba. This form of his name (there are others) can mean "son of a star".

[2] The word Ghetto came to mean "Street" (as in Juden Gasse in Teutonia). The word may be a corruption of Giudeica. (Gietto, a cannon foundry in Venice, has also been suggested.) The change from soft to hard "g" may be accounted for by the absence of "j" from Hebrew and Yiddish.

[3] The Khazars were a tribe, of Magyar affinity, active and powerful for some three centuries between the Balkans and the Caucasus. In the eighth or ninth century they were converted, by their chief, to Judaism. Eventually their power was broken by Russian and Turkish forces. A quasi-Jewish group in the Crimea (Krimchatki) is said to be the relics of what was once a kingdom. Judah Halévy wrote his great

from Mesopotamia through Africa, Spain, France, Germany, Poland, Turkey and back to Mesopotamia, there has been a discernible, permanent, cohesion, the cohesion of defence, only disintegrating under extreme pressure or (more rarely) in complete freedom.

In the ghetto political aspiration became sublimated into personal Messianic hopes: but group solidarity was perpetuated by the presence of enemies almost permanently at the gate.

The pattern of the story, and of the group whose story it is, can be described as a dramatic conflict between personal dedication and assimilation, until (and even after) the social changes of the nineteenth century made possible a new nationalism. By then the Jews were long reconciled to political nirvana. So that when Zionist devotion again endeavoured to call the Jewish spirit back to what may be its proper home, the new pioneers found that they were conjuring a reluctant revenant, a name without a local habitation, a ghost which, unlike that of Samuel, was reconciled to not being laid. Nothing less than a world upheaval, comparable to the Rabbinic vision of the rolling of the corpses,[1] threw the Jews back into political reality.

In the intervening centuries, between ancient and modern Israel, the wandering Jewish spirit has acclimatized itself to

philosophic work in the form of conversations held by the King of the Khazars. That the thing is not mere legend is proved by evidence collected by (*inter alia*) Harkavy, and, recently, Professor Dunlop. Incidentally, although it is said in the Talmud that "the land favours proselytes", and allowing for the military aspects of some Hashmonean pronouncements, the Jews were never propagandist. Yet the Khazars were not unique. In the period before the Moslem invasion of Africa several Berber tribes—notably the Jerua—adopted Judaism. These, later, fought bravely against persecuting, conversionist, Islam.

[1] T. B. Kethuboth 111a. (A theory to solve R. Eleazar's problem: how the righteous "from outside the land" could participate in the Resurrection.)

hazardous group dwellings in alien territories: "to a sojourn there", as the Midrash has it, rather than to settlement;[1] to occupancy which, however long it lasts, is transient; to a dependent independence, fragile between the poles of external inhuman nature; trembling between the threat of extermination and the temptation of assimilation.

The history of the Jewish group became, during, and even before, Christian times, the story of the play of psychological forces which have created that ubiquitous, unlocalized, aggregate of streets (ghetti) which is Yiddishland; the land of Judaeo-German, or Judaeo-Spanish, or Judaeo-Turkish, or in the distant Kwang-lun of the Mings, Judaeo-Chinese. The forces that wall these shifting territories are the external force of Jew hate, and, internally, the Jewish obsession: that is, the Jewish psychological anti-body to the effects of that inveterate endemic hatred which is Anti-Semitism.[2]

The ghettoes are all different, and all similar. The massacre of York in medieval England, the blood libel[3] which gave at least one English "Saint"[4] to the calendar, the murder of a

---

[1] The thought is exploited in the Passover Haggadah. *See also* Genesis XXXVII.1 and the commentaries, *ad loc.*

[2] Anti-Semitism is, of course, an inaccurate word, and is only used in this book because it is conventionally established. Jew-hate is pre-Christian and not confined to "Aryans". In point are the writings of Manetho, the Egyptian, who accused the Jews of Ass-Worship, and of Apion who accused them of a taste for blood. To these writers Philo and Josephus, respectively, replied in celebrated essays. There are also many Latin texts with anti-Jewish content, but little religious bias (e.g. in Tacitus). There is reason to believe that the hostility to early Christianity on the part of the Roman emperors was due in a degree to their hatred of things Jewish.

[3] Blood Libel: (*see* Note at end of chapter).

[4] Little St. Hugh of Lincoln (1255) known, in effect, to readers of Chaucer's *Prioress's Tale*. (*See* note at end of chapter.) Another "saint" in English Blood Libel literature (there are 5 cases) is St. William of Norwich (1144), the first of the recorded medieval accusations.

Rabbi at the coronation of a romantic English king,[1] are phenomena indistinguishable in essentials from Jew murder, oppression, and libel in all places and at all periods, whether by Romans, by Spaniards, by Teutons, by Slavs, Zendist Persians, Moors, Arabs, or other "Semites"; by Legionaries, Storm Troopers, Iron Guards, or any of the varieties of brutal Crusaders under crooked crosses. There are always local and temporal explanations of the persecutions; but these have it in common that they rationalize a hate directed against a familiar object of hate.[2]

The ghetto wall, physical and spiritual, which is built as a siege line, or as a defence, surrounds a group that is always conscious both of its physical transience and its spiritual permanence. Every ghetto, however long it lasts, is impermanent. Inside it culture is vivid, but always incomplete: expressed in a language which is not the original language of Israel, nor the true language of the environment, however socially adequate: but a jargon.[3] That jargon is rich, and species of it have achieved significance as vehicles of the best literary expression. But the vocabularies all contain one key word, which is GOLUS[4]—exile—a word which explains the heterogeneity that prevails among the other words.

[1] *See* note to p. 11 *supra*.

[2] I should add, an irrational, subjectively created, hate—to be distinguished from the more understandable hate that can exist between opposing sides in war, or lesser rivalries. To what degree anti-Semitism influences men such as Nasser (directly or indirectly) suggests interesting speculations.

[3] So Aramaic was the spoken tongue even when Hebrew was official, as in the period of the Second Temple. Old Aramaic prayers are retained in the Jewish liturgy. The Meturgeman (translator) has disappeared: but it is still orthodox tradition that one should read, each Friday night, the weekly pericopes, twice in Hebrew and once in Aramaic. (For women there are Yiddish translations.) As to the nature of Yiddish *see* note at end of chapter.

[4] Or GOLUTH (by scholastic usage). In Israel pronunciation (a sort of Sephardic) GALUT.

In Yiddish-land, or any land of jargon—in all the Jewish colonies, so to speak—is to be found an immense variety of life and culture; at the same time a solidarity, ranging from a reluctant to a voluntary acceptance of a certain separateness from the world outside the walls. This solidarity gives unity and continuity to an historical process. It characterizes for a time—for a sufficient time—any "remnant" that escapes from one place to sojourn in another; and it serves as a tie between the various groups, even between those that remain within some pale of settlement and the frequent outliers from the tribe.[1]

In this tie a function of unity? Said the Rabbis, about the Jews in Egypt: they did not change their names; they did not change their language; they preserved a moral purity; and they did not betray each other; therefore, they survived. In that statement the proposition that they survived is probably the only completely accurate one.[2] But the pattern is a true one. For certainly we have seen in many lands

[1] It adds to the complexity of these matters (though not in the degree that might be expected) that as between Jews there are considerable linguistic differences even when they are speaking Hebrew or jargon. The Sefardim have (*inter alia*) Ladino: the Ashkenazim Yiddish. In Yiddish, there is great diversity of pronunciation (as between "Lithuanian" and "Polish") to say nothing of German, Rumanian, Ukrainian variations. This is due to differences of tradition in the transliteration of "umlaut" words, and the origin of Jewish groups in places where the umlaut had different effects. So the Vav and Yod as vowels become differently pronounced in Yiddish—and in Goluth Hebrew. So a Pole says BURICH (Blessed) instead of BORUCH. Strangely, there was a group in Lithuania which was defective in the Shin, as were the Ephraimites of old. However, none of these differences amount to the generic, and they cause no difficulty in the recognition of Jew by Jew.

[2] See (*inter alia*) Vayikra Rabbah: XXXII.5. There have been many times and places where the Jews were forced to wear special garb, such as the famous yellow hat (pursuant to an order of the Fourth Lateran Council, 1215, under Pope Innocent III): others where the Jews con-

ee of
larly,
classi-
e. But
descrip-
aracter-
descrip-
at which
ction of
"Gentile
group is
n group is
identity of the

n, where reincarnations of the boy from the
ws have risen to power; in Persia of Daniel
cording to Holy Writ; in Spain of Ibn
Abrabanels; in the Ottoman of Haim
of Baron Ginsburg; in the Britain of
many lands where great Jewish in-
een honoured, we have seen that
because of, and in the form of, a
nded of foreignness and transience
ied with the cohesion that resists
dership (for the bones of Joseph
at the exodus), not the shepherd, but
of the sheep, constitutes the psychological
moving, changing mass. This solidarity,
imperfect and impermanent, yet never completely dissipated or crushed out, is something without which the fame
of individuals as Jews would be meaningless. The vizier
would achieve nothing by suffering mutilations at the hands
of the cruel Pasha,[1] if the lives that he protected were the

sciously retained a special garb: e.g. European frock-coat for Sabbath
use among the orthodox, more special garments among the Chassidim.
Among the latter, Streimel, Gartel, Kapote (large hat, girdle, gown) and
white or blue socks, set off the beards and ear-locks and fringes of the
conformist. For the rest, Asiatic and African Jews were famous for their
Sabbath dress.

As to names, Jewish surnames are often derived from localities or
trades, and, therefore, are European words. First names vary. In "culture
periods" Jews tended to use the names popular in the environment.
Alexander and Nicodemus (conqueror of the people) have special
origin. (Alexander was the name given to all boys within a year of
Alexander the Great's visit to Jerusalem. The Midrash (*loc. cit.*) does
not seem to approve—"in Egypt Benjamin was not called Alexander".)
Saadyah is Arabic (Said), and Ibn replaces Ben in such names as Ibn
Ezra. It is a strange gloss on the verse "a good name is better than good
oil", that Shemtov (which means good name) can appear among orthodox Jews in the Greek form Kalonymos.

[1] The reference is to the sufferings of Haim Farhi at the hands of

lives of individuals not made significant by some degr
inherence in some significant historical reality.[1] Simi
without this background an "alien patriot" could be
fied (by his father) as a "curiosity of literature".

Group solidarity, not individuality, is of the essen
the term solidarity does not constitute a sufficient
tion of the life of the group, or groups, whose ch
istic it is. Nor is it a sufficient (though it is a useful)
tion or definition of Jewry to say that Jewry is th
is the object of Jew-hate, and the enduring fu
resistance to the effects of that psychological
problem".

Yet when a function of unity for the Jewis
sought, the researcher finds it very elusive. To the Jew—
and to him belongs the criterion—the word Jewry is a
container, not a sieve.[2]

Inclusive, not exclusive, the Jewish religion affords a
continuum along which events are aligned in the history of
Jewry. The abandonment of the religion has been the

Mehemet Ali, who used the loyal services of the man whom he de-
lighted to torture. (*See* Sokolow, *History of Zionism*.)

[1] So we find Mehemet Ali, in 1840, suppressing the mob violences
stimulated by the Damascus Blood-Accusation.

[2] From the orthodox standpoint, a real Jew is a conforming Jew in
every formal and spiritual way: and that is the criterion that is applied
when persons seek admission to Judaism: or (often) when Jews are
praised as Jews. But the standard bearers of Judaism have always found
themselves leading masses (Erev Rav) and have not been able to apply
the exclusive tests that a spiritual Gideon would wish to apply to his
followers.

Ethnically, the problem is made more difficult by records of mass-
conversions to Judaism—e.g. of Berber tribes in the sixth and seventh
centuries of the common era: of Magyar-Tatar tribes (Khazars etc.)—
and by casual exogamies. For the rest, social herding is incompatible
with selectivity. External pressure refines (as the Darshon would put it:
"pure oil crushed for the lighting"), but prevents the prior choosing
of the material to be refined.

recognized way which Jews have adopted in order to separate themselves from the community. More important, religious conversion has been the only means of access. But recent events have made it clear (and it was known in Roman and Inquisition times alike) that the Jew-hater does not recognize a doctrinal test for Jewishness. This refusal may, or may not, be scientifically valid, but is an historical fact which is part of the data. To it must be added the fact that, even from the orthodox Jewish standpoint, the religion is one that declares a loyalty to its own back-sliders. It is a religion, moreover, without a practical catechism.[1] A religion, this, much involved with group memories of, and group aspiration to, nationhood; a religion which, although not, in recent centuries, missionary, has accepted strangers; withal, at most periods, a tolerant religion, even of heresies.[2]

So tolerant is this religion that, in modern times, in the thickly populated proletarian masses of the larger ghettoes, the leaders of the religion have recognized that the dominant fact of group life—myriads of oppressed people, with problems of survival and aspirations to emancipation—has changed the standards and traditions of orthodoxy from tests of loyalty into spiritual consolations. There is also a recognition that these are not as the days of the first Hashmoneans; that now, in the defence of Jewry, the forces of money-power, and even successful hooliganism, cannot be ignored.

A more important factor than theological doctrine is the

[1] The thirteen "I believes" of the early Maimonides are published in the Siddur (liturgy): but their pronouncement is not made obligatory by any sanction.

[2] There have been many periods, and many manifestations, of intolerance. But the outer limit of tolerance is only reached (according to the best opinion) when denial of the unity of God is actively propagated. Private belief is not "inquisited".

historical fact that religious Jewry has fostered endogamy from within, and has had endogamy thrust upon it from without. But in twenty-five centuries, allowing for all social and biological factors, and the accidents of conversions and violations, it is impossible to claim any strong physical affinity between the ancient inhabitants of the Bible lands (themselves very mixed stock, as the Bible shows) and the modern dwellers in the Diaspora.[1]

The researches of modern ethnologists, which admittedly concern themselves with the trivial externalia of human beings—the head measurements rather than the mentalities

---

[1] Of what colour were the Jews described in the Bible? We know that the word for "beautiful" is cognate to the name Japhet, applied to the Northern peoples. The apology of the dark, Bedouin-type, Shulamite in Canticles suggests that to be black was not desirable. She explains that the sun has "tarred" her: and protests that, though black, she is comely. (This is a possible interpretation of the text: but is not dogmatically presented.) Other indicia include: that the word Laban means "white". Was he exceptional? or the representative of a white group among coloured peoples? More helpful is the description of David in the book of Samuel, as ADMONI—"ruddy". Whether he was florid or red-haired, the implication is that the "stock of Jesse" was white. As to the mixed nature of the "stock" of ancient Israel, it is clear from I Samuel XIII–XIV that the Hebrews (the stock of Joseph, who in Genesis XLI.12 is described as a Hebrew) were only part of the Israelites, and that some Hebrews and other Israelitish tribes lived among the Philistines.

If, as has been claimed, Jewish characters are recessive, much will have disappeared of the original stock type. But the biological question is obscure. And it is doubtful whether there was ever a stock type.

In the present world, among other functions of diversity, there are differences of colour among Jews. Black Jews are found in North Africa and the Yemen. Also to be considered are the quasi-Jews: viz. the Falashas of Abyssinia (black men preserving rudimentary Jewish tradition) and the Indian Beni-Israel (brown men, more obviously related to the main stem). The Falashas—and with them, the Ethiopian Royal family— hold traditions of the Queen of Sheba. This is interesting in the light of the Rabbinic opinion that there was no Queen of Sheba; what the Bible text refers to is "Kingdom of Sheba". (T.B .B.B. 15).

—seem to establish that all the European varieties of Jews differ from the Semites, as the brachiocephalic from the dolichocephalic. The Jews, if they ever were Semitic, are Semites now only in so far as they are the objects of the Anti-Semites. For the rest, although researchers, following Galton, have drawn up composite pictures, showing high cheek-bones, heavy eye-lids and heavy lower lips, they have at best described a Mediterranean or a Slavonic group, and have not achieved any biological formula to denominate the many varieties of Jews among the Caucasian stocks.[1]

In other words, although there are aggregate types, there is no "Jewish body". Indeed it seems as if the sheep and the goats on whom the Patriarch performed his experiments in genetics, at the expense of his father-in-law, are avenged upon his descendants, by reason of the rapidity with which the endogamous Jews seem to assimilate the outward physical appearances of the nations among which they dwell. Even where a pure strain prevails, biologists, at the present stage, can only isolate trivial factors in the description of human appearances. Nor does biology account for the changes in facial appearance that are caused by behaviour, by the imitation, for example, of the Teuton stare, or the American mouth. A more rigid feature, such as the Jewish nose, beloved of caricaturists, happens to be characteristic of the western Slavs, as well as of many middle eastern stocks. The Jewish nose is less characteristic of Jews than are Jewish eyes, which are so often softened by anxiety and a consciousness of tragedy.[2] This is a function of

[1] One composite picture, made in the late nineteenth century, in New York, was said to resemble the young Spinoza. But Slavonic is a better description. As to Nordic, and other, influences, even in the old Jewish belt (Baltic–Black Sea) there were blond types and Tatar types. In the Carpathians were many red-haired Jews. As to source, a Polish researcher (Zajaczkowski) claims that some family names found among Polish Jews are of Khazar origin (i.e. with Magyar affinities).

[2] "The eyes of Leah were tender" (Gen. XXIX.17). In the best

psychology, not biology. So, too, is the "Jewish back", the "expression" of resignation that seems to fall on the figures of ageing Jews like a mantle.[1] But there are no significantly Jewish biological isolates.

In brief, then, there does not seem to be available a standard "Jewish body" for the purposes of classification. What makes Jews physically recognizable, in most places, is the fact that, in any given land, the Jew is likely to be the progeny of immigrants. In the western lands they are mostly immigrants from the Slav lands. In the Slav lands, in turn, they were mostly immigrants from Central Europe;[2] and there they came from Italy and Spain. In the Slav lands they were recognized by Teutonic names, in Teutonia they were known because they ate Italian dishes; in Italy they wore Levantine dress.

Everywhere the significant identification was by conduct; by mass separatism, by recognizable garb or custom, by the bright eye and the will to live. Psychologically, Jewish "expressions" are easily recognized by fellow Jews, who are suffused with the same Weltschmerz, or by the keen perception of the hater, who frequently recognizes, as a Jew, the man who talks the language of the country with more polish, greater accuracy, even apter idiom, than do the ordinary inhabitants. In the modern world the Jew has been further recognizable because he has outstripped the *bourgeoisie* by all *bourgeois* standards. The Jewish immigrant to the western slums comes to his new ghetto equipped with an energy, a mental activity, a recognition of the transience of homes and dwellings, that make it possible for him to move

Rabbinic opinion, the word is "tender" not "beautiful". The Scriptor is not saying that they were her only feature of beauty, but that they expressed her sorrows.

[1] A super-gloss on the well-known homiletic interpretation of "in the evening you shall eat unleavened bread".

[2] Some Russian Jews originate in the south-east, i.e. Western Asia.

rapidly from poverty to plenty in a way psychologically impossible for the indigenous population of slums. The very hostility of the populace is a spur. Once again the identification is by conduct and character, by a degree of liveliness not unmixed with melancholy; by a Weltschmerz; by a Chutzpah that deflates the values of pomp: by the intuitions that come with affection and hate.

Evidently these attitudes and this equipment, that make Jews recognizable, are elements in a psychological, not in a biological, study of this group.[1] We are left, it seems, without any physical criterion of Jewishness. We know, empirically, that those are called Jews who adhere to the Jewish religion in some degree, or are connected by blood with those who adhere; and, nowadays, those who claim and receive the nationality of Israel as Jews. But, for scientific purposes, this is not the definition of a species, only the description of an aggregate.

Within that aggregate, is there a function of unity? The next question is too obvious. If there is no Jewish body, is there a Jewish mind? Are the Jews characterized by some mental quality—that they possess a peculiar brain, peculiar mental resources? As to this, let it be said immediately that, granted the distinction between mind and body, or between brain and body, it seems quite impossible to base any group identity on any mental characteristics that are scientifically measurable.

At our present level of psychological inquiry we cannot isolate any special (or even general) factor of pure intelligence in data to be collected from individuals; who vary, as all individuals do, in their life histories, in their training, in the accidents of environment.

Certainly no Jew who knows the Jews can fail to be aware that all degrees of intelligence, from very high to very low,

[1] For Jewish "peculiarities", *see* note at end of chapter.

The Jewish Mind

are to be found in any aggregation of Jews. Admittedly ghetto Jews are often, indeed usually, much higher in intelligence than the proletariat or slum dwellers amongst whom they dwell. But there has been, and can be, no comparison of family histories, or even individual histories, between Jewish intelligentsia and non-Jewish intelligentsia, so as to reveal some special characteristic. When the intelligent Jew enters into conference with the intelligentsia of the Gentile, he and they are speaking the same language, and probing the same problems. Morover, if a large number of Jews display great success in these realms, display great efficiency and, often, great originality, the explanation need not be the dogmatic one that they are better equipped as a species. If there is a better average among them, it may be that historic circumstances have made possible, or necessary, the survival of a relatively large number of intelligent Jews; not that they carry in themselves some special mental equipment that makes for intellectual success.

The Jew, be it understood, makes no claim to the status of "chosen" in any invidious sense. In order to be made moral, he was "selected from among nations and emancipated from language".[1] If he uses, in his prayers, words like "exalted", the context is of ethical aspiration. The meaning is that he has been "elected" to be the best behaved among the nations, and his language has been made the vehicle of great ethical thought. It is also an historical fact that in life spent under constant pressure, and under the hostility of the most diverse enemies, united only in their enmity, the Jews have, willy nilly, become particularly law abiding; consequently, exquisitely civilized. As *bourgeois*, they illustrate the forgotten truth that *Bourgeoisie* (Bürgerschaft) literally means "urbanity" or "civilization".[2]

[1] I paraphrase the Kiddush.
[2] Those who speak of Wandering Jews should not confuse them with nomads, such as gypsies, who love the life of the townless.

In this way, undoubtedly, it has come about that the Jews have thriven as intelligences; not the possessors of a Jewish mind, but a group of people whose life is the life of the mind, if only because they have too little to expect from the forces of the earth.

Already in Talmudic times the Jew was reconciling himself to the life of the mind, recognizing, as a moral fact (or, a cynic might say, by way of rationalization of failure), the superiority of the mental to the physical realm. His kingdom was not of this world.

It is told of Resh Lakish, a gladiator[1] who became a great master of religion, that he leaped across a river in order to study the law with Rabbi Jochanan, and, having studied, could not leap back.

This story seems to symbolize a change in the destiny of Jewry from the vigorous physical life of peasantry, to a history of *Luftmenschen*. And that is confirmed by the commentators of those days, who would make Jacob a man of peace. Onkelos and his fellows (as we shall see) could not appreciate the reality of a Jewish physical life, communal, limited, agrarian, uncharacterized by individualism, unsuffused by an individualistic fear of death.

From those days onwards the Jews were condemned (or dedicated) to the life of the mind. In the life of the mind are to be found their triumphs, and, only there, no failure.

Here then is a field of investigation.

In this realm, which is sufficiently unexplored to leave scope for adventure and speculation, it is tempting to try and trace any common factors that have emerged among Jewish thinkers. That there is Jewish thought, we know. Jewish literature and learning is voluminous enough to constitute one of the major sectors of thought. Is there, it may be inquired, some characteristic style or method in that

[1] *See* p. 271 *infra*. Note that Resh Lakish is also referred to as Ben Lakishor Simeon ben Lakish.

aggregate of learning to equip the Jews specially for intellectual tasks?

If that be the case, a further question follows. Is there any biological process by which generations of human beings, trained in a certain way, can transmit a modification in the form of heightened subtlety, enhanced mental sensitivity, increased capacity for synthesis, for the apprehension of the fine distinctions, or for the grasp of an integrated whole?

At the present stage of biological inquiry, it might be answered that intellectual acquisitions are not transmissible. But there is no room for dogmatism here. *Credat Judaeus Weissmann, non ego.* In the nature of the subject it is impossible to conduct experiments, because the subject-matter consists in generations of human beings.

There appears to be reason to believe that the children of musicians are apt to be quick at mastering music; that the children of mathematicians find mathematics easy. This cannot be made the basis of an inference, but is suggestive of analogies. Certainly Jews, who for generations have been obliged to acquire more than one language, seem to be good at the acquisition of languages. That capacity, incidentally, involves the most fundamental type of synthesis, and one common to many intellectual activities. If this synthetic power is biologically transmissible, then it is arguable that the Jews, by reason of their mental life, have achieved the perpetuation of a better than average intellectual capacity.

That, be it repeated, is matter for speculation. But the thought is well enough grounded to justify an inquiry into how Jews have thought in the past, how Jewish intelligence has been trained; what has been the subject-matter; what style or method has been consciously adopted.

One difficulty in this inquiry is evident at the outset. Much of the Jewish contribution to thought has been in fields that cannot be classified as Jewish fields, assuming, indeed, that there are Jewish fields. Given that prophetic thought is Jewish, and that the Talmud is Jewish (and more than a body of case-law or an essay in legal codification), it cannot be disputed that philosophy—natural and theoretic —and all the sciences that have crystallized out of that matrix are not Jewish fields. Yet Jews have achieved great triumphs and creativity in them.

To those who would grasp Jewish history in one comprehensive formula, it is tempting to treat the Jews as the intellectual exponents of a function of unity in the world of thought.

The Prophets (orators) saw life in a great conspectus; in a bright glass, as the Talmud has it. That clear and all-inclusive comprehension gave power to their utterances, and raised them intellectually above the level of priests and lawyers, and above the analytical critics of institutions, who were unguided by any clarifying light.

By analogy, it may be suggested that the Jews who, at later stages, have made great contributions to thought, have possessed this capacity for unifying the world of experience. So the great codifiers created a perfect circle of law. Outside the specifically Jewish context, a philosopher of Jewish birth and education, such as Spinoza, brought into secular thought a magnificent unity of intellectual construction. It may be suggested that, in more recent times, some scattered lines of Western research were gathered by a Jew, Marx, into a comprehensive (however inadequate) formula; that Bergson expressed a fresher, and Freud grasped a wider, concept of Mind than had ever been contemplated; that Einstein sought to orchestrate the discords of physical experience into a harmonious whole.

For a universal Jewish continuity of mental pattern there is, however, little scientific basis. Any claim made for the Jewish genius must be more modestly stated than in terms of a transcendent capacity for unification.

35

Jewish intellectual history is, unhappily, not of the prophetic. The modern nomad has not been able calmly to contemplate the desert heavens. He has been a wanderer in the crowded ways of life.

In his ghettoes, even in the early ghetto which was a land of Israel subordinate to Gentile powers, the Jew has had his vision directed, not to the great unities, but to the differences. The unity of God he has defended and maintained. The intransigent plurality of life around him he has been unable to unify. Its multitudes have oppressed him.

Thus Jewish thought has been driven to self-searching, and to discrimination between self and others, self and the external world; driven to the organization of spiritual defences in the fastnesses of tradition and ritual, which are the easiest defences to fortify.

The spiritual leadership of Israel devolved, then, on the unprophetic, on priests, on lawyers, on the teachers of traditions. That these achieved great spiritual performances is not to be denied. That they manifested an extraordinary mental sharpness is clear from their written works.

Since the fall of the Temple the most bigoted of priests has not been a ritualist in the pattern of the idolators. The Rabbi, who took over the leadership from the priesthood, has been a teacher of laws and customs against a spacious background of human ethics; an analyst with vision.

Under the influence of Rabbis the education of countless generations of ghetto Jews (and the times of emancipation from the ghetto have been relatively short and few) has been "on the Book".

No claim can be dogmatically made that this education has created a mentality. But if it is biologically and psychologically possible that the training of generations may facilitate, in some way, some intellectual process, then clearly it is of interest to investigate the ways of thought that have been traditional for many centuries among the people of the Book.[1][2][3][4]

[1] In these pages the assumption is made that the Jewish mind will be best revealed in realms of thought intimately related to the standards and problems of the Jewish way of life, as distinguished from non-Jewish ways of life. There is, of course, a great overlapping. But the author has not concerned himself with such matters as Jewish successes in finance, mathematics, chemistry, military tactics, boxing, chess, medicine, politics, etc. etc. Rothschild, Ehrlich, Sylvester, Monash, Mendoza, Lasker. These are names of Jews who achieved great things in realms of general endeavour. Let Gilbert be described in the history of the theory of magnetism, Disraeli in the annals of personal magnetism. Their lives are of interest in the same way as lives of Jews who travelled early to China, or fly now to the moon. Thus there are Jews living (named Swiff or Swift) whose ancestors Napoleon (the emancipator!) used as guides (he called them Juifs!). This is interesting (and relevant to the history of oppressed Russian Jewry) but not integral to the theme. So for these purposes Abrabanel is the name of commentators, not of Iberian statesmen. Schiller-Szinessy is referred to as Talmudist rather than as freedom-fighter with Kossuth. Perhaps the second aspect of the man is relevant to the refutation of the charge of Jewish timidity. Similarly, the brave Colonel Joselowicz, who fought for Kosciusko, is part of Jewish history. So, perhaps, Kahina Dihya, Jewish warrior, princess of the Berbers, who fought heroically against the Moslems. But one must set a limit. Jewish brigands and adventurers are of interest; but not thematic interest. So I do not decry romantic facts; only their significance here. That there were Jewish warriors and poets in Arabia before Mohammed: that a Jew achieved the Papacy (Alexander III or (more likely) the rival Pope Anacletus II): that an eccentric English nobleman (Gordon) adopted Judaism for no good reason; that a Jewish boxer became the head of an African Federation: that an American financier-statesman is the son of a Polish immigrant who became a medical officer in the Confederate forces: these are sets of romantic facts to illustrate a platitude: *quae regio in terris nostri non plena laboris.*

[2] *Jewish peculiarities:* in studying the idiosyncrasies of Jewish conduct as observed by non-Jews, one must recognize certain distinctions.

(a) Manifestation of foreignness, or foreign tradition, or outlook, in any given environment.

(b) Less variable: manifestations due to religion, and customary interpretations of religion. In point are the beard and the earlocks of orthodox males: the covering of the head—and, among the Ashkenazim, the married woman's wig. The gown and girdle of the Chassid, and his retention of a medieval headgear, are sectional developments in Jewry.

The Sabbath, the Festivals, and the many fasts are noticeable in orthodox groups: and, very widely, the dietary laws: which are not only a restriction on species of animals and fish for food, but include ritual requirements deriving from the prohibition of blood. These (and the involvement of laws about crockery, etc.) are neatly summed up in the demand made by the Jew in the railway buffet: "Madam, if you serve Bovril in cups, please give me milk in a glass."

The above are instances of obedience to law and custom. And so, if a Jew is seen with Tefillin, with Tallith, or with the fringes of Arbah Kanfoth, or carrying (at Succoth) Lulav and Ethrog and myrtle leaves, he is obeying certain laws.

(c) But there are also observable, in many Jews, habits at the psychophysical level: the NIGUN and the SHOKEL; i.e. the sing-song of argument (though the Hebrew word has a wider meaning than that): and the shaking, or weaving, or swaying, of the body in learning, prayer, and the concentration of thought. These habits seem to come very easily to Jews. They may be orientalism. There is a theory (mentioned by Judah Halévy in his Cuzari) that the body movement (and it may apply to the sing-song) developed in times when manuscripts were scarce, and many students learned from one manuscript only. A student would lean forward, memorize a sentence or passage, and sway backwards to permit another student to see the text. The students would help their memories by intoning what they had learned, and intoning it in such a way as to distinguish question, answer, further question, and so on. The only difficulty of this theory is that it may be said to postulate the possibility of transmission of acquired characteristics.

For the rest, hand gestures (with the possible exception of the use of the thumb in learning) are continental. Special gestures may develop, but most "talk with hands" is not peculiarly Jewish. As for the lisp of the "stage-Jew", this is completely fictitious.

[3] *Blood Accusation.* As wicked as absurd, this suggestion that the Jews seek Gentile blood, especially for the Passover, has a history from Apion of Alexandria to Streicher of Munich—and beyond. There have been, in Christian Europe, some two hundred famous—infamous—accusations, usually accompanied by tortures and massacres. Confessions have been extorted. Jewish renegades, have, on occasion, participated. The European occurrences start with the case of William of Norwich (1144) in

which an apostate named Theobald of Cambridge was a prime-mover. Since then, there have been cases every century, though many leading Christians, even Anti-Semitic Popes such as Innocent IV, have ridiculed and condemned the charges. A striking revival of the accusations took place in late Tsarist Russia, where Anti-Semitism, as taught in Germany, was State Policy. The last cause célèbre was the case of Mendel Beylis, a brickworker of Kiev, accused of killing a child that had, in fact, been murdered by its guardian. Evidence for the prosecution was given by a professional Anti-Semite (Pranaitis). Rabbi Maseh, friend of Tolstoy, gave evidence for the defence. Much of the argument was as to Jewish (Talmudic) tradition, of which Beylis knew little. E.g. It was made clear by Rabbi Maseh that Jewish law forbids the use of corpses. He also explained away the Biblical sacrifices as a stage in Evolution, and incurred orthodox displeasure for doing so. But all this was less clearly in point than the fact that there was no scintilla of evidence against Beylis. An interesting feature of the case is that one of the defence counsel was Andrey Kerensky (later head of the Provisional Government). After the acquittal of Beylis, Kerensky and other defenders were persecuted by high authority.

As to the "theories" propounded by Blood Accusers, these vary. Chaucer's *Prioress* (end of fourteenth century and speaking with Chaucer's knowledge of history) speaks of the existence of "Among the Cristen folk a Jewry. Sustainèd by a lord of that contree for usury, and lucre of felonye." The child in that poem was killed because the Jews were annoyed by his sweet singing of the Ave (which he did not understand).

The popular theories, however, were that the blood was required either sacrificially, or medicinally, or ritually. So seriously was the last belief held that a commentator to the Shulchan Arukh (Rabbi David Halévy in *Turé Zohov*) advises Jews not to drink red wine at the Passover Seder.

Honest Christians, of course, never initiated the accusations. The Emperor Frederick II held an inquiry and found the belief to be without foundation. The Franciscan monks dissuaded Henry III of England from continuing the murders that he had initiated at the time of the Lincoln defamation. And there are many other examples—including refutations of the Blood Accusations by established Anti-Semites.

In conclusion, let it be mentioned that a large number of places (Frankfurt, Arles, Regensburg, Polna, Corfu, Venice, etc. etc.) retain memorials of the trials, tortures and burials. The variety of the names indicates the universality of the propaganda. It is to the everlasting credit of England and of the present Dean of Lincoln (Rt. Rev. D. Colin Dunlop) that he has declared the grave of "little St. Hugh" (there was a big one as well!) to be merely that of a child buried in the Cathedral, and has dissociated his Chapter (and Christendom) from a savage superstition. On the other hand, an historian such as Sir Francis Hill has "scientifically" preferred not to abandon the mean burden of an old "romantic" ballad.

⁴ *Yiddish*. The "jargon" used by North European Jewry. Substantially this is a blend of Middle German, from which are excluded many of the refinements of High German grammar, and into which have been absorbed a considerable number of Hebrew words, to express matters of particular concern to Jewry. This started nearly a thousand years ago as the dialect of Jewish Kahals in the Rhineland. (Rhenish and Provençal words are used by Rashi in frequent parentheses.) In established Yiddish approximately seventy per cent of the vocabulary can be described as German. The relation to High German is illustrated by such features as the following: that the Yiddish plural of Tag is Täg: that Yiddish preserves many old "ge" forms of the past participle (e.g. worden is rendered geworren); that while the German "schreibt mit einem federn", the Yiddish speaker "schreibt mit a penne" (the original Latin "penna" that was used when the Jews came to the Rhineland!): that he asks 'far voss' (für was=pourquoi, or potchomu) instead of warum: that Yiddish uses double negation: "Ich (sometimes pronounced Yich) hob (habe) nicht (frequently nit) kein mazzol."

That this language has its own structure is clear, and it is a literary medium. Two main modes of pronunciation—the Lithuanian and the Polish—may derive from changes in the German matrix, and the development of different sounds from the umlaut. These differences are very important, but do not affect the literature. Buch is written as Buch even if pronounced BICH. But very interesting and important is the fact that the different renderings of the vowels in the species of Yiddish are reflected in the consequential differences in the pronunciation of Hebrew by the speakers of Yiddish. [So if a Jew pronounces kleid in the German way, he will render the Hebrew vowel TSEREH as Ī (in "time") not as ā (in "gate"). The Lithuanian Jew will use the latter sound, which is believed to be the original. Similarly, U is rendered by the Polish and Ukrainian as Ī. Strange influences (including Dutch) cause some London Jews to pronounce Shabbos as Shobbos, olom as owlom, etc. And there are other singularities. Let it be added that no good Hebraist or Yiddishist is prevented from understanding by the differences of pronunciation.]

In the literature the problem is one of vocabulary. Learned Jews bring too much Hebrew into Yiddish, against the doctrine of those who say that only well-established Hebrew terms (e.g. ritually important ones) should be allowed. Thus Buch is a book: Sefer (Hebrew) would denote a book of religious etc. significance. Gebrennt is burned. Nisrof (Hebrew for someone, or something, burned) is not necessary, except possibly to describe martyrdom.

Again, Jews long settled in Russia and Poland have introduced much Russian and Polish. "Ended" in Yiddish is, properly, "geendigt". Much used, however, is gekontchet—a Russian root in a German frame. English Jews have been known to use absurdities like ge-finished. This is, however, only absurdity because (a) a proper Yiddish word exists, (b) the innovation is not supported by over a century of usage, as is the occasional Russian word.

The Russo-Polish Arbeiter Bund (founded in the 1890s) made great efforts in two directions:

(1) To preserve Jewish identity and language inside Socialism.

(2) To preserve the Yiddish language from over Hebraization, Russification, etc. etc.

Logically, a balanced Yiddish is a proper vehicle, notwithstanding its composite nature. Its literature is immense and valuable. Today, Soviet Russia tolerates Yiddish poets. An extreme development, in the Soviet, is to use Yiddish phonetic spelling for Hebrew words—even those validly admitted, like Shabbos and Yomtov.

For the rest, among the Sefardim, Ladino (Spanish with Hebrew contributories), corresponds logically to Yiddish. This, too, has a literature. Judaeo-Persian (very rich) and Judaeo-Greek are among other common jargons. Several Yiddish words (including so important a one as DAVEN (pray) have not so far been traced to sources in other languages.

CHAPTER TWO

THE PEOPLE OF THE BOOK

T HE Jews are called the People of the Book. By that name they were known as long ago as the days of Mohammed, and were so described by him. But they have never appeared as minstrel custodians of poetic narrative comparable to the early Greeks. As a group—and a group not barren of literary creation—they rarely apprehended their own literature lyrically or dramatically, as spectators do, but always as the repository of ethical refinement and homiletic; as something to be infinitely expounded in order to reveal moral and legal principles; or to unfold secrets of their own history significant for the conduct of their lives; or even to demonstrate, to the possible doubter, the inspiration of the Bible, its unity, consistency, and truth.

For this is the Book wherein each one seeks that which he wishes to find. To the mere spectator the whole stark narrative of the literal Bible, and its harsh-sounding nomenclature, must seem nearer in spirit to the Biblically-named townships of the hard Western plains than to the civilized, intellectual Jewish communities of Europe and the East. The epic event and the heroic character, suggestive of the Pagan, un-Semitic, Iliad (more carefully studied by Gentile theologians than is the Bible), sound more truly in the tents of the ungodly than in the houses of the Lord. In the synagogues of the ghetto the meaning of the text of the Bible, seen, as it were, through a garment of allusion and elucidation, "comely between strings of pearls", takes on that beauty in familiarity which shines in the faces of well-loved human beings. The mortal clay of the Bible is never contemplated—only the spiritual expression and ornament: and those so truly emanating, and so unmistakably fitting, that they, rather than the literal text, constitute for the Jew the substantial reality.

That the literal text was nothing without interpretation is an historic attitude older than the technique of the so-called Pharisees. Thus, at the peak of the Prophetic tradition, Isaiah established (for Atonement) a different interpretation, from the literal, of whatever spoken or written rules of fasting and penitence then existed. From the moment when Prophecy gave place to Scripture, and the sons of Prophets degenerated into a kingdom of Priests, the written law and the written narrative conjured, as if in compensation, a spirit of imaginative interpretation which was destined to make possible the evolution of Jewish law from Mikra[1] to Shulchan Arukh[2] and beyond, and to inspire a hundred generations of commentators and homilists.

In the very beginning, in the roots of the Bible itself, as we have it now in the Masoretic text, there is revealed, in the hand of the Scriptor, a syncretic talent. Strange names, like Moses, are given a Hebrew significance.[3] The Egyptian name attributed to Joseph is Hebraized.[4] The name of

---

[1] Mikra—"the reading"—comes to mean the Pentateuch.

[2] Literally, "The Prepared Table"—the last of the great codifications. It was made by Rabbi Joseph Caro and published in 1565. Later, Rabbi Moses Isserles added glosses called Mapach (table-cloth) relating to customary practices and interpretations.

[3] Exodus II.10.

[4] Gen. XLI.45. Zophnath Paanaach is Hebrew for "revealer of

43

Benjamin—in the oriental "lucus" meaning "left-handed"
—is interpreted "child of old age",[1] in order to express the
special position of that late emerging tribe of (left-handed)
warriors. Sometimes the purposes of the synthesis is defeated by the redaction, as when the interpretation of the
name Saul seems to be given in explanation of the name
Samuel.[2] But throughout there is evidence of a thoughtful
purpose in the words and phrases of the text, suggesting
that some, at least, of the Scripture writers wrote "inter-
pretively", and that their writing justifies interpretation.

Significant, at the outset of interpretation properly so-
called, is one who was probably the first writer to be called
Evangelist; that is to say Onkelos[3]—one of the earliest

secrets". In Egyptian of a fairly late dynasty is to be found the form:
ZT-P-NTR-E-F-NKH, meaning "Saith the God: he liveth". Incidentally, it is not known exactly at what period the Jews were in Egypt.
We know that Hyksos (Shepherd) invasions went on for a long time
during early dynasties up till the XVIIIth. The Egyptians never completely
assimilated them. The book of Joshua seems to indicate, for example, that
the Egyptians never adopted circumcision. The story of Moses and Zipporah corroborates this. We know that in the XVIIth–XVIIIth Dynasties
the Egyptians were temporarily affected by a monotheistic influence
(the period of Akenhaten). The Tel el Amarna inscriptions are consistent
with the belief that the Jews were a force in Egyptian affairs during those
dynasties. It is only from that relatively late period that evidence exists
of the use of the word Pharaoh to mean king. (Earlier it meant sacred
house.) Assuming that King Solomon's relations were with the XXIst
or XXIInd Dynasties (for which there is evidence) one can date the
Exodus in the fourteenth to twelfth centuries B.C.E.

[1] Gen. XXXV.18. But *see*, for the old tradition, Judges XX.16.
Incidentally, the notion of "lucus" may be a Jewish one. Sagin Or—
"too much light"—is Aramaic for a blind man. Analogously, the Tractate of Talmud relating to funerals is called "Rejoicings".

[2] I Samuel I.20. Kimchi defends the text by observing that the word
SHMUEL contains all the consonants of SHOUL M'EL (borrowed
from God).

[3] Probably a transliteration of Euangelos. (Suggestion of Schiller-
Szinessy.)

translators from Hebrew into a vernacular. As was mentioned, he refuses, this pioneer exponent of a traditional Jewish contempt for force, to recognize that Jacob captured his land "with sword and bow", and translates the Hebrew words, ingeniously, to mean "with praises and supplications".[1] Many centuries later the philosopher Maimonides pointed out that the same Onkelos had always endeavoured, by paraphrase, to avoid any suggestion in Holy Writ of the corporeality of God.[2] By paraphrase, be it noted, not by emendation.[3] And, since few commentators have been so bold as the translator Onkelos, it follows that,

[1] Gen. XLVIII.22. It is to be observed, however, that nowhere in Genesis do we find any record of a military campaign by Jacob. That fact may have puzzled the translator and influenced his rendering. (I am indebted, for this observation, to that excellent scholar, my friend the late Rabbi Hyman Klein.)

[2] E.g. "God manifested himself" (instead of "came down") Gen. XI.5. Similarly Gen. XLVI.2. "A word came from God". Even more strikingly, in Gen. III.5, not "ye shall be like God", but "ye shall be like Princes". In the same tradition the Targumist of the Hagiographa (not Onkelos) renders "under his feet" as "under the throne of Glory". Contrast the attitude of some Amoraim who were prepared to interpret the word "man" in the Bible as referring to God: by Gezerah Shoveh from "The Lord is a man of war" (Ex. XV.3. *See* T.B. Sanh. 96b.).

[3] The case of Samuel's nomenclature has been mentioned above. A similar case, where a slight emendation seems called for, is in I Samuel XVII.12, where the words BO BA'ANOSHIM ("went among men") appear a probable corruption of BO BESHONIM ("advanced in years"). For the Rabbinic explanation ("popularity") *see* Kimchi, and Gersonides, *ad loc.*

The Rabbis, be it added, were aware of the dangers of "the fly that defaced this page", but did not apply the thought to Scripture text.

It is to be observed about the book of Samuel that, whereas other books of the Bible succeed in the synthesis of what were probably different narratives, the editorship of Samuel fails to unify, for example, the two stories of the emergence of David (Chap. XVI and XVII respectively), or the two different explanations of "Saul among the Prophets" (I Sam.X.11, I Sam. XIX. 20–23: *see also* I Sam. XVIII.10).

in the centuries of commentary, the aim has been to explain the text in the light of theories and beliefs, but not, by scepticism and history, to "explain it away".

Onkelos was called a "righteous stranger".[1] That description ("righteous") was not applied specifically to his work. But in every generation commentators have followed a tradition which asserts the permanent rightness of the homiletic attitude. One may, therefore, apply to him the Midrashic thought, quoted by the commentator Rashi, which endeavoured to establish virtue for Noah; "not righteous by the standards of his generation, but righteous by high standards even in that generation".[2]

Contemporary with the early Targumist is the early Midrash. The Midrash is "inquiry"; not inquiry as we have it now, into the history of the manuscript and its authorship, but exegetic inquiry into all possible thought that can be derived from the text. If there is apparent discrep-

---

[1] A convert (GER TSEDEK. Distinguish GER TOSHAV—as it were the "domiciled stranger" a status attributed by the Rabbis to Naaman the Syrian (T.B. Sanh. 96b and Gittin 57b)). Little is known about the personality of this leading Targumist, if indeed the name is not eponymous. He has been, but should not be, confused with Akilos (Aquila) a name occurring in the Talmud and belonging (*inter alia*) to a Greek translator of scripture. Rabbi Azariah dei Rossi (author of *Meor Enayim*, etc.) explored that possibility in the sixteenth century. It requires to be added that a person named Akilos raised questions about the benefits of conversion: and this fact may have been the cause of confusion among the editors. There may even have been more than one Aquila: but there is no reason for confusing the two names. Origen, in his polyglot Bible (Hexapla), has preserved some of the Greek of Aquila. This is terribly literalistic, and shows the strong influence of Rabbi Akiva, whose pupil Aquila seems to have been, and who would not allow any particle in the Bible to be regarded as insignificant.

[2] Gen. VI.9: Rashi ad loc. (I have "adapted" this.) One reason for Rashi's elaboration is that the verse is pleonastic. A recent homilist has explained "righteous in his generation" as meaning that he gave rise to a pious posterity. The Scripture hardly supports this.

ancy, then an explanation must be sought; an explanation calculated to keep the Bible a perfect whole; just as, centuries later, the Tosafists (according to Rabbi Solomon Loria) made the Talmud itself into a perfect circle.

Always the aim is harmonious exegesis; not history, never emendation.

No emendation, that is to say, after the text was settled. The consonantal text ante-dates the Rabbinic period: and very early it was assumed to be unlawful to recite the Law rather than read it. But before what we call the Masoreh[1] was finally settled (and that was long before vocalized and cantillated texts were published) there was scope for variation in the reading[2]. In the Masoreh itself there survives the occasional difference between KERI (reading) and KETHIV (writing). (This is due to (inter alia) the fact that two of the Hebrew consonants—Yod and Vav—operate also as vowels.) Among the Rabbis there was occasional challenge to the Masoreh (the "editorship") from the accepted Mikra—or familiar reading. Generally, the Mikra (the familiar reading) was preferred. (YESH AYM LEMIKRA.) Also the Rabbis played with possible vocalizations.[3]

[1] "Traditional Text". Derived from a root meaning "fetter": but consistent with a derivation from "handing over"—tradition proper. What form the Masoreh took is not at all clear.

[2] Thus Spinoza—a fine Hebraist and first of the "higher critics"—points out (in Ch. VII of *Tractatus Theologico-Politicus*) that the author of Epistle to the Hebrews is relying, in XI.22, on a different vocalization of Gen. XLVII.31 than the now generally accepted one. In our reading of Genesis, Jacob was leaning on his bed (MITAH): the New Testament writer was reading MATEH (staff)—which Spinoza thinks to be the more likely original.

[3] There are rare instances of consonantal variation. E.g. where Resh Lakish appears to misquote Zephaniah (T.B. Sanhedrin 18(a)). This may have been a homiletic effort.

An excellent example of a self-conscious playing on words is the Rabbinic comment on Ex. XXXII.26. "The commandments were inscribed on the tablets." Inscribed is CHORUTH. But the Rabbis, who

"Played" is a *mot juste*. Not a determined effort at emendation this. It was rather as if, once they had been extruded from the Temple and had made the Bible their home, they were polishing and adorning the furnishings. This, be it observed, was not an awful proceeding. The Rabbis treated the Bible with something of the respectful familiarity with which Chassidim, then and now, have treated God.

In some instances there was a wish to derive a statement of Halacha. So the Amora Samuel would read not TASHICH (bite: i.e. charge interest) but TEESHACH (be bitten: submit to a charge of interest)[1]. Usually, however, the purpose is homiletical and not meant as serious emendation: as when the Rabbis say (of the verse "Peace to thy sons"): Don't read BŎNAICH—thy sons, but BŌNAICH—thy builders![2]

What could not be done with Holy Writ was alteration, or abandonment, or challenge, on the ground that a text seems to contradict, or differ from, another text, or be otherwise inexplicable. There could be no doubting of

regarded the law as liberating say: "don't read CHORUTH (inscribed), but CHEYRUTH (freedom)."

[1] T.B. Baba Mezia: Chapter on Interest. Modern authorities treat the text as Hiphil (Causative). "Let the stranger exact interest: not your brother". I.e. give interest to strangers, not to Jews. (Sci. Take interest from neither.) The Bible rule occurs in Deut. XXIII.21 and elsewhere.

[2] Where this is quoted (in the liturgy) a stronger example is quoted alongside. "The pathways of the world are his". In Hebrew "Halichot olom lo". This is rendered by revocalization and apt punctuation: "Halachot (Laws)—the world is his": Videlicit: If he studies the laws— the next world is his. This was no doubt conceived as a pun, with a homiletical purpose. In this kind of verbal experiment is to be found the origin of the Pshettel. Chassidic Rabbis (some of whom have been more witty than learned) are famous for their homiletical punning. E.g. "many oppressions surrounded us, We called on thee, O God. You were far away from us in our sins", has been rendered (by the dexterous use of a "causative" form)—"many oppressions surrounded us: we called on thee, O God. You made them far away. (Back) in our sins".

acceptability. If the text poses a problem, the student must find, by legitimate exegesis, an explanation, even if the effort drives him to fantasy and myth creation.[1]

On occasion when a reference is not understood a legend is wrought. Thus Ur of the Chaldees, not then known to be a place-name, was translated by the Rabbis into "the fire of Chaldea", and a story was told that Abraham had been condemned by the idolators to the stake, and had miraculously escaped.[2] Similarly, when the Psalm (attributed to David) deploring the dead is contrasted with a statement, in the mouth of Solomon, praising the dead, and when Solomon himself is found independently inconsistent,[3] an account is given of incidents which explain the statements and reconcile the differences; and the attitude of the Psalmist

[1] Sometimes unnecessarily. Thus the authors of the Midrash (Bemidbar Rabbah 4) are puzzled by the text of Joshua IV.11. If LEPHNAI means "before", then there is contradiction about the movements of the Priests, relatively to the army of Israel. So an extra miracle is extrapolated. But if Lephnai means "in the presence of", there is no difficulty. English readers, who have the Authorized Version, benefit from the rational attitude of Kimchi and Rashi, studied by the translators, who give the easier version. (*See* Manasseh ben Israel :*El Conciliador*: ad loc.) For fanciful exegesis no better example can be cited than the happy speculations recorded in the Haggadah. "This is the finger of God," said the Egyptians, and at the Red Sea we learn that "the hand of God" was on the waters. It follows that, if there were ten plagues in Egypt, there were fifty over the sea. But, as four, or, according to another school, five words relate to the Lord's smiting of the Egyptians, so that each plague was four- or five-fold, there must have been forty or fifty plagues on the land, and two hundred or two hundred and fifty on the water. That analysis kept the Rabbis up all night at Bené Berak.

[2] This story is developed by the commentators to the Koran (at Sura 17). They portray Abraham as in conflict with Nimrod, who had him cast into flames, which miraculously became a garden. It may be proper to suggest that the Koran itself is an Aggadic Midrash of sorts.

[3] It will be remembered that most of the Psalms are attributed to David: Proverbs, Ecclesiastes and the Song of Songs to Solomon (T.B. Baba Bathra 14).

and the Wisdom writer to death is restated in the language of an age with a more elaborate eschatology than was invoked by the Scriptural authors.[1] Again, when we are told that the horses of Pharaoh were drowned in the Red Sea, the Mechilta inquires: were they not killed in the plagues? And the answer is found: that the Jews protected the animals of friendly Egyptians, who later betrayed them; a truth of history, if not an historical fact.[2]

To the pioneers of the Midrash the words of the Bible appealed for imaginative interpretation. This verse says: "Inquire into me". (Rashi: Gen.I.) As the stone cried out from the walls to Habakkuk, so the stone—or stones—with which Jacob made his pillow called out to the Rabbis for explanation.[3] Why first the plural—then the singular? Because the stones fought in the night as to which should be honoured with the head of the Patriarch: and peace was

[1] The verse: "The dead shall not praise the Lord" expresses David's regret that Death exonerates from duties. The verse: "I will praise the dead that are all already dead" refers to the colloquies of Moses with God. Only when Moses invoked the memories of Abraham, Isaac and Jacob did the Lord forgive the Israelites. The verse "for a live dog is better than a dead lion" was said at the death of David. David by prolonging his studies had contrived to elude the Angel of Death until the Sabbath—a better day on which to die. Solomon was advised that though he could feed the dogs on that day, he could not minister to the corpse of his father. (T.B. Shabbos 30.)

[2] Mechilta to Beshallach (Ex. XIV.17–XVIII.16). (Mechilta, with Sifre and Sifra, constitutes an old Midrashic commentary on parts of the Pentateuch. It deals with laws as well as narrative.) The Rabbis expressed their disgust in the words: "The best of the Egyptians are for killing". Some manuscripts gave "Gentiles" instead of "Egyptians", and (although Tractate Soferim explains "in time of war") that text has been the cause of great suffering to the Jews. I was impressed by the vigour with which the late Chief Rabbi Schleifer of Moscow assured me that the original said, and meant, Egyptians.

[3] *See* Gen. XXVIII. vv. 11 and 18. (The word Rashi is the acronym of the name of the great commentator Rabbi Shlomo Yitschaki (1040–1105)).

established among them by a miracle that turned them into one stone. Even if this be taken as poetic metaphor, it is valuable above aesthetic imagery.

Did Sarah live for "a hundred years and twenty years and seven years"? Rashi (eleventh century), applying early Midrash, explains that as she was at seven, so was she at twenty, and so at a hundred. Since seven was the oriental zenith of beauty, we learn that her beauty did not abate: and Rashi and other commentators are keen to show that there is also a comparison for virtue, between Sarah at a hundred and Sarah at twenty (since two comparisons, not one, are made): and so the exegesis of this verse grows into a body of literature on which the Biblical (literal) account of Sarah's life reflects a smile.[1]

[1] Gen. XXIII.1. *See* Rashi, Nachmanides, Ibn Ezra and others, ad loc. From another standpoint Sarah's earlier years were made romantic by adventure which did not interest the moralists. Thus there are three instances in Genesis of strange Patriarchal conduct when the wife is described as sister. The archaeologists find possibilities in this. (*See* Buber: Moses.) That it did not escape the Jewish commentators is evidenced by Rashi's gloss on the verse: "These are the generations of Isaac: Abraham begat Isaac". (Gen. XXV.19.) The extra words (i.e. the second half of the sentence) convey to us that God caused the face of Isaac to be the exact replica of Abraham's face, so that none should attribute his parentage to Abimelech.

The commentators treat Sarah humanly and sympathetically as a woman whose life was a difficult one. "And the life of Sarah was . . ." (Gen. XXIII.1). The word "was" (VAYIHEYU) has a numerical equivalent of 37. Isaac was 37 when Sarah died, and only in those 37 years could she be said to have had a life. We are told, further, that the immediate cause of her death was the shock of her hearing that Isaac was being sacrificed.

Abraham valued her, but he mourned her intellectually before he wept, and he wept little (Bachya ben Asher and others on Gen. XXIII.2). His grief was moderated by his pleasure at hearing of the birth of Rebecca, which meant that his son would not be compelled to marry a Canaanite. Isaac, apparently, did not attend his mother's funeral. He was recuperating from the Akedah. A simple, or cynical, commentator

Seven centuries after Rashi we find the same tradition vivid, which Rashi had inherited, through many generations, from the Midrash. "What does it profit us," asks Judah, "If we kill our brother and conceal his blood?"[1] To the dramatic critic, this is the weighty speech of the same man who later challenged, with dignity, Joseph's arbitrary and unaccountable behaviour. But to Malbim the apparent superfluity of words challenges explanation. And he explains that Judah is dwelling on three possible motives for murder. There will be no profit: no blood vengeance (for it is their brother): no glory (for they intend to conceal his blood).[2]

The three periods from which the three examples are drawn (the periods of the Midrashim, of Rashi, and of Malbim) are not discrete. That tradition is continuous over two thousand years, by which Jews read into the text, and through the text, and beyond the text, seeking what they wish to find, and exercising the kind of imagination that discovers richness and subtlety in a world of words.

The early impulse is two-fold, legal and spiritual, but flowering first in a period when the legal and spiritual were not so clearly separated as they are now.

makes Abraham send Sarah to die at Hebron so that he would not have to explain why he wanted the cave (where Adam was buried) for her grave.

[1] Gen. XXXVII.26.

[2] The commentators do not find the story of Joseph easy. First, they must reconcile some textual difficulties about his sale, by Ishmaelites and/or by Midianites. A doctrine of agency is invoked. But more serious is the question, could the fathers of the tribes have been so wicked? Joseph reported their evil deeds (Gen. XXXVII.2). With the aid of an analogy with Numbers XIII.22 and other texts it was suggested that Joseph made a mistake. He thought they were eating living flesh. In fact they were eating (lawfully) a calf found *en ventre sa mère*. Because of such events Joseph was made to suffer, and, in so doing, initiate the exile.

"Turn in it (the text), turn in it: for everything is in it".[1]
The scholars of the early exiles, seeking refuge from an
oppressive world, found in the Book an inspiration and a
comfort. This was the redemption of their lives, and the
preservation of it even beyond the grave. To give less than
a full devotion to the Torah (The Teaching) was to waste
eternity. Therefore it was not fitting for a man to look up
from his meditation and say, "How beautiful is this tree".[2]
Indeed, although the Rabbis were capable of beautiful language in their meditations and their mourning, they held
that it could be unseemly to admire the beauty of the sacred
text. David, we are told, was punished because he said: Thy
laws are my song.[3] So the imagination was concentrated
into an intellectual world, but a very rich one. The product
of that imagination is a literature of Halacha and Aggadah:
Halacha, the creative analysis of the legal "way": Aggadah,[4]
the narrative of the real life through which the "way" was
hewn: and the world that was explored, and charted, and
organized was the Bible world in which they continued to
live. So the missionary takes his civilization with him into a
heathen wilderness. So the tortoise takes with him his shell.

Aggadah, then as now, is the world of the Book explored:

[1] T.B. Avoth. V.25.

[2] T.B. Avoth. III.9.

[3] T.B. Soteh. 35a. This Rabbinic thought is not inconsistent with a
reference in Tractate Eruvin (18b) to scholars singing as they learned.
There is, I think, no need for the gloss of R. Samuel Edels (Mahrsha)
that it was proper to attract attention to the learning. There is authority
(Rabbi Jochanan) that to read the Pentateuch or Mishna without melody
is against the spirit of the law (T.B. Megillah 32).

The verse of Psalms for which David is criticized is CXIX.54, from a
part of the Psalter which one traditional text, at least, does not attribute
to David.

[4] An Aramaism, either from a Hebrew root meaning "gather" or
from a Hebrew root meaning "narrate". The second derivation is
implied in the word Haggadah—a name given to a Midrashic book
used at the Passover Seder.

but *ex hypothesi*, not expanded by any new cartography. In the Book there is ample scope—indeed a constant challenge.

Was Noah really good? Did the patriarchs sin? If, as in one tradition it was taught, the patriarchs studied the law in the academies founded by Shem and Eber, how then could Jacob marry two sisters? An answer is that the law was stated for the land of Israel, not for Syria: and we know that Rachel died as they crossed the border.[1]

How did Moses become defective in speech? In the Court of Pharaoh the child was suspect. Pharaoh had been visited by an ominous dream. So a synod of wise men was appointed to investigate the matter, the members being Jethro and Balaam and Job. They devised a test: that the child should be offered the choice of dull gold and shining hot coals. If he made the intelligent choice he was to die. The child stretched out its hand to the gold, but an angel guided it to the coal, which the infant transferred to his mouth, spoiling his speech and saving his life.[2]

These are typical of legends galore recorded in Talmud and Midrash: most of them centred round a text, or designed to fill a lacuna in the text, or to resolve a contradiction.[3]

[1] Gen. XXXV.18. Rachel, whose sad history was known to Jeremiah, is the subject of many Rabbinic stories and conjectures. Thus: she gave her maid to the elderly Jacob (he was 84 when he wooed her) because Sarah had given her maid to the elderly Abraham. She was discreet, not betraying her bargain with Leah. Therefore her descendants, through Benjamin down to Esther, were discreet.

[2] T.B. Soteh 11a. Sanhedrin 106. Shemoth Rabbah XI.3. One Talmudic legend—about the infant Moses knocking the crown from Pharaoh's head—is related by Josephus (Antiquities: Ch. IX). Josephus knew a great deal of Aggadah.

[3] The Rabbis may have had access to some books mentioned in the Bible, but not extant: e.g. the Book of Jasher. A book of that name was printed in Venice in the sixteenth century by a publisher whose introduction is an amusing lament on the woes of publishers. But this book so obviously coincides as to its content with Talmudic narrative that

Who was this Ethiop, wife of Moses, referred to in Numbers?[1] We are told a story of Moses' life in Ethiopia whither he escaped from Egypt after killing the Egyptian and being informed against. There he rose to great military rank. (And Ethiopic traditions of untraced origin support this.)

Who were the dead that Ezekiel called to life? They were the tribe of Ephraim, who left Egypt too early. They had calculated the four hundred years of exile from God's promise to Abraham, and not from the birth of Isaac. And they perished at the hands of the Philistines in the Vale of Ascalon.[2]

How did the water behave in the cleavage at the Sea of Reeds (Red Sea)? A Rabbi was told in a vision by Serach, the long-lived daughter of Asher, who witnessed it. The water was like a latticed wall.[3]

Was Phineas right to kill Zimri and Kosbi, and how did he achieve this? Miracles were wrought so that he should

it is clearly a compilation: and it has been traced to a Provençal writer of the thirteenth century.

Also there is a large Apocalyptic literature emanating from Alexandria, third century B.C.E. to second century C.E., the contents of which may include stories handed down through many generations.

It cannot be suggested that all Aggadah is "deduced" from Scripture: only that it is all integrated to the text, and that "sources" are unknown.

[1] Numbers XII.1. It is not clear from Exodus XVIII.9 whether Moses divorced his Midianite wife Zipporah (according to the legend, his second wife).

As to the archaeologically interesting incident between Moses and Zipporah ("bridegroom of blood") the Talmud seems to anticipate criticism by saying that Moses himself was born circumcised (Soteh 12a). More historically minded critics point out that not only did he not circumcise his own son, but it was left to Joshua to circumcise the people. Clearly, whatever the origin of Moses, his culture was Egyptian. Against this, observe that Moses uses the metaphor "uncircumcised" to describe his own lips and quotes it (Lev. XXVI.41) to describe Jewish hearts.

[2] T.B. Sanhedrin 92b.

[3] Pesikta de Rab Kahana.

find them *in flagrante delicto*, because only that situation would justify killing by the sword. A flash of Talmudic (and political) humour is seen in the story that Phineas was opposed by the angels when he sought entry to the holy realm, because he had executed without formality. But God said: "He is a Zealot and the son of a Zealot", and Zealots have their own standards.[1]

So all the characters of Holy Writ abide a Talmudic or Midrashic questioning. In some cases (What became of Daniel? What happened to the three youths from the furnace?) the answers are unintelligible.[2]

But in every case that matters the story is integrated with text, and frequently accompanies an exposition of law.

Torah means Teaching. The laws and the lives of the law-givers, the acts of saints and sinners, are alike the subject of the teaching. Then the Temple grows dim. One of the most touching passages in the Talmud is "Tell me about the Temple": and the answer: "He who did not see the Temple never saw beauty all his days. The colours were like the waves of the sea. . . ."[3] With the fading of the colours, the narratives also fade. What survives is the traditional law: and for near two millennia the law takes on a greater importance than the history. The teaching becomes subordinate to the derivation of legal rules. Since the sanctioned tends to survive the unsanctioned, the powerful instruments of exegesis, and the technique of hermeneutics, became applied to the statement and application of clear duties and penalties. The change, however, was one of emphasis only.

Be it remembered that the religion, even in the theological

[1] T.B. Sanhedrin 82b. Incidentally, it is good law that had Zimri succeeded in killing Phineas in self-defence, he would not have been guilty of murder.

[2] Ibid. 93a.

[3] T.B. Baba Bathra 4a.

sense (not isolable in Judaism), is in the content of Torah. A Mishnah in Sanhedrin tells us that among those who forfeit the future life are the ones who deny that the Resurrection is implicitly stated in the written word. The Gemara points out that the anathema is not on those who deny the Resurrection, but on those who deny that it is attested by the Pentateuch.[1] So the controversy is between Pharisee and Sadducee: between two parties (rather than creeds); and the crux is Rabbinic authority, which, under pressure, claims title from the Scriptures. In the triumph of hermeneutics, the Rabbis took the leadership of Israel from priests and politicians. The long continuum of Biblical exegesis from then till now forms a not inglorious trail of that triumph. Viewed from that standpoint, the Talmudim and Midrashim are more than "curiosities of literature".

Even in early Mishnaic times, when the life of the Temple was falling into party strife, and after the Temple itself had fallen, it was clear that "the Jews a headstrong, moody, murmuring race"[2] would ever prove intransigent to personal authority. Any legislation, therefore, required to be

[1] T.B. Sanhedrin 90a, et seq.

[2] Dryden (*Absalom and Achitophel*). Moses had called them "stiffnecked": Solomon, "difficult": Jeremiah had called them "the people of a revolting and rebellious heart". Let it be added, "for favour", that without obstinacy the group could not have survived for two thousand years without land or Temple. The Bible gives us to think that the mentality of the Israelites was Bedouin. This people's laws dealt more favourably with the open robber than with the hidden thief. They were unpolitical and intransigent in the early days: and later evolution only brought out their individualism. An elaborate legal system weakened their original tribal vigour: but it did not give to the people, as a whole, the political sense that must be developed in the process from the life of the village to the life of the state. Significant is the strength of the law against informers, and the prevalence of that breed in Israel. (The best-known examples are, of course, apostate defamers, of the Pfefferkorn type.)

To revert to Dryden's shrewd summary of the Jewish character, the

well-grounded in the Scriptures. All the legislation, whether by legal fiction or equitable device, or direct authorization or prohibition, was rooted in a code: a code far too limited to carry the crop of laws of a developing society, had it not been enriched by the imaginative efforts of those who found depth to compensate for lack of superficial extent. Not of the Jewish Bible was it said: "the couch is too short for stretching".[1] The coverlet could be made to accommodate the most restless of sleepers. So Rabbi Akiva was expressing, in extreme form, an already established tradition, established by lovers of a text which was their only domain and their only source of sovereignty, when he declared that there was no superfluous word in the Torah.[2]

Long before Akiva, arguments had been based on the similarity of expressions in different parts of the law, and practical analogies had been derived from those verbal similarities. Akiva stated no new principle, but was more pedantic in its application than was the more scientific

word "headstrong" is peculiarly well chosen. Not only does it describe the zealotry of the people on occasion, but it stirs a Talmudic echo. In Tractate Kerithoth (112a) the Jews are described by a Sadducee as "headstrong" (AMA PEZIZAH) because "they let their mouths anticipate their ears". (They said at Sinai: "We shall do and we shall hear.") *En passant:* Dryden's understanding of the problems of Jewry—or of an England that had such spiritual affinities to Jewry—is brought out in his reference to the character who "never broke the Sabbath but for gain".

[1] Isaiah XXVIII.20.

[2] Akiva went so far as to say that every particle ES (ET) in the Pentateuch is significant. He found it difficult to explain the particle where it prefixes the Divine name. His teaching was adopted by Aquila, whose Greek translation is consequently very awkwardly worded.

In Akiva there was something of "the enthusiasm of the convert". Till he was forty, LO SHONO, he learned no Mishna. He was Am-Haaretz or Apikoros (*see* note on p. 166 *infra*)—in effect, a Sadducee. Then he realized that in the Rabbinic life lay the salvation of Jewry; and he lived to be the great hermeneutist of Pharisaism, and a martyr to the Zealot cause.

Rabbi Ishmael. "And the people saw the thunders and the lightnings". Rabbi Ishmael was content to say: "They saw what they saw, and they heard what they heard" (because the Torah uses the relatively loose language of man): but to Akiva the words implied a miracle by which the waves of sound were made as visible as the lightnings.[1]

Allowing then, for differences of degree of intensity in the cultivation of the verbal text, it is true to say of the whole Talmudic and later Rabbinic period (which has now not ended) that the text was sown with ingenuity in order to produce justifications for otherwise "unwritten" laws.[2] When the new law appeared to do violence to a common-sense interpretation of the text, and when that law was disliked, or the Rabbis who pronounced it were disliked, then the phenomenon of Sadduceanism, or Boethianism, or later Karaism, developed by way of reaction. But it is noteworthy that even the Sadducees and Karaites never reverted to "pure" literalism. Nor was pure literalism ever valued until Mendelssohn (an orthodox and Rabbinic Jew[3]) gave to a rationalistic generation of German Jewry his

[1] Exodus XX.18. *See* Mechilta, ad loc. This is a good example to show that pure "literalism" can be expository—can constitute Peshat in the sophisticated sense. Observe also that intellectual pressure on the text is not limited to the Pentateuch. Throughout the Talmud, the words of the Prophets and Hagiographists are exploited Halachically and Aggadically: even the words of the three latter-day Prophets (vide, e.g., T.B. Yoma 22b.).

[2] And, as we have seen, for doctrines such as the belief in the Resurrection, or the immortality of the soul. "The land that I promised to your fathers" is cited as proof of the former doctrine. So, too, "I kill and I return to life" (Deut.32) and other verses. In every case the interpretation is challenged for ambiguity, and for specificity of reference.

[3] His descent was from Moses Isserles, a glossator of Shulchan Arukh and a bulwark of orthodoxy. But his masters were Abraham Ibn Ezra, (1092–1167) and David Kimchi (1160–1235), both of whom had great respect for the grammar of the text, and the rational meaning. (Kimchi was used by the makers of the Authorized Version.)

translation of the Scriptures.[1] It is significant that this
translation has had considerably less effect on the history
of Judaism than the translations of Wyclif and Luther
exercised upon Christianity.[2] The genius of Judaism was
Rabbinic in a nation of scholars: the genius of Christianity
failed to be priestly in a world of peasants.

In two flowing impulses, then, and those never completely divided, the Jewish genius exerted its dynamic
activity on the Bible. The Bible, with the aid of exegesis,
was the source of Halachah—the law. The Bible, with the
aid of exegesis, was also the source of Aggadah; that is to say
—narrative, legend, homily, and Biblical novelty for its
own sake. What does this verse mean? Very rarely is the
answer: "Its meaning is what you hear it say". The very
questioning implies that the literal meaning would need
to be established by argument.[3] Usually, the answer is a
change of stress from the normal reading, or an elaboration
of the meaning of particular words, eliciting a distinction or
an emphasis.[4] This is called Peshat.[5] Within, and out of,

[1] Since the Septuagint and Onkelos there had been other Jewish translations: Saadyah's translation into Arabic: some translations into Spanish,
Persian, Modern Greek, etc. and into Yiddish.

[2] Mendelssohn inspired the Biurists, careful commentators on gram-
matical-linguistic lines in the Spanish tradition. But Mendelssohn,
though orthodox himself, is also looked upon as the inspiration of
Reform movements.

[3] As in the case of the verse interpreted literally by Akiva (*see* p. 59
supra). Judah ben Ilai condemned all persons who read the Bible literally!

[4] Typical is the (post-Talmudic) explanation of "an eye for eye"—
Ayin Tachat Ayin. By punctuating this: Ayin—Tachat Ayin, we can
translate: "For an eye, the value of an eye", etc. That it was the value,
not the eye itself, is accepted doctrine at a very early stage. Some
historically-minded apologist might argue that "an eye for an eye" in
its crudest meaning was still an improvement on the blood-feud, and
superseded practices from an earlier level of culture (e.g. the story of the
concubine of Gibeah).

[5] Many authorities use the word Peshat to mean "the literal sense"—

Peshat develop more elaborate expositions of text, ranging over widely scattered verses, and sometimes presenting a new ethical theme, even a myth. This is Drash, a root signifying inquiry, and the word can cover some very profound expositions. Later generations artificially elaborated and classified, distinguishing Peshat from Drash,[1] from Remez[2] and Sod,[3] these latter being Kabbalistic speculations, employing (*inter alia*) mechanical ingenuity in the use of the numerical equivalents of letters. This is called Gematriya.[4] We also have notarikon (acronyms) i.e. the significance of

and a usage in Chullin is cited in support. But it is doubtful whether the language of Talmud and exegesis contains a word to denote simple restatement in other words. The use of the circumlocution "it means as it sounds" suggests the absence of such a word. From this fact one deduces no special significance. A relatively undeveloped language is not likely to contain sophisticated words like "paraphrase", because the operation is not much required at that level. The author, throughout this essay, uses the word Peshat as bearing an exegetical overtone. Thus usage is justified by the general use, in Yiddish, of the word Pshettel (diminutive of Peshat) to denote a clever interpretation.

[1] In Sanhedrin 27, there appear several uses of this word, including: (1) a search for the reason of a law: and (2) speculative inquiry and exposition. The latter is the usage of the commentators.

[2] Hidden reference. E.g. Through a play on a word in the Targum, Lot is found to be the incarnation of the Serpent; and, with his daughters, symbolizes the workings of the YETSER HARO (Evil inclination).

[3] Secret: mysterious reference. Thus, whereas the masters of Peshat and Drash elaborate the story of Abraham and his visitors (Gen. XVIII. 1–10), explaining e.g. that he killed three oxen so that each visitor should enjoy the middle of the tongue, "mystery" commentators (medieval) see the whole narrative as a symbolical description of the approach of the contrite soul of the righteous to Paradise and its reception there.

In this kind of speculation much use is made of Canticles and Psalms that lend themselves to metaphor and allegory. Ezekiel's "chariot" is, of course, always relevant.

[4] Gematriya is not a transliteration of Geometry, but a mistransliteration of Grammateia—the science of letters. Gematrioth are often "arbitrary" selections of phrases numerically equal. Sometimes they

individual letters as possible initials[1], and other devices. These have been harnessed to metaphysical constructions accounting for the Creation and the Chariot. This riot of intellectual blossoming has neatly, and characteristically been described as The Orchard.[2] In the Orchard many went astray: critics like Elisha Ben Abuya[3] (indoctrinated with pagan philosophy) who failed to find the answers they required. But to most scholars the blossoms made the ways of the law into pleasant paths. Of these blossoms the simple clear Peshat is the typical flower. Everything else is elaboration. The insight of Peshat is the same refinement of perception that made the Rabbis of the Talmud, and later periods, into exact and subtle disputants. Hence a technique pervading the Jewish educational system (of which the centre was the pulpit of the Darshon) which has endured for centuries,

are very apt, e.g. "Shiloh comes" (Gen. XLIX) is equivalent to Messiah. Similarly, in Gen. XIV.14, the number of servants (318) is equivalent to Eliezer.

[1] Of Notarikon, a neat example is HAMISHPATIM Judgements—which can be made an acrostic of the Hebrew words meaning "The Judge must essay an arbitration before he decides the issue". HADAYAN METSUVEH SHEYAASEH PESHARAH TEREM YAASEH MISHPOT. Similarly: BERESITH: Bereshith Raah Elokim Sheyekablu Yisroel Torah. (In the beginning God saw that Israel would receive the Teaching.)

[2] PARDESS in Hebrew: being formed from the initials of Peshat, Remez, Drash and Sod. This is an instance of a familiar Rabbinic mnemonic system. E.g. MITSVAH (Commandment) is analysed into M—Mezuzah—T S—Tsitzith (fringes)—Vav—Utefillin.

[3] Known as a great scholar, teacher of Rabbi Meir, Elisha ben Abuya is often described as Acher (The Other). One of "four who went into the orchard" he emerged on a wrong path. The other three were Ben Azzai, who died; Ben Zoma who lost his reason; Akiva who lived on. Some forgotten history lurks within this allegoric statement. A simpler account of Acher is that he saw a man "spare the young" from a nest. Instead of receiving the Biblical reward (long life) he was bitten by a scorpion on his descent from the tree and died. Akiva could account for this eschatologically; Acher could not.

and is responsible for traditions of subtlety in Jewish learning, life, literature, down to the most plebeian levels of Yiddish humour.[1] In this way a mind is formed. When it is also
endowed with a great capacity for integral thinking, then
the mentality, subtilized by Peshat, realizes itself in the work
of great jurists; more rarely philosophers, since philosophers
think in systems more difficult to hold together by ingenuity: and philosophic analysis strikes into the soil of the
historic systems in which Peshat and Drash are sown and
nurtured.[2]

[1] Thus a character in the works of Sholom Aleichem justifies his
boasting as follows: " 'Let others praise thee: not thine own mouth.'
That means let others praise thee: not (that is to say, if not) then thine
own mouth" (This is an old Rabbinic idea). Similarly, the Prayer-Book
praises Him who holds in hand the principle of Justice: and this is
humorously rendered: "He who holds in his hand (that is) the principle
of Justice". More seriously, there is a good popular comment on the
sceptic. The Psalmist says, "No counsel, no wisdom, no understanding
is comparable to that of (literally, over against) God". This is rendered:
"He who has no counsel, no wisdom, no understanding, is against God".

[2] It must not be thought that the thinking of homiletics is mentally
far removed from philosophic thinking. The philosopher draws fine
distinctions. E.g. Samuel Alexander, a Jew who wrote excellent philosophy, quotes, from Hermann Grimm, a distinction between "knowing
by means of the senses" and "knowing through the senses". This kind
of distinction appeals to the exploiters of text, and appeals to lawyers.
Again, a large description of a system is an imaginative effort comparable to an elaborate Drash, or to a piece of juristic system-building.
The important differences are, however, as follows:

(1) The philosopher is involved in making cohere groups of wide
concepts, postulates and propositions about the orders of being and
knowing. He is more concerned with a frame than a picture (not
that the two are separable).

(2) He aims at reduction of terms, not their increase.

(3) He is reluctant to accept any one proposition as a basis. All basic
propositions are possible bases.

In contrast the masters of Peshat and law prefer firm foundations and
love detail. Thus the types of thinking are movements in different
directions, rather than different modes.

The history of Jewish Thought is largely, then, the history of exegesis. Not wholly so, be it added: for Jewish jurisprudence developed a creativity in legal concepts before the Mishna was closed. But it is fair to say that in Bible commentaries, and in legal analyses, consists almost the whole of that literature which can be called "Jewish and nothing else but Jewish". Nor is this a dry field of verbal analytic. That impulse to an imaginative conception of the unity of things, and the transience of human distinctions, which was the Prophetic impulse, was not extinguished in the Jews when the Temple Priests lit their smaller lamps. Nor did the settling of law into parchment prove as stultifying to the Jewish spirit as the German critics of the nineteenth century seem to have believed. Legal analysis need not be "dry as dust" pedantry. The best analysis presupposes an imaginative synthesis: and the masters of Peshat and Drash were thinkers not limited by words: they mastered the words. Their effort was to save the world of Israel from being bounded by a Book: and in order to do so they made the Book into a world and a source of life.

For the Peshatist, or the Darshon, finds in the text what his imagination requires him to find. Illuminating is the treatment of any given verse by different exegetists of different periods or of different schools. Thus we are told that Jethro, the father-in-law of Moses, "heard all that God had done for Moses, and for Israel his people, that the Lord had brought forth Israel out of Egypt"; and, later: "Moses told his father-in-law all which the Lord had done unto Pharaoh on account of Israel: all the hardship which had come upon them by the way, and how the Lord had delivered them. And Jethro rejoiced over all the goodness which the Lord had done to Israel, that he had delivered it out of the hand of the Egyptians". To all the commentators these verses are rich in pleonasm that calls for explanation. The ordinary Peshatist (of whom the greatest is Rashi) analyses what news came to Jethro, and in what order it came; in what degrees of significance the various items appealed to him, and what Moses added. And this is much elaborated by Nachmanides and others. Some centuries later, we have the Darshon Ephraim of Lenciza, writing at a time of great theological speculation in Europe (the time of the Reformation), and explaining that these verses taught Jethro that the world was not divided between some Ormuzd and some Ahriman—a principle of good and a principle of evil. The same power was responsible for the evil that befell Egypt (and in a degree Israel) and the good that Israel received.[1] And another theologian puts a neat interpretation on the next following verse: "Now I know that the Eternal is great above all other gods". The Hebrew word that is translated "above" literally means "from" (or, by analogy, "than"). What Jethro said was: "Now I know that the Eternal is great from (my experience of, or comparison with) all the (putative) gods".

The literature of Jewish Bible commentary is, consequently, important in the light it sheds on the evolution of thought. Each commentator brings to his work something of the spirit of his age. Thus the first century Midrash, examining the Ten Commandments, expresses something of the "mystery" tradition of that period; a tradition that was to flower, so differently, in Gnosticism and in the Kabbalah.

The Ten Commandments start with Aleph. The Bible starts with Beth. The Aleph was offended by not being the first letter of the Pentateuch: but God explained that the world was created for the sake of the law: the Aleph would open the Commandments.[2] That thought is the text of some elaborate, and ethically interesting, homilies.

How different is the rationalistic analysis of the

[1] Ex. XVIII.1, et seq. Commentators, *ad loc.*
[2] Midrash Rabbah to Genesis.

Commandments on the part of Ibn Ezra—a product of the high culture of Moorish Spain, impregnated with Graeco-Arabic philosophy. Why does God describe himself, not as the creator of the world, but as the one "who brought you out of the land of Egypt, out of the house of bondage"? The explanation is that God is showing himself to be, not the arid "primal cause" of the metaphysicians, but the manifestor of "particular providence".[1]

Again, Ibn Ezra, in his capacity as textual critic, and many Peshatists besides, exert themselves to explain the textual differences between the commandments "spoken" in Exodus, and "remembered" in Deuteronomy. There were Rabbinic homiletics in plenty. But the great Spanish exegete demurs (most respectfully and scientifically) to these. Thus he rejects the suggestion that "remember" and "keep" (the Sabbath) were "pronounced in one utterance": and works out juristic reasons for the differences of language in the two statements in the Decalogue.[2]

Earlier than Ibn Ezra, but more rationalistic (in the spirit of Aristotle) we find Gaon Saadyah endeavouring to explain away miracles. Not the serpent or the ass spoke, but

[1] Exodus XX.2. Ibn Ezra, *ad loc.*

[2] It may be mentioned, further, that Ibn Ezra, being an astrologer, brings astrological theories into his commentaries, as well as the philosophical and psychological theories of his period. Thus he explains Balaam's skill as that of a stargazer making correct forecasts, and denies him (what others grant) the status of a prophet. (Ibn Ezra on Numbers XXII.28.) Astrology, be it noted, was never regarded by the Jewish philosophers as a magical system. Astrophysical influences, of a putatively scientific type, were the common stock of "natural philosophies" until, including, and after, Kepler. On the topic of the commentator's metaphysical background, it is worth noting that Nachmanides (Ramban) in the twelfth century was imbued with the neo-Platonic Kabbalistic learning of his period. He uses the terms of this system (spirits of fire, etc.) to describe the performances of the Egyptian magicians and Moses, respectively, when they demonstrated before Pharaoh.

angels through them, and angels (messengers) were more acceptable.[1] We have it on the authority of Ibn Ezra that Saadyah's opinion, being challenged, was supported by the Platonist Ibn Gabirol.

The philosophers of form and matter interpreted the Bible in a more sophisticated way than the masters of the Midrash. "Let us make man in our image". An explanation attributed by Ephraim of Lenciza to Nachmanides is that God co-operated with the earth so that Adam should be in OUR image, participating in the earthly, participating in the spiritual. And so, for each mind, and in each generation, there are special theoretic interests; and all these find expression in Bible exegesis and in homily based upon it.

To the commentators the Bible was a world for exploration: and a world with a unity to be established by thought, where there might appear to be discrepancy. What is said in one part of the Bible is inseparable from what is said in another. Moses said: "Hearken ye heavens . . . and hear O earth". Isaiah said: "Hear, O heavens, and hearken earth".[2] Because, explains the commentator, Moses was higher in the degrees of Prophecy than Isaiah: to Moses the Heavens were nearer: to Isaiah the earth. And the Rabbis were keen to notice, in Holy Writ, the difference in intimacy in the style of language that God seemed to use to Isaiah, and the style used to Ezekiel. "For Ezekiel was like a countryman who came to the capital to see the King. Isaiah was a townsman who saw the King every day".[3]

On the same theme: God demanded of Moses: "Cast thy shoes from thy feet, for the ground whereon thou standest

---

[1] To the commentators of most periods it was accepted learning that the messengers of God had appeared in the guise of men: had eaten. (As with Abraham. When Moses ascended among them, he did not eat.)

[2] Deut. XXXII.1: Isaiah I.2.

[3] T.B. Chagigah 14a.

is Holy". Of Joshua: "Cast thy shoe from thy foot".[1] Because, says Malbim, explaining implicitly (and following) an analysis of Prophecy by Maimonides, Joshua was to retain more of the earth in his composition than Moses. The mind of Moses came nearer to a direct intuition of the godhead than any other Prophet attained.

So to the theologian theology, to the historian history, to the moralist ethics, to the lawyer law, were metals to be mined from the text of the Bible by the sinking of intellectual shafts into the words. At times the claims to value in what was delved were fantastically exaggerated. By some schools the Bible was regarded as more holy, less human, in its language than is claimed in the Bible, or by the Rabbis to whom the Bible was freshest.[2] Thus the Kabbalists (and others) invested the letters of the text with significance. "I sojourned with Laban".[3] The word "I sojourned" is numerically equivalent to 613—the number of specific laws in the Pentateuch: and the interpreter will have it that the laws were revealed to the Patriarchs. Any departure by the Patriarchs from the Mosaic code, as given later, required to be explained with ingenuity that rarely proved unequal to the magnificent task. This method is not confined in its application to the Pentateuch. When there is an apparent contradiction between the accounts of Hannah's children (7 and 5) one explanation given is that the word for seven is numerically equivalent to Samuel. Also, at another pole of the Bible, in the Wisdom literature: "Wine goes in: Secret goes out". The word for Secret is numerically equivalent to the word for Wine. On coincidences of this

---

[1] Ex. III.5: Joshua V.15.

[2] On the legal side, "The law is not in Heaven" was always a maxim of interpretation, even though in the hands of some jurists it received the narrow, limited, and rare application that the maxims of Equity receive in English jurisprudence.

[3] Gen. XXXII.4.

type theories of the Bible are synthesized that verge into mysticism and mystery. Few among the great commentators emphasize this method: yet one of its greatest exponents was also one of the severest and most exact and careful of Jewish jurists.[1]

It must be remembered that, in the Jewish culture, the texts were mainly legal; and the homiletic, ethical, social aspects were developed in the matrix of a law that was, *ex hypothesi*, a thing of ethical perfection and human delight. The law itself is largely the creation of Peshat, so much so that the literal Bible law reads strangely in the light of the later codes. But always the theory was "exposition", just as for centuries the English Common Law pretended to be

---

[1] Jacob ben Asher, the compiler of the great codex called TURIM (lit. "lines"). He lived in one of the dark ages of Israel, when German Jewry was seeking escape into mystery and eschatology. (His father, the great Asher ben Yechiel, one of the first to epitomize the Talmud, had emigrated from Germany to Spain.)

On the topic of Grammateia, etc. it is to be observed that not only numerical equivalence and initials were significant, but the number of words used could be interpreted Aggadically and Halachically. E.g. when it is said of the Jews in Egypt that they multiplied (literally: swarmed like fish in the midst of the earth—and one commentator says they lived underground!), six words are used (Gen. XLVIII.16, et seq.)—to imply that sextuplets were born by each woman. Again (Halachically) four words of salvation (and some say five) are used in Exodus. Therefore four glasses of wine at the Seder—and a fifth doubtful (to be decided by Elijah). *See* p. 341.

At this stage it is pertinent to observe that the Jews have no monopoly of exegetic skill. Shakespearean cryptograms are *vieux jeux*. More simply, the text of the allusive Milton ("blind mouths") and of Shakespeare ("this sun of York"—a reference to heraldry) has been ingeniously interpreted. The difference is of degree and of relative importance. Much literature is allusively intended. In Peshat, the allusion is not obviously intended. Peshat was the Jewish normal: and an essential instrument in the extraction of laws. On the legal side, Statute interpretation in Europe has been casuistic: but never so imaginative, or so desperately ingenious, as in Talmudics.

existent from of old and rediscovered afresh in the bosoms
of Judges. At the best, the Bible law was inexplicit, and
effort was necessary in order to develop latent significance
and to make possible the working out of detail. Thus: what
was the Pentecostal tabernacle to be like? The Scripture
(Lev. XXIII.42, 43) employs the word tabernacles (Succoth)
three times: twice defectively spelled, once *plene*: there-
from it is curiously inferred that there were required two
walls and a section of wall; not more (T.B. Succah 6b.)[1].
And there are stranger examples.

The Rabbis were conscious of the strain imposed on the
text. "Some laws hang in the air, like mountains suspended
from hairs".[2] A vigorous community, achieving its institutions at a time when writing was not systematically
practised, developing laws; borrowing laws from Greek
merchants, and Greek and Roman occupation forces;
withal a litigious and anti-authoritarian community, found,
when it later achieved the levels of academic legal analysis,
that it possessed much law and little guiding authority other
than the Biblical codes and precedents. Therefore in the
colleges of Palestine, and (later) Babylonia, the task was to
deduce authority. Some laws were accepted as traditional:
oral law: law "given on Sinai" and not written by Moses, but
conveyed by Moses to Joshua and from Joshua to the Judges,
thence to Prophets, thence to Elders, and so by devolution
to the "Men of the Great Synagogue".

[1] Something turns there on the difference between MIKRA and
MASOREH as bases of exegesis.

[2] (T.B. Chagigah) It should be noted that not all derivations of law
by verbal methods are "deductive", or relied on as if they were deductive.
Thus the washing of the hands is supported by a verse in the Psalms
calling for "clean hands" (in another sense). This is ASMACHTA—
a "support" rather than an authoritative basis.

That the Rabbis were conscious of the dangers of the "verbal"
justification is evidenced by the witty comment: "If you must hang
yourself, do so from a strong tree".

But the later Rabbis (who remembered the scepticism of the Sadducees) found more acceptable that law which could, by effort, be extracted from the "written law": and, apart from firmly established traditions, strict extraction from the written law seems to have been required as a method of derivation in the self-conscious days of the fully developed academies. Once the Temple was destroyed, the Holy Spirit had departed from men. No one thereafter could find new law. The generations of Yavneh and Sura would not tolerate additions, by their contemporaries, to the Torah and the small body of already accepted Mishna. Yet within the four walls of text considerable juristic creation was to be achieved, especially by the Babylonian Schools.

After the fall of the first Temple, some Biblia came to the knowledge of the people. After the fall of the second Temple, the Bible came to life. A kingdom of Priests, translated into an academy of lawyers, found solace, inspiration, and a guidance for their lives, in writings which they knew that their ancestors had neglected. And the Rabbi, succeeding the Priest, and anxious to avoid the dogmatism and arbitary conduct of the old hierarchy, dedicated himself to an impersonal and devoted articulation of the legal principles so transmitted, and to learning which he regarded as of much more importance than his own will and the will of his own or alien rulers.

By the time of Ishmael and Akiva scientific minds had worked out many of the principles of interpretation which must be used by any jurist whose task is the analysis of codes. They arrived (with or without Graeco-Roman inspiration) at such a principle as Ejusdem Generis: the principle that, where a general rule is followed by particular cases, the latter limit the operation of the former. Indeed, in the absence of evidence to the contrary, it is arguable that the Rabbis of the first century of the common era were the discoverers of this rule, which is now a well-known doctrine of jurisprudence. It may be added that other principles laid down eventually by Rabbi Ishmael—elaborating the teachings of Hillel—are not out of place in a mature jurisprudence. But, in the derivation of Halacha, scientific principles are only part of the intellectual equipment of the Peshatist. Verbal analogies (of which one species is Gezerah Shaveh) play a part that is peculiar to Talmudics. Thus the expression "a Jewish Slave" is ambiguous in Hebrew (Eved Ivri): it can mean "the slave of a Jew" or "a Jew who is a slave". But in another context we read: "if thy Jewish brother is sold to thee in slavery". From this the Rabbis infer, not along any strict line of inference, but through an aesthetic principle, that the law relating to Eved Ivri was limited to the Jew who was a slave. Similarly Hillel "derived" a law he had learned from his teachers, allowing the Passover sacrifice on the Sabbath, from the occurrence of the words "at the appointed time" in the context of the Pesach sacrifices, and also in the context of the daily offering that was known to be permissible on the Sabbath.[1]

The Rabbis were careful to set limits to these methods, and would not allow new substantive law to be founded on

---

[1] On the Aggadic side, Gezerah Shaveh is very freely used. E.g. In Baba Bathra (16b) Esau is accused by the Rabbis of defiling a betrothed maiden, because Esau "came in from the field" (Gen. XXV.29), and the defilement described in Deuteronomy takes place "in a field" (Deut. XXII.27). More romantically, an anonymous match-maker in Baba Bathra (15b) marries Job to Dinah the daughter of Jacob, because a word occurs in her story (Gen. XXXIV.7) similar to a word used in his (Job II.10). Compendiously, it may be said that Gezerah Shaveh is one inspiration of a good deal of Drash. Thus when Jacob meets "a man", it could have been Gabriel, because of the language of Daniel IX.21. Similarly that Ezra "went up" suggests analogies with Moses. Other sources of Drash (and Peshat) are questions suggested by the immediate text itself. E.g. Why did the angels go "up and down" the ladder, instead of "down and up". Because they had been on duty guarding Jacob, etc.

72

analogy. Yet they defended much accepted oral law (which was Rabbinic law) in this way. Articulations of the law (which do not involve a new principle) can be supported by the method of verbal analogy and other pressure on the text. But the process is hard to restrict. Indeed, it happens in the Talmud that new law is derived from the mere proximity of verses. Thus in Deuteronomy a verse about false witness is followed by a verse on the powers of the laws to punish wrongdoing: from which it is deduced that, apart from the specific law relating to the "scheming" witness, there is a general power of flagellation to be administered to witnesses who fall short of the first degree of HAZOMOH, for which the penalty is capital.[1]

Many quite substantial sections of the Rabbinic law (Day of Atonement: Levirate marriage: and many others) are so scantily referred to in the Pentateuch that imaginative effort was necessary to achieve their elaboration, or to justify the elaborations of centuries of pre-Talmudic Jewish life. As the law developed, the principles of derivation became more rigid and scientific. The Masoretic text, becoming settled, resolved many disputes founded on variant renderings. The Mishna, once codified (third century C.E.), settled the essentials of oral law. From that time onward a high degree of mental energy was devoted to the reconciliation of Mishnaic traditions, the case learning of the Tannaim and their various pupils. That task was the burden of Talmudic scholarship until the great codes were made; and was continued thereafter.

The source and the consequence of Rabbinic method was an Idealism which included a belief in the unity of the Scriptures, and the unity of the entire law. Discrepancies between similar texts were rarely resolved by the theory of different authorship—in the case of Bible texts, never. Thus, one Biblical statement runs: "Honour thy father and

[1] Makoth 2.

thy mother": according to another verse: "Thy mother and thy father shalt thou fear". Not two different sources these, as modern critics would hold, but one elaborate message. The normal, say the Rabbis, is to honour the mother and fear the father. The purpose of the two scriptural verses is to redress this natural imbalance.[1]

Later, in the field of jurisprudence, this method of reconciliation became a task and an intellectual strain; and, in compensation, created a system of learning which at once accentuated subtlety and challenged mental capacity to grasp the system whole. No legal system has ever been studied with an intensity or to a standard which is the normal of Talmudic study. And this is to some extent traceable to the early Jewish method of legal thinking. Thus the Amoraim and Sabaraim, who studied the Mishna and the teachings of the Tannaim and all the case-law available to them, tended from the earliest days to assume complete consistency and coherence in what they learned. If there was apparent conflict, they restated the conflicting views in contexts which made them consistent. They extrapolated circumstances to make one judgement cohere with another. If the conflict was too clear to be resolved, then they classified each conflicting view and showed it to be coherent with a system Tannaitically approved. The conflict between Tannaim was irreducible: but even if one school of thought was followed in preference to another, that other was never regarded as fundamentally wrong. Rather there were empirical conditions that made one line of learning more applicable to human material than the other. If Shammai gave way to Hillel in authority, it was because Shammai was too strict for an incapable generation.

To the modern student of law, who is prepared to say: this doctrine is old, and this is new; this was wrong, and this

[1] *See* the Decalogues in Ex. and Deut. for the familiar, and Lev. XIX.3 for the other, form.

is right; the Talmudic method constitutes a waste of intellectual energy. From another point of view, it is excessively difficult, if only because a language without grammar is bound to be more difficult than a well-articulated language. If the Talmud is a mass of detail ingeniously held together, it cannot be mastered by those who wish to grasp only a few principles. Nevertheless, the Talmudic law has been codified, and brilliantly codified; but that achievement has been the work of the very few, and at long intervals of time. Most of the commentators on Talmud have occupied themselves with the exposition of what is obscure, and speculation on what is not explicit.

Many have conjured problems and apparent conflicts, and sought to reconcile them, but never claiming more than could be proved by clear reference to established authority. An occasional outstanding legal luminary such as Rabbenu Tam (the grandson of Rashi) or, nearer to our own day, Rabbi Elijah of Vilna (1720-97), has been able to combine the maximum of conciliatory ingenuity with an ability to see the law as a whole. Such a one can show that particular disputes have been unfounded, have been based on ignorance. But, in the whole history of Talmudic research, few in any century have achieved the intellectual confidence and recognition that makes possible the great simplifications. And the greatest approach the task humbly. Even in our own day the dominant masters of the Law are very conscious of being its servants.[1]

It follows, then, that the mature Jewish scholar of today—and indeed any Jew who lives within Jewish tradition—is heir to a learning, legal, moral, and intellectual, which is profound, which is intricately articulated, which is authoritarian. The entire tradition is spun and woven with threads of imagination and ingenuity, which, being continued,

[1] The Rabbis described themselves, in Talmudic times, as "Pupils of the Wise". (Compare the word "Scholar".)

constitute considerable intellectual forces. The moving spirit is evidently quite different from the analytic, atomistic, historically framed learning of Western Europe, which was founded by the anti-traditionalist physicists of the seventeenth century, who are responsible for most contemporary philosophies.

Of Jewish philosophy, let it be said at this stage that the same keen light that illuminates the interstices of a sacred text, is at times spread more widely to form a bright frame for the world of things. A vein of rationalism runs deep through the strata of Jewish law and legend. The name of Hillel is outstanding as one who, through the accidents of accreted tradition, saw the essentials, and was able to invent devices which gave expression to the spirit, while preserving the letter, of the ancient law. That rationalistic tradition, estimating human ethics higher than formalities, is the inspiration of one Jewish philosophic tradition, which, developing through the work of Saadyah, the poet Judah Halévy, Maimonides and many others, consists in the statement of those fundamentals that are the differentia of Jewish life from the life of the world.

But in metaphysics (in the modern sense) the Jewish heritage is a tradition dominated by the Book; ironically an unmetaphysical book. The Rabbis read into the mind of Abraham an argument for monotheism which is, in effect, the Ontological Argument in rudimentary form. He looked to the Sun, and the Wind, and the Water, and needed something beyond them. Something prior and greater is required by thought: must be, therefore is.

In the main, their thinking was not systematically speculative in matters of cosmology. Their theology was too intimate to be philosophical. In the spirit of a Book in which the only proof of the Godhead is by revelation, they thought of God as near and not remote, as humanly thinkable, not as a comprehensive predicate of reality. That spirit has remained as a permanent factor in Rabbinic tradition, and has been refreshed, from time to time, by Chassidic movements ranging from Essenism to the Chassidism of the Baal Shem in the eighteenth century.

The God of the Chassid is an intimate God, living now, as then, in communion with his people. The Jew is not ashamed to pray to him—to make requests for help in his personal life. Although the liturgy is largely praise, thanksgiving and meditation, some of the oldest prayers are entreaties. Even, on occasions of peril, the Psalms are recited by way of invocation. The Jew does not require the apologetic of philosophers who say that his prayers are an elevation to a high Hegelian level of religion. Some are that as well: but the Jewish God does not resent entreaties. He claims, says the Chassidic Rabbi (perhaps in a spirit different from that of Ibn Ezra) to be, not the Creator of Heaven and Earth, but the one "who brought *you* out of the land of Egypt." A Holy Spirit which, as the Midrashic (now colloquial) expression has it, is "in exile" with a people whose history is exile.

To orthodox Jews (and not only Chassidim—for the Essene is only the extremist Pharisee) the thoughts that are important about God are ethical thoughts. Speculation about the nature of God they derive, not from any rationalist tradition, but from the unsystematic, and rich, lore of Aggadah and Midrash.

Out of this "crystal store" a treasury could be collected simply of the conversations to which the Rabbis made the Lord a party. Everyone disputes or discusses with Him. Angels give him arguments against making Man. An overflow of their resentment is felt in the actual Bible text of Job: and in the Talmud (Baba Bathra 16) Job seems to be asking God whether He has confused the word IYOV (Job) with OYEV (Enemy), and God meditates on this. The exile Rabbis seem to have regarded God's attention

77

as directed to individuals rather than the nation. So, Adam wants to see the future and is prepared to sacrifice years of his own life so that God shall prolong the life of David. David, in turn, was to hold colloquy with God—on one occasion, as we have seen, about the duration of his own life.

Very characteristic are the extra-biblical colloquies of Moses and God. When God says, in reply to his entreaty, "I cannot", the word in the text is in feminine form, and the Aggadist attributes to Moses the bold challenge: Are you, like a woman, afraid of opposition? This spiritual Chutzpah, two millennia old, is in exactly the same spirit that animated in modern times the famous Berdichever Rebbe in those many recorded soliloquies which consisted of appeals to God to argue the matter on a rational-ethical basis, to show cause why Israel is being made to suffer, to prove the justice of the matter. In another vein the Rabbis point out that when Moses said: "Strike out my name from what thou has twritten", his name was left out of the current section of text when completed.

God, according to the Rabbis, prays, lays Tefillin, wears a Tallith (Berachot 6a): makes vows, and asks to have his vows "released" (Shemoth Rabbah XLIII). Even He is imagined as ritually unclean at the moment of burying Moses (Sanhedrin 39a). How much more personal can God become?

Abba Shaul (grave-digger and medical man!) interprets the word ANAVEHU (in Exodus XV.2) to mean: "I shall be like unto him".[1] This is not in the spirit of those philosophers who explain away anthropomorphism: but it may have inspired the modern Chassid, Rabbi Nachum of Tchernobil, who, when his congregants took action against

[1] Conventional translation: "Adorn Him". There is a speculative possibility that a name of the Deity is being used (cf. ANI-VE-HO, in the liturgy).

a recipient who had abused the Rabbi's charity, said: "I was trying to catch hold of the hem of His garment, 'who is good and does good to the bad and the good', and you prevented me."

In this spirit most of the great commentators discuss the questions of Divinity that are suggested by the text. They do not ask how Deity is possible, or how the concept of Deity is stateable in a world full of evil. What they undertake is to explain God's words and works, so as to make His utterances cohere—as if, be it said unblasphemously, He were a human authority. "Come and hear", as the Talmud has it. When God said to Moses that He had revealed himself to Abraham, Isaac and Jacob as El Shaddai, but that in His proper name he had not made himself known to them, the problem for the Darshon is to reconcile this with some of the revelations in Genesis, where divine names are spoken. Evidently much can be read into the expression "had not made himself known". The patriarchs had not been given insight into the deep realities that lie beneath the names. As to the names, a typical Peshat is that one name signifies the characteristic of mercy, another signifies power, another justice. In the light of these distinctions, the revelation to Moses can be distinguished.[1] At this stage, be it observed, philosophy of a certain degree is guiding the commentator: but not a philosophy that investigates the cosmology in such terms as the Judaeo-Arabic philosophers of Spain were to adopt from the Greeks. Nor is that speculation philosophical which derives meaning from the letters of the various names, or which finds, as Ephraim of Lenciza did, evidence, in the word Shaddai, of a promise of a future life.

On the famous verse "I am what I am" (any translation

[1] Maimonides points out that, in His revelations to the Patriarchs, God had never called upon them to speak prophetically, or to lead people, as Moses was being called upon to lead them.

will beg a question) the typical Peshat is Rashi's: "I was with you and I shall be with you". Not until the age of Maimonides are we offered the explanation that God is declaring himself as essentially existing—a Being of which Existence must be predicated. That Kabbalists (theosophic rather than philosophic) have worked much on the names goes without saying. But in so doing they incur a criticism for a fault against which the text declares a warning. Both Maimonides and Nachmanides come near to, yet fall short of, the truth perceived in our time by the more historically-minded Martin Buber: that, in refusing to give a name, the Lord was distinguishing Judaism from the cults of Magic. "A name to conjure with." That is not offered. This thought—perhaps the most substantial contribution to theology made by the strange modern, existentialist, Chassid—coheres with all the realities and appearances of the Bible. The Bible is full of evidence that cults of magic were superseded by a religion which has no sorcery in it— a process of adoration, not of conjuration. The phallism, the sacrifices, the sacred lots, the very serpents of Semitic cults, are transmuted in Biblical Judaism into a ritual accessory to adoration and dedication. It was left to Ophites and other Gnostics to disinter from the Scriptures evidences of a Demiurge, and mysterious forces of good and evil struggling for supremacy with magical weapons. In contrast the spirit of the Bible, as we have it, is a belief in the complete dominion of a benevolent power. What the Unity of the Godhead meant to the Jews was that there was only one Good, only one Right, only one ultimate appeal for guidance. A human conception of the Godhead expresses this belief: and that belief is hard to state in terms of a metaphysical system based on the world order of physics, in which good and evil can so easily become devalued as merely human predicates.

From the original Jewish spirit, the Talmudic development is not to metaphysics: rather to mystery.[1] This dangerous development is possibly a safer one than the ways of pure reason.

The Talmud (which is a literature—not a book) records alongside the Halacha, and interspersed with it, some of the legends, the dreams, the speculations, the pre-critical world constructions of men in exile, endeavouring to find in their minds the sources of comfort and confidence that had possessed the Prophets. This inspiration they could not recapture. But they gladly wove into their Biblical traditions much of the speculative thought that was stimulating the heaving culture of the lands between East and West. They accepted, and stated in Biblical terms, some of the angelology that was moving between Persia and Alexandria. Michael, Raphael, Uriel, these are Hebrew names. Elijah is a prophet turned angel. So is Enoch. Metatron[2] (the angel behind the throne) is the Greek name of an angel who only appears in Hebrew literature. But the stories about these angels, stories such as fill the pseudepigraphic Books of Enoch (the man who, like Elijah, never died) are legends in the context of Biblical events—at the Reed Sea, in the desert, and at many Biblical battles and disasters.

The Talmud, being mainly a legal work—more accurately, a centuries-long study of Jewish ethical-legal duties—only hints at the speculations of the period: and the Rabbis, even then, were conscious of its dangers. They feared the consequences of inquiring into the Creation and the Chariot.

[1] Mystery, be it emphasized; not mysticism. In mysticism man lets himself be lost in the Universe. In mystery, the Universe is concerned with, and affected by, individual man.

[2] Perhaps a judaized form of Mithras. Observe that some angelology is Biblical. The Jacob narrative, and Jacob's blessing of Ephraim and Manasseh, refer to MALAKH (Messenger). Also, we have the experiences of Balaam, stopped by an Angel, and of Abraham, Lot and Joshua who encountered "Men". But no Biblical Messenger is given a name.

They said, in effect, that it was easier to enter the "orchard" of thought, than to return. But some of their speculations are known.

There is evidence that the great Rabbi Akiva ben Joseph was inspired, in his hermeneutics, by a theory of the sacredness of the letters of the alphabet. This is part of the Chaldaic learning of a long period, in which participated the Pythagoreans and the Alexandrians. From that time is derived the inspiration of a very old writing, the Sefer Yezirah (the Book of Creation) which, for centuries, was treasured and annotated by orthodox Rabbis. It contains, according to possible interpretation, a theory of the revolution of the earth on its axis, which is believed to have been known to the Hindus. But this is the only book of pure cosmology that has found its way into what may be called the Rabbinical Canon. All else is Midrash, or Aggadah, concerned with a Biblical subject-matter. Even the body of learning which was centuries later to be embodied in the Zohar (The Book of Light), was stated, indeed conceived, in the terms and spirit of Midrashic commentary.

The Zohar itself is a commentary on the Pentateuch, and to that all its ancient eschatology and neoplatonic superstructure are subordinate.

So, it is in such accounts as that of the death and burial of Sarah, and the purchase of the cave, that we are told of the orders of spirit and soul. In another context, the voice of the turtle is the voice of the angel who musters the spirits of those about to be born. It is as if the Bible story is being told from the standpoint of an observer among the Heavenly host. This is an extreme development of a Talmudic-Midrashic tradition in which angels were more imaginatively described than they had been in the unsophisticated Biblical references to the messengers of God.

Typical of Aggadah, and typical of Midrash, are (as we have seen) stories of conversations between God and the angels, studded with quotations, by all the disputants, from Biblical text. But the metaphysical, here, is always sub-ordinate to the ethical theme.[1]

How different is the approach of the metaphysician proper, trained in the critical apparatus of the Greek Schools. His task is to explain away the "human" mani-festations of the Godhead. The purpose of Aggadah and Midrash is to multiply them.

But the Jewish metaphysicians proper have also been spiritually bounded in the Book. Philo, the Alexandrian, was the first of the great Jewish apologists, striving to reconcile Jewish traditions with Greek science. He based his system on a doctrine of Logos, the creative word. His work (which escaped the Rabbis but strongly influenced the Christians) is valuable now mainly as an analysis of some methods of exegesis.[2] A thousand years later, one of the latest, and himself the greatest, of those that can be called Jewish philosophers—philosophers of the Jewish tradition—Maimonides, brings exegesis to its limits as a philosophic instrument, and virtually abandons it in his ultimate re-liance on a theory of a Bible written anthropomorphically for the benefit of simple people. With the aid of this doc-trine (the tradition of Ishmael, not of Akiva) he is almost able to turn the "numenon" of the Bible into the noumenal abstraction of Aristotle. Perhaps it was right that some of the lesser Rabbis of his period, conscious as they were of the merits of this greatest of Jewish jurists, wished to declare his philosophic teaching anathema.[3]

[1] The Talmudic redaction seems to have eliminated from the records some instances of speculation for its own sake.

[2] It has been argued that Philo knew no Hebrew; that his Bible was the Septuagint. This seems to be evidenced by his misunderstanding of some phrases, which the Septuagint had translated clumsily. In that case it is remarkable that he showed a flair for Peshat, away from the sources of its inspiration.

[3] In his treatment of the arguments of Alexander of Aphrodisias,

Maimonides made one of the last great efforts to state a philosophy which would be reconciled with a positive exegetic attitude to the Scriptures.

After Maimonides—in logic more than in time—Spinoza. Spinoza (well read in the works of the great Spanish master and of his critics) seems to have begun his thinking with critical speculations that grew into a critique of the Bible in terms that anticipate the historical approach of later centuries.[1] To Spinoza, philosophy is once again criticism: criticism grounded on an awareness of the human brain as the organ of knowing, and the human heart as the organ of obedience. From that standpoint the Bible is a book among other books. Its value is in its pieties: the exegetists are wrong to read too much into it: Maimonides is wrong in rationalizing its ancient mysteries.[2] Spinoza, in short, was an unbeliever. Consciously, or unconsciously, he sums up his attitude to two religions in one sentence. "Final causes," he pronounces, "like Virgin births, produce nothing."

After Spinoza, philosophy did not "cease out of Israel". Mendelssohn, we shall see, was to inaugurate some kind of philosophic revival. But it is fair to say that, since Spinoza, philosophy of a critical-metaphysical type has moved away from the Book. Those writers who discuss the relative

Maimonides leaves his view on immortality to be conjectured; and exposes himself to the criticism that he is not accepting the derivation of the doctrine from Holy Writ.

[1] *Tractatus Theologico-Politicus.* In this work Spinoza reveals an extensive, if incomplete, knowledge of Judaica. He is familiar, *inter alia*, with the text of RASHI (whom he refers to as Rabbi Solomon Yarchi—lit. of Lunel) and of Ibn Ezra. He knew, and owed much to, Maimonides, whose world-picture may well be reflected in his own. (Dr. Leon Roth has written an excellent essay on this topic.)

[2] One of Spinoza's points of departure is Maimonides' account of Prophecy. Spinoza accepts the analysis, but treats the Prophet as a man possessed of a high degree of quite human insight—not outside the order of ordinary cognition.

importance of nationality and religion in Jewish tradition are historians rather than philosophers. *Exceptis excipiendis*, let it be said that since Spinoza outstanding Jewish philosophers have been Jews who were philosophers simpliciter: and include, in the last hundred years, great conspective thinkers in many fields: systematizers in science like Bergson, Marx, Freud, Einstein, each of whom may owe something to an intellectual spirit, mysteriously transmitted, but whose genius is, only in a biological sense and with the aid of metaphor, a manifestation of the Jewish Mind.[1]

[1] There have, of course, been many Rabbinical philosophers: but none of recognized magnitude in the secular sphere. Isserlein, Sirkes, Solomon, Loria, Isserles, Eybeschütz and Hirsch deserve mention among others. The late Rabbi Kook, Chief Rabbi of Israel, wrote law philosophically. Famous Maggidim (Homilists) have been aware of philosophy: but have preferred the more personal pictures of good and evil, such as Midrash and Kabbalah afford, to the intellectual abstractions. As moralists they found that "evil spirit" meant more to a congregation than "base material". On the other side, among the abstractionists, we find that, since Mendelssohn, Jewish philosophers have been more concerned with the justification of Jewish survival, and the justification of specific institutions, than with Jewish metaphysics.

CHAPTER THREE

HOW PLEASANT IS THIS TREE

To the poets of this latter-day century, inhaling the culture that pervades the blossoms of leisure, and exhaling the sense of freedom which fills the nostrils of the emancipated, the Bible flowers call greeting from Canticles. A light shines gently which is not the fire of Sinai, and there is sweetness unknown to Samson in the voice of the turtle dove. So, when Tchernichovsky stood in front of the statue of Apollo, admiring the myrtle-wreathed god who had sung to the lust of youth, but not of Jewish youth, he conjured also the image of a Jewish god who had once been young, when Israel was young, and before they bound him and themselves with the bands of the tefillin.

In that poem the poet is also expressing some historic truths: a truth about the history of Israel; a truth about religion and life and art; a truth about the place of the Bible in Jewish life. Truths, these, such as Ben Lakish experienced after he had leaped across the stream; truth expressed in the reproach to David for treating the law as a song:[1] truth latent in the warning given to the student not to ponder the beauty of the tree: whether that tree was the one outside the window of the Yeshivah, or in the

[1] T.B. Soteh 35a. *See* p. 53 *supra* and note thereto.

distant grove of Mamre: not to be admired: not to be worshipped.

As the Scriptor himself fuses into the story of the growth of Judaism all references to the cults of groves and serpents, of phallism and taurolatry and human sacrifice, that are the background of the Pentateuch narrative, without dwelling on them, without describing them, so the recipients of the Scripture read the content and truth of the message without thinking of the persons concerned as ordinary human beings, and without meditating on the natural background of people and land.

In that spirit the words and language and stories of the Bible were to be understood as law and morals and faith and mystery: not to be admired as poetry or narrative: not to be appreciated, not to be criticized. Not the art of words was looked for in the Book, but, as the lawyers have it, "words of art".

Consequently, as was recalled above, the Jews did not become—what the Greeks were—the minstrel custodians of a heritage of song and epic. Just as the Bible is a text-book of politics—and from it the Jews completely failed to learn politics—so the Scriptures are rich in models of clear prose and narrative, of lyric and elegiac, of declamation and diatribe, even of intellectual drama: but that was not their appeal to the ghetto Jews, even when the ghetto was being formed in their own land. For the Jews have loved the Book in such a way and with such an intensity, they so belong to the Book, that they never could, as a group, stand away from it and contemplate it as spectators do.

They are involved in a spiritual struggle to which the Book is introductory. That involvement is expressed in the Book itself with its emphasis on wrong and misfortune. That Omri ruled a happy kingdom,[1] is a fact totally

[1] For a contrary view: *see* Josephus (unreliable for the period), in *Antiquities*, Ch. XII.

87

obscured by the long account of the errors of his son Ahab. The successes of the latter mean nothing—are not even shown as dramatic contrast—in the story of his misdeeds and their retribution. As the writers were, so have the readers been.

The law, the ethics, the misfortunes consequential on wickedness, the occasional triumphs of righteousness, these were always too much part of their lives, and thought, to be aesthetic spectacle. The God of Israel was too near and too important for his works to be regarded in a detached way, as the audiences of Aeschylus and Sophocles could regard the patterned workings of the fates and the caprice of the pagan gods. For the Jews, the sufferings recorded in the Bible were not the sufferings of others removed in time and place, but the inveterate and perpetual sufferings of the living group.

And as they viewed the deeds, so they heard the words. "How beautiful on the mountains are the feet of the messenger with good tidings" (Isaiah, LII.7). A poetic thought this, not inferior to a line in Sappho. But to the audiences of Isaiah, the meaning of the message was too vital to allow of any appreciation of its aesthetic form.

So, generally, in respect of the message of all the poetic prophets, the language of the Bible itself, urgent with a sense of futurity, and the desperate hope and belief, on the part of the ghetto Jew, that his circumstances are transient, combine to make the Jewish attitude to the beautiful words too intense for the purposes of aesthetic appreciation.[1]

In other words, the aesthetic judgements, the enjoyment of the world of eye and ear, the contemplation, with controlled emotion, of tragedy, the relaxation of the mind in

---

[1] Intellectual appreciation is there, as when a Jew says of a Peshat, or Drash, that it is "sweet as honey". There is an aesthetic satisfaction in that, but the strong appeal is to thought.

humour, these are the experiences of groups not pre-occupied with the attainment of righteousness and the avoidance of sin, not timelessly involved in a desperate plea for salvation. Aesthetic judgements are the functions of the spectators of events, not of a protagonist. Suffering Israel clung fiercely to the Bible for comfort or promise of comfort, for guidance, for the direction that is given by laws and customs, for some authority to lead them through their waiting lives. Being all that, for the Jews in exile the Book could not be literature.

That the Jews are not lacking in the aesthetic qualities, in eloquence, in artistic endeavour in many fields, in the irony of intellectual detachment, we know from the works of Jews in alien fields. They have been set to watch the vineyards of others; and those they have cleverly cultivated. But Jewish aesthetic effort in a Jewish context has not been the normal mental activity of Jews. Jewish poets there have been, at all periods, especially in the rare phases of emancipation. More will be said of these. Suffice it here to observe that those who dwell in a heritage built of words cannot entirely escape from the blandishments of words.

Music there was once. But we know as little of the martial tunes to which the Maccabees marched and set their Psalms as we do of the songs the Sirens sang. When the Temple fell, instrumental music (whatever it may have been) was banished from the Jewish ritual. The Nigun of the Cantillations is old, more than a millennium old, and so are many Synagogue melodies—some even older than the Plainsong of the Catholic Church, which owes much to them. An old Yigdal has given at least one melody to modern Christian services.[1] But of secular composition by Jews to express the Jewish spirit there was nothing of note until the light-

[1] A Rabbi of Amsterdam discussed old Jewish hymn tunes with Sir Thomas More, and cited a Passover Seder tune (Adir Hu) as among the most popular.

hearted Sulamith of Goldfaden in the nineteenth century, and the more important works of Bloch in the twentieth. It has been said of Bloch that he wrought a cassock with fringes showing beneath. For the rest, when we call Bloch's melodies Jewish, let it be remembered that nobody knows what elements of Arabic, Slavonic, Magyar, are blended in traditional Jewish synagogue and folk-tunes.[1] Yet there are those who can feel in the music of Mendelssohn and Meyerbeer that Jews are speaking to them: who can listen to Offenbach and discern a lyrical extravagance that might delight the emancipated son of an orthodox Chazan.[2]

Of painting and sculpture let it be said that they were the victims of the Second Commandment. If, in the Jewish view of the Godhead, there was any change from ancient sternness to modern humanity, it could not be expressed as the Christians expressed their changing theology, in the works of painters. Thus, Christian painters have achieved the transmutation of their stern deity of the Middle Ages into a being expressing the softer humanity of easier days. But the Jews had no Botticelli, no Angelo,[3] no Millais.

[1] The aggregate of Chazanic melodies which is called the Scarbova Nigunim—the stock of European cantors—undoubtedly contains much that is very old. The absence of MS. music before modern times unfortunately makes proof of their Palestinian origin impossible.

[2] Of Jewish sentimental singing there is no lack. Very well known are such songs as Eli, Eli, and Tayere Stane. But Jewish instrumentalism is better known than Jewish singing. Jewish instrumentalists favour the violin (a portable instrument!) as was found when the great Israel orchestra was founded by Huberman. And though great competence has been shown in many idioms and styles, the majority reveal an impulse to virtuosity and lyric performance, and a flair for emotional interpretation. Of Chazanuth, Caruso described the late Chazan Sirota as one of the greatest voices in Europe.

[3] Angelo is interesting to Jews because his magnificent Moses is marred by horns, owing to a Latin mistranslation. For KORON OR PONOV (the skin of his face shone), the Vulgate (reading KEREN) offers: cornuta facies ejus (his face was horned).

Jewish evolution has been literary—not pictorial. So now, when there is Jewish painting, we cannot say of it more than that some of it is Jewish because it is about Jews, and some of it is Jewish because it is by Jews. Solomon J. Solomon painted well in a British tradition. In contrast, Chagall has enriched surrealism by symbolizing Yiddish expressions. (The beggar on the roof tops *"geht über die haüse".)* Up to the present none of them—not Chagall, not Soutine, not Modigliani, not Reuben—have produced an Hebraic study to compare with the Jews of Rembrandt. In the adjacent field of sculpture, the experts have not yet established what tradition of Jewry or Jewishness was revealed when Jacob Epstein endeavoured in his "Genesis" to express the canons of an aesthetic Deuteronomy.

Ornamentation was permitted by the Law and has been a Jewish art. As well as the love of embellishment, which derives from the East and the South, there has been among the Jews great craftsmanship. This is one reason for the prevalence of the Jewish goldsmith, jeweller and clockmaker. But their greater craftsmanship has been in words, in the art of allusion. In the world of words, however, the creative impulse has been, for most Jewish intellect, legal, ethical, religious. That, under the compulsion of special emotional impulse, in conditions where expression to an audience has been possible, the Jews have achieved great poetry and great prose is a fact not well known to traditional Jewry. Even learned Jews do not treat their liturgy as a literary treasure: which it is. As for the Bible, the Prophets in it may not have known that they prophesied: their hearers certainly did not know that they were listening to poets.

Intensive emotive conditions made possible the writing of the various Scriptures at various periods. These writings only began to be valued when the Exile was already imminent. Their content was then revealed as a moral lesson: and that lesson was too overwhelming for the readers and listeners in the synagogue to appreciate the music of language, the fine rhythm of the parallels, the elemental majesty of skies and mountains conjured by the words.

By the spectator at a distance, by the reader of the Authorized Version, or of Luther's taut German translation, the poetic values of the Bible are easily recognized. Are poetic images desired? What poet does not respond to the "hart pining for cooling streams", or the pilgrims asking to return "as do the streams of the South", or to the voice of "deep speaking to deep" of "day communing wordlessly with day, night with night"?

Are effects in question? Antithesis? "From the narrows I called to the Lord. He has answered me in the wide spaces of the Lord" (Psalm CXVIII.5). Parallelism? "The Heavens recite the glories of the Lord: the firmament tells the story of His greatness".

In the Hebrew the assonances of the Psalter and the Prophetic books possess a beauty that is incommunicable in translation. Even a "narrative" prophet, such as Jeremiah, aims at, and achieves, tonal effects.

Yet by an irony, the poetic values that have been so appreciated in the translations have been almost ignored by the custodians of the melodious original.[1]

---

[1] Some of the poetic and verbal effects of the Bible are, necessarily, lost in translation. In point is Isaiah V.7 (MISHPOT—MISHPOCH, etc.). Again, Jeremiah's prophecy on the almond tree involves a verbal play on the word SHOKED—the word for almond, and the participle of the verb "to hasten". (This is a legitimate literary device, used by Greek poets: e.g. in the famous line about Helen, Hellenaus, Heleptolis, Helandron—"ruin of ships, ruin of towns, ruin of men".)

But even Hebraists have at times failed to appreciate less difficult poetic effects. Thus "the sea saw and fled: the Jordan turned back". Because the Biblical past and future tenses are confusable (by reason of the "imperfective" form) this can be read as meaning "The Jordan will turn back". And one commentator makes the gloss "The sea fled

Even more striking than the absence, from traditional Jewish thought, of literary appreciation of the Bible (with the attendant dangers of literary and textual criticisms) is the failure of Jewish writers, who were subtle in their assessments of human motives, to value the Bible characters as human beings.

What manner of man was David? The Rabbinic obsession was with the question whether he had sinned. There are schools of thought holding that he did not sin with Bathsheba, but that he was lacking in piety toward Saul.[1]

But what of that charming shepherd boy with the catapult? Let the Midrash (on Moses) provide the Jewish artistic treatment. " 'The Lord trieth the righteous' (Ps. XI.5): and by what? By the feeding of sheep. He tried David by sheep and found a good shepherd. 'And he took him from the "restraints" of sheep' (Ps. LXXVIII.70). (Follows a digression on the meaning of the word, with a citation from Genesis.) David restrained his sheep. He brought out the

before Moses: The Jordan will turn back for Joshua". (Cf. In the meditation Perek Shirah, "Moses will sing" as a translation of Ex. XVII.1.) This kind of comment suggests an indifference to the syntax, at least of poetry.

It should be added that the great commentators, especially of the Spanish period, had full understanding of grammatical and rhetorical forms. Thus Moses Ibn Ezra wrote a treatise on rhetoric. But the application of these studies to the Bible was not systematically made until the period of Mendelssohn and his Biurists. Worthy of study, to those who have access, is Mendelssohn's introduction to The Song of Moses.

[1] Interesting is a touch of "realism" in Tractate Berachoth 3b. After David had studied all night, to the music of the wind playing through his harp, his advisers approached him with economic questions. "The nation needs income". "Go and make a living out of each other". They replied "A handful of grain does not satisfy a lion: and a pit cannot be filled with the earth extracted from it". "Well then: let us mobilize". After which exercise in pre-Keynesian economics, he returned to meditation.

young sheep to feed on the tender shoots, the older sheep later to feed on the coarser. Wherefore the Lord said: 'He who understandeth to feed sheep let him come and feed my people'. As the Psalm has it (LXXVIII.71) 'From following the ewes great with young, he brought him to feed Jacob his people'. And so Moses. When he was feeding the flocks of Jethro a kid ran away: and Moses followed it to a mountain pool. He carried it back saying, 'I did not know that thou didst run away because thou wast thirsty'. And God said: 'Because thou wert compassionate among the sheep, belonging to mere man, lead thou my flock'. Therefore it is written 'And Moses was feeding the flock'." (Shemoth Rabbah II.)

In beauties of homiletic exposition, not in the beauties of appearance—the things of which one says "this looks beautiful"—are the Rabbis creative.

And what of the magnificent Solomon? To the Tannaim, who knew Hadrian and remembered Herod, killer of Rabbis, he was a King with all the vices of Kingship. The later Rabbis valued him more highly. But the trend of thought about him is best expressed in the comment of Judah ben Ilai (second century C.E.) who said of the famous "judgement" "Had I been there I would have put a rope round his neck".[1]

So with other characters that play their parts on the stage of Holy Writ. Unless an ethical or political judgement can be passed on them (like the description of Phineas as a zealot) they are not studied in the human round.

What manner of man was Balaam? A prophet with strict limitations. We are told of his intellectual problems. And Job? Those Rabbis (of whom Ben Lakish was one)

[1] Clearly the case of the babies is not to be decided according to the rule of "two who found a garment" (Division). What rule of evidence is applicable? Onus on the Plaintiff? Was the Rabbi wrong in thinking that a test for truth may not be made prior to a decision on pleadings?

come nearest to literary criticism who offer the suggestion that he never existed, was a figure of legend. And there is some implicit dramatic appreciation in those comments which make Job VII.9 (the finality of the grave) into a question posed in order to be answered. Others provide us with speculative biographies and ethical explanations for Job's sufferings—his failure to act positively in favour of the infant Moses. Of some Bible characters we find fantastic deeds recorded (e.g. the miracles achieved through Phineas) and fantastic measurements are attributed to such figures as Og of Bashan. But Rabbinic assessment, then and later, never takes the form of presentation of a human being realistically and dramatically, as Wellhausen described Amos at the Court of Jeroboam II, or as Ewald describes the black-browed Absalom.

Even when the Bible itself speaks of physical love or beauty the commentators write no panegyrics. The matriarchs are assessed as Prophetesses, oracles of truth, not objects of human affection. We are told that Rachel was fair of form and face.[1] But is the Bible telling us in the same verse that her eyes were inferior to those of Leah? Or are we being told that Leah was beautiful, too, but that her eyes were weak with weeping for her emotional failures? To have dwelt on the beauty of women and the virility of men would have been not merely un-Jewish in some religious sense: it would have been strange to the Jewish genius by reason of the difference of that genius from the Greek.[2]

[1] Gen. XXIX.17. It is of interest that some of the Rabbis were unsympathetic to Rachel because she spoke before her sister. (They were twins, but Leah was the senior.)

[2] Characteristically Jewish (of the period) is the argument of the author of a Sibylline poem, that the Greeks had originally been believers in the Jewish religion, until Homer came with his lies and romances to corrupt them. Christian claims (textually based) have been made for the Jewishness of Virgil: Spanish Jews claimed Aristotle for Jewry.

Among the Greeks—i.e. the Jews who lived among the Greeks—there was more literary appreciation.[1]

In Alexandria and Asia Minor there was an impulse to fanciful development of Midrash, to the construction of myths: also to the poetic "wisdom", and to pseudo-prophetic poetry. Significantly, this never became part of any Jewish canon.[2] Again, during some part of the Gaonic period, when the Jews were so strong in Mesopotamia that they could raise armies, such as Mar Zutra led against Persia, there was an impulse to prose and poetry. Saadyah, a pioneer grammarian, and a great thinker, later expressed some of that culture.[3]

The utilitarian—or purposive—prose of the Jews was good at all periods. The Rabbis, in their meditations (of which some are in their liturgy), in their laments (for example, so beautiful a HESPED as Bar Kapparah pronounced over Rabbi Judah), in their imaginings, in their parables (some elaborate, some homely), were speaking the stuff of poetry without knowing that they were minstrels. Later, in the Middle Ages, Hebrew continued to be used by masters of language. Between the ninth and sixteenth centuries Jews were travelling and writing their reports. The imaginative, tendentious or fictive, Eldad the Danite gives us literature, not history. He sought varieties of prac-

---

[1] But the translators of the Septuagint version seem to have been tone-deaf to parallelism. Hence that great mistranslation (now part of literature) "a voice crying in the wilderness". (Let it be added that another theory is that the unpunctuated Greek "The voice of one crying" etc. is true to the Hebrew: and that the misquotation in the New Testament is a DRASH.)

[2] The Talmud contains a quotation from the Hellenistic, but good Jewish, Ben Sirach as Hagiographa. This is an accident less remarkable than the early Christian inclusion of Philo among the Fathers of the Church.

[3] Incidentally the Jews in Arabia produced Arabic poetry before the days of Mohammed. Some of this is extant.

tice in distant lands and found them. He also claims to have found, in Kush, the sons of Moses dwelling by the River Sambatyon,[1] which ceases to flow on the Sabbath. What mattered to his readers (and this is traditionally normal) were the features of ritual among the discovered tribes. Of Rabbis, only Ibn Ezra and Meir of Rothenburg dismissed his work as fictitious.

In contrast, against the records of Benjamin of Tudela, who describes for us the lands of the twelfth century, nobody can suggest unreliability. And he is one of many who, in describing their travels, made the Hebrew language into a useful medium of description.

In Moorish Spain, during four centuries, the Jews became poets and philosophers in the Arabic manner and achieved high standards in that age of high standards. When they wrote Hebrew it was grammatical and unpedantic. The tradition of good prose moves into more modern times. A cultured Italy produced Immanuel of Rome (the friend of Dante), Azariah dei Rossi and later, Moses Chayim Luzzatto.[2] He wrote ethics in very pure Hebrew, as well as excellent dramatic verses. Over a century later, an emancipating Austrian Empire produced Samuel David Luzzatto. Two very great, unrelated, poets these and masters of simple speech. The German emancipation gave opportunity to Mendelssohn and Wessely—the latter a considerable poet as well as a scholar. That *Aufklärung*, communicated to the strengthened masses of Russia and Poland, inspired, together with nationalist aspiration, a century of Haskalah (Rationalism) which culminated in a vast Hebrew and Yiddish literature, achieving naturalism and romance

[1] Corruption of Sabbataion. Such a river is mentioned in the Talmud, Sanh. 65a, and by Josephus and Pliny.
[2] The Italian Rabbis (including Jacob Sforno and Obadiah Bertinoro) are important, also, because they knew Greek and could recognize it in the Talmud.

on the high levels of literature, in the prose of Smolenskin and Abramovitch the novelists, and in the poetry of Bialik and Tchernichovsky at the end of the nineteenth century.

These names are of men who achieved literary peaks, climbing out of the deep (let it not be said dark) valleys of Rabbinism. In the valleys there was legal learning of great depth: profound homiletic thought: also mystery and eschatology. Some of the Rabbinic productions have literary value: but they were not written consciously—or self-consciously—as literature, in the way that Gabirol and Halévy and the Luzzattos wrote. Moreover, although the Luzzattos and others wrote dramas on Biblical themes, it was psychologically difficult for any writer or thinker not on the levels of emancipation to contemplate the Jewish heritage—the Bible in particular—as a collection of literary models, as stories, poems, and dramas to be admired as such, and to inspire artists with the original impulse that had animated the writers of old.

"Cause us to return, Lord, as the springs in the South". This has been described by an English litterateur (Day Lewis) as a striking poetic image. To the Jews it has been a line in a prayer.

Similarly, to nearly a hundred generations the Psalms were prayers and the stories truths, with moral bearing on contemporary life. The "wisdom" was wisdom—not wit.[1] The Song of Solomon was explained by nearly all the commentators as an allegory expressing the love of Israel for God, or of God for Israel. "Stay me with flagons" meant "teach me Halacha", "sustain me with apples" meant "teach me Aggadah". Such an expression as "the breasts"

---

[1] Rabbi Dr. Isadore Epstein expresses the Rabbinic view in words to this effect: that the Prophets directly imbued the people with the message of God. The "wisdom" gives them practical reasons for accepting it.

was ascetically (certainly not aesthetically) explained as a metaphor for the tablets of the law.[1]

Yet the Jews have always loved the language of the Bible, almost as if for itself. They used the Bible copiously in their literary activities at all periods. Hebrew was never a dead language. It was written by authors, and correspondents, for centuries, who put more life and subtlety into it than the ignorant monks could put into medieval Latin. More will be said about the evolution of the language. So far as the Hebrew Bible is concerned, let it be observed that, for most writers, over many centuries, the Bible, while not a literary model, was a living source of phrase and allusion.[2]

One aspect of Jewish writing—and it is to be observed in

[1] By mystic writers as Moses and Aaron.

The role of the Song of Songs in Hebrew tradition is fascinating. As we shall see in another chapter, such a verse as "thy navel is a round goblet" is legally used, as a symbolic indication of the roundness of the Sanhedrin.

Homiletically, the Midrash quarries the Song for metaphor. The method of the Midrash Rabbah—the great Midrash, which grew alongside the Mishna—is to synthesize verses from the Hagiographa (including Canticles) with the Pentateuchal text that the homilist is expounding. So "the scent of thine oil" inspires Rabbi Berachia to compare the virtues of Abraham to those of the juice of the balsam tree, and to explain this in detail.

Of the direct commentators, all write on the assumption—stated explicitly by Maimonides—that there is nothing erotic in Holy Writ. Varying degrees of mystical allegory are read into it. Even Rashi tacitly approves this. Perhaps the best insight is that of Malbim, who does not strain the images into symbols; but sees in the Book seven episodes, in each of which the peasant girl escapes from her princely spouse or master back to the simple loves of the desert. This the commentator treats as poetic allegory to describe seven departures of Israel from her pledged allegiance.

Let it be added that the Catholic Church has always treated Canticles allegorically.

[2] Mr. Daiches has recently pointed out the consequence that some Hebrew poetry is characterized by what appears to be mixed metaphor, but is the weaving of Biblical threads (other poetries are not free from mixed metaphor).

Jews, such as Heine, Disraeli and Zangwill, writing in European languages—is a flair for neat allusion, a capacity to invest the written page with the suggestion of analogies, and to adorn it with relevant learning. So do scholars write, rather than simple lyric poets or direct narrators.[1]

When one considers the poems with which the Rabbis[2] of the Spanish period adorned the prayer-book, and when one reads some of their works in lighter vein, the reader may become aware that the critical problem is the inveterate problem of all classical composition, of all Augustan verses. In what degree is the idiom inhibiting free utterance? In great poets the discipline of form, even of phrase, does not prevent great utterances. But it may well be true that, to apply Dunash's phrase, more "birds would twitter" in the forest than in the cloisters.

If poetry be the creation of clear images and new thoughts in the clear music of language, the best poets of the Judaeo-Spanish period suffer but one obfuscation: that only those well versed in Biblical Hebrew can appreciate their richness. There are Hebrew poets, of a "metaphysical" type, whose idiom is obscure except to the scholars of the recondite: and they are open to the criticism, which all metaphysicals incur, that great thoughts do not require an esoteric presentation. Short of obscurity, it is no fault in Dryden or Pope that they are better appreciated by those who have read Horace. Nor is it a fault in Halévy and Ibn Gabirol that

[1] The Bible in itself is not without allusiveness. So the Psalmist (in CXVIII) echoes the Song of Moses and in CX.3, the older Song of Deborah, and there are many phrases in the Prophets that suggest the Psalter, and vice versa. (E.g. cf. Psalm LI.19. and several passages in Isaiah.) Isaiah in Ch. I shows knowledge of the story of Sodom. Jeremiah knows of Rachel: and alludes to or echoes the Psalter. (*See* Jeremiah XVII. vv. 1, 2, 7, 8. etc.) Incidentally, of this prophet the epithet "melancholy" is undeserved. (It is due to the attribution to him of the lamentations.)

[2] Such a poet as Judah Halévy was Rabbi and medical man.

they are best enjoyed by those to whom the text of the Hagiographa is a part of culture.

Within limits the great ones are even translatable—though any good poem will defy restatement except in another poem.

The leading Spanish Jewish poets, Halévy, Ibn Gabirol, Al Charizi, Ibn Ezra, and others, while able to harness their muses to the vehicles of the sacred, were also familiar with the pathways of Parnassus. Love songs abound, and epigrams. Judah Halévy tells us of the grey hair which says to him, "you have torn me out and mock at me; but a thousand of my brothers are coming to mock at you." He also tells us of the little boy who "climbs on to my knee and kisses my eyes; but I know that what he is kissing is the reflection of his own face."

Nor are they lacking in works of the comic muse. Al Charizi has a poem to a flea. But the thought does not develop into the erotic as with the English poet. The Spanish Jews wrote of love, but not coarsely. If they laughed, they laughed at wine.

The late Israel Abrahams translated a drinking song of Ibn Gabirol's—a striking expression of happy mood on the part of one who contributed so much to the sad meditations of melancholy occasions.[1]

> "The feast's begun and the wine is done
> So my sad tears run like streams of water.
> Three score and ten were wine's bold braves
> But a full score more were water's knaves.[2]
> For whence tuneful note
> When the minstrel's throat
> Tastes naught but water."

[1] The occasion of the poem is said to have been a banquet given by a man named Moses who gave his guests very little wine.

[2] The numerical value of the Hebrew word for "wine" is 70: the numerical equivalent of the word for water is 90.

The poet goes on to say that "Moses turned the Reed Sea dry till Pharaoh's hosts for water cried."

> But Moses dear, why dost thou here
> Turn all to water, hated water."

This little poem is a particularly clear example of a conceit communicable across the loom of language. Incidentally, it shows that the exponents of a stern unhedonic way of life were capable of enjoying lighter moments.[1]

Interesting, too, is a poem on Chess, attributed (perhaps wrongly) to Abraham Ibn Ezra. The writer succeeds in describing the game (as it was then played) very well indeed, for all that much of the phrasing is Biblically allusive. So we are told of "The Wind" (Ruach-Persian Ruh: modern "Rook") that its ways are not "crooked ways": and the description is not made obscure by the circumstance that the Hebrew for "crooked ways" is lifted from the Song of Deborah.

Many of the poems of the Spanish masters are in acrostic form, and many exploit the subtle and difficult rhyme patterns of Arabian verse. But the good poet, in this medium, succeeds in creating what Halévy described as "verses stretched on the wings of the cherubs", "messages that could not be expressed if they were not written by the finger of God".

> "Zion, wilt thou not ask if peace's wing
> Shadows the captive that ensues thy peace.
> Left lonely from thine ancient shepherding?
> Lo! west and east and north and south—world wide
> All those from far and near without surcease
> Salute, thee. Peace and peace from every side."

[1] Needless to say, the bulk of Ibn Gabirol's poetry is solemn. Among the best of them, and among the best poems in the Jewish liturgy, is KETHER MALCHUS—a meditation for the Day of Atonement, in

Those lines of Halévy—brilliantly translated by Nina Davis Salaman—are among the best known (though not the very best) of that poet's work. They express a love of the land of Israel which suffused the poet's life and led him to his death. What is not so well known about them is that they were written as liturgy—part of a meditation for the Fast of Av, the anniversary of both the Destructions.[1]

Also liturgical are his famous poem on the Sabbath, so much warmer and truer than Heine's. Liturgical, too, are most of the greatest elegiac efforts of Ibn Gabirol, Moses Ibn Ezra, and many others who, while able to pen epigrams, drinking songs, and love poems with the best, found their strongest impulse in religious feeling. This, being recorded, renders the Siddur and Machzor into unrecognized golden treasuries.[2]

Whether the Spanish-Jewish poets recognized the Bible, and the liturgy, as poetry is a question that cannot be answered. Certainly they added poetry to the religious literature of Israel, and, in their turn, have suffered the fate that their poems are now valued only as prayers.

Historically they are important for that, in their short period, they demonstrated that Hebrew is a poetic language; and they gave it new life. Particularly, they demonstrated that a classical idiom, allusively used, is a great medium for the genuine expression of fresh thought and emotion.

Below those high levels, Hebrew was allusively, if not artistically, written through two millennia.

The mark of the writer in Hebrew has been his anxiety

which the poet expresses in verse the philosophy of his MEKOR CHAYIM (Fons Vitae).

[1] The poetic value is not diminished by the circumstance that the last few words of the lines cited are a quotation from Isaiah.

[2] Some of the best Piyutim have been well rendered into English: *inter alia* by the late Israel Zangwill, who, however, was not a close adherent to the original text.

to load the rifts of his text with Biblical gold and Talmudic ore. Thus the letter in which Chasdai Ibn Shaprut addressed the King of the Khazars opens with an acrostic in which Biblical phrases are ingeniously conjured to express the admiration of the writer for the one whom he is addressing. The reply of the less cultured King is in simple, direct, Hebrew of, possibly, higher literary value.[1]

Centuries later, when Jonathan Eybeschütz, cruelly persecuted by the fanatical Emden, appealed to the great Elijah of Vilna, the latter replied that he wished he could come to him "on the wings of an eagle". That is typical of Rabbinic correspondence.

They describe each other in Biblical phrases: living springs; and roaring lions; cedars of Lebanon.[2]

Nor did the style disappear during the Haskalah and enlightenment, for part of the task of the Hebraists of the nineteenth century was to restore the Bible itself to generations so immersed in Talmud and in commentary that, for many, the original text of the Scripture had become

---

[1] It may well be that these letters are compositions by the great artist, Judah Halévy, who published them in the Book of Khazars. (They are published with Ibn Tibbon's translation of the main text from the Arabic.) If so, he has illustrated some truths about art which are well expressed, at a humorous level, by Ernest Bramah. The latter writes of two Chinese craftsmen: the teacher wrought an intricate series of boxes, fitting into each other ingeniously: the pupil did a bird, but could not win a prize because it flew away.

[2] Often the Biblical phrase is used punningly in connexion with the personal name. (E.g. Adereth Eliyahu—mantle of Elijah.) Frequently Rabbis were referred to by names which were the titles of books they had written. It is told of the cynical Mapu that he asked a certain Rabbi "Are you the 'roaring bear'?" and the Rabbi replied: "Yes, and I believe you are 'the painted popinjay' ".

Difficulty is occasioned when the title of the book is in turn reduced to acronym. Thus Rabbi Joel Sirkes, one of the greatest of Halachists, wrote *Bayith Chodosh* (New House) and is referred to as Bach. Similarly TURÉ ZOHOV is referred to as TAZ.

unimportant except as the text of sermons, or the basis of argument. There were even students whose knowledge of the Bible was a knowledge of Talmudic citations from it. The new writers rejoiced in the Scriptures as had the Puritans of seventeenth-century England. Not in the purest literary way, be it said, for we find that the generation of Mapu and the Measefim, who (in the late eighteenth and early nineteenth centuries) endeavoured to make Hebrew into a modern vehicle of communication, failed to use the Bible as a model, but rather quarried it for phrases. Only their grammar was better than that of most of their predecessors. Even to this day it is hard for the Hebraist, who wishes to say that his hair stood on end, to do other than quote the Book of Job and proclaim "that the hair of his body was like nails".[1] Only great writers and great poets, and Jews reliving, on the land, the conquests of Caleb and Joshua, can use the Bible as artists use masterpieces—that is to say, as inspiration, not as forms to be copied—and the language as a meaningful medium, not as an aggregate of cliché.

The task, be it said, is a hard one, for many reasons. Among other things, it is difficult to abandon allusion completely without reducing the language to barren utility and technicality. Moreover, the religion, the history, and the law will always be so much part of Jewish life, that "phrase" for its own sake, phrase heavy with undertone, and sounding with overtone, will be on the pens of the writers, as surely as the text of the Bible is printed with cantillation marks. Even in Yiddish much of the literature expresses the minds of those who think in broken Hebrew phrases. But whether in Hebrew or Yiddish, the life of the Goluth is expressed in

---

[1] Other examples abound: e.g. to "unite" is usually expressed as "to form one company" (a Biblical phrase): phrases like "triple thread" are currency of political speech.

allusive utterances.[1] So Bialik, the Hebrew poet, describing the young student, rising early in the morning before he can discriminate "between blue and white, between wolf and dog",[2] is conjuring the background of law that guided the lives of millions with a detailed control.[3] In the expression of that life the allusive phrase has this additional value: that it expresses the mentality of the subject described, as well as of generations that pressed the words of Holy Writ for their intellectual wine.

The Hebrew writer, of necessity, finds himself faced with the aesthetic problem of achieving a clear medium for the description of a life which rejoices in Peshat, but indulges fully in what the Talmud calls "the life of the men of this world".

Comparable to the history of Jewish secular writing is the history of the liturgy. The original prayers were simple, the Biblical Shema: the eighteen blessings (with a nineteenth added—against informers): the Biblical Hallel: and the Kaddish, which, being understood, sheds so much light on what Christians call the Magnificat and the Lord's Prayer.[4]

[1] Yiddish is, however, more emancipated than Hebrew from Classical atmosphere. There is a large recent and contemporary Yiddish prose and verse, in which the idiom is free as in any European language: and Hebrew phrases are parts of elementary vocabulary, almost as Latin words are used in English, without any effort being made to suggest their original context. Using this language, writers are less apt than Hebraists (i.e. most Hebraists before the very modern) to aim excessively at polished phrase and felicitous effect. In the result, modern Yiddish poetry is a strong vehicle of secular song.

[2] Readers of French may know the expression *"entre chien et loup"* to describe the half-light. This may well have come into French from the Jewish culture that flourished in Medieval Provence and Rhineland.

[3] Bialik, be it observed, is using allusion because it frames the subject-matter of his poem so artistically. In other poetic efforts, Bialik's Hebrew is free from oppressive literary stress.

[4] It is typical of Jewish involvement that the Kaddish is never said intelligibly. The singing and the responses deprive it of meaning, as

These are direct utterances. So, too, are meditations, like those of Rav, that have found their way into the Siddur. But the Synagogue liturgy soon became heavy with the compositions of Payetanim, whose poems seem to us to be so heavy with Biblical phrase and allusion, with Midrashic or Talmudic reference, that the simple thought is lost. These "metaphysical" poets, from Kalir (ninth century) onwards, speak of Abraham as the "old inhabitant", of Isaac as the "righteous one", of Jacob as "the lily", of the High Priest as "the one who stood in the porch". Amongst these thickets of phrase, like roses among thorns, are occasional Piyutim of the great poets—Gabirol and Halévy— and occasional Zemiroth, Sabbath songs, in which, alone of liturgy, Jewish singers have expressed joy, though traditionally "their sweetest songs are those that tell of saddest thought".

The great treasures of the liturgy include (as we have seen) some great poetic Piyutim of Ibn Gabirol, of whom it was said that when he left the hall of poetry he threw away the key so that none could enter after: of Judah Halévy, who could picture Jerusalem as if he were praying there; and of some few others whose singing minds made the synagogue liturgy into music, rather than formal ritual incantation.

It must be remembered of these that when they wrote liturgy they wrote it as prayers, not poetry: for poetry is not the purpose of the words of praise, or of thanksgiving, or of invocation, or of appeals for aid and guidance that

tune takes away the meaning of libretto in opera. Thus the Kaddish runs: "Exalted and Magnified be his great name in the World that He created according to his will. And His kingdom will be established in your lifetimes and your days, and the lifetimes of all Israel". Now, although the Editors of Siddurim punctuate it properly, singers do not. The normal break therefore is heard after "name", and a response is intoned there, thus rendering two sentences unintelligible.

In other words, here as elsewhere, toned liturgy is valued independently of meaning, as in churches where forgotten languages are used.

help to constitute a religious service. Some considerable Piyutim—such as the Akdomuth and the Nethaneh Tokef—are poetic *per accidens*. The one is a meditation on the overwhelming power of the Lord as revealed in history; the other was said to have been inspired by the misfortunes of Rabbi Amnon of Mayence (tortured by a Bishop to whose blandishments he offered too weak a resistance) and consists in reflections on the possible fates of those who pass under the crook of the great shepherd at each New Year.

Similarly Piyutim such as "let our prayer ascend",[1] and "like clay in the hands of the potter", are good meditations in themselves: but their composers have succeeded, while putting their hearts into the thought, in expressing also their word-craft, and the verbal and imaginative forces which are the poetic impulse.

Poets they were unintentionally. They have ceased to be valued as poets among masses characterized by ignorance of advanced Hebrew. And they have lost appreciation as poets in the degree that liturgy has become dominated by vocal and choral music, which tend to be more highly valued than the words which are their burden. So the poetry suffers because of the music; and many great prayers —including the Kaddish—fail to be understood except by the learned.

As to the learned, we have seen that their preoccupation is not literary. From their point of view the meaning of words and the implications of thought are communications of religious truth—not sounds and patterns to be admired for their beauty.

In fine, the history of the prose and the verse can be summed into a paradox. Heritors of an aesthetic treasure-

---

[1] Even this beautiful acrostic elegy has been "interpreted" so as to show Biblical references where they were, possibly, not intended. (*See* Romm edition of the Machzor, with Yiddish "translation".)

house, the Jews of the past have rarely been self-conscious artists in the use of their own tongue.

The life of the ghetto, and the use of the Bible and the liturgy as an ethical escape, were incompatible with the artistic contemplation of life and Jewish literature. The ignorant among the Jews became connoisseurs of the arts: not the learned. They also became rich more easily. Those same ignorant ones made the cantor in the Synagogue more important than the preacher. On a principle stated in Canticles, the Jews in alien fields have cultivated some of the best blossoms in the European anthology. Only in the last century has their own garden really begun to blossom.

For want of a better word, we speak of the great modern development of Jewish culture as Haskalah—the period, or movement, of Reason. But the phrase is quite an apt one, because, when we look to another high peak of Jewish culture, the Spanish period, we find a preoccupation with the Rational: a preoccupation so marked in one of the great men that Maimonides' thinking has been called the Rule of Reason.

During the Hellenistic period, too, when Jews thought about personal beauty, and Rabbi Jochanan dispensed with a beard,[1] there is evidence of rationalism, as well as of aesthetics, in Jewish thinking and writing, especially (but not only) among the Alexandrian thinkers. From that period Philo survives in philosophy, Josephus in the annals of objective history-writing.

But in modern times Haskalah denotes a period which the word Rational is inadequate to describe. It was a period which, not only for Jews, but for the whole of European

---

[1] Resh Lakish said to him: "Your beauty is for women". He replied: "Your strength is for the Torah". This beauty was held imperfect by some because of his beardlessness. There is no certainty that this was intentional. (*See* T.B. Baba Mezia 84b.)

civilization, was an emancipation from the forms of formalism and an opening of the organs of expression.

After the French Revolution, for the first time on a massive scale—at least for the first time since the eclipse of Hellenism—writing became attack, became experiment, became realization of resources and resolution of difficulties.

At no previous phase of development in Christian Europe could social criticism, social reconstruction, be planned and articulated in the work of story writers. Accordingly, it was not only new in Jewry, it was a new fact in modern European literature, that if Mapu wished to deride the hypocrisy that could become entrenched in established religion he could do so in a fictitious narrative, as Reade and Kingsley later did in England: that if Gordon wished to reveal the absurdities of the status of Jewish women, he could do it in narrative satirical verses, good according to European models. In this period the novel achieves importance in Europe as a proper medium for the implicit statement, by any writer, of his world-view, of his relation to his fellow men and women, of his hopes for humanity, and of his disappointments. The way is open to the study of life, through the psychological novel, into psychology as we know it now.

This literary development, coinciding in time with political upheavals, with enormous industrial development, with increased communications including a greater circulation of wealth, afforded at once a glimpse of freedom, and an outlet for intellectual energy: of which the exercise, in itself, is a form of freedom.

It was to be expected, and it is the case, that the moving spirit of Haskalah literature was opposed to all formalism, was, in varying degrees, aggressive against traditions that bound people to narrow life and kept them to a narrow path. Inspired by a dictum of Mendelssohn that Judaism is a religion with freedom of doctrine and conformity of conduct, the Rationalists found themselves able to discard, as irksome and outdated, the discipline of fringes, tefillin, ritual baths and elaborate liturgy.

A century after the Romantic Movement, the world became aware of the truth uttered by a pioneer of literary emancipation: "Me this uncharted freedom tires". But to the Jew, gaining, in Tsarist Russia and Hapsburg Austria, his first access to secular culture, there was no suspicion of an ultimate satiety. Even now the springs of temperament and wonder are spurting strongly. In the century of Haskalah what took place was the emergence into culture of Jewish self-expression as a literary fact, with whatever normality attaches to literary facts.

In this period Jews begin to write the history of Jewry from an objective standpoint, dealing with the heresies and backslidings dispassionately, and recognizing the facts of politics and economics as determinants, and using, in their analyses, the terms of ethical, or religious, neutrality. Great names that have emerged, in the century and a half of history-writing, include Graetz, Zunz, Krochmal, Rappoport, Harkavy and Chwolson[1]: and late, but not least, Dubnow, historian of the group rather than of the creed.

These and later historians were prepared to disregard the claims of sanctity made for the Bible text—claims not made

[1] These fulfilled the criterion set by Renan for historians of religion. "They had believed, and had ceased to believe." Chwolson is interesting as one of very many who converted themselves to Christianity in order to secure admission to secular academies. When asked why he turned, he replied: "Out of conviction: I was convinced that it was better to be a Professor in St. Petersburg than a Hebrew teacher in a village". The same man is responsible for a famous pun. "Now that I have been created, it is as if I was not created" runs the Day of Atonement liturgy. It happens that the word "I have been created" (Notsarti) can also mean "I was Christianized". In that sense the humorous apostate quoted it. It may be added that, after his apostasy, he made great efforts to improve the lot of the Jews in Russia.

by the Scripture itself!—and treat the Bible as literature and history. They have not permitted themselves all the extravagances of the Christian higher critics, who were motivated by a desire to show the Old Testament as a process of spiritual development introductory to the ultimate realities which they find in Christianity.[1] But the Jewish historians accepted the possibility of textual criticism and applied it scientifically to Bible, Talmud and all the Midrashic literature. Much of their work—not all—is accepted by the exponents of traditional Jewish orthodoxy.[2]

From a literary standpoint the gift of Haskalah to the world is the re-creation of an original Jewish literary activity. Coming at the end of half a millennium in which Russian and Central European Jewish legalism had allowed the literary heritage of Spain to be forgotten, there was a completely new burgeoning of genius. Here is a generation of poets, starting with Isaac Levinsohn, who recaptured the poetic capacity of the Hebrew language as the Bible writers had experienced it, and the forgotten poets of the Spanish period.

If comparisons are to be made, the poetry of the modern period is freer and more powerful than any since the Biblical age, because it developed in an atmosphere relatively free from formalism. The poems of Levinsohn, Bialik, Tcherni-

[1] There is also a tendency to devalue the Jew. Perhaps this is why insufficient justice is done to the creativity of the Bible writers in places where intelligent synthesis is a better explanation than multiple authorship.

[2] Talmudists necessarily, in the mastery of the texts, learn some history: e.g. of the Rabbinic lives. But, apart from the suspicion that history may undermine orthodoxy, the Rabbi entertains a certain contempt for the historian—who explains away rather than reconciles, and who is, evidently, lacking in depth and subtlety. Said the celebrated Akiva Eger (at the end of the eighteenth century), "If you wish to know what kind of clothing Rashi wore, by all means ask Geiger. If you want to know what Rashi said and thought, ask me!"

chovsky and Schneour are in the Romantic tradition in the proper sense. Not erotic poetry this, but conscious of nature, aware of the pleasantness of the green tree. Its content is, for the most part, suffused with Weltschmerz and desire for emancipation. Bialik's "Skylark" is a bird that brings the poet news of the land. He asks (echoing faintly Halévy): Does the dew drop on Hermon like a garland of pearls, or does it flow down the mountain like tears? Also he sends what Jews call "a geruss" to the toilers. Much of his verse is the expressing of a spirit which found in developing Zionism the object of a love and an enthusiasm that could no longer be absorbed by the Sabbath and the Festivals and the ancient customs. That impulse is strengthened by an increased awareness of nature, on the part of pious and impious alike.[1] The whole order of natural science has now been expressed in Hebrew. Withal there is a joy in the use of a language whose poetic resources have been too long neglected. Hebrew, being a concrete language, is a language proper for poets. Those who have sung in it recently have been, for the most part, too familiar with traditional overtones. But when such a man as Tchernichovsky, scholar in all the secular cultures, adopted Hebrew as a language for his verses, he found the language rich and subtle enough for the expression of a purely lyric impulse. His translation of Shelley's "Cloud" is Hebrew lyric in its own right.

But language is more than its words. The heritage of Hebrew is in the hands, and will probably remain in the

[1] Very striking are the exact descriptions of nature in the rich Hebrew of Mendele Mocher Seforim (Abramovitch). One of that great writer's first works in Hebrew was a book of Natural History, written in a rich idiom, and amusingly synthetic of Biblical-Rabbinic science with the modern. In a Yiddish sketch called "How Pleasant is this Tree", Sholom Aleichem describes Mendele as one who was physically robust, rejoicing in the fields and in the rivers, a lover of animals, and of natural beauty for its own sake. Evidently his long years of deep learning had not prevented him from looking at the outside world.

hands, of writers who are aware that they belong to a special group, and will not be content to sing love lyrics as if they were the peasant poets of a Balkan or Levantine homeland. Up to the present the language of the Bible is being used, by novelists, essayists and poets, on themes arising from the permanent problems of the Jews: all that is inveterate: all that is ill-starred: all the struggle against the constellations.

Significantly it was the poets of a deep-seated melancholy that wrote Hebrew melodies in the languages of the world. If Gentile Byron and Moore[1] and godless Heine were conscious of the sadness; Jewish poets proper how much more so! They are the minstrels of exile recapturing the mood of those who wrote of earlier exiles. In the long period between, Jews escaped, as it were, into another world. The recent generations have escaped (if that is the proper word) back into a reality which is not less sad, not less poetic.[2]

[1] Moore is celebrated, *inter alia*, for a poem on Zion that might be a Zionist anthem.

[2] I have not been concerned in this chapter with the poetic efforts of Jews, devoted or otherwise, to express some Jewish thought in other languages than the Jewish. Let it be remembered, however, that Philo wrote his religious matter in Greek, Maimonides in Arabic, Manasseh ben Israel in Spanish. So there can be no denial of value to the poets and novelists of religious experience who write in the "tongues of the nations of the earth". (Grace Aguilar, Emma Lazarus, Nina Davis, Isaac Rosenberg, are names famous in Anglo-American literature.) Striking is the discovery by an English Bishop (Wm. White) of a beautiful Chinese epigram, found inscribed in a seventeenth-century synagogue in Kai-Feng. The poet says (in effect) that "God's law is clear and bright. So we send light up from our silver candlesticks and look upwards for divine illumination. God's Blessing is fragrant, so we send up the incense of sandalwood and await the descent of the divine fragrance." This is surely worthy of inclusion among all the beautiful religious poetry that Jews have written in English and other languages.

CHAPTER FOUR

THE PEOPLE OF THE LAW

1. *From Prophets to Rabbis*

THE original "people of the book"—that is to say the people described in the early books—were not consciously the people of "the word", or of the Law. They flourished, as spiritual and primitive communities, below and above the levels of articulated law and self-conscious institutions. This pastoral, or early agrarian, Semitic[1] group, living according to good customs, had, remarkably, been fertile in conceptions of Righteousness (fair and kind dealing) which are at once the roots and the flower of mature legal systems. Yet they were not "law-minded" as the Greeks were, and later the Romans. What the Ark contained is unknown: perhaps commandments (not necessarily the Ten Commandments[2]): certainly no elaborate writing. Elijah and Elisha refer to no code. When the Prophet denounces Ahab: "Hast thou murdered and wilt thou also inherit?" he is revealing, as orators do, the wickedness and the malignant irony of the human conduct that he is condemning. Nothing in the context or the

---

[1] This word may well be inaccurate. The word Semitic, like the word Aryan, is more useful as a description of linguistic classes than of ethnic. Even in that usage it is not scientific.

[2] *See:* e.g. Ex. XXXIV.

background suggests the modern, pedestrian, juristic analysis that concerns itself with the impropriety of benefiting from one's own wrongdoing.

The spokesmen of the Jewish spirit in those Biblical days were orators: Neviim—mature successors to the old "seers" —speaking more clearly than the wise men and women, and transmuting whatever old beliefs there were in "idiot" oracles into a tradition of affirmative and declamatory speech, through which there pulsed conceptions of right and wrong powerful enough to purge the hypocrisies of formalism in Court and Priesthood.[1] They differ from the smoother dialecticians of Greece as the torrential Jordan is different from the tideless Mediterranean. A superficial litterateur of Victorian times contrasted, unfavourably, their fire and strength with the sweetness and light of Greece. Yet there are those who think that, in the utterances of Isaiah and Moses, the fire gives forth a light, and from the strength comes a sweetness, that puts Hellenism to shame.

The well-analysed arguments of the sophisticated Greeks are based on limited concepts clearly apprehended. Prophetic oratory is animated by a different vision; a clearly grasped, albeit unanalysed, notion of unity, of which goodness is an all pervading manifestation, universally valid.

Good and evil actions (i.e. Right and Wrong) were recognized, described, respectively urged and proscribed;

[1] The Book of Samuel suggests two traditions: one, in which there were men called seers, and another describing bands of wandering soothsayers (Neviim). The latter word comes, in Samuel and later, to be used to describe prophets in the maturer sense.

Interesting is I Samuel IX.9. Also I Samuel XVIII,10, where the Hebrew commentators render YITHNABAY as "was talking foolishly". (*See* Rabbenu Isaiah *ad loc.*) In general, the association of Saul with Prophecy suggests "idiot prophecy". But Samuel's "prophecy" is in the tradition of declamation that starts from Moses (in his relatively small circle) and includes Elijah and all the orators of the Prophetic Books.

but not, in any early Jewish school, analysed or dialectically challenged.[1] Argument, at this level, is the reinforcement of what is clearly believed; impassioned affirmation, or sarcasm at the expense of the benighted Idolators. The opposition is not the intellectual nihilism of the over-educated, but the obscurantism of the primitive taboo-mongers, of the priest who has been accustomed to point to idols, and say to his folk: "these are thy gods". Such priestcraft is not remote from the story of the Patriarch who received, and acted on, the protest of Laban: "You have stolen my gods".

Remarkable to the Jew whose life is guided by a body of

---

[1] Many centuries later Maimonides, strangely, praises the Aristotelean "mean"—MĒDEN AGAN. At the Biblical stage, at least, there were no propositions about conflicting comparative "goods". If men were conscious of questioning as to their acts, then the choice was clear-cut—right or wrong. There was no balancing: no vacillation between "thresholds", no compromise. (At that stage, at least, the Jewish genius was not for Diplomacy.) A maturer society evolved the notion of Derekh Eretz (the way of the world)—the not harmful. Biblical issues were too sharp for this. A point to be observed is that the Biblical decisions were ethical rather than (or as well as) legal. The word TSEDEK—at the Biblical level—is used to denote both what we would call Justice and what we would call Charity. Only later does the notion of a duty "within the lines of the law" emerge. At the Biblical stage there was no conflict.

Yet the matter is not perfectly clear. Was there a Bible period in which righteousness did not denote kindness etc. but only a ritual, personal, purity? And what, in the early days, was meant by sin? The Pentateuch (especially Deuteronomy) is severe against oppressions of the poor and against extortions. These are RA (evil) and not compensated by the offering that is called "Sin-offering" (KORBAN CHATOTH) and is related to ritual default. Hosea speaks of stealing, adultery and murder: Samuel speaks of witchcraft, rebellion, idolatry, stubbornness (I Samuel XV.22). Later, Elijah and the prophet Nathan are clearly spokesmen of compassion—and treat its opposite as sin. Samuel is a pioneer in that he, as the much later Isaiah, does not allow formal sacrifices and ritual to be equivalent to good conduct.

Law, developed from Talmudic times to our own, is the realization (if he ever realizes it) that the historical narrative of the life of the Jews in Canaan is almost uncoloured by any shades of technical legal significance. An elaborate priesthood there was, inveterate:[1] succeeding to, or rivalling, the looser hagiocracy of the Levites.[2] Ritual we find in plenty: law only rudimentary. In the later days of the Temple, the days of Jotham, Hezekiah and Jehoiakim, there seems to evolve the notion of an ancient code. But written law only achieves substance with Ezekiel and his successors in Babylon. If "the law comes out of Zion", it only does so after having been developed in exile.[3]

That the Torah as code[4] is antedated by the Jews to the pre-Canaanite community of Moses constitutes one of the peculiar problems of Biblical research, albeit not without

[1] The Priesthood eventually became an elaborate civil service. The contents of Tractate Erachin (Valuations) suggest (not prove) that there were elaborate assessments of the sacrificial gifts, and a vast Temple book-keeping system. Tithes, heave-offerings, wave offerings, etc. came to constitute a system of taxation for the maintenance of the Priests.

An important change in Jewish Life is expressed in the fact that the Rabbi, who succeeded the Priest, was unprofessional, was amateur. Such Rabbis as Maimonides became medical men—because they did not wish to make the law into "an axe for delving". The Rabbis of Talmudic times included a grave-digger, a cobbler, a tailor, etc. They escaped, in this way, the evils of professionalism and excessive intellectualism.

[2] Because the editorship of the Pentateuch is ingenious, it is not clear which system was the earlier. The organization of the Levites, as described early in Numbers, is less dependent on established rituals.

[3] It was probably in Babylon that the Temple laws were generalized to the whole of the community. At this stage the laws relating to Sacrifice become the basis of the laws of animal-slaughter for food. This, and other, developments give a meaning to the words: Kingdom of Priests.

[4] The word Torah means teaching. Tradition is, of course, older than code.

analogies in the study of other social groups. Without accepting the Wellhausen-Delitzsch teaching, to the effect that the Mosaic Law is "mosaic" law, one may refrain from attributing the whole of Pentateuchal Law to that one lawgiver. Further, Moses himself is mysterious as a historic figure, if only for the reason, which scholars have not pondered, that, in the historic narrative which starts with Judges[1] and Samuel, there is little, if any, unambiguous, uninterpolated, reference to Moses: none to his code: and none to the man, commensurate with his importance, before the days of Jeremiah.[2] As a massive lawgiver he seems to be the creation of the Exile writers. But even as a charismatic leader he is Scripturally (outside the Pentateuch and Joshua) uncelebrated. As a prophet he is hardly cited: never quoted in the words and records of the Prophets of the Kingdom. Belonging to an age before Samuel, he is not known for his laws to the schools of Samuel. Yet, if Moses were an historic person (and the Pentateuchal

---

[1] In thinking of the Judges, it is useful to consider the Carthaginian system of Suffetes (Shofetim). Carthage, be it recalled, was founded by Phoenicians from the neighbourhood of Israel.

As to the Book of Judges, this, even to those who are sceptical of textual criticism, must appear as the expression of an earlier period than the Mosaic, or of a people with no knowledge of the Mosaic laws. Such a story as that of Jephthah and his daughter is otherwise unthinkable —even if the killing were not murder. This story, like that of the concubine of Gibeah, and some of the battles described in Judges and part of Joshua, seems to belong to the period described in the Genesis of Abraham and Lot (Cf. Akedah).

[2] The reference to Moses and Aaron in I Samuel XII may well be "editorship". It may also be the case that Samuel, from a tribe affiliated to Joseph, or with a tradition in that direction, knew something of the Exodus. There is no evidence that he knew of any Mosaic code.

Hosea may have known of Moses: and there are affinities of style between the book of Deuteronomy and the book of Hosea. The higher critics post-date the former: but there is no convincing reason for this. (*See* an essay by Rabbi Sperber in "Melilah" (1948).)

narrative is too human to be theogonic fiction) he was not only a prophet, but the greatest of them, and a great lawgiver as well. In the rationalistic analysis of the prophetic imagination that was worked out by Maimonides, Moses is shown to have achieved a degree of vision unattained by others. If Ezekiel was a countryman who only occasionally saw the King, and Isaiah a courtier and a townsman, Moses must rank as a great statesman grasping the realities of government and all the detail of authority.

The historic narrative of Exodus and Numbers, written in a style suggestive of the early historical books, and echoed in them, and even the narrative of Deuteronomy, not later in style than the period of Hosea (who may have used it as a model), indicate the probable creation of a written Mosaic tradition in the early days. What became of that tradition in the Kingdom is unknown. What became, it may also be asked, of the Ten Commandments? No prophet refers to the great "Thou shalt not"s in terms.[1] And what became of Mosaic traditions relating to the Ark in the days that saw the vicissitudes of the Ark? These, and other laws, were relevant at all times: yet were never cited in the words that are Holy Writ. Centuries later the syncretists made Moses into the originator of masses of law, for the most part out of harmony with the spirit of the period in which he flourished.[2]

As a prophet he seems to have flourished in days when the sources of inspiration were still sought in the oracular, and

[1] Hosea refers to stealing, adultery, etc. but not to any commandments.

[2] If it be suggested that the Prophet "foresaw" a settled land with a Kingdom, and Temples, and Red Heifers and curious housing problems, the answer is that the Bible does not attribute "foresight" (in the sense of detailed prognostication) to prophets. Nor are the laws relating to leprous houses probable topics for discussion in the wilderness of Sinai.

Of some of the Levitical laws, there are Talmudic dicta that instances of their application were unknown (T.B. Chagigah).

in the spasmodic utterances of wild men or idiots. "Inadequate of speech"—and that is not likely to be a *lucus a non lucendo* in the context—he only became articulate when God spoke through him; addressed him and commanded him to convey the message. An early stage of prophecy this, even if it be the highest prophetic manifestation.

That there was such a man, a leader, a creator of a national group among the Hyksos-type slaves of the Egyptians, a restorer of ancient desert monotheism, and a translator of the monotheistic belief into moral terms; that such a man existed is clear.[1] Primitive fiction does not create such characters. And in the story, which, at the destruction of the tablets, is drama in the manner of Sophocles, there are woven the early strands of the inveterate Jewish struggle between Prophecy and Priesthood; a struggle dormant at times, but reviving when the Kings seemed to take refuge in ritual: and very clear in the later days when such a prophet as Isaiah declaims: "What to me are your sacrifices?"

The life of Israel after the time of Moses was Priest-controlled and King-controlled. The prophets were not rebels against the institutions and the ritual. While valuing them, they saw through and beyond them to the spiritual realities they symbolized. Only in exile did the Priests, and their successors the lawyers, come to esteem the Prophets and look on them for inspiration, and (more practically) religious authority.

In the hieratic and monarchic phases Moses had been forgotten. Probably he had been the leader of a relatively small group, the tribe of Joseph[2] perhaps, that emerged

---

[1] The suggestion that he was not a pure Semite, based on his apparent unfamiliarity with circumcision—as in the Zipporah incident (and *see* Joshua I), is supported by the name of his father AMRAM ("lofty people").

[2] Or tribes with traditions involving the history of Joseph—history that Moses had kept fresh. There is also a Levitical tradition running

from the desert to conquer parts of Canaan, and to become isolated or assimilated among older tribes, some of whom may never have participated in the Egyptian Exile. The message of this group did not penetrate the Kingdom.[1]

The stories and writings (if any) that embody the traditions of Mosaism, varying, naturally, in the conception of the man and of his work, varying even in the conception of the commandments with which he is associated,[2] must have survived with the Passover Festival, as practised by some few tribes, but only became a national treasure when exile paradoxically turned a group of separate tribes into a self-conscious national theocratic group, and the Passover into its symbol.[3]

through the book of Judges. The name GERSHOM (Stranger—the name of Moses' son) is there given. Moses may have confided his teachings to that tribe. (The story of the emergence of the Priesthood from the Levites is difficult.)

[1] It must be remembered that these were days before the earliest known Semitic script. Writing probably existed, but not in a quantity adequate to even the smallest propaganda.

Since the above text was written, Mr. Ben Gurion, the Prime Minister of Israel, has conjectured that only a very small group left Egypt at the Exodus.

[2] An analysis by Wellhausen shows (not clearly) the existence of two very different statements of Ten Words in Exodus. The primitive set, applicable to harvesters, concludes with the exhortation to bring the first fruits to the Lord and not to seethe a kid in its mother's milk (i.e. the differentiation of the early Jewish from some Mediterranean cult). The maturer statement, which we call the Ten Commandments, is recapitulated in Deuteronomy. This later book is unlikely to be as late as the "Higher" Critics seem to believe. The language is far less sophisticated than that of the young, or early, Isaiah.

[3] For other tribes the feast was an agricultural one, said to be associated also with the rite of Circumcision. This last belief is supported by the tradition of Elijah's presence at both the Festival and the rite. There are, indeed, rational explanations, which, if accepted, reduce this to coincidence. The case affords one instance of Jewish synthesis. To this day the liturgy of the Festivals expresses dual functions. (Pente-

From the point of view even of theocracy, it is arguable that the destruction of the first Temple saved the Jews spiritually; saved them from the excesses of hierocratic exploitation.[1] Certainly, from the days of Saul to the all too late reforming Hezekiah, the Jewish ethos was submerged in the wars of conspiring princes, and crushed in the grip of extortionate monarchs and oppressive priesthoods. The protest of the prophets is always against oppression; and for most of the time is involved with a campaign against oppressive idolatries.

Idolatries were expressive of many tendencies; the recognition of local chieftains; the approval of the policy of an allied power; the desire of the King to emancipate himself from some specific control. Idolatry, which could correspond to local revolts, signified, generally, the rule of priests and kings in an oppressive way; also a disregard of spiritual values: because the essence of the various cults was ritual, justification by mysterious works, many of which were obscenities, ranging from the human sacrifice of Moloch worship to the scatophagy of the cult of Baalzephon.[2]

The prophetic protest is perpetually ethical; not in any degree legalistic. Of legal principle there is likely to be little in the early days of agriculture; only specific laws

cost, for example, is an agricultural occasion, and the anniversary of the giving of the Law. Appropriately, Ruth is read.)

[1] This could never be a Rabbinic thought. Consequently, the late Professor Lazarus, the learned author of *Ethics of Judaism*, was wrong when he translated a dictum of R. Eleazar (Berachot 32b) to mean that when the Temple (second Temple) fell, an iron wall was removed from between Israel and their Father in Heaven. The word Nifsekah can mean—and must mean here—"intervened", not "was removed", notwithstanding the contrary opinion of the German translator Goldsmid. The much greater authority of R. Samuel Edels (Mahrsha) supports the interpretation given here.

[2] This is Rabbinic interpretation, suggested by the language and the Bible text.

about the preservation of boundaries, the ritual of the harvest festivals, and the elaborate system of taxation, which is the concomitant of priesthood.[1]

Commerce, the mother of many laws, makes its appearance in Israel at the time of Solomon, when the King traded with Tyre and Sidon, using ships of "Tarshish", which may well be ships of the Tarsos type (oared vessels).

Law only becomes a clear conception under very different conditions; when the Jews are divorced from the land, and have to think in terms of the commercial life, and the slave organizations, of the nations into which they are absorbed; when, further, the priesthood loses its psychological power and only has left its moral authority; when the need for a way of life is urgent, and guidance must be sought beyond the too human survivors of a priesthood, and a kingdom, that have failed to preserve their heritage.

In captivity, and after the return, the evidence points to a change in the outlook of the Jews. Now, at last, they think in terms of Torah, or Law. The priest has always been an embryonic lawyer, because ritual and tax collection involve a rudimentary analytic technique. But after the first exile there emerges a notion of law as something transcending priesthood and kingship. In a way the prophets have achieved recognition; because the prophets always expressed an undifferentiated binding moral law valid for everyone. But the new life is more difficult and detailed than was life in the days of Elijah, Amos and Hosea, when people lived confidently on the land and were unafraid both of life and death: more difficult even than in the relatively sophisticated days of Isaiah, who knew about usury and cosmetics. The need is for a body of law: describing not only the right and the wrong, but (different and difficult) the permissible and the forbidden particulars: i.e. the legal and the illegal. At that

[1] It is conceded, of course, that the primitive is anything but simple is, indeed, highly formal. But ceremony is not yet law.

stage Jewry, emancipating itself from priesthood (as priest-hood was before the exile), and drawing some inspiration from the more secular societies of the great towns, commences the building and preservation of a legal monument calculated to outlast the memories of the Temple and the Court.

The legal tradition is better than the priestly one, but it is not the pure prophetic tradition. For by this time the orators are gone. The prophetic tradition only survives in the ability of the Judge or the Teacher to see, through the technicalities, the pervading principles of justice, and the righteousness which has been the burden of prophetic utterance. When, in a difficult context, Hillel refers to the practice of the people for authority, he is quoted as saying: "if they are not prophets they are sons of prophets". In that utterance there is, perhaps, more truth than the master con-templated. Something survived in the Jews which differ-entiated them, even in the depths of legalism, from the cold analytic exponents of the secular codes. But the saying may also have embodied the regret of a very great jurist who was conscious, more than any of his successors, that the law is not a thing in itself, but only valuable as the exponent and protection of a spiritual society.

The words of Hillel also express the problem that per-plexed the pioneers of Rabbinic Law; the same problem that was to perplex their successors, until they had built up a theory to cope with it; the problem of Authority. Jewish life in the anarchic centuries that preceded, and immediately followed, the fall of the last Temple, is characterized by something pathetically new; a craving for written, or reliably recorded, authority, on the part of those who had never accepted dictation.[1] The body of law which is in the

---

[1] In the same period "authorities" were opposed to the writing of their traditions.

Pentateuch of Torah had achieved writing and acceptance by the time of the Maccabees. The first exile had institutionalized Torah and demonstrated its value as stated. But now guidance was lacking to the Jews through the increasing complexities of Hellenistic civilized life, in which people moved about, and saw strange lands, and participated in an elaborate commerce. These things strained the ethics and institutions of an agrarian society, which had lived from Sabbath to Sabbath, and Festival to Festival, according to well-settled usages. Only a relatively sophisticated society finds the Sabbath, and the Sabbatical year, difficult or oppressive, and draws from its lawyers, devices such as the Prosbul[1] of Hillel, and the Eruvin[2] to make possible new modes of living within the framework of the old institutions.

Old wine in new bottles. In that much used antithesis we find expressed the intellectual ferment of the first century before the Common era. There were those who recognized that irreconcilable forces were at issue, and refused to compromise old values with new expediencies. These became

[1] A device by way of Assignment to the Court—which prevented a loss of accrued rights during the Sabbatical year. (The idea is that the pledges etc. are no longer in the control of the lender: so he cannot surrender them to the borrower.)

[2] The origin of the word ERUV is obscure. According to one theory, the root is "widening". Specifically the word may also mean a "cooking pot": and this was one (not the only one) of the devices used. But the popular explanation is that ERUV means a mixing (cf. Erev Rav): an intermingling of "domains" or of functions (as in the Eruv "of cooking" when one cooks for the Sabbath on the eve of a Festival that immediately precedes the Sabbath). The best known Eruv was a symbolic extension of the house, or a blending of domains, so that within the extended area there could be a fetching and carrying. One method of achieving this was to place food on the other side of the court. But a pole could also function as a symbolic extension of walls. The Eruv device has been applied so as to make travel by sea possible, as well as land journeys beyond the limit of 2,000 cubits in large towns. The device falls within the class of "legal fictions" as described by Sir Henry Maine.

sectaries;[1] at one extreme Sadducees, tending to a non-religious nationalism; at the other extreme Chassidim (Essenes) and religious Zealots. Sectaries of the latter types easily become mystics; and a mystic approach can lead surprisingly into heresy. Extremes have met more than once in Philosophy and Theology. Between the mystic who has learned, and overvalued, the proposition that the Sabbath was made for man, and the "reformer" who gives man leave to use the Sabbath according to his needs, the gap is not wide.

Over against both of them stands the lawyer; the Pharisee, against both Essene (Chassid)[2] and Hellenistic Sadducee: as the Misnaggid, in recent centuries, against both the modern Chassid[3] and the modern reformer. The way of the lawyer

[1] I use the word "sectary" for convenience. Gentile scholars have suggested, not without reason, that they can be described as members of political parties, if that word can be applied to the schisms of a theocracy. Of names, let it be observed that Sadducee is late and eponymous, though the distinction is old. When Alexander Jannaeus advised his wife, he is quoted (in Soteh 22b) as saying: "Do not fear the Pharisees or *those who are not Pharisees*: only be afraid of the hypocrites who do the deeds of Zimri and claim the rewards of Phineas". (*See* note at end of chapter.)

[2] Though the Chassid starts as an extremist Pharisee.

[3] It should be understood that the eighteenth century saw the growth of a Chassidic movement, inspired by the Baal Shem (Rabbi Israel of Miedzyboz), which involved no heresies, but emphasized prayer, and a prayer-inspired emotion (Hithlahavuth, or Hithpaaluth) and gave less value to the arid legal learning of the Yeshivoth. If there be any doctrinal characteristic, one may find it in the notion of a Holiness pervading the whole of life, and not limited to places and occasions that are sacred rather than profane. (Something analogous to Christian Pelagianism, but very different from Antinomianism.) It is assumed here that Essenism was similar in spirit to this. The word "Essene" is the Greek form of ASSI (pl. ASSIIM) which is an Aramaic form of CHASSID. The common denominator is that both the Essene and the modern Chassid are strongly orthodox and acceptive of orthodox ritual. What they add is

is to reconcile life with authority. He does this well or badly, according to his skill and his spirit; things which vary between lawyers; vary from the skill and insight of the creator of new legal procedures and useful fictions to the crudeness of the purveyors of pardons and indulgences.

The final destruction and exile decided the spiritual fate of the Jews, in that it brought about the desperate acceptance of the authority of the custodians of Torah. Already in the time of the second Temple the need had been felt for authority to cope with changing conditions. Hence the Sanhedrin,[1] sitting in the Temple to guide Priests. And over-lords had found it convenient to regard this as a Jewish Senate. But its power had been the power of priestcraft, of Temple officialdom—especially so in the Sadducean days of the Maccabean Kingdom. Once the Temple was destroyed the desire of Jews was for guidance, even from those whose control they had resented. The Master (Rabbi) is now sought, not as political priestly ruler, but as teacher. Yavneh is accepted; and Tiberias: and later, in the East, Sura, Pumpeditha, Nehardaa.

Thus from the need of exiled groups for survival came the stimulus to Rabbinic thought and life. At the same time other factors combined to add force and inspiration.

The need of the Jew for authoritative guidance—that is to say exposition of the Law for the purposes of life—coincided with the rapid development of legal institutions in the Gentile world, in which the Jews found themselves being submerged. The period of the dispersion is not enthusiasm—in some instances ignorant enthusiasm, and a tendency to mysticism or mystery.

[1] The Jewish pronunciation of a Greek word that was Sunhedrion. The late Dr. Buchler held that the Sanhedrin that was exploited by the political authorities was a separate branch, or manifestation, of the traditional Sanhedrin from that which considered the non-political laws. In other words, the Sanhedrin referred to in the New Testament was not of the species described in the Mishna.

characterized only by Alexandrian scepticism; it is also the age of Cicero and the Jurists. The period in which the Mishna grew, became codified, and outgrew its codification, generating Gemara,[1] and later developments of Sebara[2], is parallel to, if not part of, the growth of the Civil Law that culminated in the codes of Justinian.

There is evidence, in the nature of the law taught in far Sura and Pumpeditha, that the Jews were quick to absorb the dominant ideas of the Gentile age; and were skilful to frame these ideas in their own traditional categories. In this movement syncretism achieves the degree of originality which is creativity. The great Rabbis were creative jurists in their own right; and that body of legal literature which is the Talmud is an individual field in which Jewish thought becomes a special kind of legal thought, and the Jewish mind expresses itself as a highly integrated legal mind.

For nearly twenty centuries, from the time of Hillel, the fine flower of the Jewish mind was destined to be law, not prophecy; and its apprehension of the unity of things took shape from words in a book. The lawyer differs from the prophet—even the conservative prophet—as the priest differs. They look for different things. The narrower vision of the priest or lawyer is intense; but the scope is a deep well—not the sky. If the lawyer or priest realizes, as he does today, the possibility that his subject is a limited one, a function of forces which, when manifested and opposed, make it seem trivial, then either he finds a philosophy that gives essential value to the social frame, or the empirical content, of his subject; or he loses the urge to whatever creativity law and ritual can inspire.

For twenty centuries the Jewish lawyer has kept creativity alive by a faith which made the Torah into more than law—

[1] *See* p. 144 *infra.*
[2] Analysis of *rationes decidendi.*

into the very shape of creation. That is why the Talmud is not arid. Authoritarian and ingenious, it is redeemed from triviality by a faith in the moral order which the law expresses, by the reality of the moral impulse in the Rabbis, and by the perpetual impulse to make the Jewish way of life complete and adequate to the facts of a world hostile and in every other way changing.

2. *Rabbinic Authority*

The modern critic of institutions believes that the law is "too much with us". Twenty centuries ago the Jews found salvation by hedging themselves round with law; and that in the heart of a society that was mature enough to be sceptical of the forms of formalism.

Rabbinic law owes its richness to many sources; to the growing jurisprudence of the Roman world; to the need for rules in the new order of commerce; to the new needs that develop with urban life and with the notion of negotiable wealth: and to the paramount need for reconciling all these various purposes with prophet-inspired morals, and with an historic, relatively unarticulated, body of legal tradition, including the written Torah—the writing not so old in reality—and the accreted hieratic and judicial legislation.[1]

Traditional, unwritten, law is old in Israel. There were always Elders (their origin is ascribed to the advice of Jethro): and there was an obscure mode of recourse to the sacred "lots" (Urim and Tummim). The Pentateuch, of whatever age it is, presents Moses asking for guidance: and

[1] It was obviously important in days of slave-labour to expand Jewish doctrine on the treatment of slaves. Similarly, payment of wages, bailment, deposits, purchases of land were complex beyond the scope of Biblical law—to say nothing of financing: which the Bible seemed to forbid.

persons (like the daughters of Zelophehad[1]) asking for authoritative rulings.

Later, Judges of a type, and rudimentary Sanhedrins, were in being soon after the return from Babylon. Their remembered sayings are collectively attributed, by a later Mishna, to "The Men of the Great Synagogue"[2] who "received" the law, and settled the written canon of the Scriptures.

The law that they transmitted, and the later developing law, owe their acceptance, and their survival, to their defence by the Pharisees.

A famous Essene has spoken of some Pharisees in a way that has caused the Gentile world to forget that the Essenes were only extremist Pharisees themselves, and that no sect holds a monopoly of hypocrisy—or of purity.

Not that Jesus was alone. We find a later uncanonical Tannaitic text (a Baraitha) describing seven kinds of Pharisees, including many eccentric types (the "Shoulder-Pharisee", the "Wait a little Pharisee", the "Bruised Pharisee", the "Pestle Pharisee", etc.): and Joshua ben Hanania says that the eccentric types ruin the world.[3] But these things were said long, long, after those bloody struggles against Alexander Jannaeus in which Pharisee Rabbis established,

[1] Apropos of the Rabbinic "constructive" attitude to the Bible, some authorities make Zelophehad the man, referred to in the book of Numbers (XV.32), who was killed for desecrating the Sabbath. This is doubtful. Probably his daughters would not have been considered. (*See* the story of Achan in Joshua VII. But here the condemnation of the family is explicit.)

[2] More exactly, Men of the Great Assembly (or Community). It is possible that this expression is a description of the older Pharisees, who extended many of the Temple rules (details of Kashruth, for example) to the whole community of Israel. The Synagogue, in Rabbinic Hebrew, is "the house of the Assembly (Community)". While the Temple stood it was the only Synagogue: and was called "House of Holiness". The expression "Men of the Assembly" does not necessarily denote a Temple group: but does not exclude that construction.

[3] T.B. Soteh 22b.

for Israel, the rule of a higher authority than the Temple priesthood and the hereditary monarchy which exploited it.

Let it be added by way of parenthesis that modern Jewish Rabbis have, on the whole, known less than they should about their spiritual ancestry. Their work has been Halachic, the working out of legal decisions; and much of their task has been lightened by the monumental work of the Epitomists, Alfasi and Asheri, by the "strong hand" of the great codicist Maimonides, by the guiding lines of his successor Jacob ben Asher, by the availability of a "table prepared" by Joseph Caro and garnished by Isserles.

But the masters, and consequently the students, of Talmud are lacking in narrative awareness. The Talmud is the work of the descendants of Pharisees anxious to forget their enemies. Significantly, the feast of Chanucah, celebrating the victory of the great Maccabees, who founded the Priest-Kingdom, and whose descendants were Sadducees, this feast is only once, and obliquely, referred to in the entire Babylonian Talmud. Nor has Jewish learning been much on Josephus. The eastern Yeshivoth, the sources of scholarship for four centuries, were not aware of him. Hence a degree of ignorance among the Jews. If Rabbi did not learn this, whence could Chiya derive it?

But, to the Jew who knows something of his own history, the word Pharisee can never be a term of abuse. In extremes they were open to many different criticisms—they were casuistic, pedantic, unworldly, unconscious of the world. Their words were fiery, dangerous even to the birds of the air. The ordinary Jew was advised to warm himself at their fires, but beware of their glowing coals.[1] Not ascetic in the accepted sense, yet they deplored the distraction of the charms of nature—they walked head down and would not stop to admire a tree[2]—and as we have seen, they had little or

---

[1] (Avoth II.15). The danger is "metaphysical"; so is the fire.

[2] When their minds were on Torah. But that they were not blind to

no appreciation of the aesthetic merits of the "book" that they treasured. Their life's purpose was to teach a stern law to a weak generation. They said that, when Moses gave the Law to Israel, Sinai was torn from its roots and held over the people threateningly lest they refused. So the Pharisees improved their own EREV RAV. Withal they made the law a living thing, and a humane thing, preserving the spirit in those materialistic generations in which people tended to accept the letter of the law, and make profit out of its defects.

The Pharisees were interpreters;[1] they maintained interpretations of the law against the literalist Priests, and the worldly men, collectively described as Sadducees.[2]

Their interpretations are largely legal, but are not limited in scope or purpose to matters of ritual or matters forensic. Their primary effort was to establish that the law is above monarchy and priesthood; and that the law (on which they base these propositions) is more than mere text: is living tradition. Compendiously, they elevated the spirit of the law above the letter of the law, without departing from the methods and ways of lawyers.

One historic aspect of the matter is that the Pharisees were

beauty is evidenced by the existence of an old blessing addressed to the Creator of "goodly trees to give delight to mankind". (*See* Singer's *Prayer-Book*, p. 294.)

[1] This is one of the many possible meanings of the word Pharisee (from the verb Paresh). Other meanings include: Separatists (the generally accepted interpretation), and Devotees: and it has also been suggested that the word is derived from the Hebrew word for Persian, since the Pharisees may have held some Persian belief about the after life and about angels.

[2] The word is a late one. (*See* note to p. 127 *supra.*) Ignoring this fact, some would say: Disciples of Zadok (a famous High Priest). Dr. Rubin has suggested "inhabitants of Jerusalem" (the city of "right" (Tsedek).) They must not be confused with the later developing party of Zadokites, a group, cognate to Essenes, and consisting of the followers of another Zadok.

preserving a number of traditions—for the most part good traditions—and a number of well-grounded developments of tradition against the politically intransigent and the socially untrusting.

Law there was: much more than in the Mosaic Code. This was handed down from Master to Student: and there was a reluctance to the writing of the Halacha. "The way" of life, was, in a degree, too subtle for writing: and scholars shrank from the dogmatism that is associated with written text.[1]

The formula with which the Rabbis protected their learning, whose origin was remote in time, is: ORAL LAW (TORAH SHE BE'AL PEH). This is also called HALACHA LE MOSHE MI SINAI (The law (way) [shown] to Moses from Sinai). To any Jurist who is aware of the traditional reluctance of Judges, and even of early political authorities, to legislate changes in accepted law, this formula is readily understandable. To men who believed that their predecessors had not "added to or subtracted from" the Mosaic code, there was doctrine to reinforce the formula. At a later stage, when hermeneutical methods, applied to the written text, became the accepted way of justifying tradition or adding to it, the notion was never abandoned that the revelation on Sinai had revealed the unwritten as well as the written. "Everything that a pupil

[1] One of the problems of the jurists is due to the belief that the bulk of Talmud was, for centuries, never reduced to writing. Many textual problems could be solved if there were certainty as to this.

To believe that students remembered the masses of learning, mixed with homily and small talk, which make up thirty-six tractates of Babylonian Talmud is not impossible to any who have witnessed the colossal achievements of erudition for which the Yeshivoth have always been famous. Characteristic of the Jewish attitude is the colophon of every tractate of Talmud: "learn again tractate Berachoth" (e.g.). And the conclusion of any tractate occasions a SIYUM at which the contents of the treatise are thoroughly discussed.

will ever demonstrate to his master was shown to Moses on Sinai."[1] Evidently the modes of exegesis were also revealed: and that gave them a measure of authority, even when there was difference of opinion as to the proper methods of interpretation in particular cases.

In practice, the oral law in all Rabbinic times—certainly from Yavneh onwards—was drawn into, and submerged by, the derived law—the law that was extracted, by analytic methods (including verbal methods), from the Scriptures.

The evidences of dissension between Pharisees and their opponents belong to a period when hermeneutical methods were developing. The Pharisee reads the text differently. At an elementary level, since the text is consonantal, it is possible to read it with differences of vocalization. There could be a traditional reading, a "Mikra", which could be challenged by other traditions of reading, and challenged by references to some consonantal text (one of which texts was later called Masoreh), especially where the issue might be whether a semi-vowel (a Vav or a Yod) were present or absent. "There is strength in the Mikra", "there is strength in the Masoreh", became, indeed, conflicting principles of exegesis between two great Pharisees (Akiva and Ishmael) both of whom worked out elaborate hermeneutical methods.[2]

As between Pharisee and Sadducee, the former interpret the Scripture with the aid of all the devices available to the exegetist. The Sadducee, except in rare cases when exegesis fits in with his purpose, will not accept from the written code anything that is not clearly set out in it. He is sceptical

---

[1] It is worth mentioning that one at least of the great Posekim, Asher ben Yechiel (twelfth century) holds the expression Halacha le Moshe mi Sinai to mean: valid *as if* given to Moses on Sinai. This is a formula which is not un-Talmudic (*See* e.g. T.B. Niddah 45a).

[2] The N.T. references to Scribes and Pharisees may, conceivably, refer to two schools of Pharisees, corresponding to their attitudes to the text. It is also possible that the expression "Scribes and Pharisees" refers

of law given to Moses on Sinai: he is equally sceptical of methods of construction applied to Holy Writ in order to support doctrine that he does not wish to accept.

From that conflict Rabbinism, emerging triumphant, acquired confidence in its own ways of thought, in its own methods of interpretation. So Peshat and Drash became conventional, in the legal as well as the homiletical process, even when these two diverged, and long after the conflict with the Sadducees was forgotten.[1]

To mention some of their legal pronouncements and interpretations; the Pharisees did not act upon the literal duty of automatic compensation for damage as it is stated in Exodus and Leviticus. From the stupidity of a slave they exonerated the master. To them the expression "An eye for an eye" called for interpretation, and subtle application. They were reluctant to inflict death except (in the Biblical tradition) on the political enemy. On the whole their interpretations were the more humane. Yet no pronouncement of this type can formulate the differences. Very interesting is the fact that in the case of the scheming witness (ED ZOMEM, whose crime is called HAZOMOH), whereas the Sadducees held that the criminals could only be executed if the victim had been executed, the Pharisees seem to have held that only if the victim had not been executed could the schemers be executed. "If they have not slain, they are slain; if they have slain, they are not slain."[2]

to one group, characterized by their learning (Soferim-Bookmen) and their interpretations.

[1] In the eighth century, Karaism developed to remind them of it.

[2] (T.B. Makoth 5b. The Biblical verse is Deut. XIX.19. *See* Sifre *ad hoc*.) The theory that the Pharisees held the view expressed in the paradox has been described (by Kaufmann Kohler relying on SIFRE) as an absurdity. But it seems to be adopted as the law by Maimonides (Yod: Eduth XX.2) and the Codicists. That death penalties do not depend on "inference" is Talmudic commonplace. Yet it is hard to find a reason for the exoneration of the successful schemers. The classical suggestion is:

In less spectacular issues they applied the words of the Scripture dexterously, and with much use of analogy (HEKESH, GEZERAH SHOVEH, etc.). In divers ways they built up the still contemporary laws of Shechita (applying the rules of the Temple ritual), of the Tefillin, of the liturgy, and the Sabbath, as well as a corpus of civil and criminal laws. The general result of their labours seems to be a large number of apparent differences between practice and the Pentateuch.

let there be an end to blood-letting. Another explanation is that the Lord would not have allowed the Tribunal to condemn and kill unjustly. This, let it be said respectfully, seems bad argument. Murder happens in the Lord's world.

The author's suggestion, for what it is worth, is that once the Tribunal has acted, the witnesses cannot be said to be causative. (Analogously, in the Common Law, if a Court has imprisoned, the false complainant is not guilty of "false imprisonment"—only of malicious prosecution.) But the stated Talmudic argument is confined to the interpretation of the Scriptural text.

Interesting, in this connection, is the question: does "burn out the evil" imply that the "schemer" shall be burnt? (i.e. in practice, have molten metal poured down his throat). No, the verse says that the witness shall suffer precisely the fate designed by him for the victim.

Incidentally, the law of HAZOMOH seems to be, uniquely, an Halachic case of the punishment of intention. There is an overt act—the testimony—but this can come to nothing.

As to the nature of false testimony, the Talmudic distinctions are interesting. First, let it be remembered that evidence was not on oath, except on the part of defendants in civil (not criminal) issues (Lev. VI.21) and a few protected plaintiffs (workers suing for their wages; suitors for declarations of immunity from liability to minors, etc.).Witnesses other than parties were unsworn.

Their evidence could be factually false. Then they were guilty of HAKCHOSHOH (deception), which was serious but not capital. Complete fabrication, refuted by the proof "You were not there but somewhere else at the time", is the type of HAZOMOH—scheming—which was Capital: and the only capital offence for which guilt could be pronounced against a person "unwarned". (In the nature of things, a false witness is hardly in a position to be warned.)

Yet it must not be thought that they did intentional violence to the text. Some of their disputes with King Alexander Jannaeus are evidence to the contrary, perhaps evidence of a politically inspired pedantry. But, on the whole, they read the text in an interpretative, purposive way.[1]

It is to the Pharisees that the Jews owe their, admittedly not very good, Divorce Law. Some of them read the verse that gives the right to deliver the Get more generously (to the male) than did the Sadducees. In this respect the latter had the sympathy of the Essenes, as readers of the New Testament will appreciate. But, while giving great scope to the divorcing male (against the opinions of that stern Pharisee, Shammai), the Rabbis did much, that the Bible does not appear to contemplate, by way of mitigating the dangers to unprotected women. The instrument which is the Kethubah ("writing"—marriage contract), with its clause for the return of dowry, is one degree of protection.

Also, while not allowing a female initiative, the Rabbis used what powers they had (and they could be great among the religious) to cause relief to be given to unhappily married women. Let it be said, compendiously, that Pharisaic law was human, when human standards did not include egalitarianism between the sexes.

They were a stern group: yet they liberalized much.

Thus they liberalized the Sabbath, allowing the Sabbath candles[2]—now such a feature of Jewish life—allowing the "Sabbath day's journey", allowing (later) the Eruv which turns the village into a house for Sabbatical purposes. In this they were aiming, according to their lights, at the fulfilment of Isaiah's appeal to "call the Sabbath pleasant".

---

[1] In the modern phrase "tendentiously".

[2] To this day, Jewish women, lighting the candles, make gestures of welcoming and delaying with their hands, creating the fiction that the Sabbath does not arrive until the fire has been kindled and that the blessing has been said on its arrival.

Not least of their achievements is that, before the Destruction, they defeated hierocracy. They cleansed the
Temple as Phineas, whom they extolled, had cleansed the
camp. In the course of this long campaign, they claimed
that the progeny of proselytes—some of the great Rabbis
were that—and even illegitimates[1] who knew the law, were
equal in dignity and merit with the High Priest. The
Priesthood they thought of as Temple Servants, not
Masters. For the rest, aristocracy of intellect was greater
than aristocracy of blood.

The defeat of the entrenched hierocracy was also of great
theological importance. A considerable Gentile scholar
(G. E. Moore) has recorded the well-grounded judgement
that it is impossible to state completely or compendiously
the Jewish notions of Resurrection and Immortality.
Talmudic theology is unclear. But one thing is certain.
The Pharisees insisted that some doctrine of an after-life
is to be deduced from Holy Writ. That is not to say that
they excommunicated those who did not believe in that
eschatology. What they secured was the emancipation of
Israel from too narrow a nationalism, and from the des-
perations of thwarted hedonism.

An addendum to Mishna (Avoth de Rabbi Nathan) relates that when Antigonus of Socho, centuries before,
declared that one should obey, not as a servant for reward
but without the purpose of earning reward, his two pupils
Zadok and Baithus[2] were outraged by what they thought

---

[1] The Pharisaic definition of bastardy according to the Torah is very
narrow. The bastard is the child of a married woman from free co-
habitation with a man who was not, at the material time, her husband.
The Jewish "bastard" is not *filius nullius* (as the Roman and English)
but has property rights. He cannot "enter the congregation". That
means he cannot be married Halachically.

[2] Although Josephus refers to Baithusim, the term may well be
eponymous. Possibly we have here a corruption of Boethian, the Greek
expression for a stupid peasant type.

was the implied hopelessness of the good life, and became hedonists, Sadducees. This is probably not an accurate account of any historical event: but it reveals a traditional truth. Be it added that the Pharisees were not the inventors of eschatology, nor did they purvey it as opium to the masses. But, apart from their own belief, they were keenly aware that the flesh and blood of a group requires an eschatology. Few, be it added, have ever been able to look steadily at a hopeless future, and see it bright, as through the lenses of Spinoza.[1]

To the leading Pharisees, then, the people looked for guidance and called them "masters". In the time of national collapse it was the masters—the Rabbis—who saved the remnant of Jewish culture. Jochanan ben Zakkai, according to the legend, escaped from beleagured Jerusalem in the bier of a corpse. From that bier Rabbinism came to life. With the Temple fell the Priests, who, thereafter, were to fulfil less function in Jewish life than does now the Brahman caste in the life of Europeanized India.[2] The seat of judge-

---

[1] The insistence on an eschatology by such a man as Akiva does not imply any weak-mindedness. His life and death were characterized by great courage. Such men do not invent ideas for their comfort. Akiva said that dying for the Holy Name gave meaning to the Bible text, "love . . . with all thy might". Akiva's example, be it added, was gloriously followed by the many East-European Rabbis who, when they might have escaped, preferred to accompany their congregations to the German murder-sites.

[2] The member of a priestly family (such a name as Cohen or Katz —KOHEN TSEDEK—can be an indication) enjoys certain privileges and suffers certain restrictions. He is called first to the Reading of the law, followed by the Levite. He can pronounce the blessings on the congregation (the ceremony known as Dukhan). He takes part in the vestigial ceremony of the Redemption of the First Born (which is in itself a memory of a compromise between the ritual claims involved in primogeniture and the claims of the priesthood). He inherits, from Temple priesthood, the duty of special cleanliness: so that he must not go near a corpse. Nor may he marry a divorcee. (Readers of Zangwill's *Children*

ment was now legal—not priestly: and centuries of judgements, and of questionings and answerings, and debates and
disputations, became the subject-matter of the Talmud.

Every page of the Talmud reveals the mentality of spiritually lively and naturally free-minded people, endeavouring
to consolidate authority. The law that is laid down in any
case that comes before the Rabbi—or that is settled in any
disputation—must be consistent with many things: must be
consistent with the written Torah or must be grounded in
tradition; must be consistent with other accepted tradition,
which, as we have seen, is venerated as "torah she be'al
peh" (oral law) and described as "the way shown on Sinai".

These descriptions, it was said, are survivals of the struggle
between the struggling parties. It is important to add that
the Sadducees gained one victory; namely, that the tradition had to be well authenticated to survive. Hence the
perfection of hermeneutic methods. This tradition of analysis, from Hillel onwards, is a great phase of jurisprudence.
In later days, the influence of Akiva and Ishmael brought hermeneutical processes so much into the foreground that the
oral source of the tradition became a less important consideration than the possibility of deriving it, or support for
it, by exegetical methods from Holy Writ.

As the period of the Tannaim ends (third century C.E.)
and the period of the Amoraim begins, the Rabbinic task
is crystallized. To derive law from text, or from already
derived law. As to the derivation from text, the hermeneutical methods of Hillel, expanded by Akiva and Ishmael,
were themselves regarded as accepted oral laws. These
methods, which include rules of analogical reasoning (in
some cases verbal), rules of induction along the line from

of the Ghetto will remember a rather unreal, but dramatically excellent,
story worked out of this rule.)

Apart from these formalities, he is indistinguishable from the ordinary Israelite. He enjoys formal privileges—and no powers.

weak case to strong case (Kal ve Chomer), principles of classification (Binyan-Av), principles for the construing of the interaction of the general and the particular (Kelal and Perat), are recognizable as the logic of jurisprudence. The Jewish methods are special only in that they are biased by the doctrine that the Scripture is completely significant: that none of its pronouncements are superfluous; that, from the point of view of Akiva, none of its words are wasted.[1]

The Rabbis who settled the Mishna—the Tannaim—stated traditional laws, in some cases based upon delivered judgements, but, for the most part, in the form of general propositions. The students and successors of the Tannaim were analysts of these laws, and appliers of the law to specific cases. They were jurisconsults—judges on occasion—answerers of questions, the first of very many generations of what are called Posekim, deciders of the law. The continuity of the tradition is maintained through libraries of Shaaloth u Teshuvoth (questions and answers). In the present the Posekim are still at work, solving such problems as are set by the modern demand for grafts of living tissue, the need for autopsies, furnaces, burning on the Sabbath, etc.

At the time of the Gemara, i.e. the work of "completion" which is the bulk of Talmud, the subject-matter is logically the same as it was before and after: viz. the application of laws. The task is to state the law applicable to the situation: and that means to derive it from general statements and from precedents, all of them believed to be, or required to be, consistent with a meagre written text.

We see also in the Talmud some operation of the implicit juristic requirement that judgements must be consistent with principles of logic and common sense: and with legal principles, as they were then apprehended.

The problem may present itself in the terms: "who has

[1] Even the particle (ES) in "thou shalt fear the Lord" is interpreted: to signify the need for deference to the learned.

an oath". This is an early stage in the development of principles of proof, comparable to the finding of formulae by the Roman Praetors. That kind of problem and the learning involved (of which examples will be given) are valuable to any student of the evolution and logic of laws: and generally the Talmud is valuable because, problems of ultimate authority being solved, the discussions are readable as legal exposition: much of it belonging to a high order of juristic thought.

3. *The Rabbi as Lawyer*

Many important legal principles are only imperfectly articulated in the Talmud, because the Talmud is nascent law, a language in which the grammar has not been worked out and systematized. It follows that the Talmud, to its creators, and to its students (its creators called themselves students), is an intellectual effort analogous to the mastery of communication among peoples who have no clear accidence or syntax; for the authorities and the jurisprudence of Talmudic times were fluid.

The need for establishing authority is made clear in any section of Talmud. First we have a Mishna (the "learning", as distinct from Mikra, the "reading", of written Torah): that is to say a statement of law handed down from Tannaitic times, i.e. from the period of the Tannaim (Exponents)—the Rabbis who rescued the law from the anarchy of the centuries of Herod and Vespasian. Tannaitic law is authoritative, unless (*per impossible*) it be in conflict with written Torah. But Tannaitic law is not always clear, and there are many Tannaim; and the paths of doctrine can seem to lead in opposite directions. A decision can be a cross-road of irreconcilable doctrines, the difficulties only becoming clear when the roads part again, and when the principle of the judgement is sought in order to be applied in a different context. Given Tannaitic doctrine, the task of the student is to apply it, and to reconcile the application with all other Tannaitic doctrine; and, if Tannaitic conflict is suspected, then, so to clarify the opinions as to reveal the sources of difference in the clear pronouncements of opposing Tannaim; a disagreement of the doctors.

The Mishna is stated; the text that then follows is Gemara, which means (*inter alia*) "a completion". That text, the compilation of Sebaraim (analysts, centuries later, of the *rationes decidendi*) contains collated learning from various sources; from other Tannaim, from Tannaitic texts of lesser authority (Toseftas), from Amoraim (the generations of Masters of lesser rank than Tannaim, lesser, if only because they flourished after the closure of the Mishna)[1], and from the Sebaraim themselves. The text of the Gemara

---

[1] Second to third century of the Common era. Rabbi Judah Hanassi (the Prince) at that time collected a canonical Mishna. Some of the Amoraim may have been of greater mental stature than the Tannaim, but as authorities they were subordinate. Abba Areka (Rav) whom Rabbi Judah Hanassi appointed to Sura was at least equal to his appointer. The latter, however, did not confer on him the title Rabbi, the alleged reason being that permission to judge and appoint could not be exercised outside Palestine. (There is evidence—the case of Bar Kapporah, e.g.—which suggest that Rabbi Judah was not above "personal" discrimination.)

Amoraim, generally, used as a prefix (if any) the word Rab, rather than Rabbi. But the absence of a prefix is not a safe guide to status in the degrees of authority.

It must not be assumed, incidentally, that Rabbi Judah Hanassi constitutes the authority of the Mishna. He was only the *redacteur* working along lines set by predecessors such as Rabbi Meir. The importance of the Mishnaic text (no one knows when it was reduced to writing) is the exclusion from recognition (as clearly authoritative) of doctrines not stated in the text. In other words what Rabbi Judah had not included in his edition lacked the powerful support that his reputation lent to whatever he recognized as good tradition. (Observe that he recognizes and includes much with which he himself disagrees.) He is editor but only one of the authorities.

resembles modern case-law with this distinction; that it is almost impossible to solve a problem by dismissing a Tannaitic dictum as wrong.[1]

The task is to derive the law, deducing it from the clearest sources, if possible from the Torah itself; and to that end the Rabbis developed (as we have seen) principles of interpretation, many of them scientific by modern standards.

By that time the Hebrew and Aramaic languages had become abstract enough to express notions like the "general rule" and the "particular case". This type of distinction made possible a much more scientific view of the text of Torah, and of the language of tradition. But, in addition, the Rabbis were always ingenious to force the text of the Scriptures in the traditions of Peshat and Drash. (The "Peshatist" is skilful in the perception of legal distinctions, and latent ambiguities, by virtue of his very skill in the control of words.) In many cases the use of Scripture must seem strange to modern eyes. How do we know that the Sanhedrin was to be seated in a circle? Because of the verse in Canticles: "Thy navel is a round goblet". A more practical example. Can I infer from Ex. XXIII.5 that I am obliged to help to unload a beast of burden without pay, but that for loading it I can expect to be paid? (Note the pressure on the text: what the text does not say is almost part of it.) There is difference of opinion on this. A point to observe is that at this stage there is no distinction of mode of

---

[1] Another important aspect of Talmud is that many of the disputations are on hypothetical questions, and on problems of classification. Rabbi I. H. Weiss, the author of *Dor Dor ve Dorshov* (a monumental history of the oral law), points to instances of quite fantastic questioning: e.g. what should a man with two heads do in the laying of tefillin? (T.B. Menachot 37a.) In this connexion there is (in another part of Talmud) an amusing legend about King Solomon, who was asked by a man with two heads to declare him two persons (entitled to two portions). Solomon poured hot water on one head and the other head screamed. That threw cold water on the claim.

obligation drawn between what we now call the ethical and what we now call the legal. At all levels the text is a guide to right conduct.

Such exploitation of Holy Writ is available to explain any tradition, any practice. From, and alongside, these ingenuities, a science of analysis of legal texts is also developing: including principles of limitation. What is the scope of the expression: "Thou shalt love thy neighbour as thyself"? It grounds duties like that of burial. In other words the Rabbis were working towards what we now call principles of construction: to legality: and the later generations were expert in the perception and isolation of reasons for decisions. But, more than any secular school of lawyers, the Rabbis are bound to seek and find unity. The task is to harmonize the law, even while discovering or creating it: to reconcile conflicts. And this movement is a complex one because each generation seeks to find perfect the works of the previous generation; and the emphasis is always on the transmitted word: there is little scope for restatement in the light of history.[1] Let it be said, however, that so sound was the standard of Rabbinic judgement, that the masses of accumulating learning yield clear principles in excess of unreconciled conflicts.

The argument of the Talmud, when allowance is made for excessive verbal ingenuity, and the inveterate determination to reconcile,[2] is legal argument. The Masters of the Gemara thought like lawyers.

[1] There are references in the Talmud to errors committed by early Sanhedrins, before the destruction of the Temple. But there is little claim to authority from that period. Articulation of authority begins later against a background of anonymous tradition. The history is a history of Schools. At the time of the Destruction Rabbi Jochanan ben Zakkai obtained from the Romans permission to found a school at Yavneh. Only then began systematic statement, and the selection, from tradition, of the authoritative.

[2] This effort to reconcile will be seen to characterize the efforts of the

The Talmud is important in the history of thought, because it reveals the evolution of laws, and the development of legal thinking, among people who were not consciously lawyers, from sources ritualistic and formal and sub-legal, or super-legal, and with an inspiration religious and ethical. The documentary basis was slight.[1] A significant passage in Chagigah tells us that, whereas some laws are well grounded in the written Torah, others hang on very slender threads, or float in the air. One explanation is that for centuries before the Common era, and for centuries thereafter, Israel was permeated by the Graeco-Roman civilization, which was suffused with legal notions, and which had created a secular, disciplined, way of life in a setting of politico-legal institutions: had suffused everyday life with laws.

One of the celebrated Tannaitic conflicts is interesting in this connexion. Beth Shammai (the conservative Palestinian school of legal thought) held that, if a beam were stolen (converted) and used in the structure of a building, the building must be dismantled so that the beam could be restored to its owner. This decision, not accepted by the more progressive, or practical, thinkers of the school of Hillel (who sought to encourage restitutions), happens to be an article in the Roman Twelve Tables. That fact, in isolation, suggests one source of the inspiration of Rabbinic law-making, or law-finding. It is reinforced by the fact

Philosopher-Rabbis who sought to equate the teachings of the Greeks with the teachings of the Prophets. (*See* Ch. VI.) (Since writing the above I have discovered that the same thought is expressed by Weiss in the *Dor*.)

[1] Laws about the laying of Tefillin, etc. are stated in the Pentateuch but all the detail is Rabbinic and, apparently (as the Karaites point out), against the plain meaning. In another field, the duty of the brother-in-law of a childless widow seems clear in Pentateuch—and the exoneration is by Chalitza. In Rabbinic practice, however, a brother-in-law would not be allowed to marry the widow, however devoutly that consummation might be wished. Again, the laws of theft and conversion

that the Talmudic laws of inheritance, insofar as they add to the Scriptural, embody the principles of agnation common to the ancient world. In default of issue there was a tracing back to the common male ancestor. Moreover, the later levels of the Talmud are rich in Graeco-Roman legal notions; and Greek words such as hypothecation are accurately used by later Rabbis, who knew no Greek[1] and sought ingenious explanations of the sources of the strange words.[2]

Much of the Talmud is Rabbinic legislation, by Rabbis who refused to admit (or believe) that they were legislating. They were applying law, acting according to traditions, which they held to be derivative from written and oral authority of respectable antiquity. But the reality of their task was "judicial legislation", such as takes place in the modern Anglo-Saxon system. In discharging that task

are so elaborated in the Talmud that they seem to oppose the apparently clear laws stated in Holy Writ.

[1] Greek was forbidden by the Rabbis of the second century C.E. to all but the college of Gamaliel.

[2] Thus they rendered Hypothec (which they understood, correctly, as a mortgage of chattels left in the possession of the mortgagor) into APO TEHE KOAI (let it stand here). Similarly, DIATEKE (obviously the Greek Diatheke, a Will) is rendered DA TEHE KOAI: "This shall stand" (after the death of the testator). It has been suggested, by that great authority Rabbi Yomtov Lippman Heller (Tosafoth Yomtov), that these "explanations" were not due to ignorance, but were pragmatically desirable.

In another context, the author has speculated that, if Rabbinic ignorance of Greek were fully appreciated, at least one Jewish ritual item would be different. If AFIKOMEN, is, as the author believes, derived from EFIKNEOMAI (I have had enough—cf. AFEKEI, the word used in the New Testament garden scene), then the rule that one does not utter AFIKOMEN after the Pesach means that it is wrong to stop eating after the Pesach ceremony. The Jewish practice, on the other hand, is cessation—surely out of keeping with the tradition of the "protected right", which the Rabbis (released from the night SHEMA) celebrated intellectually until the time for the SHEMA of the dawn.

they thought like lawyers; and many decisions are available that could only have been made or found by men who had achieved a legal method of thinking.

In point are some striking rules and decisions. A man has lent a beast to another on hire; and the hirer has lent it gratuitously to a third person, in whose custody the animal dies. Now the hirer can exonerate himself for any death not due to his negligence. On the other hand the gratuitous bailee is absolutely liable to the hirer. According to one school of thought (semble, Rabbi Judah, opposed by Rabbi José), the hirer keeps the proceeds. From this it is worked out that if an owner borrows a beast from its hirer during the term of the hiring, for a period less than the hiring term, and the animal dies during the period of lending, then the owner becomes liable to restore a beast to the hirer. What happens thereafter is not clear, but a case is adumbrated (rather ingeniously) in which an owner might lose more than one beast to a hirer who only hired one. Whether this is good Halacha (established doctrine) is not clear: but the thinking is legal thinking, since there is a clear recognition of the distinction between "capacities", and some understanding of the distinction between proprietary rights and duties on the one hand and contractual rights and duties on the other.[1]

The notion of legal principle is also implicit in a decision in the law of finding. Seeing is not legal finding: taking hold of something can be finding; and seeing something lying within four ells of oneself can be finding. But the man who throws himself on all fours over an object without actually taking hold of it, does not acquire by finding, because he had not relied on the doctrine of four ells, and he has not taken hold. Therefore he has established no legal claim.[2]

[1] T.B. Baba Mezia 35. The examples worked out are probably an attempt to reduce Rabbi Judah's contention to absurdity.

[2] T.B. Baba Mezia 10a.

Rab Abba advised on a point about a man accused of converting a bar of metal. A witness saw the defendant take it. The latter pleaded: "I took it; but what I took was mine." Now, had the man entered a simple denial, he would have been allowed an oath to "contradict the single witness", and, on taking the oath, exonerated. But his defence made it impossible for him to contradict the witness; and there was no recognized oath available to him. Rab Abba ruled that the defendant should surrender the metal.[1] Evidently this, too, is strict legal thinking. There was no legal defence open. The argument that here a man suffers by his honesty is not legal argument of the first order: it is an argument from possible results, not from an acceptable principle; not from a text, or a recognized *ratio decidendi*. The accused man's plight may be an absurdity comparable to that of the owner restoring beast after beast to a hirer; but *reductio ad absurdum* is not the best legal argument.[2]

Much Talmud is concerned with law that is now obsolete: (that was, even then, obsolete); of sacrifice and impurities, and penalties stated in terms of sacrifices. But they are legally stated: that is to say, there is exact thinking about the duty and the penalty. This mode of thinking is now basic in the Jewish religion. In the modern codes, laws about prayer and fasting, etc. are stated juridically. "This is a positive commandment from the Pentateuch, and the penalty is . . ." "This is a prohibition and the penalty is . . ." "This is Rabbinic ruling (Takkana—legislation within the four corners

[1] T.B. Baba Bathra 33b.

[2] In English law, *reductio ad absurdum* failed, as argument, in the famous Russell case where rules of relevance applicable to peerage claims were not allowed in a divorce process brought by a peer.

Reductio ad absurdum does occur in Talmud, e.g. where, while they are making special provisions for the High Priest during the week before the Day of Atonement—special dwelling, etc., they do not accept the suggestion of an "emergency" wife: "because if so, there is no end to the matter". (T.B. Yoma 2.)

of accepted Halacha) . . ." etc. So questions such as: What overrides the Sabbath or the Day of Atonement? are legal questions: and the relative severity of duties is judged by their stated penalties.[1]

At the Talmudic stage, it must be remembered, there was no full articulation of the difference between Criminal and Civil process.[2] Indeed the Graeco-Roman civilization never achieved this analysis perfectly. Nor was clear distinction achieved between ethical or religious, on the one hand, secular, on the other. Indeed, the Jewish system of thought would hardly have tolerated that distinction. (In point are laws against "overreaching".)

Nevertheless, there is enough recognition of relative importance of degrees of culpability, etc. to enable us to describe large areas of the text as fields of civil law in one of the senses in which we use the term today. Indeed, in this field the Rabbis were responsible for a fertile growth of concepts that are important for all jurisprudence.

In the development of notions of civil rights and corres-

[1] So the prayers are legally (and very logically) ordained. The hundred blessings that are said each day are prescribed as to their occasions: and an "empty prayer", or "wasted prayer" (i.e. on an inappropriate occasion) is a minor blasphemy.

The Chassidic tendency to multiply and improvise prayers is, of course, not wrong, but would not be regarded as "duty" by strict authority.

[2] That a rudimentary distinction was appreciated is clear from the rule that where penalties were sought (always of course by private suit) oaths were not administered to the defendants. The wrong was of a type that tainted them. (The theory perpetuated for so long in the English Common Law.)

Of the modern distinction, between, on the one hand, process at the will of parties, terminable at the will of parties, and, on the other hand, process by or for the State, terminable only on the motion of the State, we can say that the Rabbis knew it in the context of Homicide. Indeed, we have the distinction drawn, for Homicide, in the Pentateuch (Numbers XXXV.31) which forbids the private release of the killer.

ponding duties, we find the Rabbis working out clearly the differences between the Public Domain and the Private Domain (Reshuth Harabbim and Reshuth Hayochid). Clearly different considerations apply in the determination of liability in these respective situations. In respect of title and ownership it has been suggested that such a rule as *Cujus est terra ejus est ad caelum et ad inferos* is of Rabbinic origin. Certainly they thought much about Accretion. In the law of chattels they were masterly. Finding is well analysed. Indeed in the basic notion of acquisition by finding —the notion of abandonment—there is Rabbinic analysis that is unparalleled in other systems. The notion of "unconscious abandonment" or, as modern lawyers might express it, "presumed abandonment" is the subject matter of collated case-learning around the names of Abaye and Rovo, which, restated in modern terms, would carry the hallmark of the best case-law.

On the passing of property in chattels, there is elaborate and practical,[1] and very lawyer-like, learning. Does gold acquire silver? If gold is currency and silver is commodity —yes: but Rabbi Judah lived through times in which gold ceased to be the currency and went into the class of commodity. So, if gold were given for silver, the property in the silver would not pass automatically to the would-be acquirer.

Again, those who are acquainted with the learning of Holt J., as expressed in the judgement in Coggs *v.* Bernard, can possibly learn more in the Talmudic classification of Bailments. (T.B. B.M. 98.) There are four classes of bailees; gratuitous bailees; hired watchers; hirers and borrowers. Their liabilities, of course, vary. The one who looks after a thing for nothing only has to swear that he did not interfere with it. The hired watcher and the hirer are liable if the thing is lost through straying or clandestine theft: the bor-

[1] T.B. Baba Mezia. Perek Hazohov.

rower (for no consideration) is liable in all contingencies except natural causes. Though linked with Bible text, and stated in terms of available oaths,[1] rather than pleas in the modern manner, such an analysis constitutes juristic thinking *par excellence*.

The Rabbis of Babylon as well as Palestine seem to have been thoroughly equipped with Graeco-Roman legal ideas.

Roman notions like Usucaption are well articulated in the Talmud, and well analysed. The communities of those days lived in conditions in which the landowner might not be able to live on his land for a long period. Therefore squatters' law (law of Chazoko—"holding") was important; and principles of "protest", and similar evidence of intention, were worked out in detail. Further, mortgages of many types were known.[2] The notion of security is treated for what it is, a factor in developing commercial enterprise.

Some of the notions are cramped in their development by the inveterate Rabbinic determination to reconcile the new with the old. Moneylending at interest is resisted even more strongly than it was, later, by the Canon lawyers. We find Samuel, the Babylonian Amora, "pointing" the text in Leviticus to mean: by the Gentile you may be bitten (charged interest) not by thy brother.[3] Lending is a form of charity. Charity must not be rewarded—even by thanks! The Greek word Oneia[4]—benefit—is used in the Talmud to

---

[1] E.g. They swear to the facts that show they committed no breach of duty. In a sense, this is one case of oath in respect of "partial admission".

[2] Indeed, all advances were presumed to be secured. A failure to mention security was treated as a "clerical error".

[3] *See* p. 48 *supra*. Since the "pointing" of published texts is a late development, the pointing of Scripture (at least in quotation) was traditional-oral. This gave scope to many who sought to read their own thoughts into Holy Writ.

[4] For the Talmudic word there is a possible Hebrew root in a word signifying mischief or deception. But the theory of the Greek origin is

signify illicit benefits vitiating not only commercial exchange but good deeds. Eventually, capitalization by financial advances for profit was made possible by the fiction of
partnership; a legal fiction considered also by some Canon
lawyers, and used by Jewish moneylenders up to modern
times in their dealings with Jews.[1]

In many aspects of life the Talmud reveals the rich and
rapid development of legal notions to frame an expanding
urban society. But this development took place within
traditions, and great subtlety was required at all stages to
allow the legal notion free play among intellectual restrictions.

Thus, just as the Halacha (the legal and substantive part
of the Talmud) is characterized, even in the context of
exact legal argument, by frequent recourse to the methods
of Peshat, so, in the classification of opinions of the Rabbis,
there is a function of ingenuity as well as of science. There
is always authority to be reconciled; and, if necessary,
conjectural contexts and textual refinements are examined
in order to facilitate distinction and analogies.

A Mishna in Nezikin[2] runs as follows: "Two persons are
holding a garment; one of them says 'I found it' and the
other says 'I found it': one of them says 'it is all mine' and the
other says 'it is all mine'. Then one shall swear that his share
in it is not less than half, and the other shall swear that his
share is not less than half: and they shall divide it."

Now the first task that the Sebarist (the redacteur) takes

preferred, because what is proscribed is not a mischief or a deception,
but an enrichment that is not approved.

[1] The formula is known as HETER ISKA—permission of enterprises.
It was used by orthodox Jews when they undertook some of the financing of Zionism. (The late Rabbi Rabinovich of Liverpool drew up the
form). Of course it must be understood that much moneylending has
been done by those who do not try to reconcile their practices with
Jewish orthodoxy!

[2] T.B. Baba Mezia 2.

upon himself (or the first argument that he records) is verbal analysis. Why the duplication? Why "it is all mine" as well as "I found it"? Are we to infer something from this? One suggestion is that the duplicated language of the claim makes it clear that finding is not completed by the mere seeing of a lost article. This inference is not clear; and preference is given to the theory that "it is all mine" extends the doctrine to a situation in buying and selling; the only case that is analogous being one where two people claim to have bought and paid for the same article, and the vendor is conscious of having been paid by one but does not know which one. The further possibility that the language of the Mishna is dramatic or pleonastic is not for one moment considered.

After this the law as law is debated (or the points are arranged as if they arose in debate). The debate is actually a series of citations from other authorities, and their comparison, contrast, and reconciliation with the doctrine of the Mishna.

Why, for example, is this not a case of burden of evidence on the plaintiff? Because the seizure was simultaneous, and both are plaintiffs. How does it differ from a proposition by Symmachus, who had ordered a division of disputed money without an oath? Or, on the other hand, from the doctrine of the Rabbis who had opposed Symmachus? (The fact that Symmachus enjoyed great personal authority is irrelevant.) How does it cohere with dicta of Ben Nannes against the danger of perjury? Or with Rab José who would leave the question "until the coming of Elijah"[1]

---

[1] The formula is TEKU—which may be short for a word meaning "you will let it stand": but is almost certainly an acronym of words meaning "the Tishbite will answer questions and problems"—TISHBI YETARETS KUSHIYOTH VEABAYOTH. (Incidentally, Israel chess players use the word TEKU to mean "drawn"! This is unscholarly: the term is only apt to an "adjudication" of special difficulty.)

(i.e. to remain unanswered), rather than risk the accrual of a benefit to the wrongdoer.

These questions are resolved by demonstration that the decisions, or dicta, in question were in different contexts. Each demonstration can be, and is, challenged. Some alternative restatements of the case law require to be considered for the achievement of consistency among the authorities. A student may well feel that too little scope is allowed for genuine differences among the authorities. That, however, is only to observe that the standard is an authoritarian one. For the rest, in the course of the argument some very close reasoning is followed, and a fine logical discrimination is everywhere evident.[1]

Much of the research in the Gemara is, in effect, legal case-collation, with some differences from modern case-learning; e.g. the fact that the categories for classification were not clear in Talmudic times: that the legal language is without a clear grammar. Also the period of Talmudic learning is a longer one than is covered by English case-law, and there is a greater reluctance to abandon the antique.

Writers of great authority and great conspective grasp, such as the Tosafists[2], Ezekiel Landau, Eybeschütz, and Elijah of Vilna, have pointed out that some laws must be

---

[1] From the student of Talmud, in the orthodox tradition, the intellectual effort called for is the holding in mind of a number of possible combinations of the explanations of the decisions that are cited. Two words of praise show an interesting distinction. The man of comprehensive knowledge is BOKI. The sharp, original percipient of distinctions or new syntheses, is CHARIF. A "genius" is ILUI. When distinctions are very finely drawn the process is called PILPUL (Lit-Pepper. At times there has been excess of this.)

[2] The Tosafists (the word TOSAFOTH means "Additions") were mainly a group of French and Rhenish (twelfth century) Rabbis, whose comments on the Talmud are, to an extent, amplifications of the commentary of Rashi. Their comments are always subtle, incisive, and lawyer-like. The greatest of them was Rabbenu Tam, Rashi's grandson.

treated as late (and valid) developments, of which earlier authorities had not known the principle. Thus the Babylonian Rabbis understood better the concept of Bererah[1] (a feature of joint ownership) than had the Palestinians. Again, agency was analysed, and re-analysed, at many periods. The Babylonian Rovo was much more chary of accepting the full notion of principal's authority than his predecessors had been. (Perhaps that was because he was further from the centres of Roman learning.) He took more seriously the problem of the supervening death of the principal.[2]

Again, there was an evolution, recognized in the Talmud itself, in the doctrines relating to oaths. At "Talmudic Common law" so to speak, witnesses were unsworn; only defendants (and not all of those) were allowed oaths. These were oaths of exoneration—available only when there was lacking the testimony of two witnesses to the issue in support of the plaintiffs. (The law of oaths is derived from Exodus XXII.7-10 and Leviticus VI.21). A plaintiff was regarded as a person who, if he could not be believed unsworn, would not be believed on oath. The defendant was little better. His not to deny. He was called upon, not to contradict a statement of fact, but to testify to the unknown facts. Thus, it being admitted that he hired the animal and

---

[1] T.B. Baba Bathra 54. A celebrated civilian has described joint ownership learning as the filigree of law.

[2] There were, it should be noted, two growths of Gemara: one in Babylon, one in Palestine. By common consent, and according to the high authority of Alfasi, the Babylonian Gemara (of which more is extant) is better learning. There was some communication between the Schools, though one Palestinian Amora spoke of Babylon as a land of darkness where people saw obscurely. An amusing story describes how a great scholar came from Babylon to hold discussions with the Palestinians. The local Rabbis said to their representative: "The lion of Babylon is upon you". After the discussion had gone some way, one of the spectators observed: "This lion that you spoke of has turned out to be a fox".

that it had died or disappeared, he could swear that he had done no breach of duty.

There was no oath to be administered in respect of simple claims, based on simple statements of fact, such as a claim for the return of money lent. The onus being on the plaintiff, he had to produce witnesses or fail in his claim provided that the defendant entered a simple unsworn denial. Evidently this was a great hardship on honest creditors. So the Rabbi's invented, for such cases, an "oath of inducement" to be taken by the defendant, since they held that, on the one hand, no one was impudent enough to bring totally unfounded claims, whereas a defendant might only be entering a denial in order to gain time. They extracted from Bible text an oath to a defendant making partial admissions. They also granted oaths to certain plaintiffs when the defendant was ineligible for an oath (a minor, etc.). They granted an oath, also, to a defendant, in order to refute a single witness. (This was their nearest approach to conflict of testimony). They invented an "added oath" so as to enable a defendant to answer a second claim, when he is under primary obligation to swear to only one. In this way there developed an equipment for the handling of testimony that operated to prevent the bringing of doubtful claims, and gave a hope of redress to honest claimants faced with denials that were legally irrefutable.

From the juristic standpoint, then, the Talmud is not a perfect system, rather a legal system evolving.[1]

That in itself is a merit: and, in the evolution, great juristic achievements are evident in the Talmudic corpus. It is clear from the examples already given that they worked out, from practical and ethical considerations, many of the

[1] This is not the traditional Jewish view. But that the great scholars were aware of an evolution is evidenced by the comment of Rabbi Solomon Loria (MAHRSHAL) on the method of the Tosafists; that they sought to make a perfect circle.

important features of Agency, of Bailment, of Pledges, Securities, Purchase and Sale, and generally, the legal constituents of urban commercial life. Some inspiration comes from Roman sources: but the Jewish working out of doctrines is individual, and is often characterized by greater subtlety than is the work of the Romans.

In point is a Mishna on what the Romans call Specificatio.

To the Romans the doctrine was easy. They had their legal "grammar". To the Rabbis, early decisions had to be analysed so that the principle could be articulated: and always there were many possible classifications of the learning.

"If one misappropriates pieces of wood and makes utensils out of them or pieces of wool and makes garments out of them he has to pay for them according to their value at the time of the misappropriation".[1]

This is a departure from the Pentateuchal law (Leviticus V.3), that "he shall return what he took by robbery". Clearly the case must be different from the simple Biblical position, because the written law is immutable; but at the outset the new principle is not clear.

The opening criticism is typical of Talmudic reasoning: pressure on the words used. "By speaking of garments and utensils do you imply that if wood were merely planed, or wool bleached, the material itself must be restored to the owner? But there is a Baraitha (an uncanonical Tannaitic text) to the contrary: viz. that when converted wood has been planed or wool bleached, the converter pays the value of the material that was misappropriated as at the time of the misappropriation."

Another way of putting the question (an historical approach) would be to ask what the Mishna adds to the known Tannaitic tradition.

A suggestion (which meets both approaches) is made

[1] T.B. Baba Kamma 93b, and see p. 147 *supra*.

that the Mishna deals with manufacture executed in such
a way that the completed article can be dismantled and the
materials restored as they were. The argument is that the
Mishna allows an extension of the doctrine of specification
here, as a Rabbinic indulgence to make it easier for conver-
ters to admit their wrongdoing.

But that is not accepted as the explanation of the Mishna.
Strong opinion is expressed that the Mishna is the authoritative pronouncement of a school that allows all changes in
converted materials to cause a transfer of ownership. Many
texts are collated and examined to show whether what they
were considering was change at all; or some special degree
of change: or an indulgence to facilitate restitution. The
analysis concludes with a recognition of two main schools of
thought. Later the medieval codicists were in some doubt as
to how the law stood. Modern critics are prepared to re-
arrange the citations so as to show the historical development
of a notion which was not indigenous to Jewish law.[1]

In this field, and many other fields, the Rabbis were
creating law from difficult traditional material in order to
accommodate the expansion of life in a sophisticated world.

That they were committed in advance by Scripture we
have already seen. Also they started handicapped by
certain rigidities of procedure. Given a horror of perjury,
the problem, in many issues, was, how can an oath be
administered? How can people be made to attest without
the possible supervention of perjury? The task of the Rabbi
in that context was analogous to the task of the modern
advocate when he tries to present a case, if possible, without
a conflict of testimony. (The problem is also similar to that
of the Roman Praetors when they sought for formulae;

[1] This line of law is of particular interest because it implies an understanding of civil claims, and principles of mitigation of damage, in
contrast to the Biblical law with its overtones of moral condemnation,
and its fixed penalties.

but the Jewish difficulty is less formalistic.) We have seen that the Rabbis were skilful, on behalf of honest claimants, in causing defendants to take oaths in denial of claims.

It must be understood that a Jewish trial never took the form of a direct conflict between witnesses. That modern (European) form is the result of a long legal evolution. The witnesses (two to establish a fact) were cross-examined (in the presence of the parties). There was an interrogation as to their position in time and place when they witnessed the event (this is called Chakira): and there was an interrogation as to the details of what they saw (Bedika). A flaw in their testimony revealed by the first form of interrogation was regarded as much more serious than a confusion revealed by the second form of interrogation. That he saw confusedly was understandable; that he was not where he said he was could go to the root. Both modes of cross-examination could invalidate testimony. False testimony of the first class, however, could amount to corrupt scheming (HAZOMOH).

Proof of the corruption of witnesses was difficult because the procedure did not allow the person attacked to swear against two witnesses. Other witnesses could testify in contradiction. Failing that, the defendant on a criminal charge was in a sorry plight. The only convincing refutation of scheming witnesses was the testimony of other witnesses that they (the schemers) had been elsewhere at the time in question. The Jewish alibi was a proof that the witnesses were elsewhere. The attacked witnesses could, in turn, call witnesses, but after that conflict no one could reasonably be convicted.

In the development of the Jewish civil law, many important notions of evidence were worked out from first principles. Evidence was direct (two witnesses according to the Pentateuch). Hearsay was not accepted, though in civil matters provision was made for sickness, etc. Circumstantial

Evidence (i.e. inference) was not allowed to establish facts. Thus if a woman was seen in "maidenly garb", that did not prove, or help to prove, that she was not a widow. (T.B. Ket. 2nd Chapter). Documents were accepted subject to proper production, but as "deeds" rather than as records of events. The problem that beset the Rabbis was the difficulty of the Pentateuchal law as it affected the Burden of Evidence. Simple and just claims could fail for want of witnesses independent and unrelated to parties. The simple logical burden of evidence was a commonplace. Subtler, and typically Rabbinic, are the arguments (embodied in law) to ground credibility; presumptions, of sorts; e.g. that such a defendant should be believed; that such a defendant should be trusted with an oath, and another not. For example, a gambler is not trusted on oath. A defaulting debtor is given an oath, a defaulting depositee (denying the deposit) not: because the debtor may have been seeking to gain time, and will not go to the extent of perjury: the depositee, however, must have done some wrong to be in his position: so his conduct in denying the deposit is inexcusable: one who has so behaved is likely to commit perjury. Different considerations arise and are entertained, when the depositee pleads that the thing deposited has been stolen. Where, however, the denial would go to the root, it seems that the claimant can only succeed with the aid of the two witnesses that are required to establish a matter.

Again, and this covers a large range of issues, including bailments, a partial admission allows the defendant an oath because he could have made a total denial, leaving the onus on the plaintiff. But it had to be clear that he had nothing to gain by his concession.

These are refinements disregarded in a world in which all persons are competent and compellable, and the cogency of their evidence equally suspect.

A Rabbinic form of argument (not necessarily confined

to oaths, but appearing much in that context, because the burden of evidence is one of the most frequent of questions) is the argument from the strength or weakness of the facts under consideration in relation to analogous situations. This is, in effect *a fortiori* (or *a minore*) argument, as we know it today, and is called KAL VECHOMER (literally, light and heavy).[1] The mental act is the apprehension of a line of thought relating two situations. (This logical form is also one of the hermeneutical methods of deriving law from written text.)

A simple example is the following: If a paid bailee, who is not liable for injury to, or death of, the animal, is yet liable in the event of theft, or loss, surely the borrower, who is liable for death or injury, is also liable for theft or loss.

More complex is the following. The claimant says: "You owe me a hundred zuz". The defendant says: "I owe you nothing". Two witnesses say that the defendant owes the plaintiff fifty zuz.

Now had the defendant admitted fifty, he would have been given an oath in respect of the remaining fifty. So the question arises: Do two witnesses to part of the claim make the defendant liable for an oath when he enters a total denial? On first principles there seems to be no justification for an oath, because the man might be a perjurer. On the other hand the Rabbis were anxious, without being arbitrary, to help the plaintiff in this unsatisfactory position.

An argument, *a fortiori*, or *a minore*, is then adumbrated. If the word of a man's own mouth, which would not oblige him to pay a fine, can make him liable to an oath (as in partial admission), then surely two witnesses, who can cause a man to pay a fine, can make him liable to an oath.

But an answer is made: the two witnesses are not stronger than his own mouth, because two witnesses can be refuted:

[1] A mode of thinking not unknown to the Scriptors. "He who planted the ear, shall he not hear?"

an admission can never be refuted. So there is no valid argument available from weaker to stronger.[1]

Then another approach is essayed. If one witness can inflict an oath (to deny the witness) surely two witnesses can inflict an oath. But that is not acceptable argument. Because, it is replied, when one witness asserts, the oath contradicts his assertion: but here the oath in question is not to contradict the witnesses (that would not be allowed, in any event) but to cover a state of fact as to which they do not depose (i.e. the question of the other fifty zuz).

In this particular dispute, an ingenious solution is found: and the "common factor" between the two *a minore* arguments (from "one witness" and from the witness's "own mouth") is accepted to vest the defendant with an oath.

The logic of the solution is not easy to follow. But the whole argument (quoted from the first chapter of Baba Mezia) is typical of the mental activity of acute legal minds.

Also typically Rabbinic is the Miggo (perhaps the underlying principle of "Partial admission"). Personal property is being claimed. The defendant says that he owns a share in it. Being in possession, he could have denied altogether that anyone else had a share. Therefore he is credible on oath.

Quite a volume of learning is involved in this argument. Suffice it to say that the Rabbis (at least in the later Talmud) were mature enough lawyers to see the need for the limitation of this line of argument. They held it valid for defendants only, not for plaintiffs. Incidentally, it is a typical problem for the Talmudical student to isolate such a distinction from the plethora of Miggo cases.[2]

For the rest, let it be said that the development of Rab-

[1] In hermeneutics the rule is stated (about this and other types of analytical argument) that you cannot deduce what does not spring from the premises. Analogies must be exact.

[2] The Tosafists, in the twelfth century, made the position clear.

binics stopped before the generalization of litigation to its present frame: i.e. simple issues between plaintiff and defendant on sworn evidence, directly tendered, and probably conflicting. That was not achieved before the nineteenth century (unless it be right to conjecture that the old Athenian system was like that).

In substantive law, the development is better than in adjective law. Varieties of damage are well analysed. The Rabbis did not, however, quite arrive at a full doctrine of Negligence. Accidents due to animals are classified. The distinction is drawn between TAM (unwarned) and MUOD (warned). But a free man is always MUOD. Certainly liability is not stated in terms of duty of care. (*See* first chapter of Baba Kamma.)

Similarly, the Talmud and its exponents never achieved the clear articulation of a criminal code, impersonally penal. There is a clear distinction, from the Torah itself, between compensation and penalty. But the "claim" is always of the same type except in respect of the major crimes which are breaches of some of the Ten Commandments. Below that level, in very few cases can the principle of retribution be isolated from that of compensation. Nor is the rudimentary Halachic criminal process easy to distinguish from the laws of flagellation etc., that belong to the ritual, ceremonial codes: i.e. what would today be called religious.

In other words, the Halacha is not evolved to the modern secular degree. Subject to that consideration the Talmud can be described as good law. Subsequently to its closure several generations of commentators and codicists preserved the juridical tradition. Until the most recent times, this legal learning (Talmud and commentaries) formed the intellectual training of Jews in all their settlements. It never lost importance because there were many occasions for Rabbinical decisions, many occasions for the exposition of law in answer to questions. Be it remembered that Talmudic law is still valid Jewish law. Even in this age, the Posekim still fulfil a function; and in more than one place in the Goluth Jewish law is (by consent) still administered in the Talmudic tradition.[1]

[1] In the State of Israel, Talmudic law is the only law of Personal Status available to Jews who live there. Not the least important field is Divorce.

Before one leaves the discussion of Jewish law, the point is worth mentioning, which Rabbi Kagan has so well made, that Jewish law was always unitary: was never divided into jurisdictions—as between Consul and Praetor, Courts of Common Law and Equity. The Law was an articulated whole, with no principle of conflict between tribunals. This being said, however, it does not appear that the Monism in the system amounts to a claim of superiority for the Jewish law over other mature bodies of law. (Other virtues would ground more significant claims.) Indeed, there are those who wish that the Rabbis had been more vigorous Praetors, more powerful wielders of the weapons of Equity, bolder claimants to legislative power. Further, it does not appear that the formal unity—the unity of the system, of the jurisdiction—corresponds to any perfect internal unity in the empirical content of Halacha. Between the generations, as well as on simultaneous planes, doctors of Talmud have disagreed. They continue to do so.

Note on the opponents of the Rabbis (and on Rabbinic Greek)

The terms Pharisee and Sadducee have, on account of New Testament writings and the works of Josephus, acquired what may be a disproportionate importance. As we have seen, Jannaeus did not use the latter term. In Tannaitic times the poles of culture or tradition were, on the one hand, the Rabbi—or Chover (literally Companion): on the other hand the anti-Rabbinic AM-HAARETZ. This word, in later development, comes to mean ignoramus. Talmudic anathemas, however, are inconsistent with this translation. Ignorance would not justify the Rabbinic wish to gut the Am-Haaretz "like a fish" or the desire of the Am-Haaretz "to bite the Rabbi with the teeth of an ass".

The matter may well be explained in an epigram after Porson

> The Hebrews in Greek
> Were sadly to seek.
> All save the Greek Jew
> And he knew no Hebrew.

In the author's view Am-Haaretz is precisely what the Greeks called

EPIKORIOS—"man of the country", "backwoodsman"—i.e. the reactionary.

In Hebrew this is *transliterated* APIKOROS: *translated* AM-HAARETZ.

The popular translation of APIKOROS as Epicurean is unwarranted. There is nothing in the teachings of Lucretius to warrant the contempt felt by the Rabbis for the APIKOROS—the unbeliever—the derider of so many Rabbinic beliefs.

Nor is there reason to believe that Epicureanism was particularly known to the Jews as Hellenic doctrine. Stoicism was better known at that period.

If it be understood that, originally, the conflict related to Rabbinic authority, and that the words AM-HAARETZ and APIKOROS carried the same connotation—viz. reaction against Rabbinic authority—then much light is shed on many curious Talmudic dicta. It also explains why the word Sadducee is little used in the Talmud. That word was not an important formal description of the opponent of Rabbinic authority. Out of the large class of backwoodsmen who opposed the teachings of the sophisticated—even foreign—Rabbis (Hillel was from Babylon!), the Sadducees mentioned in the N.T. constitute one late-named group that did not endure. (As to the meaning of the word, *see* note to p. 158 *supra*.) For the rest, confusions are obviously due to the fact that, in the later levels of Talmud, the old identity of Apikoros and Am-Haaretz is lost: and the words become pejoratives to describe differing types—the unbeliever and the ignoramus respectively. So does the semantic whirligig bring in its changes.

CHAPTER FIVE

THEOCRACY WITHOUT
THEOLOGY

1. *The Old Wine*

ANYONE who chances into Yiddish-land can hear, in the mouth of some bearded old man, or some bewigged old woman, a strange lament: the Shechina is in Goluth (the Holy Spirit is in Exile). This is said with more intentional significance than any accidental literary allusion, as when some rustic note strikes a chord in Homer or Shakespeare. Yet the speaker knows nothing of the metaphysical implications of the sad pronouncement. Certainly he, or she, means to impose no limitation on the Godhead, nor to suggest a degrading anthropomorphism. For these are people who, though they know of Asmodeus and the creatures of Persian mythology, have not learned, and would not accept, the statement that Jehovah is the specific name of a tribal god, or Elohim a generic description. One word to them is ineffable. Other words for God, including all the synonyms and literal substitutions, are words not lightly to be used. To treat them as comparable to human names, or as class names, would be blasphemy.[1]

[1] The word represented by JHWH was, in Temple times, only pronounced by the High Priest in the Holy of Holies. What the pronunciation was is unknown. In the Hebrew pointed text, the pointing is as

To the average dweller in the ghetto, it is not known how Maimonides speculated on the difficulties of thinking about the Godhead. The God of the ghetto is numinal, not noumenal. The worshippers try to know God, not to know about Him; to believe first, to understand later; or as the Bible has it, to "do and hear", not to "hear and do".[1] In return their God is a God of real deeds, not abstract words: of righteous and benevolent action, not of logical qualities and relations. His attributes are manifestations of kindness and justice.[2] When, therefore, they speak of man as made "in the image of God", they are elevating the human rather than compromising the divine. Not anthropomorphism this: but the impulse to that Imitation of God which is true religious experience. In that effort they are assisted by the imagining of God as active in human affairs. Even, they imagine HIMSELF as giving utterance to Prayer.[3]

They speak of God with a familiarity and a pathos that suggests the attitude of a loving child to a father: a father to whom the Midrash is applicable: he is to be loved as well as feared. He is old, but yet all-powerful; and though all-powerful, a giver and a recipient of sympathy. He said, "Comfort ye my people: Comfort ye with me".[4] For their suffering is His suffering. To this day the Chassidim—

of ADONOY (My Lord) and the word can be so pronounced. But the orthodox shrink from this and say (except in the liturgical use) ADO-SHEM or HASHEM (The Name). Also they tend to pronounce ELOHIM on secular occasions as ELOKIM. This sensitive avoidance of a suggestion of blasphemy contrasts oddly with the frequent references to God in "God preserve us", etc.

[1] This is not obscurantism, so long as the Law is the object of affection.

[2] The thirteen MIDDOTH (derived from a text in Exodus) are set out in the Prayer EL RACHUM VECHANNUN. They include COMPASSION, KINDNESS, PATIENCE and the VINDICATION OF RIGHT.

[3] T.B. Berachot 6, et seq.

[4] A beautiful Midrash, made possible by the fact that the letters of

the emotional, mystery-living, Jews—refer to God with an
East European endearment: they call him Gottenu. But even
the sterner Misnaggidim would not denounce this as blasphemous; for they too believe that God is within their
midst immediately as well as eternally; not only in the
whole of the Universe, but with His people in Exile.

Perhaps no other people in the present world, or in the
history of the world, has entertained a notion of the Divine
Being comparable to the Jewish. The Jews arrived early at
monotheism, with the aid of an intuition both pre-philo-
sophic and greater than the philosophic. It was the idea of
an age in which the abstract had not been isolated and
specialized. The Talmud, indeed, rationalized the legend of
Abraham into a search for first causes. That is already too
critical. What is certain is that some early Jews realized that
the forms and practices of idolatry were incompatible with
the idea of any divine being which is higher than earthly
bodies, or earthbound spirits. The unity of God as understood by the Prophets was not the empty logical consequence of an ontological argument. God was one and all,
because only in that oneness and allness could be vested the
ethical qualities that distinguish the supreme moral dominion of the Universe from the arbitrary actions of local and
rapacious human powers. God is one because there is only

AMI—my people—are also the letters of IMI—with me—describes how
the Lord sent each of the twelve minor prophets to Jerusalem with
words of comfort. But each message Jerusalem rejected, because each of
those prophets had made terrible prognostications. Thus Zephaniah
was sent, and Jerusalem said, "What have you in your hand?" He
replied, "It shall come to pass that I shall search Jerusalem with lights".
But Jerusalem said: "Only yesterday you told us 'a day of dark and
gloom'. Which shall we believe?" And so Jerusalem (quoting chapter
and verse to each prophet) could not be assured as to which saying to
accept, the auspicious, or the dreadful. Therefore the Lord said "I will
reassure Jerusalem: and so, through the prophet Isaiah: "Comfort ye my
people, comfort ye with me". (From the Pesikotho.)

one RIGHTNESS. If argument had been required to mediate the apprehension of God by the early Hebrews, that argument would best have been stated in terms of the right against wrong, good prevailing over evil; and not in logical terms, of the greater and the less. God embodied the justice of Abraham in contrast to the unscrupulous pleasure-seeking of the cities of the plain. God expressed the anguish of the slaves in Egypt: the timeless claim of those who were temporally oppressed. The word of God was most clearly heard in reproach to oppression: hast thou murdered and wilt thou inherit?

Such a conception of God, in its best expression, is more than anthropomorphic. So much more that the anthropomorphism is unimportant. The people whose story is reflected in the Bible were primitive enough, and later, materialistic and chauvinistic enough, to express thoughts about God in terms of the lower levels of experience: boasting of His powers and His favours, and invoking fear in a crude way. But the higher tradition, the tradition of emotional sublimity, was early, and was never lost: and in the Exile it gained strength.

At no time before the first Exile was any serious attempt made by the Jews to debate the nature and qualities of God critically. "Show me a sign", the Prophet was human enough to ask: but it was his own worth he was doubting, not the divine power. Not Prophet, not Priest, not King entered into disputation about God even when they disobeyed. Unique among nations, this critical people worshipped without inquiry, and preserved a recognition of a personal God without degrading the conception. From all but the most primitive levels of the Bible, and later writings, there emerges clearly the idea that God works among persons, but is not to be thought about as personally defined: a humane—not a human—God.[1]

[1] This thought—the humanity of God—is embodied in the paramount

In the early history of Jewish thought, comparatively little effort was made to state the nature and qualities of God philosophically. But they knew His works, and believed that they ended in good. The irony of Isaiah against those who manufactured their gods from wood is perpetuated in the ironical indifference of the Rabbis to all the approaches of Hellenic and Roman critics, and their invitations to logical argument. They refused to drag the divine name into the sophistic arena; and many times suffered for that refusal.

Through this, their philosophic reticence, was perpetuated a theocracy without a theology.

The Jewish substitute for theology is superbly expressed by a Christian scholar (Dr. Driver): "The Jews believed in the abiding presence of an unseen power that makes for righteousness". To this may be added a corollary: that they denied all other Godheads because they were only thinkable as principles of unrighteousness.

God is the Jewish King: Our Father our King—in the Jewish as well as the Christian liturgy. Whatever conflicts have disturbed the Jewish group from time to time, disputes about the nature of the Godhead are not among them. Jews did not fight as the Christians did when, by chance, Greek met Greek and there was battle for an iota in Homoiousion. Nor did they joust in theoretical fields in order to determine the modes of obedience, and to distinguish between the merits of faith and the merits of works.

doctrine that human life is prior to the law. Thus at a time of cholera epidemic the saintly Israel Lipkin (Salanter) insisted that his congregation should not fast on the Day of Atonement. To impress his wish on them, he ate in the pulpit. (And pronounced a blessing on the food, so as to demonstrate that he was performing a duty, not taking advantage of a concession.) On the other hand it is good law that the Sabbath (which is the most important) and all other festivals may only be broken for real emergency. The doctrine that the Sabbath is for man must be carefully interpreted.

Being lawyers, the Rabbis recognized the intimacy of intent and action. Consequently, although they were familiar with the "charitable" hypocrite,[1] they took for granted the faith behind the good deed, and expected bad conduct from the cynic. Even in the modern disputes between orthodoxy and reform, the psychological factors in Jewish behaviour have not been polemically treated as doctrinal issues. The reason for this is that even the most orthodox of Rabbis only claims to be the exponent of a system of law. Those who obey it should do so for its own sake: but the knowledge of purpose is in the obeyer. On the other hand, all that the reformer asks is reform of the law. He does not allege that orthodoxy is mere ritual or formalism: and neither disputant claims an insight into the relations between God and man, or a power to mediate between them.[2]

Significantly, Jewish doctrine takes much more seriously the sins against man than the sins against God. The sins against man are, of course, also sins against God: but, unlike simple sins against laws that do not affect human relations, these are not expunged by prayers or other forms of atonement.[3] Because man is treated as an end in himself, there follows as additional reason why the Jews have not been inclined to dictate to each others' minds. Jewish obedience has been determined by social and personal enthusiasms

[1] T.B. Avoth. *Passim.*

[2] If ever (say in the eighteenth century) there were dangers of a dispute in Jewry between the exponents of Faith and the advocates of Works, it was prevented from developing by the historic fact that the Jewish Counter-Reformation preceded the Jewish Renaissance.

[3] Only by the forgiveness of the person wronged. Incidentally, the Jewish modes of atonement, TESHUVAH, TEFILLAH, TSEDOKO, conventionally Repentance, Prayer and Charity, would be better expressed if translated more exactly: RETURNING, PRAYING AND DOING RIGHT.

and influences rather than by authority.[1] "Thou shalt teach thy children": "diligently" add the translators in the Authorized Version, perhaps trying to express in English the Piel form of the verb, and possibly conscious that the root of the Hebrew word for "to teach" is similar to the root of the word meaning "keen". Certainly in the ghetto the teaching of customs is the principal duty of parents. Some do it gently, others cruelly: and so it is with the Hebrew teachers, the Melammedim who are such a part of Jewish life. Diligence is always in evidence.

But the Jewish tradition is for gentleness, and the learning is not the inculcation of answers to a catechism. Children are taught to love these customs. That is why the customs survive. Oppressive teaching inculcates an obedience which does not survive the emergence of the youth into manhood. The reason for obedience is acceptance, affection. One sanction of obedience has been the psychological difficulty of breaking away from custom. That psychological difficulty implies affection rather than fear, because people fly from fear. Very subtle, therefore, is the authority of the MINHAG[2] and praiseworthy. Doubtless, this feeling will not be absent from the principles of obedience which are making possible the resurrection of the homeland.[3]

[1] But though open sin be impudence, surreptitious sin was generally regarded as aggravated sin. (Avoth.) This may be in the tradition that holds theft worse than robbery.

[2] Customary law, in effect.

[3] Unhappily, Jewry everywhere, including in Israel, contains elements of what the Rabbis call MUFKER (abandoned): that is to say the reactionary from the decencies of orthodoxy; the escaper from pressures associated with ghetto-environment; as well as the assimilationist driven back; the "secular" idealist; the refugee from everywhere; "the remnant" in a pejorative sense.

To most of these are lacking the Jewish "bourgeois" standards: "Baalhabatishkeit", Edelkeit; the concepts of Yichus, Zechuth Avoth, etc. etc. These come to the land, or grow up in it, with less than the necessary

Authority of a political type the Jews have not enjoyed for any long term in the long term of their history. Some of the nearest approaches have been realized in those systems of collective responsibility imposed on Jewry by Gentile authorities. Such was the famous Council of Four Lands. This kind of authority has been essentially synagogal, and mediated by religious acquiescence. Secular control of Jew by Jew is a rarity.[1] But now that some part of Jewry is achieving political reality in Israel, we are presented with a paradox—the compulsion of the voluntary. In matters of urbane behaviour, the norms are the norms of Western Europe, including criminal and civil laws. Of the "peculiarities" (the laws relating to dietary customs for example), either these need no enforcement, or cannot be enforced in great detail. The Sabbath is, formally, publicly observed, but its ancient rules are too intimately within the scope of

minimum of that traditional heritage which is conservative of the human values.

To these it is difficult to distinguish between Sabbath and weekday. Nor can they realize (for most of them are blinded by ideology) what they lose by not regarding themselves as "elected" for merit above the grasping self-seeking which is ineradicable from materialism, above the emotional cheapness that is free-love.

To these the psychologist can, but does not, explain that behaviour has more principles than the social logical. The uncultivated Jew would say, more simply, of their conduct: "es passt nicht".

[1] The familiar authority of Beth-Din, when invoked civilly, is, in most places, comparable to the authority of an informal arbitrator. For a civil dispute to be solved by Beth-Din implies the acceptance of the Tribunal, and later, loyalty to its verdict.

In civil disputes in the State of Israel the authority of Beth-Din is little different from its authority in e.g. England. But it is much invoked. Lately it has been called upon to cope with many (Halachically) novel issues and has dealt well with them. When e.g. a Defendant claimed that, since the Plaintiff was insured, the Damages should be less, the Court, working from first principles, arrived at the same solution as that found over a century ago in the Common Law; that Insurance is irrelevant.

private life to be the subject-matter of public legislation. That distinction—between public and private domains—is not new. (Rab Shesheth in the first century refused to accept dictation as to the form of his prayers.) Such a distinction, moreover, is now part of the pattern of the politics of free lands, mainly because religious conflicts have left it clear that, when doctrine is calmly contemplated, few religious doctrines are other than benevolent, and the fundamental decencies emerge as part of modern civilization.

A Jewish State, however, reveals the vestiges of theocracy in older form, in so far as old laws, like the Divorce Laws and the Levirate Laws, and the doctrines relating to Aguna,[1] are recognized by the State; which gives its assent to their perpetuation by leaving the law of Personal Relations outside the Statute Book. Continued are the ritual and the customs, in that the State reduces interferences with them to a minimum. Even the soldier in battle may, if orthodox, fulfil his religious obligations—the prayers, the Sabbath, the Festivals, the Fringes, the rule against SHATNEZ (mixture of materials in clothing), and behave, generally, as in an orthodox civil life, save when the paramount dangers and military necessities make conformity impossible. As it was with the Maccabees, so now. Thus Israel caters for Judaism as Britain for Christianity. If one stresses the lack of mass compulsion, it may well be asked: Where is theocracy today?

The answer is that all life is theocratic in a slight degree now: ghetto life in a higher degree.

If political theocracy has disappeared, except in some of the strongholds of Islam, it has not been completely driven out; but has left much of its doctrine embedded in the structure of politics. For the Jews, in so far as Judaism calls for a high degree of ethical conduct, for that attitude to the Law which refuses to take advantage of the letter of the

---

[1] The "grass-widow" who does not know whether her husband is alive or dead. There is no "presumption" available.

law,[1] in so far as it calls for charity and magnanimity, the obedience is uncontrolled; for these are things that politicians have long since recognized their inability to control. Nor has this aspect of life greatly concerned them.

The theocratic function has seeped out of politics, in the degree that politics is content with minimal standards of obedience. That is the case, even now, when the theoretically high requirements of collectivism are minimally stated in economic quanta. But, because a residue of ethical behaviour is left in the laws, some slight dynamic of the Scriptures continues effective in the movements of society.[2]

Theocracy, indeed, is one of the great unacknowledged contributions of Israel to the common politics of the world. The English political philosophers, who, in the seventeenth century, deduced the categories of the modern nation state, drew more upon the Hebrew Bible than upon the lore of the sophisticated Greek Republics. Paradoxically, it was the English Church, not the English State, that came to prefer the pagan classics as a spiritual inspiration. The English political thinkers found in the stories of Samuel, Saul and David, the rich raw material of politics.

But the anointing of kings is not the important Jewish legacy. More vital, and less observed, is the tradition of ethics which has prevented some of the erastian states from

---

[1] The Talmudic expression is Penim Me Shurath Hadin ("inside the line of the law"). There is a Talmudic dictum that the Temple fell because the Jews did not live up to that standard.

[2] Probably nobody sensitive to sentiment would accept the Shavian view that Socialism makes charity undesirable. A Jewish doctrine like "The hand of the worker is uppermost" (i.e. that the master should concede to him) hangs on thicker strands than the present economy of trade unionism.

Readers of Sholom Aleichem may remember a pretty study (in the story *KONKURRENTEN*) of the cynic who collects for the unfortunate Jewish hawker, and the "man of principle" who defends their right to flourish, but refuses to contribute!

becoming completely secular in the materialistic sense. When the jurists speak of "Natural Law", they usually mean "God's Law". When they speak of the behaviour of Christian princes, they are actually stating Jewish doctrine; *viz.* that there is a moral law behind and above the conduct of statesmen. In our times only avowedly materialistic atheistic orders, such as modern Germany, have understood the State as an unethical thing in itself, a power from whose purposes, only, any axiological values are to be derived. In the Christian states, the difficulties of rendering unto Caesar have been solved in Caesar's favour. But Caesar now stops short of the arbitrary bloodsheds and enforced idolatries, in protest against which the Jews and Christians of the Roman Empire suffered martyrdom.[1]

In modern terms, it is easily proved that Society is not content with a system uncharacterized by righteousness. Thus Democracy can be described as the counting of heads, as the mechanical result of voting, as representative government according to numerical determinants. But if a despot arises and intimidates masses of people into voting for him, the world does not treat the voting as democratic. They are not content, then, with the counting of heads. They hold that it is the heads that count.

The modern Western state is not theocratic as the Jewish kingdom was, or should have been. But when we see the shaping of new nations, with theocratic traditions, such as Pakistan, and the modern State of Israel, it is clear that the differences are not so vital, between Theocracy and Demo-

---

[1] I admit that this sentence is optimistically written.

In the modern issues between the forces of idealism and materialism, or between differing ideologies, the Jew manages to preserve a priestly compromise, what though the best spirit is of prophetic protest. In point was American slavery: in point, today, is Apartheid. For the Jew the problem is complicated by his own need to preserve himself in a hostile environment. Whether in this way he does justice to himself and to others is a difficult question.

cracy, as a secular political philosophy might be expected to pronounce. The difference between the Western democracies and the Eastern theocracies is one of degree only; because, unobserved by pure politicians, the values of religion have crept so deeply into Western thought that most political orders acknowledge an ethical minimum in their laws and customs, even in the most modern statutes. This tradition has entered modern history through many channels; through the Christianized Roman law, through the Canon Law, and through the direct study of the Bible, which was made part of the heritage of the modern world at the time of the Reformation. All these have been channels of Jewish example.[1]

In this theocratic tradition that tinges Western political thought, the dominant doctrine is the ethical nature of the Godhead. Whatever God is metaphysically, he is a God of righteousness and mercy for ordinary human beings. This teaching did not impress itself strongly enough on the Kings of Ancient Israel. Hence their degrading moral involvement in the meshes of intrigue. The irony of history is that Jewish thought, of the generations of Jews in exile, has never abandoned this belief in the ethical standards of life. So they were set to guard the vineyards of others, after their own vineyards they had failed to watch. In their own lives the Jews of the ghetto have lived the theocratic life: and their own laws are integrated with the laws of God. These are mediated by a doctrine, which the Rabbis pronounced as well-grounded, that the Civil Law of the nation in which the Jew is exiled is binding law.[2] That is

[1] In exchange, Zionism and Israel have acquired the machinery of Representative Government, as taught to their leaders in trade unions and the London School of Economics. They have adopted, latterly, the concept of "party-lists"—a method of P.R. involving dangers of totalitarianism. But they are careful.

[2] One reason given is that the civil law preserves from riot and disorder.

179

why the Jews, during the last few centuries, have not been confronted, in civilized countries, with the difficulty of dual loyalty. They have lived according to their religion, which sets high standards of generosity, against a secular background which, in demanding law-abidingness, calls only for obedience to a lower, a minimal, ethical standard; and, in civilized times, does not call upon its citizens to behave wickedly.[1] As for the enemies of the Jews, they guarantee that Jewish conduct is above the average. That conformity intensifies their hostility. So integral are Jewish values to modern civilization that we find, whenever a given civilization is mature—having left anarchy behind, and not yet having reverted to it—that that civilization draws the Jews from their group solidarity by the social osmotic processes which are assimilation. Then they become, for short periods, ordinary citizens of particular secular nations, but adhering to the Jewish ritual in some degree or other—Ruritanians of the Jewish Persuasion. The degree of orthodox conformity in those circumstances is unpredictable. It increases with external hostility, varies with economic difficulties, changes with education, and may be expected to be higher in the lands where religious observance is strong than where the inhabitants are indifferent to religion. Thus at recurring periods we find Jewry achieving great heights, both of Hebrew and secular culture, followed quickly by assimilation. So the son of Moses Ibn Ezra drifted into another creed: the descendants of Luzzatto became ordinary Italians, the children of Mendelssohn Germans.[2]

---

[1] The duty, in totalitarian (and other) states, to "inform", is usually stated as moral obligation—higher duty. It is a practice very much against the spirit of the Jewish laws.

[2] The witty Moses Mendelssohn (he who told the resentful poet Frederick of Prussia that if he erected skittles he should expect them to be knocked down) said of himself: "I know I shall die a Jew, I know my grandson will die a Christian. But I don't know in what religion my

Within the last century and a half, however, the pattern of evolution has changed. Heavy industrialization has increased the size of the ghetto. Then nationalism intensified anti-Semitism, and made the ghetto walls of Eastern Europe more rigid.[1] In turn, within Jewry, a nationalistic and some socialistic movements redistributed the emphases in Jewish solidarity, and redirected faith from the sanctuary which was the crowded Synagogue in the direction of a broader based mutual reliance. The old Jewish doctrine that even a sinner is a Jew developed into the feeling that Jewishness is wider than the life of the Synagogue. The rejected stone became the corner-stone. In this inevitable process the theocratic element in Jewish life was reaching a nadir, until reviving anti-Semitism, directed against all aspects of Jewish aspiration, reasserted the conviction that the Jew, even in his own State, is the creation of an exile, which is an exile of the spirit.

During these centuries, living with a God in Exile, the Jews have spread the idea of a God-guided life, but (at first sight strangely) have not contributed much to the philosophic investigation of the nature of God.

Creatures of a theocracy, they do not declare, nor define their purposes by, any detailed theology.

The Jews took God for granted. Much of Jewish philosophy was written in "assimilative" periods, and is concerned, not mainly with questions about God, but with the deduction of the minimum number of principles required to distinguish the Jew from the God-fearing Gentile.

Saadyah, Maimonides, Albo, are great names in this

son will die." The son actually died a Christian. He said: "For half my life I was the son of my father: for the other half I have been the father of my son". (That son was the composer Felix Mendelssohn.)

[1] Early rigidity had been, to some extent, due to the difficulties of travel. Only with the development of transport does the question of freedom of movement enter seriously into the laws.

mathematical tradition of thought. A typical problem is whether the Jew is required to believe in the survival of the soul. The Bible is lacking in evidence of the doctrine. It is most unlikely that people such as the Jews held no such belief; but they lived the kind of life in which the fear of death is not omnipresent; and the writings show only that necromancy was regarded as a bad practice. The old woman of Endor knew that those who gain the next world are apt to lose it.

The writings do not offer immortality as a reward. But the Rabbis deduced such a belief from God's promise to Abraham to give him the land, and from similar texts. Later the notion of eternal beatitude as the lot of the righteous became orthodox doctrine. That was possibly a concession to a humanity incapable of achieving the standard of Antigonus.[1] The most disciplined of Jewish thinkers, Maimonides, made immortality the logical consequence of a life of mental development in the Torah, and the peculiar of the intellectual.[2]

The topic was a perpetual one. But Jewish thinkers were, for many centuries, dominantly legal thinkers. When they undertook the philosophic task of stating the fundamentals of faith, they were undertaking something which, in the Jewish context, is an unrealistic speculation. The Jews, we have seen, are indefinable: only describable—and that in terms of world-history, not of any local space-time. Their religious loyalty is to a large body of developing tradition that has emerged from the writings of generations of undogmatic, rational, lawyers. To these the life of the group was always something greater than the rules of obedience. The tradition of Rabbinic rationalism enabled Judaism to be

[1] See p. 139 *supra*.
[2] This may be Maimonides' solution of a problem set by Alexander Aphrodisiensis and the author of *The Letter of Aristeas*. (*See* next chapter.)

preserved by all who lived a loyal, rather than an orthodox life.[1] If these rational doctrines are isolated as common factors, then very little content is available to differentiate the ethos of Jewry from the conduct of the "righteous of the nations". Only, with the Jews the standards and the conduct go to constitute their function of unity.

Excessive thinking on basic principles, then, participates in the error of those philosophers, whom Maimonides refers to, who would seek, in a few abstract ideas, a short way to the knowledge of the world of things. Many generations of Rabbis avoided this error, and spent their energies in the exposition and application of a full legal system, without investigating the ultimate terms of the system. Thus Judaism, which was never Theology—as are so many obscurer systems—was also not Philosophy; that is to say, it was not the subject-matter of any such continual metaphysical effort as that which characterizes the traditions of Catholicism. The reason is clear; that Catholicism is founded on a metaphysic. Judaism on the other hand, is inspired by ethical notions, which may be metaphysically challenged, but are too well grounded in the heart of humanity to be disturbed by the conflicts of logomachists.

In the light of Jewish tradition it is not difficult to explain why the Jews (who have, indeed, produced great philosophers) do not seem conscious of having produced a peculiarly Jewish philosophy to be compared with Greek philosophy, or with the medieval schools, or the work of the Cartesians.

The Jew has not doubted the Righteousness of God or his own sinfulness. Belief he has: what he needs is hope. A certain other-worldism offers him this, but he hopes for

---

[1] Excommunications, e.g. of Spinoza, and of that strange character Uriel Acosta, have been directed, not at the men as heretics, but as propagators of heresy. Thought has been free: speech not so free. (As Dr. Johnson understood, speech is also conduct.)

salvation in this life as well. As a group the Jews have not reconciled themselves to loss. The belief in a Messiah is an obstinate refusal by the Jew to accept that he is the fool of the Proverbs, who loses what is given to him. At least let the loss not be irretrievable. Therefore he will come, in the future, who will restore the peace and the holiness. And every Jewish mother hopes that her son (sci.: her first son) will be the Messiah.

These are hopes, and are not the subject-matter of much thinking. As the Jew ages he reconciles himself to the melancholy truths that the Messiah will not come in his lifetime, that the life beyond the grave is beyond the grave.

These distresses and disappointments may or may not amount to ultimate doubt. But, strangely, the doubts do not weaken Judaism. In doubt, the tried Jew tends to remain Jewish. And, as the individual is, so has been the group.

Apart from the circumstance that for many centuries Jewish culture flourished in a world culture which knew no philosophic systems such as the Greeks created, they lived a life of enforced practicality and legality: modes which are unfavourable to over-critical speculation. In those centuries natural philosophy was an aggregate of many kinds of learning, including theology; and the sciences were not differentiated. The Jews participated in the learning of the nations in all matters that did not involve the dogmas and doctrines of Gentile theology. Their own religious thought was not brought into this secular learning, and was differently inspired. Being concerned with behaviour, the Jew thought only of the behaviour of God, not of His nature. God did good things and his people must do good things.[1]

Towards God the Jew was acceptive, not critical. Jewish

[1] The typical Jewish Credo is the Kaddish—the mourner's prayer, which is also a synagogal meditation. It has been compared above with the Christian Magnificat and "Lord's Prayer", which spring from similar sources. The theme is man's acceptance of God's goodwill.

religious genius was expressed in the apprehension of the greatness of God's charity, not in the analysis of descriptions, nor in attempted definition. The long avenues of Aggadah are full of blossoms that spring from fertile imagination. The dreams of Abba Bar bar Chana and Joshua ben Levi are early examples of this imaginative wealth; and continuous with them are the fantasies of the Kabbalistically inspired Chassidic Rabbis. Jewish speculation on God is phrased in the poetic forms of shining analogy. This imaginative richness is expressed in the homiletics—in the commentaries on the Bible, in the works of the Darshonim. Remarkably, the same Rabbis, who preserved rigid thinking in the Halacha, allowed themselves a riot of poetic expression in their homilies; with this difference from the works of mystics, that they ingeniously worked their fancies into the text of Holy Writ, or into the frame of accepted Midrash.

And always their theological speculation shows God in the process of working out the application of his principles of justice and mercy. God sits and learns: and his learning is in the subtleties of kindliness within the law. The Zoroastrian, and later Christian, speculations about the co-existence of good and evil, only find the slightest echoes in the cosmic speculations of the Rabbis.

Philosophy and Theology, in anything like the modern sense of those terms, are largely the product of periods of emancipation[1]—those in particular when Jews had access to Hellenic learning. In the early days of the exile, we have found Philo of Alexandria systematizing the modes of

---

[1] And of individualism. The Jewish conception of group suffering and group responsibility calls for less speculation as to the status of the individual, who is the centre of most philosophy. Individualism is the spirit of the *Aufklärung* when Moses Mendelssohn, in his *Phaedon*, argues for immortality on the lines of platonic dialectic. (Mendelssohn held that Judaism is doctrinally free—but requires conformity of behaviour.)

exegesis and homiletic, and framing his method of Bible exposition in the theory of the Word—the Logos. Yet Philo, like the Hellenistic historian Josephus, leaves barely a ripple on the surface of Jewish thought. The great commentators of Africa, Spain and France, make no mention of his work.

Between Philo and Saadyah there is a period of a thousand years; and there survives from that time no record of any constructive Jewish philosophy in the Philonic tradition. But something was happening. The language was changing, becoming, under external influences, subtler and more abstract.

The Bible is concrete. The Talmud is sufficiently abstract to express the "general" and the "special" cases of the law. Not until we approach the Spanish period do we find expressions (such as Ibn Ezra uses) to express abstract ideas like "particular providence" and "general providence". Jewish adaptability made possible the use of Biblical roots to express, first the legal, later the scientific and metaphysical.[1] By the end of the Gaonic periods, therefore, the language was available to receive and express developing Graeco-Arabic thought.

With Saadyah commences awareness of, and response to, the intellectual challenge of the Greeks, increasingly available to the Jews through the Arabic translations, and through the Latin writings to which Jewish apothecaries and savants had access.

Of the philosophy that began with Saadyah and culminated in Maimonides, it may be said, compendiously, that though the strong effort of Jewish thought, and some Jewish style, is evident in it, yet it does not seem to belong to

[1] So the Philosophers used the Biblically noted word HASHGOCHO —overseeing—in the more abstract sense "Providence", and there are many analogies to this. In our own day the latest stage is achieved, in which the abstract word is reconcretized into the technical. Such a word as HISTRADRUTH illustrates that process.

the continuum of Jewish tradition, and leaves little mark on the subsequent generations. To the orthodox Jew, the great Maimonides is the codicist of the Law, not the author of the Guide for the Perplexed. By the philosophically minded, among Jews and Gentiles, Maimonides was undervalued as a philosopher: and the Jewish philosopher, *par excellence*, was "recognized" in Spinoza. Spinoza, it may be added, called his philosophical work *Ethics*. To the Jews Ethics was the only proper philosophy.

Is there not, it may be asked, at least some guidance to be derived from the Jewish thinkers on the basic question of Jewish identity?

If the evolution of Jewry has stopped at the high level represented by the ghetto of Amsterdam, when Spinoza wrote, the resources of the Jewish thinkers of the Diaspora might have been adequate to the solution of any problem of Jewish identity that presented itself. Am I a Jew? Does my birth and do my beliefs entitle me to be called Jew? The question would have been answered in the terms of Halacha, interpreted with varying degrees of humanity according to the humaneness of men and periods. Occasionally the answer would be a counter-question: are you a propagator of heresy?

But in the last century a stage of development (not necessarily a higher stage) has been passed through by the wanderers in the ways of European life. "What is a Jew?" became a different question when addressed to the leaders of the growing masses of Russo-Polish Jewry. What shall a Jew do? Particularly what shall he do in order to express himself Jewishly and help to preserve the Jewish group? Not his bare identity but his purpose is in question. Here the thought of men was lost, as it were, in the sixty kabs of social pressure that were put upon him. Jews were revolutionaries, nationalists, socialists, everything. The criteria, to the humane Rabbis of that period, had to be, not a person's orthodoxy in practice, nor his statement of belief, but his association with the group. In this atmosphere several intellectual movements (conflicting movements) became facts of life.

It is a period described in a title of an essay by Achad Haam (Asher Ginzberg)—*A Parting of the Ways*. Other titles from the same period are suggestive. Peretz Smolenskin called his fictitious autobiography (his *David Copperfield*) *"Astray in the Ways of Life"*. He expresses in it all the Haskalah bitterness against the formalism and ritualism in which too many were seeking refuge. More positive responses are expressed in Pinsker's *Auto-Emancipation*, and were later to be strengthened by the writings and campaigns of that greatest of publicists, the Viennese Herzl.

In social economic terms two sets of attempts at organization came, at this time, to be made. One was the union of Jewish workers for economic ends in such a group as the ill-fated Bund: the other was political Zionism. Seed from both these stems was sown in what is now the State of Israel. In the transition and the grafting, made urgent by intense persecution and pogrom on a Teutonic scale, strange growths came to fruition. In some intellectual hothouses that survived the destruction, many of the new growths were regarded as strange and alien weeds. Very orthodox Jews were associated with Zionism, but others of the highest orthodoxy, Misnaggidim as well as Chassidim, could not reconcile the new development with their conception of a State of Israel revived by a Messiah. At best this new phenomenon could only be a phase in the wars of Gog and Magog: at best a harbinger comparable to the Messiah ben Joseph whose reign would be one of blood.[1]

[1] This attitude contrasts interestingly with the reception given at many stages of Jewish history to Pseudo Messiahs such as Alroy, Reubeni, the saintly Molcho, Shabbatai Tsevi, Frank, and others. Their appeal was always through religious mystery to masses whose suffering was desperate.

From the other extreme, other questions. What is Jewishness in a political entity containing voters who are Christians, who are Moslems? to say nothing of Jews who are militant atheists, regarding the State of Israel as a misadventure in the course of the triumphal march of world proletariat.[1] Who shall lay down law for all these conflicting tribes?

To state it another way, what guidance do Jewish traditions offer at a period when, out of the group life, there crystallizes a political reality? If there is a Jewish State, in what sense is its statehood Jewish? Not, we find, in the aggregation of a number of persons called Jews. That such an arbitrary agglomeration is not sufficient in itself becomes clear when the elementary laws of nationality, that every nation needs, come to be considered: when, in a modern context, questions arise relating to the admission and treatment of criminals and traitors, as well as to the welcome Stranger within the Gate.

This problem is not peculiar. Moslem States are experiencing it, experiencing the conflict between their traditional Sharya—their Halacha, so to speak—and the differently derived requirements of the political-economic environment. But in the Jewish case, typically, the degree of complexity is higher: if only because Jewish tolerance is unique among theocracies; and the intransigence inveterate, characteristic now as it was in the days when Moses found the people stiff-necked and Solomon found them heavy.

If the rulers of Israel were the rulers of a liberal Levantine republic, democratic and erastian, the problem would be soluble. The place, like Jewry as a whole, would be a receptacle not a sieve. It would be conceived as a dwelling place for persons describable as actual or potential objects of

[1] Socialist thought has not yet decided whether or not to accept Hegel's teaching: that unity is a synthesis of differences, and not an abolition of national, linguistic, etc., distinctions.

anti-Semitism: and though that formula does not express any inner ethos, it constitutes an adequate account of any settlement of Jews.

But if this were so, any refugee from a concentration camp, labelled Jew by the Nazi, would be Jewish: a gift, as it were, from the Devil. To some, at least, of the Jews, the tradition of Ruth and Naomi is a lively enough oracle to cause them to resent these gifts.

In reality, the rulers of Israel are not in the easy position of rulers of a Levantine republic. Rather are they comparable to Princes of the Exile, Chiefs of Hashmoneans, Kings of Khazars. They cannot be as exclusive as Gideon was: but they also know the dangers of the Erev Rav, such ill-bred masses as came out of Egypt.

How shall they select? If only by way of selectivity for its own sake, they are pressed—morally—to an exclusive standpoint. The difficulty is that the criteria of exclusion are either too exclusive or not exclusive enough.

At the present stage of development, it is clear that one born of Jews is a claimant to Jewish identity. Jewish tradition is lenient enough for that criterion to be generously applied. Children and descendants of converts are accepted, provided that their blood is traceable through Jewish female branches, and themselves wish adherence to Judaism. At the present time an extra indulgence allows recognition to one who claims Jewish blood and is not adherent to any other religious denomination. The thing is reminiscent of "the common factor that is in them", known to the students of Talmud.

But at some stage the factor of religion will bring with it a religious problem. If Jewish religion is relevant to Jewishness, then, in the absence of catechism, in the absence of theological apparatus, some traditional ruling must be found to distinguish between sheep and goats. Some Halacha is required, subject to the difficulty which besets many codes—namely, that the code contains no machinery for its revision.

The Halacha admits Jews to Judaism by voluntary immersion; in the case of males, voluntary circumcision and immersion. In the case of young infants, where *ex hypothesi* there is no volition, Jewish parentage is the *sine qua non*. Allowing the problems of the backsliding parent to be soluble, what of the product of miscegamy? Here the Halacha is clear. The child of a Jewish woman by a non-Jew can be Jewish. One of the reasons for this is, possibly, the old presumption that the erring Jewess is the victim of violence: and the offspring of a ravished female suffers no taint. On the other hand, the product of a Jew out of a non-Jewess is not Jewish, because, *inter alia*, the birth is the product of licence. On this issue, there has been disagreement between the secular Jewish authorities of Israel and the religious authorities. Quantitatively, the problem is not a great one. Nor need it produce conflicts such as ruined the second Kingdom. But behind it lie the greater problems that have agitated Jewry for very long: namely, all the accumulated demands of an age-old religion which has never theoretically acknowledged that its textual law can be reformed. On the other hand, let it be remembered that authoritarian systems are well equipped (by experience) to deal with demands for their reform, or for the invention of new devices to meet new situations. Old wine is poured into new bottles, rather than (what is less desirable, according to Avoth) new wine into old. Do the bottles break? Surprisingly they hold their contents. The worst consequence is an accidental strange ferment. In the Jewish case, the tolerance and rationalism inherent in the system carry occasional consequences which defy ingenuity, as if to prove that kindness is a creator of problems as well as their solution.[1]

[1] To those who speak easily of Sanhedrin as a reforming authority, it should be pointed out that even a Sanhedrin constituted "Kehalacha",

2. *The New Bottles*

The Maggid of Dubno showed great juristic insight in one of his famous glosses. "Stay me with flagons and refresh me with apples". Why do the Rabbis (whose homilectic attitude to the Canticles has been observed) declare that the flagons signify Halacha and the apples Aggadah? Why not the contrary? Because, explained the Maggid, Aggadah, like an apple, is the better for freshness: Halacha, like wine, is valued for its oldness. This is good law. Even in England, where it is now accepted learning that modern Judges have made novelties, it is still held desirable to derive authority, if possible, from the ancient sources of Common Law. So it has been in most municipal systems. Evidently in the theocratic systems the principle will not be weaker. Jewish law, in particular, though it has been well analysed, well classified, and thoroughly articulated by the modern Posekim, retains the old criteria of validity: this is the text: or this is the oral law: or this is convincingly deduced by means of the canons of interpretation.

That, in the distant past, Rabbinic interpretation amounted to legislation was never admitted by the legislatorial Rabbis themselves, and has not been conceded by their successors. Yet we find something close to legislation when we consider what they did with such a simple pronouncement as that of Moses to the gatherers of the Manna (on

and accepted by all significant elements of world Jewry, would not abate any word of Pentateuchal law. The best they could do would be to find "devices" to cope with difficulties.

In the consideration of authority, it must be remembered that the Rabbinate itself, in the Goluth (including the State of Israel), is something less than it was in the days of the Temple. At about the time of the fall of the Temple, SEMICHA (ordination conveying the full authority of the ordainer) ceased out of Israel. One of the ten martyrs is said to have ordained five pupils as he died, so that Torah should not cease. But full Rabbinic authority does not exist in the Exile.

the Sabbath): "let each man stay where he is: let no man move from his place". This is read by the Rabbis as applying to all Sabbaths and not merely to that occasion. But the prohibition is then declared to restrict the movement of persons outside the town, not outside the dwelling: and so it becomes the basis of the rule as to Sabbath day's journey: *videlicet*, not more than two thousand cubits beyond the boundary. This is not the most violent instance of Rabbinic interpretation: but it represents an authoritative pronouncement as to the sense of the text, where a different sense is clearly conceivable. Honouring the precept "not to add nor to diminish", the exponent has declared something unknown: in some opinions has only stopped short of repeal. More conventionally "non-legislative" is the legal fiction of the Eruv which extends the Sabbath day's journey by the technical annihilation of distance. This can be equated with all legal fictions in all systems, where judges wish to adapt the law without changing it. The Rabbis also allowed themselves the right of making an occasional restrictive decree, within the law. That is called Takkanah. Thus when the categories of work are surveyed, it appears that travelling in a vehicle propelled by an animal is not work, and apparently, not work on the part of the beast. But travel of that type on the Sabbath is forbidden by Takkanah, lest an axle break and the traveller be involved in the work of repair. Decrees of this type are well known.[1] They form Hilchatha de Rabbonon (Rabbinic law) as opposed to Hilchatha De Orayetha (Code law). Takanoth are binding by reason of the accepted authority that is

---

[1] An example is the prohibition of drinking any milky-appearing liquid, such as almond juice, with meat, lest someone be deceived by the appearance into thinking that milk may be so drunk. Already mentioned is the dictum of the TURÉ ZOHOV that Jews should not drink red wine at the Seder (in those days), because it has been made the basis of Blood Accusations.

behind them: but two of them cannot be invoked in one situation: and they carry lesser penalties than do the provisions of the law proper. Analogous to them are declarations of Rabbinic displeasure against those whose conduct is not expressly unlawful yet savours of injustice: also the pronouncement, against breakers of promises, that they will incur the fate of the generations of the Flood and the Babel: and, better known in modern times, the Cherem, or decree of Excommunication, against those who contravene such a Rabbinical decree as Rabbenu Gershom's prohibition, to his Ashkenazim (in 1000 C.E.), of polygamy.

It is possible to argue that Rabbinic decrees of the type described can be set aside by other Rabbis: but this power would not avail against "derived" law, as distinct from Takkanah. Short of Sadduceanism or Karaism, it is not possible for a Jew to maintain that all the laws "derived" by the Rabbis are of lesser weight than those contained in the Mosaic Code. Along those lines distinctions are tempting. Thus blood is taboo in the Pentateuch. The laws of Shechita are Rabbinic deductions carried to refinements of minute detail. Again, certain animals are not to be eaten because of Pentateuchal proscription—such as do not combine ruminance with cloven hoof—but animals incorrectly slaughtered are forbidden because of the laws of Shechita. Yet no Rabbi will contemplate the possibility that such a distinction might make one breach of law less important than another. It follows that there is no question, from the orthodox standpoint, of permissibility on the ground that the law in issue is only derived law. In the last analysis, any attempt at restating the law in terms of such a distinction would amount to Karaism.

It follows that very large masses of Rabbinic law are, for practical purposes, as immutable as the clearest of Pentateuchal pronouncements. Nor is there any possible repeal by any Synod or convocation of Rabbis, however eminent, of any law that can be traced to a declaration of law accepted by Tannaim. Many laws less than the Tannaitic would be virtually on the same level.

Conceding that Karaite heresy is theoretically compatible with Judaism, because Judaism is lacking in dogma, and conceding that all the developments of Reform and Liberal Judaism are not to be condemned as apostasy, the analyst of Jewish religious law as a factor in Jewish life has to deal with the problems of orthodox Rabbinic Judaism and no other. All others beg the authoritarian question. Therefore when such an aggregate of Jews as the State of Israel finds itself working out the implications of Jewish religion for the State, the religion that it has to consider is orthodoxy—conventional misnaggidic orthodoxy. The higher demands of some sects of Chassidim are not irrelevant: but the relatively lesser requirements of Reformers do not constitute any problem other than that of tolerance. Let it be added that what applies to the State of Israel applies to all Jewish communities and families, which are specimens of the State of Israel writ small. To all of these the problem for solution is the satisfaction of the demands of the religious consciousness in a world where the Jewish ritual and ceremonies seem too heavily laden with the trappings of antiquity.[1]

During the last century it has come about that the banners of Jewry have been bravely carried by non-conformers in the religious sense. In the achievement of the aims of Zionism, orthodox Jews have co-operated vigorously with

---

[1] It is, of course, clear that orthodox Judaism does not value the many attempts that have been made to demonstrate the rationality of the Chukoth—the arbitrary laws—or of Rabbinic edicts. That Shechita is conducive to social health: that the entrails of the swine are rich in deleterious microbes: these propositions may well be true. To make them the basis of the law is to make the law conditional. As for their apologetic purpose, that is not required by those who value Jewish life.

the informal representatives of all the degrees of deviation and disobedience: with those who believe but do not obey the formal laws: those who do not accept the old forms but would modify them: those who deny their basic validity: even those who have no religious belief at all: in a word all the varieties of sinner, of sectary, of heretic. Yet when the toilers are asked about the purpose of their efforts, they are unanimous in admitting that they are seeking the welfare of a group of which one outstanding characteristic, and one cherished possession, is an old-fashioned religion.

Unless it be possible to conceive of Israel as the home of a new race of Canaanites—that is, indeed, the bold claim made by a very few partisans—then a specific religion remains a factor in its political life.[1] From the standpoint of the orthodox Jew this is an added responsibility. The exponents of Judaism, as it stands now, have, strictly speaking, no need to admit that there are any problems of adjustment: because a religion can be, indeed should be, stern and exacting in some degree. But it happens that Judaism contains many provisions for human weakness, such as the relaxation of duties for sick persons, and the right of a person to pray in any language that he understands. These, and many other, provisions (rather than concessions) are in keeping with a system whose inner core is kindness and humanity, however hard may seem the external shell of ritual and conformity. It is also in keeping with the spirit of the religion that, among its greatest jurists, the lenient tend to outnumber the severe, and are better regarded.

At this stage we must distinguish the impact of the Halacha on the State itself, from its impact on individuals (apart from the question of their allegiance to the State).

[1] A proper comment on the term "Canaanite" is that the Rabbis (adopting a relatively rare Biblical usage (e.g. Isaiah XXIII.8)) employed the word to signify "merchant". Here is "economic nationalism" —and nothing else.

In the field of what is conventionally called religion, the field of ritual and some belief, it is clear that, when all concessions are made, and when the limits of Rabbinical authority are reached, the religious problem will be that of the individual obeyer. No one can sell him pardons or indulgences. If he finds the morning service too long, the Grace after meals inconvenient, the Tefillin tiresome, the Arbah Kanfoth a nuisance, and acts accordingly, he is, quite simply, breaking some of the precepts that relate to Prayer. He cannot delegate the duty, or buy himself out of it. On the other hand, nothing coerces him, except his own awareness of duty or his sensitivity to whatever social opinion prevails. That is the situation in the Goluth. There the Jew has to decide for himself whether he will make the sacrifice of time and effort involved in the laying of Tefillin,[1] whether he can feel enthusiasm in the process. In the Goluth the Jew has to decide whether he will keep dietary laws, observe festivals and fast days. He may feel himself inconvenienced on that very day when he should be relaxed in a religious enjoyment—the Sabbath. There are those who must make economic sacrifices for the Sabbath, and their lot is a difficult one. At many phases of Jewish life the laws against the kindling of fire on the Sabbath have been oppressive—for example, in the very cold countries; and the Sabbath Goy, lighting the fire voluntarily, knowing that he will be paid, though he is not being employed, embodies a happy collection of legal

[1] This word describes the leather containers of sacred text which male Jews bind on their arms and brows at the time of the morning prayer—in fulfilment of a law in Deuteronomy. Sometimes they are called "phylacteries". But, as Professor Hermann Cohen has pointed out, this is bad translation. Phylactery is a Greek word connoting the magical protection afforded by an amulet. The Tefillin are not amulets (for which the Hebrew word is KAMEOTH—from "cameo"), but symbols worthy to be used in the creation of the atmosphere of prayer.

fictions.[1] At a more homely level, a product of benevolent legality is the Chalunt (from French *chaloir*), a stew that can be kept hot in a sealed oven from the eve of Sabbath, because the breaking of the seals is held not to be work. The history, and the sweet melancholy, through which moves the Sabbath spirit, are, unhappily, lost among generations to whom the kindling of fire is the easiest of possible acts, and the concomitant of pleasure: to whom travel is effortless: to whom the prohibition of carrying means deprivation of personal comforts, and who cannot reconcile themselves to a day without the use of the MUKTSEH[2] which is money.

To these it can be replied that ritual is a discipline: that if you do not say the Amidah properly your backbone turns, in seven years, into a snake;[3] or that the rituals that have preserved our identity are so valuable that they justify loss and sacrifices on the part of those who preserve them.

Another answer is afforded by the example of obedience which may, or may not, be socially normal in the environment of the questioner. Much religious conformity is social conformity.

So far, the ritual difficulties of the Jew in the Goluth. His solution is usually in the nature of compromise. Where the environment is not congenial for beards, beards are not grown.[4] Fringes are concealed. Wigs (the monstrous

[1] It is told of Sir Moses Montefiore that he was conversing with a Polish Jew who told him that he lived in a village of three hundred souls and ten Shabbos-Goyim. Sir Moses told the Pole that he came from London, which held some 100,000 Jews. "How many Goyim?" "Five or six million." "Why so many Shabbos-Goyim?"

[2] MUKTSEH describes articles that are used, normally, for weekday purposes (Wochedik). There is no suggestion of uncleanness. Thus Tefillin are MUKTSEH—not used on Sabbath or major festivals (though Rabbi Akiva would allow them then—T.B. Menachot 36).

[3] T.B. B.K. 14b.

[4] If those Rabbis are right who hold shaving illegal for the laity (and

creations of custom, not of law) are not imposed upon his women.[1] As for his liturgy, he obtains a certain spiritual satisfaction from praying in a language that he does not understand.

But the situation of the Jew in Israel is different. The bottles into which the old wine is poured are fragile Jewish bottles. The ritual discipline of the Jew in Israel is not purely personal: nor merely social. Here there are political implications. The State is secular: but strong elements of population are religious: and some of the state law is, therefore, religious law. The Jew in Israel can conceivably find himself compelled to "remember" the Sabbath, if not closely to "observe" it, because it may be the educational policy of the régime to foster the example of Sabbath observance. On the other hand, the orthodox Jew makes a demand on his government that such a policy shall prevail. Evidently this is a situation where that tolerance which is so easy against a Gentile background cannot be preserved.

If, in those circumstances, some ritual conformity is exacted by the State, then theocracy has not gone further than in those Christian countries where a Lord's Day is preserved by statutory restrictions on conduct. More serious for the exponent of Judaism is the realization that religious laws that could be ignored in the Goluth cannot be ignored in Israel, with the consequence that one way of compromise is closed. In point are not only the laws of Sabbath and Holy Days, with their disciplines, but all the laws of personal status. The Divorce Laws of the State of Israel are the Divorce Laws of the Rabbis. In the Goluth a Jewish woman can take the initiative in a secular Court and secure a

not merely for the practising Priest), at least they have not found, or declared, any penalty for the practice.

[1] Apparently, among the Sefardim (Jews of the "Spanish" tradition— i.e. Levantine, N. African and Asiatic Jews) the wig (Scheitel—a German word) was never known or used.

divorce. Unless the husband gives Get she will lose the right to a valid remarriage according to Jewish law. But she will not be regarded by the political authority as other than single. Evidently in the State of Israel a woman cannot achieve this degree of emancipation from the *vinculum matrimonii*. This instance, whether important or unimportant in itself, is significant as an illustration of the proposition that in Israel some Jewish religious law becomes sanctioned: becomes binding on those who are unwilling to be bound. Whether this is a good, or bad, development is obviously not a question on which partisans will agree. What is evident, however, is that there now becomes projected into practicality all the jurisprudential difficulty of a rigid system.

Let problems arise relating to divorce or levirate marriage. The Rabbis maintain, what they have exercised for centuries, a moral authority which influences husbands to grant formal divorces, brothers-in-law not to make unconscionable demands. Given a friendly political authority, the Rabbi in Israel can obtain reinforcements such as the Kingdom lent to the Sanhedrin.[1] But there can be no certainty that political authorities will always be friendly. The more satisfactory development, from the standpoint of jurisprudence, would be religiously valid legislation calculated to abrogate the need for clever devices, neat formulae, and moral coercions. Yet this development is precisely the one that all the prevailing Jewish theory renders unlikely of realization. Hence the phenomenon of a State receptive of a religion, and well disposed to it: but faced with the problem that the religion is not malleable, even for the purposes of a social administration that the most religious

---

[1] Authority backed by some civil power, of the Jews themselves; was enjoyed by the leaders of medieval KAHALS. Then Rabbis could force men to grant GET or CHALITSAH. Readers of Zangwill's *King of Schnorrers* will have a fair picture of the secular authority exerted among the Sefardim by the MAAMADOTH of their congregations.

Jew would hold ethically desirable. To say that this position is not worse than that of Moslem or Catholic nations is insufficient answer. Those religions do not contemplate an integrated life on earth. They are religions to die by. Judaism claims to be a religion to live by: therefore cannot abandon its spiritual problems. The old formula, that the questioner must wait for Elijah, is inapplicable to the dwellers in a theocracy that is struggling in the present to survive.

If this (the difficulty of delay) is true of the problems in Israel that relate to the ritual religion, how much more pressing are any unresolved problems that arise for the Halachist in respect of the State itself.

Here, for example, is a body of Jews enforcing a criminal code.[1] As a fact that criminal code is European, and as a fact that European code is Christian in substance, and, therefore, not unJewish. Yet how can a Talmudic lawyer, whose view of the capital penalty is so strict, accept the possibility that in Israel there might be a law of murder stated in European terms, and with a capital penalty that does not depend on the warning of the criminal before he committed his crime?

If the State of Israel be a land in which there are (*inter alia*) Jews, then the thing is Dina De Malchutha. But if the Halachist regards the State as a Jewish State, ruled by persons who should obey Jewish law, then he has the problem of reconciling himself to something that he holds illegal and wrong.

We have seen that the Talmudic law of murder was stated late, and long after Sanhedrins had lost their practical powers. It was admitted, even then, that something should be done to the unwarned murderer; and there was a technique for dealing with him. Yet, as it stands, the Halachic

---

[1] The *civil* jurisdiction of Beth-Din, depends on consent of parties. But let it be remembered that Baté-Din have been active for many centuries.

code is clearly inadequate to the violences of modern society. Nor is it thinkable that the Halachist could wax indignant if any "unwarned" participant in the murder of 6,000,000 Jews were put to death in European fashion.

Logically, however, there is a difficulty here that can become important in the future. How shall the orthodox Jew (who may be participant in active government) reconcile himself to a criminal code which is not the Halachic? There, in the lime of any hanged murderer or traitor, "a dog lies buried".

To return from that difficult specific problem to the general change that seems to be made, by the regeneration of Israel, in the life of Jewry, let it be said that the problem of the survival of Jewish life is a larger one, and perhaps for that reason an easier one, than the problems of any one community, or any one state. The State claims to solve nothing—only to exist: and its social reality is not different from that of the Diaspora. The fact that there are problems of Jewry to be solved in Israel, problems of Israel to be solved in Jewry, proves the intimacy of land and Exile. The nexus between ERETZ and GOLUTH is more than an umbilical cord, to be broken. The two are one continuous entity. They are aspects, both, of the long continued worship, in Exile, of a God in Exile.

But the Exile is not something transitory, to be thought away by dialectic. It is reality, the reality of struggle, achievement suffused with sorrow and happiness. Its dwellings are the traditions that people still treasure. In the adherence to them, and outside of adherence, they conjure nostalgia. Reforms do not alter them: disobedience does not destroy them. The paths of tradition along which travels the Wandering Jew in time are roads that go on for ever. Difficult though they are, they may still be described in the language of the Proverbs: Her ways are pleasant ways and all her paths are perfection.

CHAPTER SIX

GOD AND THE JEWISH PHILOSOPHERS

THE Midrash tells us that the Pentateuch opens with an act of divine mercy—God clothed the naked.[1] It may be said that medieval philosophy performed the contrary act—human denudation—in stripping the notion of God of all the qualities which our emotional nature attributes to the divine. At the outset the Jewish vision of God was a prophetic one; an act of imaginative insight such as makes the inspiration of the poet, even of the scientist, who, in a creative moment, sees the whole round, as the poet does, and gives to airy nothing a local habitation.

In contrast, the logician treats God as a verbal concept; that than which nothing greater can be conceived; that to which nothing is prior; that beyond which is nothing; the cause prior to all causes, and inclusive of all causes and effects. How different is this from the apprehension of a loving God: a God who pities the widow, the orphan and the captive, comforts the sick and buries the dead; who is in the outstretched hand of the poor; who dwells in the four ells of the traditional law; who mourns the Temple and shares the Exile.

[1] And the Pentateuch closes with another act of divine mercy—God buries the dead.

Appropriately, it was a poet-philosopher, Judah Halévy, who protested, against the medieval logicians, that God for whom the spirit longs is different from the God who is reached by cold speculative thought. But even Halévy, in his brilliant colloquy, the *Book of the Khazars*, was committed to the implications of his own (and the traditional verbal) acceptance of the incorporeality of the Godhead. Once that was stated, too much of verbal consequence seemed to follow.

Centuries later it was a Lutheran philosopher—Kant—deriving perhaps some inspiration from the Jewish sources of Lutheranism, who demonstrated that verbal processes become meaningless or contradictory when they are extended into notions of infinity and eternity—the realms of no origin and no end.

This is not to say, and Kant did not contend, that there are two orders of truth, a rational and a revealed. To say that is to beg all questions.[1] But there is much in the universe that cannot be proved. Indeed most events, and most propositions of cause-effect, cannot be proved—cannot, that is, be reduced to a mathematical equation of identity.[2]

[1] The distinction between two orders of Truth—a revealed and a discovered: an emotional and a rational, etc.—is an easy formula which many philosophers, ranging from materialists to idealists, have adopted in order to avoid a decision on the reality of God. This may, conceivably, be a solution; but it does not appeal to the ordinary thinker who wishes to think about God in relation to the Universe and to himself. That the solution is incompatible with the principle of Occam's Razor is not a refutation of it: but that it plunges the thinker into mystery makes it unacceptable—*ex hypothesi*—as a solution. To the thinker in Metaphysics or Theology the important guiding question will always be: Is this true? And for his own mind he only has one standard of truth. What does not conform to this is either a false proposition to be discarded or an unknown quantity to be further investigated.

[2] The identification of the relation of Cause-Effect with Ground-Consequence (and the reciprocal hypothetical proposition) is, in the author's view, a major fallacy, vitiating much traditional philosophy.

If, then, human beings have experienced, in many ages, and at many levels of civilization, the feeling that there exists, in or above or around the order of things, some unseen power that makes for righteousness, it does not follow that we are able to demonstrate the truth of this feeling in words, or that, failing such proof, the feeling, or the belief, is a false one, or an illusion. So to hold is to confuse the truth of a belief with the proof of its truth. The Jewish lawyer philosophers and doctor philosophers of the Middle Ages should have known that the two are different.

In Jewish thought, regarded as a whole, there is a constant experience of divine assertion. At different levels of the Scriptures the experience is differently stated. There are manifest differences of cultural evolution between the fear of God in the wilderness, and the love of God that is possible to a people that has emerged from the terrors of the wilderness. The Bible knows Terror and Affection. The Bible knows God as the pronouncer of the recognition: "thou art my people", and later, the declaration of disappointment "this is not my people". The Bible includes the early conception of a God leading an army to triumph: and the later thought of God asking for an abatement of pride, and abandoning the people that has proved to be unworthy of its triumphs.

Maimonides has shown that there are differences of degree of clarity in the apprehension of the divine by the Prophets: that Moses saw more clearly than any other. But, however the visions be graded; the simple protest of Elijah, or Amos, or Hosea, the "rural" speculation of Ezekiel, the urbane recognition of Isaiah, the all-comprehensive yet intimate awareness of Moses; they all have this in common: that the revelation, or the perception, is of reality, not of abstraction.

The analogies in which the prophets express their thoughts

(*See*, on this topic, the author's essay—"The Verb to Cause" (*Philosophy*, 1946).)

of God are human analogies; not only because "the word of the Law is in the language of man"; but because their experience, being human experience, lent itself to those metaphors.

Even the sceptic of the Hagiographa—the author of Job—still thinks of God as the master of the good, and the guardian of humanity. His problem arises from the deeper realization of a truth that the Psalmist has expressed; what is man that thou shouldst remember him? At this stage the Scripture tradition is not changing its conception of God directly; but is losing its confidence in Man as the object of God's activity.

At all levels of the Bible—even in the hideously misnamed Wisdom literature—the mode of expression is in concrete imagery, not in abstractions. The Hebrew language at that stage was a concrete language, corresponding to the Greek of the epics. But even later, in Rabbinic times, when the language was being adapted to express legal concepts of a high degree of abstraction, the Rabbinic expression of the experience of God continued unabstract and poetic. Indeed Maimonides finds difficult a saying of Rabbi Eliezer: "How were the heavens created? He took part of the light of his garment and stretched it like a cloth, and thus the Heavens were extending continually: as it is said 'He covereth himself with light as with a garment: He stretcheth the heavens like a curtain' (Ps. CIV.2)".[1]

We have seen that there was an evolution of the Hebrew

[1] Maimonides was a highly disciplined thinker who emphasized the dangers of the figurative (what we would now call the "phantasmal") imagination. To him this imagination is the mental process that prevents the scientist from really appreciating that the world is round, because there is difficulty in imagining people walking upright on the underside of the sphere. That does not imply that this philosopher was lacking in imagination: only that he did not realize how active it was, or that his own conception of prophetic vision is of something mentally continuous with, not discrete from, less disciplined imaginings.

language, through the legal abstractions necessary to Tal-mud, to the philosophic abstractions of the Middle Ages. But, by the time this was achieved, Jewish belief in God was firmly crystallized in ethical and emotional terms; which seem better adapted to express the human experience of the transcendent, or immanent, forces than is abstract logic.

The vision, in the later days of the Kingdom, was a view in a dark glass. Mystery enters, descending from the un-Hebrew chariot of Ezekiel. That mystery (different from logical speculation, different from the abstract mysticism of the Indian East) developed into a Jewish tradition, per-petuated in the concrete imagery of the Kabbalah, and in the sense of wonder that inspired Chassidim, alike in the days of Jesus and of the modern Baal Shem. Extreme is such a tradition as that two Rabbis, Chanina and Oshaia, using the magic letter formulae of Sefer Yezirah, were able to produce an edible calf each Friday. To others also have been attributed such powers: e.g. Maharal—*der hohe Reb Loeb*—creator of the Golem of Prague. Let it be said that these stories, like the wonder stories of the Chassidic Tsadikim, have not been seriously accepted, by the intelligent, as his-tory of religious experience. But they have stimulated "enthusiasm". Beliefs of this kind have been serious at the times of the false (or deluded) Messiahs. But the more systematic "mystery" that descends through the Aggadah is still not philosophic in the technical sense. It is speculation in categories that have not been subjected to criticism, specula-tion redolent of an age in which the world of knowledge was undifferentiated and unorganized.

In the light of modern analysis certain distinctions are clear: perhaps too clear. There is a sense of the word "metaphysics" which people apply (and understandably apply) to the mystery of things. Metaphysics is also the critical logic of the Sciences. In the discussion of Jewish philosophy, the stricter, critical, usage involves verbal consequences which must be accepted, but which can lead to false assessments.

How shall we classify that vast body of literature, beginning with writings like the Testament of Abraham and the Books of Enoch (which themselves embody ancient traditions), continuing in some Midrashim and in the writings of Jewish and Christian Gnostics, including in its scope the alphabetical mysteries, the Sefer Yezirah, and all the traditions that were absorbed into the Zohar? Is none of this philosophy? The answer, for analytic purposes, could be: theosophy rather than philosophy. To apply a Jewish distinction, philosophy can consider the creation of the world: but those who consider the "Chariot" are mystics, are theosophists. Applied to such thinkers as Halévy, Ibn Gabirol, even Maimonides, the distinction might be said to involve semantic difficulties. But, surely, these must be classified among philosophers rather than mystery-makers, although their writings are not lacking in fancy, and the speculative imagination that they try so hard to discipline.[1]

In a word, all that can be associated with the evolution, or the long continuance, of Jewish mystery thought is, in the arbitrary classifications of modern semantics, not philosophy—however philosophical some of its great exponents were. In the Talmudic phrase, this theory hangs on thick strands. If philosophy is an analysis down to ultimates, and a rejection of all surds (as it need not be), then there is Jewish tradition that wishes for some mystery, and rejects logical infallibilities, and is, accordingly,

[1] The distinction between philosopher (including "mystic" philosopher) and "mystery speculator" becomes clear if one compares Ibn Gabirol's account of Emanations from the Godhead (in Platonic terms) with the descriptions of the Sefiroth given by the Kabbalists. (*See* p. 252 *infra*.)

rejected by the purist. On the other hand there are Jewish traditions of extreme Rationalism.

There have been at least three intellectual watersheds in the flow of Jewish thought. One when the Rabbis (at unascertainable date) turned their backs on speculation because it was "min": i.e. Gnostic, or Christian. From such a period dates the pronouncement of Simeon ben Yochai (to whom some have attributed the Zohar) that those were under a curse who spoke of "sons of God" with the sexual characters of human beings.

Another watershed is that which separates the hard thinkers of Spanish Jewry from the Kabbalistic traditions that flourished in Spain and resulted in the Zohar. The third is revealed in the sceptical attitude adopted by the Misnaggidim to Chassidic mystery speculation. This developed strongly out of the conflicts round the pseudo-Messiahs, and culminated in the stern rulings of the great Elijah of Vilna.

But when it is remembered that great Halachists, like Nachmanides, Jacob ben Asher, Joseph Caro, the Gaon of Vilna himself, were enthusiastic Kabbalists, it becomes difficult to be confident of any pronouncement as to the relationship between Rabbinism and Philosophy, or between the Jewish philosophers proper and all the Jewish theosophists.

To speak of Maimonides, and his philosophical contemporaries and followers, is clearly, to speak of Philosophy in a strict sense.

Philosophy (in the modern view) is an operation with words in the context of a world revealed and expressed in words. The technique, as we know it now, originated in Greece, and constitutes one of the greatest of the many Hellenic contributions to the human stock. The maturer Greeks stated their speculations in a critical setting. In Greek philosophy there were (as there are in modern philosophy) two discernible purposes, which the systematic thinker integrates. One is an endeavour to achieve the whole of knowledge, and to perfect existing knowledge, by speculation on the things that are unknown to (what we should now call) contemporary science. Hence metaphysics, the subject that is studied "after physics",[1] and after Natural Science has been mastered.

The other dominant purpose is criticism; criticism of institution, of beliefs, of authority, of our means of knowing.

Thus, at one pole of investigation, the philosopher seeks unknown truths. At the other pole he investigates the notion of truth as such. In the maturer systems this critical pole is the more important: and that criticism may appear stranger to the believer in God, or in any theophany, than would be speculation about Space and Time and the heavenly bodies. That explains the complete divergence of understanding that was manifest when the famous Chassid said to the sophisticated Roman: "I am the Truth". And the Roman was asking, "What is Truth?"

To the Greek philosophers, speculative and critical, the notion of God was either unimportant or metaphorical. To Plato and the Platonists, the critique of beliefs had led to the development of a theory of universals. They hypostatized a world of universals—the general concepts that dominate the various branches of knowledge: and that world they equated with a world of reality, of truth, in contrast to the world of dim apprehension which is the world revealed to the senses, the false world, the world of error; also the transient world, as contrasted with the timeless world of the Ideas.

If there is a place for God in such a Philosophy it is to be found among the Ideas: the greatest good, the great unity, the principal purpose above all purposes: the harmony of all true knowing; and, by speculative synthesis, the harmony

[1] Its position in the Aristotelean canon is not accidental.

of the outer spheres, wherein subsist the purest constituents of being, and the clearest articulation of reason.

Notwithstanding the sublimity of argument with which Plato and the Platonists demonstrated the unreality of the apparently real, and the reality of the unseen and the purely intellectual, the system is unsatisfying; because it does violence to the data of experience, and it does not "save the appearances", in the common sense of that expression. Involving as it does a confusion between (or at least a failure to discriminate between) the act of understanding and the object of the understanding, between Reason as an objective set of relations, and Reason as a mental process, it fails to teach the thinker how he thinks, and his relation to vulgar reality when he thinks. Consequently Plato and the Platonists have succeeded in emptying reason of its proper content, and divorcing it from that material subject-matter which controls and inspires the reasoner when he reasons. A remote system!

But, having driven God from the nearer skies, the Platonists experienced a theophany of sorts among the Spheres. The God of the Platonists remains transcendent, creative, thinkable in the myths of the Timaeus. Notwithstanding the mathematical obsession of the students of the Academy, it is not a Platonic god who "geometrizes eternally". The spirit, if not the logic, of Platonism can easily be made handmaiden to Religion.

Closer to reality (and to scepticism) is the Aristotelean system. Aristotle's Ideas are the forms and classifications, of real things, that suffuse and give pattern to reality. His universals are "in re"—not "ante rem". He does not divorce the world of real things from the world of thought. But in his world there are degrees of abstraction, in the nature of scientific classification. As Plato did, so Aristotle valued more highly the more abstract features of reality, valued more highly the intellectual operation which extracts wider and wider concepts from the detail of life. If there is a god in Aristotle's system, that god is the abstraction of all abstractions. He is also the purpose of all purposes, the cause of all causes; not the Creator of the Universe, because matter to Aristotle was primeval and eternal; but an object of attraction to which all things are drawn, and which inspires the movements of matter by an eternal urge analogous to love. That love—that unerotic, unamiable love—causes, or inspires, the spheres to revolve in their places, the world to go round.

To any religious person it might seem at first sight that the philosophy nearest to religion is the Philosophy of Plato; that the sublime being, the Really Real, the ultimate Good; the One from which all things emanate, and to which all things aspire, is a Divine entity: that the actualization of its thoughts into Ideas is a mode of creation such as God would manifest, that its transcendence beyond the orders of sin and error is precisely what all true religions teach, and all believers believe.

Let it be said, however, as a matter of history, that the majority of, and greatest among, the religious thinkers of the Christian world and Islam have adopted, as the archetype of Philosophy, not Plato but Aristotle. It seems as if Aristotle offered no rivalry; Plato offered that rivalry to religion, which is Mysticism—an absorption in the impersonal unity of things: a mode of thought that can become Pantheism. Among the Jewish philosophers, the great Maimonides (1135–1204), his eminent predecessor Saadyah (892–942), his almost contemporary Ibn Daud (Rabad I 1110–1180), and his masterly follower and critic, Levi ben Gerson (1288–1344), were outstanding exponents of Aristotle; but they do not completely accept the arid theology of the Stagirite, inconsistent with the Jewish conception of a constantly active creative force. Other great Jewish thinkers of the period speak in the spirit of the Platonists: and no Jewish philosopher at all is completely identified with the pedestrian pedantries of the "peripatetics". It may, compendiously, be true to say that if Philosophy has made any contribution to Judaism, the contribution is (accidentally) more Platonic than Aristotelean. But no particular classification is justified: for the subject is religious thought. Not mysticism, but mystery, enters the more easily into the heart of the religious man. The distinction, in the Jewish context, is between a mystery tradition, with some Platonic influences, and rationalistic tradition reinforced by philosophers who had absorbed Aristotle, and made mystical by a few who had absorbed the spirit of Plato. Logically first is the less philosophically-pure "mystery thinking". Such a tradition is the Kabbalistic literature. The Zohar, a medieval work with ancient sources, synthesizes, with typical Jewish ingenuity, the Aggadah and homiletic, latent (for the commentator) in the Bible text, with a doctrine of two, or more, worlds united by emanations from the higher to the lower. This spiritualism, if not thought of Plato, draws some inspiration from neo-Platonism, a strong school of speculation, among whose founders may be numbered the Alexandrian Jew Philo. Of that tradition more will be said. Suffice it here to observe that it diverges from Platonic speculation of the philosophic type, and from the logics that appealed to the sophisticated Spanish Jews.

Among the maturer exponents of Platonism proper is Ibn Gabirol (1021–1069), the great poet, now known to be the same as Avicebron, and the author of one Jewish philosophical work—*The Fountain of Life*—which is not stated in terms of Bible exegesis.[1] Nor are the beautiful prayers

---

[1] MEKOR CHAYIM, or Fons Vitae, written, originally, in Arabic, was known to contemporaries, and later critics such as Ibn Daud, as Jewish work, and the work of Ibn Gabirol. In Latin translation it was attributed to Avicebron (a corruption of Ibn Gabirol) who was thought to be an Arab; and in that form greatly influenced all the major Schoolmen.

which he composed for the liturgy exegetical in style, though they are not lacking in Biblical allusion. Ibn Gabirol's theory is of a Universe pervaded by matter (spiritual and physical) and form: the form differentiating the functions and values of all parts and aspects of the Creation, and being the manifestation of the Divine activity —the Divine will. This theory is unacceptable to those who would more radically distinguish matter from spirit. Those who think with Ibn Gabirol regard the whole Universe as blended with spiritual purposes and suffused with spiritual activity. There are spiritual forms acting on less spiritual forms. But the element of matter is ultimately unreal. The whole order of the Universe is a procession of degrees of spiritual reality manifest in forms. These emanate from the Divine Being by reason of His Will. This is not the theory of Plato, but is Platonic. It is sharply distinguished from the thought of those who regard forms as the fixed shapes of material things, arranged in logical order, and included in a comprehensive, but rigid, classification. Exponents of the latter system (the Aristotelean) require a difficult account of Creation. What the more Platonic philosophers, Halévy, Ibn Gabirol, the Ibn Ezras and Crescas, have in common is the conception of God as a Power exercising the Divine

From then on it was not thought to be of Jewish authorship until Professor Munk finally established the identity of the author.

The MEKOR is criticized for not being linked to Bible texts or, indeed, to religion. (The Sefer Yezirah, also unlinked to the Bible, is cosmology of a different kind, but, like the MEKOR, has been suspect of Trinitarianism.) However Ibn Gabirol wrote other works which are co-ordinated with Scripture. Very interesting is his treatise on the *Improvement of the Moral Qualities* in which he links various virtues and vices with the senses. Thus Pride belongs to Sight: Wrath to Smell: Love to Hearing: Joy to Taste. There is Peshat here. Wrath in the Bible is AF (the nose). As for love—the words "thou shalt love" follow "Hear, O Israel". For all its far-fetched analogies the book is subtle and deep.

Will; and His Emanations are Acts of Will. This is a different conception from that of the Peripatetics, whose God is an ultimate, a totality, of which everything in the Universe is a timeless logical derivative. Where existence is mediated, as for the Jewish thinker, by an Act of Creation, evidently the other (Platonic, or neo-Platonic) conception is more acceptable thought. It allows better answers to problems of cosmogony, to such problems as the compatibility of the finite with the purity of the infinite, than does the Aristotelean conception. On the other hand, the Bible, with its doctrine of fixed species, and the Jewish laws, with their appropriate logic, seem to cohere more with the rigid (Aristotelean) system than with the looser Platonic. Also, to Judaism, as to Christianity, the Platonic is suspect, is dangerously pantheistic. Consequently, though Ibn Gabirol, the Ibn Ezras, Judah Halévy, and later, Crescas, were Platonic in spirit, none of them can be said to have adopted a formal neo-Platonism. They allow to Man a greater significance than does, for example, Plotinus.[1] On the other hand, they were all, in a degree, Talmudic lawyers, all exact reasoners, not acceptive of vagueness or metaphor for its own sake. Also, they accepted a strong tradition that God is not to be compared to Man. Maimonides goes further. He is suspicious of the anthropomorphism involved in the word "Will". He lays it down that a theory of emanations solves no problems, because it only articulates creation into phases.[2] Being a scientist, a lawyer, and a logician, he seeks

[1] The English "Cambridge Platonists" are nearer to the Jewish philosophers in spirit, because they, too, had a religious purpose.

[2] This criticism is, perhaps, too easy. Maimonides, like most philosophers before and since, was treating the category of Causality as if any causal proposition determined the totality of events. Ibn Gabirol's conception of the emanation of a Divine Will is a rich one. It was probably not fully known to Maimonides, who himself recognizes that the Actions of God cannot be described in a formula of Quality. Ibn Gabirol conceives the Will of God as something that emanates and

exact unmetaphorical statements. Unlike the poetic Halévy, he accepts the task of thinking with precision about God and Man: and he is equipped with all the resources of the Aristotelean discipline in his thinking.

In this approach he expresses, undoubtedly, the spiritual implications of the relatively mature natural science of which he was an exponent, of the jurisprudence that he had so convincingly mastered. He is also following in the footsteps of the great Saadyah (892–942) whose *Emunoth ve Deoth* (*Belief and Knowledge*) is an early attempt to state Jewish doctrine in Aristotelean terms.

Before dealing with the somewhat exceptional phase of Jewish thought realized in the period that includes Saadyah, Maimonides and Levi ben Gerson, one should reflect on the long period of Jewish speculative thinking which they crown, or terminate.

At all phases Jewish thinking, *Kat' Exochin*, has been on the words of the Scriptures, not on the words of natural science, not on words in the science of logic. Thus to the lovers of Kabbalah, the theories of emanation are secondary to the value that the theory gives to the revealed narrative as a sacred story, and an additional justification for seeking, among the words, such mysteries as the seeker desires to find. From the Jewish (Rabbinic) standpoint the "Holy Zohar" is a Midrash. Its teachings, in the main, are, like the teachings of the Midrash, ethical rather than metaphysical; in this case, ethics mysteriously inculcated. When full allowance is made for the neo-Platonic influence, the old mystery, or mystical, tradition in Judaism is of a Personal God (i.e. a God of human persons). The God of the Zohar remains the Jewish God, familiar to, and with, his people.

That distinction, between the personal and the impersonal,

returns. This description of its actions (as phases in the life of Godhead, not in the Creation) does not destroy the conception of Unity.

is the vital one in any explanation of the failure of philosophy to dominate Judaism. That great Halachist and great
Maggid Jonathan Eybeschütz—himself no stranger to
metaphysics—points out how differently the philosophers
treat the problem of evil from the way in which it is treated
in other lines of Jewish tradition. In the Bible there are evil
men. In the book of Job we find an evil spirit, though the
Rabbis explain that, like Peninah who scoffed at Hannah,
Satan was fulfilling a worthy purpose. In the Talmud the
spirit of evil, the YETSER HARA has developed strongly
from that saying in the Bible that the inclination (YETSER)
of the Heart of Man is bad from his youth. And Yetser Hara,
from then onwards, is an important concept in Jewish ethics,
emerging with further mystery in Kabbalah; and, even without this, picturable as an activity to which the moralist can
point, and which men who learn notions such as conscience
can appreciate. Against the YETSER HARA he must
harness his YETSER TOV.

The philosopher, on the other hand, wants to dismiss
evil, to think it away. Evil is unformed matter, or a crude
level of being, or a negation, or an illusion. The philosopher,
therefore, can rarely appeal to that audience which the
moralist exhorts. Admittedly he will never fall suspect of
superstition, or condescend to the gratification of superstition, to the making of amulets, such as involved Eybeschütz himself in distress and persecution. Nevertheless,
his approach seems unJewish, seems more compatible with
the ethical neutralism which is behind all Greek speculation,
than with the uncompromising fight for Righteousness
which is the history of Jewish morals.[1]

The entry of Jews, as Jews, into the realms of Greek
Philosophy took place twice: at two mutually remote

[1] I am indebted for stimulus along this line of thought to a relatively
unknown, but praiseworthy, book—REGESH AMORAYNU—by
the late Rabbi G. M. Boyarsky.

periods; in Alexandria, before the beginning of the Common era; and nearly a thousand years later, under the civilization of the Moors in Asia, Africa and Spain, and in the high culture of Provence.[1]

The first age is the age of the Ptolemies. In the highly sophisticated society of Alexandria the Jews had achieved freedom and great secular culture, had indeed fallen into danger of forgetting Hebrew. The impulse that sent these Jews to philosophy was the same secular impulse that sends intellect, of all peoples, and at all times, to Science. These Jews who felt the appeal to learning and speculation, and who had participated in Jewish learning, are responsible for a remarkable body of literature. Some part of this is to be found in the Wisdom literature of the Apocrypha. Another part is in the mass of what the scholars label Pseudepigrapha: being pseudo-prophetic writings in terms of Bible characters and incidents, but Hellenistic in style, and Greekly speculative in purpose. These writings have value, but have not survived as Jewish literature, though Jewish may be a correct epithet to describe the ingenuity of syncrisis employed in their composition.[2]

How active the philosophic speculation was among the Alexandrian Jews we can guess from the large growth of Gnosticism—a mystery cult, in which the Jewish name of God is held to be that of a Demiurge: creator, but not all powerful ruler, and whose struggle with evil is not necessarily successful.[3] That polytheistic system became

[1] The Emperor Charlemagne invited the Byzantine Emperor to send Jewish scholars to his dominions. Hence a great flowering of Jewish (and Gentile) culture in Provence, as well as in Northern France and the Rhineland.

[2] Some fanciful Midrashim, collected by Jellinek in his book *Beth Midrash*, are from this source. At far remove, the Koran (with its Aggadata) is in this tradition.

[3] This theology is prettily expressed in *Les Dieux ont Soif* and other works of Anatole France.

absorbed into some of the schools from which emerged
metaphysical Christianity. Of this, and of much Jewish
thought of that period, small relics only survive.[1] Among the
fragments of philosophical value are some writings of
Aristobolus, and the famous *Letter of Aristeas*, which relates, among other things, legends about the seventy-two
elders who translated the Scriptures into Greek. The work
of most of these writers—blended with Midrash—is
important, but not philosophically massive.

Most important and lasting of the Alexandrine Jewish
learning is the work of Philo—known as Philo Judaeus.
Much of his work is, happily, extant. Philo is a Platonic
philosopher on a great scale. He was the first, or one of the
first (for few doctrines flow from any one man), to intro-
duce the concept of the Word of God as that force which
mediates between the world of reality (that is, the realm of
Ideas) and the lower world known to the senses. The
"word" participates in both realms. The "word" is a phenomenon which carries in itself the mystery of the synthesis
which holds between the order of particulars and the
order of universals: a synthesis which Plato himself had
failed to resolve into simpler terms in the Parmenides and
the Theaetetus, two of the greatest of his dialogues.

The contribution of Philo to Jewish thought is that he
found in the Jewish Bible a field of research in which to
demonstrate the nature and action of God through the word
of God.

Already in Philo's time (as we have seen) there were
commentators. There was abundant Midrash. There were
some Targumim, translations into dialect (the Yiddish
of those days); and these translations had been at pains

[1] Survive because of the Jewish practice of burying SHEMOTH—
manuscripts etc. containing the Divine name—and not destroying them.
Hence such archaeological treasures as the Egyptian GENIZOTH, in
which the late Dr. Schechter found a wealth of Judaica.

to state the Bible in "urbane" terms wherever possible.

This last tradition is the one followed by Philo. Philo lays down principles of interpretation; lays it down that the Bible speaks in Trope, in Analogy, in Allegory and other modes; that these are trappings in which the spiritual reality of the word is revealed, variously, to those with varying capacity for its understanding.[1]

Philo's commentary is, then, homiletic, but in Platonic terms. The ingenuity, and the sustained effort after coherence, are typical of the Jewish commentators, although Philo's subject-matter reads so differently from theirs. A thousand years later, Maimonides made a parallel effort to read the Aristotelean metaphysic into the Bible. But no other commentator has so strongly sought to subjugate Holy Writ.

In Jewish history, Philo has suffered a very different fate from Maimonides. The work of Philo has almost passed out of Judaism. In the ninth century the Karaites[2] who had access to all the Byzantine learning, seem to have known Philo's methods and preferred them to the Rabbinic. That is a strange eddy in history. In the direct current, the doctrine of the Logos survived in the later gospels, and among the fathers of the Church: not in Talmudic Judaism. Its after glow is discernible in Kabbalah, of which the ultimate origins are the sources of Philo's thought. When the schism came the Philonists found themselves to be Christians.[3] Among the Eastern Christians, Philo was read for

---

[1] Philo is also a "numerologist" and describes the Sabbath as participating in the essence of the number "seven", which the Pythagoreans valued.

[2] Karaites. (*See* p. 225 *infra*.)

[3] Philo himself was included, by some writers, in the list of Fathers of the Church. The Patristic literature, which is syncretic in the Jewish tradition, contains the interesting claim that Orpheus (figure of the "mystery religions") was a pupil of Moses.

many centuries. In the West, Philo and all Platonism lost their appeal to Christians when Augustine and the lawyers defeated Pelagius, usurped the domain of the thinkers, and elected Aristotle to the position of official pagan philosopher.

But if Philo was lost to the Jews, Jewish influence marks his work. A trivial example illustrates his indebtedness. Philo's "primal man", the archetype of humanity, is androgynous. This belief is commonly thought to be inspired by the *Symposium* of Plato, in which love and art are described as the attempts of a divided being to reunite. But its nearer source is in the traditions of Midrash. The Midrash finds two conflicting accounts in Genesis: that "male and female created he them", but that, in the history of Adam, the extraction of a rib was an afterthought to satisfy Adam's need for a partner. Therefore the Midrash, and Philo following the tradition, describes Adam as androgynous. Philo's dexterous integration of this thought with the mystical possibilities of the distinction between pure and impure is an example of that talent for Bible commentary which has come to so many Jews.

Philo, to resume, was displaced from Christian, if not Jewish, Theology and Philosophy by lawyers who favoured Aristotle. Law, as a mental activity, is logically prior to, and more disciplined than, philosophic speculation. When lawyers philosophize, they wish to think in disciplined terms, not in paradoxes; they require their philosophy to present an ordered pattern. Therefore the lawyers love Aristotle.

Not only does the master of fixed species give greater security to the order in which law functions than would the dialectic of Plato: but Aristotle is a logician *par excellence* —a speculator only *per accidens*. Law, from a very early stage, articulates itself logically, with logical classification, and argument controlled by the ordinary principles of logic—the avoidance of fallacies. Of this technique, Aristotle was the great exponent.

The (historically) second approach of the Jewish Rabbis to the thought of the Greeks was made by lawyers. We shall see that the Tannaim were concerned with the kind of speculation that appeals to lawyers: theories of freewill and retribution: theories of the basic requirements in Jewish obedience. When the systematic efforts came to be made, they were made by men who had found clear notions in the welter of Talmudic case accumulation, and who thought with precision about the ideas they had grasped. To these Aristotle appealed. To the Talmudist who learned the laws about lands and their fruits, and about things found upon land, notions like Substance and Attribute, Essence and Accident, are acceptable and understandable. The law of Specification suggests very easily the distinction between form and matter. Further, the laws of ritual slaughter had developed, in the early Middle Ages, with some help from Greek biology and physics as stated by Aristotle. As late as the sixteenth century we find Isserles deciding a point in the law of ritual impurity by a citation, from Maimonides, of a quotation from Aristotle; but disclaiming hotly the suggestion that he had read the uncircumcised philosopher himself.

In the first ten centuries of the Common era the Talmud, and Gaonic learning, had developed among sophisticated people, equipped with the legal and logical apparatus of a civilized world. Consequently by the time of Saadyah, the Hebrew language (which, like the Latin of the Church, never died) was in process of becoming an adequate instrument for the expression of all the known abstract ideas; and the cognate Arabic, which was the normal language of the Jews under the Moors, had become an admirable vehicle for the transmission of Greek thought.

With Saadyah begins a period of nearly five hundred years which are memorable for a strong Jewish (also a strong Christian and strong Islamic) effort to express law and religion in philosophic terms, and (less effectively) to state philosophy religiously.

From the Jewish point of view, it is noteworthy that the period beginning with Saadyah is a period, not of novelty in legal thinking, but a period of epitome and codification; the age that was to see the work of Alfasi, Maimonides (as codicist), Asher ben Yechiel and Jacob ben Asher, of the Tosafists, and eventually Caro and Isserles. Of this period it is true to say that the lawyers were classifying rather than judging. Admittedly, the mental act which is the lawyer's discrimination between cases continued to be operative. But the emphasis had changed. It was not as in the days of Hillel. Legal thinking by a codifier is rationalized, and recognizably different from the shrewd, empirical, intuition of the lawyer who is "finding" law in the matrix of facts and social relations.[1]

The period begins with the latter days of the Eastern academies. Saadyah was one of the last of the Gaonim, the Eastern masters of learning who had presided at Sura and Pumbeditha. These men were already in contact with the West; with Spain, where a Jew, Chasdai Ibn Shaprut, was high in the Court of the Calif of Cordova, and was using his diplomatic position to help to encourage the learning of Jewry to perfection.

It was a period of great intellectual curiosity in the active Arab world, and among the Jews of Mesopotamia and Spain alike. That general ferment was beginning which was later to make possible the Renaissance; and the Arabs and Jews were becoming aware, before the Christian world, of the presence of great pagan intellectual forces that could not be disregarded. The movement of Eastern Rabbis to

---

[1] A good example of a codicist using philosophic classification is afforded in the writings of the English Coke. "Land, like water, cannot ascend." The reason, of course, for the English law of inheritance is feudal, not formal-logical.

Spain and Africa was symbolical.[1] Learning was in motion.

The philosophic impulses that make this period so important, and, as it happens, of more enduring significance in Jewish history than the Alexandrian Age, were more than an inclination to speculative thinking. At this time there was consciousness of the presence, force, and temptation of other religions. Other religions, particularly Islam, were endeavouring to reconcile their traditions, their records of miracles, their peculiar practices, with the secular learning that some Arabs were spreading. The Kalam, the philosophy of the Mutekalamim (literally Rationalists or Disputants), was an effort to save the Moslem religion from any criticism based on Aristotle; from any criticism based, that is to say, on a doctrine of forms and the belief in eternal matter. The Kalam is a fantastic atomistic occasionalism, in which God is supposed to be for ever holding together the particles of the Universe, and determining their movements by perpetual recreation. (Not the rose changes colour: but we have a different rose, and a different shade.) One of the greatest contributions of Maimonides to philosophy is his convincing refutation of this system in a special section of the *Guide for the Perplexed*.[2]

The Kalam was one of the challenges that called forth

[1] There is a story that four great Rabbis were sent out by the Babylonian Academies as Meshullachim (agents sent to organize aid) and were captured by a Spanish corsair, and sold in slavery: but being discovered by Jews they were given positions of honour. A Rabbi of Cordova abdicated his position in favour of one of them.

[2] They, and some other Arabian Schools, brought *NOMINALISM* into Europe: i.e. the notion that abstract ideas, concepts, are human efforts to classify, and are not well-grounded in reality. This very important teaching, which has left its mark on philosophy, is echoed in Saadyah when he writes, about "evil", that human beings do not really know what it is, but use words to express their personal valuations. There is also an element of nominalism, or conceptualism, in Maimonides, in the context where he distinguishes between ideas generated by the mind, and real objective relations.

Jewish philosophy. There were many others. There was Karaism. An eastern scholar named Anan had, in the eighth century, revolted (for personal reasons) against Rabbinic authority, and preached a return to the literal text (Kera). He rejected Talmudic authority. Very soon the Karaites (as his followers were called) developed their own artificial interpretations of Holy Writ—far from the literal: and Karaite philosophers (notably Nahavendi (ninth century)) developed a kind of Gnosticism. This movement of thought called for refutation. Even more urgently the Jews were conscious of a need for rationalizing their continuance in Judaism under the recurrent pressure of militant Islam and the Church militant. They wanted to be sure of the essentials of their faith. To that end all the Jewish philosophers, from Saadyah onwards—Bachya[1], Ibn Daud, Judah Halévy, Maimonides, Albo, Crescas, to name some of the greatest—made it an elemental purpose of their work to deduce the categories of Jewish belief: to state the principles which a Jew must hold in order to be a Jew; and which, being abandoned, would distinguish Jews from him, so that he would not be merely a sinner in Israel but a stranger.

Saadyah's work, at the beginning of the movement, lays the ground plan. God's laws are revealed. Some are evidently rational; others could not be deduced by the light of nature. But there is nothing inherently irrational in the notion of a deity who lays down laws for nature and for humans; who lets the world run according to the regularities known to science, yet Himself does creative acts, such as the Creation of the World, and the Revelation of the Law. There is no need to believe, with some of the Mutekalamim, that everything is fortuitous. On the other hand, there is nothing, in the logic of things, to exclude

[1] The reference is to Bachya ben Joseph Ibn Pakuda, author of *Duties of Hearts*, not to the later, and quite famous, exegete, Bachya ben Asher.

the conduct of God as it is described in a properly interpreted Bible, once some crude anthropomorphism has been
thought away. In this kind of answer to sceptics, Saadyah
is creating a philosophical pattern. But, in that pattern, one
important feature deserves isolation and emphasis. The
religion, according to Saadyah is mental-spiritual, not mere
ritual; something internal not external. That line of thought
may be the common factor that makes all philosophies
dangerous to the eyes of the guardians of an unphilosophic
orthodoxy.

Of the existence of God, Saadyah, like most of the Jewish
thinkers after him, states proofs which are either cosmo-
logical (Design) or (logically the same) ontological. God is
He than whom nothing greater can be conceived. Such a
Being is a logical necessity basic to the order of Things. (The
looser Cartesian statement is that perfection entails existence.)
That argument, though not in those words, is the teaching
of most of the philosophers. What the moderns call the
physio-theological argument (from "experience") is suggested in Halévy. How they differ from each other is in
emphases. All of them derive, immediately, the deductions
of incorporeality, supremacy, ultimate causality, and inde-
scribability in human terms. They differ in the importance
they give to man—and at most, that is little. Saadyah will
make Good and Evil into human illusions, though he concedes Free Will. Others explain away evil in familiar philosophic ways. All are unanimous on the Purity of the Divine
Nature, and have difficulty in finding a place for many
Jewish traditions. Their accommodation of Bible narrative
is, in every case, ingenious—in every case difficult.

Slightly diverging from the Saadyah tradition is Halévy
—prepared to rest his belief on Revelation. When he deals
with Attributes, he is back among the Abstractionists—but
that is not the burden of his teaching. It is only Ibn Gabirol,
of the great names, who, thinking Platonically rather than

in an Aristotelean way, keeps to logic, yet pictures a Universe that holds a place for Man. The infinity and eternity of God, as apprehended by Ibn Gabirol, are full, not empty, concepts. In this infinity and eternity a spirit moves. Yet it must be conceded that Ibn Gabirol is not significant in Jewish thought because he does not write as a Jew. All the other philosophers are concerned with the defence of Jewish thought: with the analysis and justification of Jewish belief, with the preservations of the Jew from the temptations of other systems. That function they discharged: though in doing so, they lost something of the warmth and richness that belongs to a religion, to a life, that needs no apologetic because it is real.

It is an interesting thought, and an important fact in the study of Jewish history, that the flowers of Jewish philosophy blossomed in Egypt and Spain, where there was, intermittently, great freedom for the Jews. A considerable historian of Jewish thought, Rabbi Simon Bernfeld, has pointed out that when the persecutions came, the Jews of France, and what is now Germany, defied the Christian authorities and perished. The Spanish Jews, under both Islamic and Christian persecution, compromised; pretending to adopt the dominant religion. It has been said that Maimonides spent most of his life as a nominal adherent of Islam. This belief, derived, by Graetz and others, from an Arab historian, has been rejected quite cogently by historians of the first rank, including Zunz and Rappaport. One essay attributed to Maimonides, *Iggereth Hashemad*, accepts the possibility of nominal apostasy to a religion, such as Islam, which is not a form of idolatry. Whether Maimonides wrote this essay has been doubted. But whoever wrote it certainly expressed the Iberian, rather than the Northern, spirit. He expressed what, from one point of view, would be described as a recognition of the inner realities of religion, and the relative unimportance of ritual forms when life is at stake. From the point of view of the strict ritualist, this attitude may be condemned as unworthy; may be condemned as violation of Jewish ultimates. Whatever be the true Halacha, certain it is that our liturgy provides, in the Kol Nidrei, a form of recantation for compelled apostates: and an introductory prayer in which the congregation seeks leave to pray together with the backsliders.[1] And what history of Marranism and crypto-Judaism generally, is conjured at the Passover service, when the words are pronounced: "Pour out thy wrath . . ." and the door is thrown open, either in caution or in defiance.

Perhaps philosophy, with its potentialities of intellectual adaptation, made possible the retention of faith without the forms of obedience. If that was its purpose, then, in a degree, it succeeded.

Whether the philosophic impulse in Judaism was a creative force is another question. Biblical Judaism was not a metaphysic or a theology in any systematic sense. To look for basic doctrine other than the simple belief in the Unity of God—the unreality of idolatry—is to seek for something that tradition does not supply in any abundance. It was always difficult, even in Talmudic times, to distinguish the Jew from the Gentile except in ethical terms; and that when Gentile ethics were low. The Jew was distinguished from the "son of Noah" by restraint; from the righteous Gentile by not standing on the letter of the law.[2] If others could

---

[1] The Kol Nidrei is, be it noted, a very old prayer, written in Aramaic. Its effect is the abrogation of personal vows (between man and God) with the permission of a quorum. A Hebrew addendum (by Rabbenu Tam) makes it refer to future vows (within the next year). At the time of that amendment, and possibly in the earliest period when the prayer was said, the purpose of the ritual was the exoneration of forced apostasies. If it ever purported to be more general in its scope, the high authority of Gaon Amram would condemn it.

[2] The seven laws of the sons of Noah were referred to at times in the way that modern lawyers have referred to the (Stoic-Christian) natural

lend money at interest, he must not lend at interest. Charity, to him, was a duty, not a meritorious indulgence.

What he believed was not particularized. There was no formula, no magic, little eschatology. If there was one metaphysical proposition that the Jews held important, this was the belief in an element of Free Will. But there were no great discussions on it in early Rabbinic times. What we find are clues: for example, in certain Rabbinic references to astrology. There were those who thought that the whole of a person's life was determined by the constellations: that, if it were so ordained, a plague could rage and persons not die: that subsistence, progeny, longevity were according to the stars.[1] But the better opinion is that of Simeon ben Lakish who said: Israel has no MAZZOL (no constellation or Zodiacal sign).[2] Even among the astrologically minded, however, the majority opinion among Pharisees[3] was that the ethical choices were free. "All is in the hands of Heaven except the fear of Heaven". This was the only metaphysic to rationalize Reward and Punishment.[4]

law. The son of Noah (semble, progeny of Japhet) was opposed to idolatry, blasphemy, murder, theft, sexual abominations, the eating of living tissue, and failure to administer justice. But he was below the Jewish level because his justice was stern. He killed and was killed for less than the value of a Perutah. (T.B. Eruvin 62a.) (This has been shown by D. H. Muller to be old Semitic law.)

[1] The Zohar (later) sums up: "Everything depends on MAZZOL (the constellation), even the scrolls of the law in the Holy Place. (Zohar on Sedra Naso—Bk.4a.)

[2] A literal translation is: "Israel has no luck!" MAZZOL, meaning luck, is still part of Jewish vocabulary; e.g. MAZZOL TOV and SCHLIMMAZOL (in one view a corruption of SHOLOM-AZIL— "walks in peace").

[3] On the authority of Josephus the Sadducees (much Hellenized) believed that there was divine creation, but blind chance thereafter. The Essenes, according to that historian, entertained a thorough predestinarianism of what we should call a Calvinist type.

[4] If the books of Proverbs and Ecclesiastes suggest, occasionally, a

The ultra pious may not have needed this rationale. The Lord was not expected to upset his Creation even for the sake of the saintly Eleazar ben Pedath or Chanina ben Dosa.[1] But Rabbinism spoke the language of the *"homme moyen sensuel"*. It may be added that subsequent generations of Jews knew astrology well; but the disciplined thinkers of Jewry never sought any mystery of religion in it. To have done so would have carried dangers of star worship; and, of course, the idolator of Hellenic times was "the worshipper of stars and constellations".[2]

At a later stage in Jewish philosophy (after Saadyah had stated the doctrine) the problem of Free Will was thoroughly argued. Is Free Will compatible with a full Providence? Is Free Will compatible with Divine Omniscience?

The first question is dealt with by Halévy, who conceives two series of causes—only indirectly connected—the "final" series and the "natural" series. This is a subtle but difficult position. Abraham Ibn Daud, and later, Levi ben Gerson, hold boldly that God created a world inclusive of possibilities, and in which real choices are accounted for. The earlier philosopher, Saadyah, and Maimonides both seem to avoid discussion of causal problems (doubtless because their concept of cause was over-logical). They write as if the only problem is that of foreknowledge. Saadyah holds that God's foreknowledge is not to be causally involved in events; and Maimonides treats the question as based on the difficulty, which human beings have, of realizing what is meant by Divine Knowledge. God foresees all that happens and all the

certain fatalism, yet there is enough material in them to make them consistent with the belief that man holds some control over his Destiny. (Note the cautious addenda to Ecclesiastes.)

[1] *See* T.B. Taanoth, 24 et seq. Chanina ben Dosa (first century c.e.) is famous for the occasions on which his prayers were answered. He is a pioneer of the utterance, "All is in the hands of Heaven except the fear of Heaven." (T.B. Ber, 33.)

[2] AKUM, Acronym of OVED KOKHOVIM U MAZZOLOTH.

consequences of decisions, including His own Rewards and Visitations. It is conceivable that this view is the only one possible to thinkers whose conception of God is of an Immutable Being whose knowledge is also immutable from the beginning.

Others, such as Abraham Ibn Daud and Levi ben Gerson —although both Aristoteleans—could contemplate God as increasing his knowledge with the happening of events. This may be loose thinking, or a sound understanding of the meaning of possibility.[1]

Leaving the refinements of thought, in the main it is true to say that, with few exceptions, the Jewish thinkers believe in the reality of Free Will. Crescas, late (1340–1410), and alone of eminence, is a Determinist. His conception of Reward and Punishment is that these are proper to man: who makes decisions under an illusion of freedom. To lawyers, who insist on act as well as intent, this is difficult learning.[2]

For the rest it is not without interest to observe that Jews in non-Jewish philosophy include notable Determinists—

---

[1] Levi ben Gerson is rich in modern-sounding ideas. E.g. he describes spirals of intellectual development in which the higher level never completely transcends the lower levels. This is quite an "evolutionary" conception.

[2] The problem presents itself to the Bible commentators in at least two contexts—of Pharaoh and of Balaam.

Was it right for God to harden the heart of Pharaoh and then punish him? The answer of several commentators is: that Pharaoh had already incurred great guilt: that it would not have been right to allow a repentance—especially one based on mere fear—to mitigate the Retribution. Alternatively, it was perhaps necessary to put Pharaoh into a state of mind relatively free from the effect of the plagues. (On these questions, Manasseh ben Israel, in his *El Conciliador*, has accumulated a useful aggregate of Jewish learning.)

In the case of Balaam, the explanation given is that his intentions were bad: and that God only created occasions in which he could attempt wickedness and be thwarted.

—Spinoza, Marx, Freud, and Einstein. The last named resented (though not in these terms) the attempt to bring into reality, through the gaps in the quanta, the angels that Aquinas contemplated on the point of a needle. An interesting point is that none of these thinkers would be considered unorthodox merely because they are Determinists.

And so of other doctrines. They are doctrines not dogmas. The belief in the Resurrection was said not to be clear from Biblical authority, only deduced. We have seen that the Sadducees did not all accept that doctrine: did not all accept the belief in personal Immortality. The Resurrection and the Messiah and Immortality were doctrines: but not so integral that the Jew who did not accept them ceased to be a Jew.

Practices were important: circumcision, the dietary restrictions, the Sabbath, the Festivals. These, however, were the subject-matter of laws—not Articles of Faith. If it may be said unblasphemously, just as Maimonides opined of God that He could be described as to His actions but not in qualities, so the Jewish way of life is described as to its conduct, not as propositions of belief. The nearest Rabbinic approach to Articles of Faith was the proposition (one statement of which was made at a Synod in Lydda early in the second century C.E.) that a Jew can do anything at the command of the Emperor except idolatry, denial of the unity of God, adultery, or the unlawful spilling of blood. But these are mainly articles of conduct. Articles of Faith are not a Rabbinic invention.

Briefly, it may be repeated that philosophy is not a Talmudic term. One Talmudic use of the term "philosopher" describes a corrupt Judge. The Talmud is strewn with passages in which Jews are invited to debate about God. The answers to criticism are usually witty, rather than systematic. Thus Imma Shalom, the wife of Ishmael and the sister of Gamaliel, on being told of the criticism that God was a thief because he had robbed Adam of a rib, replied that it was not theft to take away base metal and substitute gold. Such answers turned away wrath.

The great master of Halacha, Akiva, was one of the few who pronounced theologically. He asserted, if not the incorporeality of God, at least the inappropriateness of most human analogies: even explaining away the phrase "image of God". That attitude was orthodox at all times. Akiva also lowered the status of angels (he lived at a time when angelology was creeping into religion), asserted a belief in Freedom of the Will, and made great efforts to answer the questionings of those who were righteous and suffered.[1]

Of the distribution of good and evil, he held that the just who suffered heavily in this life did so in order to enjoy a better future life; the happy wicked would suffer hereafter.

Akiva believed these things and maintained them, and his authority was high. But they were not rendered into dogma. The stormy times of Akiva (he died about 135 C.E.) were not propitious for the construction of catechisms. More important was the control of the conduct of men. That is one reason why Akiva's legacy to Israel was the law that he helped to systematize rather than any theological speculation. Indeed much of the rich literature of that period, rich angelology and strange astronomies, has had little effect in the main tradition of orthodox Judaism.[2]

[1] This is the background of the legend, already referred to, of four entering the orchard. Elisha ben Abuya, great Halachist and teacher of Rabbi Meir, one of the creators of the Mishna, is said to have seen a man climb a tree, take bird and nestling together—and that on the Sabbath—and apparently survive: whereas another that he watched took the bird and left the young, and, on descending the tree, was bitten by a scorpion and died. This kind of problem, presented here dramatically, cost Elisha ben Abuya his faith. Akiva, arriving at a strong belief in the after life, was proof against this scepticism.

[2] Already in those days the pseudepigrapha—such books as the Book of Enoch—seem to have become lost to the Jews. Only the Sefer

The Talmudic tradition is ethical: concerned with conduct. Hillel was prepared to say that Jewish law amounted to the precept: "What is hateful to thee, do not do to another", all else being commentary. That was an oversimplification for the exigencies of an occasion. Akiva also emphasized love as the essence of Judaism: but added, as we have seen, some positive assertions about God and the future life. Akiva's doctrine was, however, regarded as the doctrine of Akiva, carrying no more weight than the (considerable) authority of a great Tanna; it did not amount to accepted Halacha. For the rest, the more picturesque speculations of the period, including Philonism, have not left any clearly traceable effect, or impression, on Jewish doctrinal tradition.

In the third century of the Common era we find a statement by Rab Simlai to the effect that Moses had pronounced 613 laws: that David had stated the essence of them in eleven: Isaiah in six: Micah in three: Habakkuk in one: "the righteous lives in his faith".[1] A statement such as this must be understood as an ethical pronouncement, made against the background of a law-observant society, and teaching that mere obedience to laws is not enough to make a man good. The law must be obeyed in its spirit, as the manifestation of an ethical principle.

Converts to Judaism (who, except in some proselytizing semi-Christian sects in the first century, were discouraged)

Yezirah (or its early source-books) survived to influence medieval Kabbalah. That the Jews were conscious of the foreignness of some of their metaphysics is evidenced by the statement of Ben Lakish that "the Babylonians gave names to the angels".

[1] This may account for the Kabbalistic statement that Habakkuk (the word derives from a root meaning embrace) was the boy that Elisha brought to life. Most quoted among the Jews is the saying of Micah (VI.8), "He has told thee, O man, what is good: and what he asks of you is (only) to do justice, to love kindness and to walk humbly with thy God."

were told on acceptance that they must declare the unity of God, and abandon idolatry. Other instruction to them was as to conduct, circumcision, the Sabbath, etc. It was not (and is not) thought necessary to exact from them the elaborate statement of a creed. The convert Aquila (pupil of Akiva and a translator of the Scriptures into Greek) complained that the convert received nothing.

So it was in Talmudic times (there was no catechism): so in any community where the Jewish law is observed. For the Jewish life is a group life, in which conduct requires no teaching. The Jewish religion is older than, and has survived, the specialization of religion from the general law and conduct of societies.[1]

Nearly a thousand years after Hillel the spirit of the Rabbis was differently conditioned. They lived when there was no longer a practical, national aspiration. Their task was to defend Jewish intellect, not only against barbarians, but against the forces of Gentile intellect, and against the intellect itself. How does a Jew differ from those devout Christians or Moslems who also believe in God? There was also (as we have seen) the challenge of the Karaites, the medieval doubters of Rabbinic tradition, who, like the Sadducees, would rely only on the Kera—the actual Bible Text.[2]

[1] Nevertheless, when Mendelssohn says that Judaism consists in doctrinal freedom and conformity of conduct, he oversimplifies. Conscious of this he adds the statement that the "ceremonial law" brings a quickening of the mind and the heart, is full of meaning, and has the closest affinity with speculative religious awareness. The conduct, be it explained, includes the Prayers, the laying of Tefillin, the Fringes, etc. which are the special property of the Jews. The added statement implies some belief as to the relationship between God and Israel. The Reform Jews who claim to follow Mendelssohn, and carry the principle of doctrinal freedom to the point of altering the ritual and the ceremonies, are reading too much into an epigrammatic simplification, and overlooking the master's own explanation.

[2] The Bible, they held, must be read without the accepted Rabbinic

So, in turn, as we have seen, the medieval thinkers stated their philosophies and their Articles of Faith. Maimonides' articles have become part of the orthodox liturgy.

But none of these lists are dogma. Maimonides' list of thirteen Articles,[1] the nearest to authoritative, appears in his earliest major work, the commentary on the Mishna, and is not repeated by him in his later codex, or in his *Guide for the Perplexed.* He does not claim for it greater authority than his name warrants. Nor do the other analysts of Articles make dogmatic claims.[2]

glosses. E.g. the Tefillin should be placed literally "between the eyes". It is a commonplace that the Rabbinic law is not as the text of Scripture. But the Karaites developed their own commentaries; thus conceding one Rabbinic principle. The Sadducees had not been more logical. The common factor is the denial of a received "unwritten" tradition.

It may be of interest to readers to know that Karaism, one thousand years after Anan, retained some life. In the nineteenth century, a Karaite of colossal scholastic attainments, Abraham Firkovitch, with the help of Chwolson, interested the Russian civil authorities in the antiquities of the sect. Although it is believed that some of his "discoveries" were forgeries, he undoubtedly put the study of Karaism and the history of the Karaites (especially in the Crimea) on a scientific basis.

Because of his work and propaganda, land was granted to the Karaites at Troki, near Vilna, where a small community flourished until 1941.

[1] Thirteen: said (by some) to correspond with a tradition of Thirteen Attributes of God.

[2] In the fifteenth century, Joseph Albo, in his *IKKARIM*, reduces the "root-principles" to three: Existence of God, Revelation, Reward and Punishment. But he recognizes many derivative principles.

The Articles stated by Maimonides are enshrined in the liturgy in two hymns, Yigdal and Adon Olam.

They assert God's existence, unlimited by time; His incomparable unity, His incorporeality, His firstness and lastness: His unchangeability, His sovereignty: His revelation in prophecy: the truth of His Torah: the uniqueness of Moses: the Divine omniscience: the Divine mercy: the sending of the Messiah: the bringing to life of the dead. Let it be added that the bulk of Jewish teaching centres round the activities of God mentioned above, rather than the formal qualities.

Moreover, except on Monotheism, there is no convincing unanimity between the authorities in respect of any Article. Therefore, the main importance of the various attempts seems to be "apologetic" or experimental: i.e. they consist in an effort to describe the Jewish belief in God in terms compatible with reason: and in an effort to distinguish Jew from righteous Gentile.

It happened, however, that, in these attempts to solve some specific problems of thought for the Jewish communities of that period, something emerged which is important in itself as Philosophy. Out of Rabbinics, and the soul searchings of Jewish scholars, emerged systematic thought on a great scale, transcending the immediate context.

In particular, one philosopher dominates his age and following centuries. This thinker, Maimonides (1135–1204), stands like a colossus across one of the forgotten roads that lead from the ancient world into modernity. In his presence the Middle Ages cease to be medieval. Possessing a complete, indeed an exhaustive, grasp of all the learning of his age, this great lawyer, who brought order into an inchoate jurisprudence, great physician, master of contemporary astronomy, and withal disciplined and profound metaphysician, towers above some great contemporaries, and in perspective, reduces Aquinas, Scotus and the schoolmen to journeymen of speculative theology.

To the Jews Maimonides (Rambam) is a Rabbi. His thought is contained in many juristic writings, in his commentary to the Mishna, in his Code (*Mishna Torah*, or *The Strong Hand*[1]—the only work he wrote in Hebrew), in essays, such as the letter to the Yemenites, and in a book, about the Bible, called *Moreh Nebuchim* (*Guide for the Perplexed*). In the *Guide*, Maimonides tackles every problem that can beset any reader whose devout belief is made

[1] *Strong Hand*: a typically Jewish title. Yad, a hand, has a numerical equivalent of 14. The work is in fourteen parts.

difficult by his knowledge of science. In this task, he manifests great philosophic power, and incidentally, that special Jewish skill, characteristic of Jewish philosophers, which is the making of unity from apparent diversity.[1]

The *Guide* is a great, and largely successful, effort to rationalize the Bible for those believers (in a humane God and an inspired authorship of His Scriptures) who were becoming aware of speculative difficulties. To these he explains away the crude anthropomorphisms, and resolves apparent contradictions. Further, he undertakes to show the rationality of the Bible text, and its scientific acceptability, according to the standards of the most disciplined of all scientific thinkers—that is to say, Aristotle.

How can the Bible story of the Creation be accepted by anyone who follows Aristotle's arguments to their apparently logical conclusion, which include the eternity of matter? Maimonides, like Halévy is objectively minded enough to consider the question on its logical merits. He goes so far as to declare that if the case for the eternity of matter were conclusive, he would not be disturbed in his belief in the omnipotent activity of God, but would be prepared to treat the Biblical account of Creation in time as an allegorical presentation of truths about God's power. However, Maimonides works out the arguments of Aristotle, and finds them circular. The necessity for matter to be without beginning or end follows, not from first principles of reason, but from the nature of matter as it is. This logic cannot be carried to the Creator. *Ex hypothesi*, the Creator is not limited in his work by features of the result of his work. In the course of this argument, he comes very near to the statement that Aristotle's conception of Cause-Effect is a verbal one, not a real one. Short of this statement, he makes

[1] In a sense all the leading Jewish philosophers can be praised, or criticized, for approaching philosophy with the spirit of Darshonim.

it clear that there is no reason to suppose that a cause is exhaustively stated in a description of its effects.

Along these lines, Maimonides re-creates the story of the Creation and demonstrates the intelligibility of many Bible mysteries, including the Chariot. He also extracts from the Bible some completely rational solutions of many of the problems of conventional theology; the freedom of the will; the existence of evil; rewards and punishments; and the immortality of the soul.

Pure theology, speculation as to omnipotence and omniscience, he shows to be largely verbal. From the abstractions that perplexed the medieval Christian thinkers, who found it difficult even to say that God existed without feeling that they had imposed a limitation, from these logomachies the Jewish philosophers, generally, were saved by Jewish tradition, according to which the works of God are in perpetual evidence and always being invoked.

The essence of the Jewish conception of God is revealed, almost accidentally, by Maimonides when he says that to God one cannot attribute properties or relations—only acts. The God of Israel is known to Israel through acts of assistance and mercy. He helped them when they were struggling with sincerity to help themselves towards redemption. He commanded them, spoke to their minds, showed mercy to them, gave them hope. What He is was never stated. I am what I am.[1] Many Jewish philosophers seem to have been too sophisticated to accept this simple standpoint; but on thinking through the implications of giving to God attributes, they reverted to it. Even in Talmudic times, there was speculation as to what could properly be said of God, without (according to the logic of the period)

[1] Maimonides is one of many commentators who gives a rational account of the apparent difficulties in the statement made to Moses in front of the burning bush.

limiting his perfection. The medieval problem was to reconcile the Biblical anthropomorphisms, the personal appearances and the miracles, with a First Cause contemplated as ultimate, as timeless, infinite and pure beyond all human degrees of purity.

This, as we have seen, is far removed from the main Biblical-Rabbinic tradition. The Bible writers and the Rabbis had experienced questionings. "I have not seen the righteous forsaken and his children begging for bread." Even if that be interpreted, as by a witty commentator, to mean "not both together" ("I have not seen both things in one family"), it seems to be inconsistent with the experience of generations of persecuted Jews. That God permitted evil was a mystery. But the mystery would be clarified in the future. The doctrine of the Immortality of the Soul (always latent) developed in Exilic Judaism as a principle of compensation. A just God would not allow suffering to go unrecompensed, unrevenged. A doctrine of Divine Reward and Retribution was accepted by many, and is included in the principles of Saadyah and his followers. But the Rabbis of Talmudic times did not investigate the metaphysics of it; did not ask: What is the nature of God so that . . .?

Evil existed. The duty of man was not to be evil. For this choice man is free. "Everything is in the hands of God except the Fear of God". So said Akiva: and it is a good compendious statement of the Jewish view. It happens that those who do not fear God cause suffering even to those that do. That is a fact—like the Exile; perhaps the consequence of sin, perhaps of brute matter. Notwithstanding the teaching of Deuteronomy and Jeremiah, that each dies for his own sin only, it is accepted Jewish thought that the Exile and its evils are the consequence of old sins. "We and our Fathers have sinned," says the liturgy.[1]

[1] Death as an evil, is the object of differing Rabbinic approaches. God

This is a different answer, and different questioning, from the Arabic-Jewish inquiries of the Middle Ages. But not irrelevant, because most of the Jewish philosophers are in a special position. They are Bible commentators.

To the theologically unengaged philosopher, acceptive of Aristotle, an abstract perfection, stated with perfect verbal consistency, is the essence of God. To Aristotelean thinkers, and even to the Platonic, the Rabbinic belief in the ununderstandable (but good) activity of God in an imperfect world would leave much to be explained. The Rabbis are humbler than the secular philosophers. The Rabbinic answer to the question about evil would be near to that of Job. Hast thou been present at the foundation of the world?

The philosopher is one who endeavours, by explaining words, to probe experience as if he were present at the foundation of the world. But words, if adequate to state, are inadequate to resolve the problem. Either they lead the questioner to complete scepticism; or they work themselves out in barren equations; for words can add little to what is put into them.[1]

---

is said to lament the death of the righteous (it is "precious" in his eyes) as He laments the temple. He is also said to inflict Death and Suffering on the righteous as a punishment for the sins of the generation. Let it be compendiously said, There is no uniform doctrine.

[1] Idle questioning, such as whether the Lord can make two plus two equal five, is the *reductio ad absurdum* of the verbal methods. In point is a literary incident. The Government of Egypt required English texts for use in their schools. *Inter alia*, the play *Libel*, was submitted. In this, the author, adopting a Greek epigram, puts into the mouth of a character these words: "One thing not God Himself can do: unmake the past."

The Egyptian Ministry of Education asked for the deletion of this line, because it offended against the Moslem conception of omnipotence.

Academically, it is to be speculated whether, if the Lord undid the past, it would continue to be past. If we are dealing with annihilation of some time-space event, this is argument about realities. But the thing

The Rabbinic conclusion was faith, not expressed in theological dogma. But the Jewish philosophers, Maimonides in particular, gave intellectual support, and discipline, to Rabbinic faith.

The beliefs of Maimonides are the beliefs of a moralist with sentiment but no sentimentality. He sees the Jewish attitude to be in danger of anthropocentricity. What is man that thou art mindful of him? is a pertinent question. His answer, boldly given, is that man matters very little indeed.

Much of the difficulty of the problem of evil is, according to Maimonides, due to the human belief that he (the individual man) is the centre of creation. There is evil: but many so-called evils are nothing other than features of a life which includes death. That the Bible declares God to have created Evil, Maimonides explains hermeneutically. The word is BORO not OSSO. The former verb describes, as it were, separation out, rather than bringing into being. Evil is the negation of good: not a positive entity. There is, therefore, no implication that the nature of God includes wickedness. As a fact, present to an omnipotent and omniscient power, evil presents no insoluble problem. God gives free will: sees how men will behave, but does not determine their conduct. To say that this is contradictory is to confuse knowledge with power, to misunderstand the nature of freedom, and to misconceive omnipotence and omniscience.

If man is to rise to some importance in the scheme of things, he must live the disciplined life of the student: he must develop his spirit. There is an immortality of the Soul, but only for those who develop Souls!

In saying this, Maimonides is pronouncing hard doctrine, which has Jewish sources and non-Jewish. In Jewish tradi-

too easily becomes the play of words, of which Kant has emphasized the futility.

From this line of thought it follows that metaphysicians of today do not like to rely on the ontological argument.

tion there frequently recur utterances which suggest that the world, and especially the world to come, is made for the learned. Study is stated by some authorities to be valuable above prayer[1]. The ignorant man is to be contemned and avoided. Although some of the Talmudic epithets against the so-called AM-HAARETZ[2] are really directed against Sadducees, there is abundant authority, and established custom, devaluing the unlearned.[3] When Maimonides speaks of human beings whom the Bible asserts it is right to kill, he seems to be arguing the cause of intellectualism.[4]

Another source of the doctrine is the Aristotelean theory, as expressed in the writings of Alexander Aphrodisiensis, in which the distinction is drawn between the potential spirit and the fulfilled spirit—between the *Nous Hylikos* and the *Nous Epiktetos*. The latter is in harmony with the world of Ideas. But, since the spirit is the "form" of the material body, it is hard to see how that emancipation is achieved which is survival after the body. Maimonides asserts, rather than explains. Apparently, a mature soul can achieve an independent ideal reality. A follower and critic of Maimonides, Levi ben Gerson, possibly the severest and most devoted analyst among all the Jewish thinkers, asserts Immortality to be possible if the world of Ideas is real.

[1] Some of the early Tannaim hold prayer to be higher: but the other tradition has held long sway.

[2] *See note on p. 167 supra.*

[3] There is even a story in Baba Bathra that Rabbi Judah refused to feed them in time of famine. But I suspect that the ignorant persons referred to there were enemies of the Rabbis. One of the values of Chassidism consists in its protest against intellectualism.

[4] Maimonides' thought is a valuable corrective to the Jewish tendency to regard the Jews as fundamentally sinless—or completely forgiven in consequence of their Repentance, Prayer and Charity: even completely forgiven on account of the Repentance, Prayer and Charity of others. Maimonides knew that there were wicked Jews as well as good ones.

Gersonides, as this writer is sometimes described, makes it clear that a Realist (in the medieval sense) can believe in this type of Immortality. He points out that the element of Nominalism in Maimonides is incompatible with it.[1]

Whatever criticisms be directed against these metaphysics, it is clear that the charge of sentimentality is not one of them. The Jewish peripatetics constitute a stern school of thought.[2]

Unlike the majority of theologians, Maimonides, at least, is not an easy comforter. He restates Judaism on a high plane of thought. To this plane not many ascend. Rabbinic thought accepts, generally, from Maimonides, what it accepts from the Book of Job. But there remain traditions, and Maimonides does not destroy them, according to which the life of man is less stern, and more important in the scheme of things. In so far as Jewish philosophy is grounded in the Bible, there is authority for that attitude. The Jewish God is personal in the sense that he is the God of human persons. Theoretically this is compatible with the unanthropomorphic. But when the Biblical conception is worked out, and developed in Rabbinic tradition, the result is a conception that the philosophic formulae do not easily accommodate. How, in Aristotelean thought, can we frame the Rabbinic picture of "an open book and a hand that writes" and a divine record of the good and bad acts—indeed all the acts—of every individual. This picture Mai-

[1] Levi ben Gerson is an accepted commentator on the Bible. His philosophic work *The Wars of the Lord*, which is metaphysically brilliant, has been described by an orthodox critic as "Wars against the Lord".

[2] Let it be observed that Jewish tradition is of sentiment—not sentimentality. The Jews have not valued life merely as the opposite of the lifeless. Human life is valued, because only the living human can do human good. For that reason Death is lamented. The irretrievably wicked human, if any, has no value. Animal life is not valued as such. But cruelty to animals is condemned. Animals must be fed: must not be castrated: if killed, must be humanely killed. To eat "living tissue" is a crime, even for the sons of Noah.

monides did not obliterate: but it does not seem to be his picture of the Highest Reality.

Be it remembered that Maimonides, to himself, and to generations of Jews, was lawyer and Bible-commentator. His great work, the *Guide*, is substantially a commentary on Bible texts, though not in the conventional form. Formally, it is a book of Drash, arranged in topics, not in the serial order of the Scriptures.[1]

All the learning that Maimonides had in astronomy—he accepted the notion of concentric spheres, with Ptolemaic epicycles: and used them in his arguments on the proof of God's action from Design—all this was part of a comment on that verse in the Psalms (LXVIII.5) which speaks of God riding the Heavens. To Maimonides this imagery cohered with the Aristotelean conception of a Deity moving round the outer circle of the concentric spheres and mysteriously influencing their motion.

The commentary is controlled by Aristotelean philosophy. But only when Aristotle is acceptable, after being thought through, is Maimonides Aristotelean. (So, too, Gersonides on Aristotle.) If Aristotle cannot accommodate "Special Providence", he is wrong: and no effort is made to reconcile the Bible with his teaching. This is not because the Bible is a basis for dogma, but because Maimonides is certain that the Bible is not unphilosophic in its evidence of "Special Providence"; and that the Bible does not conflict with any mature philosophy in respect of the Creation from nothing.

Indeed the whole book is readable as a most fascinating

[1] Typical, and interesting, are his comments on the Song. They set me to watch the vineyards, etc. symbolizes the distraction of the Soul from its proper pursuits. Incidentally, his stern personal attitude is also expressed in his legal writings. Thus he pronounces, on the subject of dishonesty, that it is not dishonest to dice with the Gentiles: but that it is wrong for any man to spend any part of his life in pursuits which are not the perfecting of his mind or the improvement of civilization.

set of glosses on innumerable features of the Bible narrative and the Scriptural thought.

Then, in the same book, we find comments at less philosophic levels, as where the writer explains to us why that Rabbi was wrong who was bored by the genealogies. For the purposes of a campaign against Amalek, it was important to know that the sister of Lotun was Timna: because by working out the line, it can be shown that not all who live in the area of Amalek are Amalekites.[1]

In the spirit of all the commentators, he reconciles the text with the "reason" of the age of the commentator.[2] Possibly his most lasting effort (in the *Guide*), from the point of view of Rabbinic Judaism, is his analysis and justification of the laws, with all their arbitrary detail as well as their principles. Conceding the possibility that laws can pass away, that, perhaps, the Sacrifices will never be restored (this thought caused him to be accused of heresy), the philosopher shows reasons, in the nature of moral discipline, for the retention of equally empirical, equally arbitrary, detail in many other branches of the law. That it cannot be deduced from rational principle is not sufficient reason for the changing of laws. These laws that exist are probably better than other laws, or the indiscipline that would replace them.[3]

[1] It should be observed that Maimonides is equally "interpretive" of the text of Aristotle, emphasizing the philosopher's references to his understanding and his knowledge, and underlining the distinctions involved.

[2] Not, however, accounting sufficiently for the "reason" of the age of the Scripture. It could be conceded that Holy Writ "wrote down": but not that the spirit of the Scripture writers "evolved".

[3] The distinction between MISHPAT (reasoned judgement) and CHOK (unarticulated law) is a very old one in Jewish learning. The apologists who endeavour to rationalize do a poor service. Thus Shechita is humane in fact: but the technique originates in the law of Sacrifices. Circumcision may be healthy, but that is not its reason in Jewish thought.

Maimonides, in these writings, is the legal philosopher, the deducer of categories of obedience, valid for many levels of obedience. If Rabbis of subsequent generations have valued the *Guide*, it is on account of this balanced theory of the conservation of institutions that it embodies.

Ironically, then, Maimonides the great philosopher, survives in Judaism as jurist. Other destinies have been similar. Of the philosophers of his period, Halévy survives as poet, Ibn Gabirol as Payetan, Abraham Ibn Ezra as Bible commentator. The philosophic works of these great thinkers seem to swirl in forgotten eddies outside the main current of Jewish life and religious experience.[1]

The period that followed Maimonides was a dark one for the Jews. Almohades and Christians in turn persecuted them. The Zeitgeist was a force driving to assimilation, or escape into ritualistic religion. Although there were great academic Jewish philosophers after their philosophic Agamemnon (Gersonides, Crescas, Abrabanel) the tradition that helped the Jewish spirit to keep alive was the

[1] If, for example, an orthodox scholar were asked about Divine Attributes, his answer would be an analysis of Biblical words in an homiletical spirit: that Elohim suggests Judgement: that JHVH signifies mercy. (This is one of the many explanations of the text of the revelation at the Burning Bush.) If argument be needed in support, it will not take the form of speculation on the nature of Deity, but citations, from other parts of the Bible, of occurrences under the auspices of the various names. In this traditional learning all the philosophical speculation about Attributes, Essences and Accidents, counts for very little.

Among reasons for the oblivion of the philosophers, the following may be suggested:

(1) The Aristotelean philosophers and Crescas, of the Platonists, use an idiom which is hard for Jews who have no learning in the Greek philosophies.

(2) Ibn Gabirol's work is divorced from the Bible.

(3) Halévy, himself, rather derides philosophy, and, in this way, has deprived his work of controversial importance.

(4) The rivalry of the Kabbalah.

warm dark force of mystery, not the clear breath of logical analysis.

Out of Spain emerged not only formal philosophy, but Kabbalah, restated and reinforced. We have seen that only the dogmatist can dismiss the Kabbalah as unphilosophic: or condemn it, in Reinach's phrase, as "an aberration of intellect". But it never was a disciplined philosophy, even from the standpoint of a Platonist like Ibn Gabirol, whose doctrine of emanations could be so sympathetic to the Kabbalist.

The Kabbalah has many sources. Old legends associated with Abraham and Enoch were given literary form in the Alexandrian period. A Talmudic dictum that the children of Keturah were given the gift of Magic suggests the prevalence of some legendary lore, and some practices, that are now unknown to us.

From Egyptian and Babylonian sources there came angelology: and Maimonides accepted at least the Bible angels as more than metaphor.[1] Also from those sources, we have seen that there was a cult of mystery associated with the letters of the alphabet. Since the Greeks, as well as the Jews, used letters for numbers, it is not surprising that many Mediterranean speculators sought mystery in the letters of words. It is consistent with the Arabian invention (or acquisition) of the figures, that the Arab philosophers were not involved in these speculations. Hence their lack of appeal to the sophisticated, Arab-educated, Jewish peripatetics.[2] But when the star of Aristotle waned, the star of Pythagoras, in strange conjunction, came into the ascendant.

---

[1] In Hebrew tradition (and language) Malakh means what Angel means in Greek: a messenger. The Cherubim and Seraphim were differently imagined: in later writings their qualities are attributed to all Angels.

[2] They were, of course, common knowledge. We have seen an instance of their use by Ibn Gabirol in a drinking-song.

It has already been observed that, among the traditional methods of hermeneutics, Gematrya and Notarikon—the methods of numerical equivalence and construction of acronyms—are well recognized. Kabbalah extends these methods to systematic decoding. The Bible is read not only in the actual letters, but in letters substituted by artificial rules: e.g. the rules of ATBASH (substitution of Aleph by Tau, Beth by Shin, etc.), Albam (substitution of Aleph by Lamed, Beth by Mem, etc.) or the reading of the immediate next letter of the alphabet for the letter in the text (as when, in order to avoid using the accepted symbols for the Divine names, some ultra pious use the formula KUZU BEMU-KHAN KUZU). Evidently this "decoding" of the "crypto-grams" of the Bible affords possibilities for quite fantastic speculation. Nevertheless, it is to be observed that when the Prophet Jeremiah writes Sheshach, he is probably using At-bash for Babel (Jer. LI.41) and LEB KOMAY in the same chapter (in the midst of them that rise up against me) is convertible to KASDIM (the Chaldeans). And cannot the obscure word HELAL, in Isaiah XIV.12, which is rendered Lucifer, be a simple transposition of the letters of LAYELAH (Night)?[1]

In the many currents of thought that fuse in the tradition of Kabbalah this is one common factor: the belief, namely, that supernatural forces are described in secret messages to be derived from Holy Writ. Sacred names can be used to work good and to work evil. This is the tradition of the Sefer Yezirah, some of whose exponents behaved as magicians. But, short of this, the pious, who eschewed magic, who felt that magic and cognate astrology were

---

[1] Zangwill speaks ironically of the mysterious significance of the letters, with any letter being substitutable for any other letter, "as in philology". It is noteworthy that these methods were known to, and used by, the Fathers of the Church. E.g. Irenaeus analyses the word Jesus into Yod, Shin, Vav. Initials of The Lord, Heaven and Earth.

dangerously akin to Star worship (as indeed they were in Gnosticism), even these held that concentration on the letters of Scripture, and on some traditional formulae, made possible an elevation of the spirit, even to the limit of emancipation from bodily control.

That the words of Holy Writ were used for purposes verging on the magical we know from Talmud and Midrash. A Mishna in Chagigah warns against the teaching of mysteries except to the qualified: and pronounces that one who inquires into "the above and below, the before and after" is to be pitied; it were better had he not been born.

Nevertheless, there is no prohibition against study of the esoteric. "But there are things that should only be spoken about in whispers." Here, let it be observed, is the reaction of the old woman of Endor—in Rabbinical form.[1]

Perhaps it was because of the dedication of the Rabbis (especially those who followed Akiva) to hermeneutics for legal purposes that mystery remained legitimate. The spread of Christian and Pagan mysteries was a further encouragement to the mentally active and acquisitive Jews.

So they have absorbed mystery from many sources. When, in the Spanish period, Kabbalah achieves something of systematic articulation[2] there is evidence of the adoption of thinking from most of the philosophic and pseudo-philosophic schools.

The contribution of Spanish Jewry to Kabbalah cul-

---

[1] I have stated the attitude of Samuel and the old woman of Endor as the belief that "those who seek (or find) the next world shall lose it". However, it must not be supposed that Judaism is incompatible with practices like spiritualism. Some orthodox Jews have interested themselves in the cult. One could, perhaps, apply the Talmudic formula: "The Rabbis would not be pleased with them". Kabbalistic practice, in contrast, is in a religious context.

[2] The word Kabbalah—reception—is not used in this special sense before the eleventh century. In Rabbinic Hebrew the word continues to mean, *inter alia*, certification of competence (e.g. of a Shochet).

minates in the Zohar, a compilation by Moses de Leon,[1] not the greatest or clearest of thinkers, of an aggregate of learning, old and new, synthesized into the form of an Aramaic Bible commentary—of a Midrash.[2]

The Zohar must not be regarded as the only system of Kabbalah. But it happens to be the best known. When Kabbalah is referred to, a tradition is meant, not a book. Elements of this tradition are of great interest and great value.

Typical and fundamental is the doctrine of the division of the mind (accepted by Maimonides) into Nefesh, Ruach, Neshamah, in that order of ascent.[3] Although some of the distinctions are not un-Biblical, the common formula is, of course, the Platonic trinity of bodily appetite, spirit, soul. This corresponds to differences between Simple Apprehension, Understanding and Reason. At all periods of Kabbalistic tradition this analysis, in one form of statement or another, is held valid: and all Kabbalistic schools have it in common that concentration in Prayer, and deep study of the mysteries of Holy Writ, develop the high levels of the human mind, and allow some ecstatic union with the forces of creation.

This, however, is not the whole of Kabbalah: only the

[1] Died 1305.
[2] There are claims that the Zohar is the work of the Tanna, Simeon ben Yochai. Certainly some of the learning is old. But internal evidence makes the bulk of the work late. In point are references to the vowel forms (not systematized till the late sixth century), a quotation from a hymn by Ibn Gabirol (b. 1021), references to the capture of Jerusalem by Crusaders and Moslems, references to the Comet of Rome, etc. Nevertheless the work undoubtedly contains much ancient material.
[3] According to some authorities the Ruach is the lowest; according to others the highest. But the general tradition is as stated. In the Lurianic system, aspects of the spirit below Nefesh are described, Chayah and Yechida—principles of animation and physical identity: and there are spirits corresponding to all the functions of action and apprehension.

technique. The philosophical, or theosophical, statements
were developed in the Spanish period as if in answer to the
challenge of those thinkers who would not vest God with
attributes. Saadyah, Halévy, Maimonides, and the others,
would not make any predication about the nature of
the Godhead that was not negative. Thus, unity could
be stated—as a denial of plurality: existence—to deny
nonexistence. Anything else would be an assertion of
corporeality. The proposition that "He created", that "He
provided": these were descriptions of His acts, not of
His essence.

The Kabbalists, with Platonist inspiration, essayed a
greater theology. If the peripatetics had denuded God of
human qualities, the Kabbalists undertook to revest Him,
at least with a sentiment, an understandable affection for
humanity.

This was ingeniously done. God, as the perfect being, is
called En Sof (No End)—the Infinite. But the Infinite could
radiate without diminution (the metaphors of light are
rich ones): or (in later theory) could voluntarily contract
itself (the process is called TSIMTSUM) in order to allow
the articulation, within it, of the forms of the finite. Then
the metaphysical problem, like the problem that presented
itself to Hegel, is a deduction of the categories so as to
express the detail of life in terms descending from, and
ascending to, the Absolute.

The Kabbalistic categories include a plurality of orders or
levels of Being and an order of emanations called Sefiroth.[1]

[1] The word means "numbers", but contains an echo of the Latin for
Spheres, the theory of which was familiar: so that in some systems
Sefiroth are spoken of as circles. In the old Sefer Yezirah the world is
said to be created through the 22 letters of the Alphabet and ten Sefiroth.
These make up, together, 32 paths. What the Sefiroth are is not clear.
In one statement, they include the Divine Spirit, three elements and
six modes of measurement. Readers of Avoth will be familiar with the
reference to "ten words" with which God called the world into

In the system as stated by Isaac Luria (known as ARI) who flourished in Palestine from 1534–1572, the contraction of the En Sof generated infinite light. As that light pulsated there appeared a void surrounded by ten circles (the Sefiroth) through which were seen the appearances of diversity which we call the finite. The Sefiroth nearer to the void could not bear the Divine light and were shattered and reformed into figures (Partsufim[1]). These figures express the articulation through four worlds, and in a difficult metaphorical process, of Creation, of Man, of the Divine Spirit, and its conquest of evil (which exists in consequence of the shattering of the Sefiroth). The Lurianic system, with its efforts at the emancipation of the spirit from the consequences of the sin of Adam, is too individual and too detailed a system for synoptic statement. But Kabbalah generally has the following features.

Man is attempting, through prayer and piety, and all the resources of saintliness, to achieve access to the Divine. His way is along the path of experience of the orders of Being (Sefiroth) with which he harmonizes himself.

There are ten Sefiroth. A supreme one: then three of high intellectual order, and two lower triads. The light of the En Sof (according to several statements) inspires into activity; The Crown, The Wisdom, The Understanding. Each emerges from each: and these express themselves at a lower level in Mercy, Justice and Beauty: and these, in turn, are made manifest in nature in The Triumph, The Glory, The Foundation. These words are not translated into terms of human activity: but constitute an ordering of the world of experiences.

being. But at the late Kabbalistic stage the Sefiroth are conceived as entities, or principles, more elaborate, and not identifiable with, letters, numbers, words, etc. The word Sefiroth also contains an echo of the Sapphire mentioned in Ezekiel's description of the Throne.

[1] From Greek: *Prosopon*—face.

The articulation is, need it be added, very subtly worked out in terms of a rationalistic logic and psychology. But it becomes suffused with other influences: accumulates accretions.

Thus many schools (including the Lurianic) mediate the logic with a doctrine reminiscent of Gnostic Microcosm and Homunculus. They order the system into the shape of Primal Man: and the Sefiroth are diagrammatically placed at various parts of the archetypal human form. Metaphors of masculinity and feminity contrive to be used in a most unfleshly way. Intrusions into the system include doctrines of pairs (syzygies): and some quite fantastic humanizations of cosmology, in which the Patriarchs (resurrected, as it were, from Alexandria) are given roles of dominion.

The philosophically valuable element in the system is, it will be clear, a rich development of neo-Platonic thought. The theory of the contraction of the divine light is one of the most poetic statements of a very subtle idea. Apart from the quasi-Gnostic elements, the system expresses a lofty conception of the relations of the human spirit to the divine, and inspires a noble pattern for ways of living. Its Jewish value is that the whole of Bible lore is reinterpreted in interesting speculative terms: and the Torah is a constant which gives concreteness to patterns of thought that would otherwise be excessively abstract.

More important even than this is the fact, that whereas abstract philosophy gives at most a mental and moral discipline, Kabbalistic thought gives hope, and urge. Not only do the Sefiroth affect Man—Man affects the Sefiroth. Every individual man is something concrete in the Universe. His attainment of purity is not the achievement of an unpicturable eternity, nor of a mystic nirvana. It is an addition to the sum of Divine, as well as human, well-being. It follows that the After-life is a very highly articulated detailed concept in Kabbalah. Leviathan and the

wild ox are only external addenda to the joy that is
immortality as conceived by the exponents of mystery.
Unhappily, the thought is hard to maintain on a high level.
The practical manifestation of it is in the interpretation of
Holy Writ in understandable mystery terms, terms that can
be understood by those who are not learned enough to
know the "system". To these mystery seekers there have
been provided speculations about Bible events. Such stories
as that of Adam and Eve are restated with introduction of
Purities and Impurities. Evil and Good Spirits, the Light and
the Angels (who make the understanding of the light easier.)
Biblical figures lend themselves to easy symbolic treatment,
and use is made of some fairly crude mystery beliefs.

Thus from Platonism Kabbalah has drawn a doctrine of
Transmigration—as a stage in the Soul process. This, in
itself, is not in antagonism to old Jewish theory: for, as we
have seen, Rabbinic eschatology is vague. Yet, although
there had been speculation of that order (with the soul of
Phinehas metempsychosed into other heroes and Moses,
embodying the spirit of Abel, and avenging him), the stern
school of thought that developed from Saadyah to Crescas
was firmly opposed to this fanciful doctrine: and it was not
accepted by the misnaggidic Kabbalists. But in some of the
Chassidic accounts of Kabbalah the element of evil in the
world is exorcised by the continued transmigrations of the
Soul through those Incarnations.

What has caused more difficulty has been the incorpor-
ation of some demonology and some magic. We have seen,
what Eybeschütz made clear, that evil is something livelier
in Rabbinics and Kabbalah than in academic Jewish
philosophy. Kabbalists have varied in their accounts of evil.
Some of them have crowded their world with spirits to be
exorcised: among these Lilith—spirit of night—the concubine of Adam, to prevent whose temptations there is an
ascetic period of eight weeks in the calendars of the

mystery lovers. Of these spirits exorcism is wrought through ritual processes, baptisms, fastings, and the use of amulets.

More dangerously, some Kabbalists carried these theories of evil, of Shades and KLIPPOT[1], to an almost Zoroastrian extreme. The SITRA AHRA—the other side of Godhead—tends to become an independent force: and we are living again in the world of Ormuzd and Ahriman.

Other features of the system are beliefs in Possessions, in Wandering spirits, to be put to rest by the piety and the prayers of those who encounter them. Asmodeus, the King of the Demons, who, in some of the Midrashim, is described as a temporary victim of the clever King Solomon, comes to power again in the syncretic demonology of the later Kabbalists.[2]

These developments, be it said, are not in the works of the great Kabbalists. The practical Kabbalah, as practised by Isaac Luria and his pupils, was an ascetic ethical system characterized by strong belief in the efficacy of Prayer and Concentration (KAVANAH) as means of TIKUN, the purification of the Soul. Their doctrines are essentially of love, and reminiscent of the best Essene teaching, with which they may even be historically continuous.

The essence of the best teaching is Purity. Rappaport (Ansky) in his play, *The Dibbuk*, describes a typical ethical thought, of this school, in a homily spoken by the Chassidic Tsaddik. The world has many places, none so Holy as the

[1] "Shells", fragments of the unreintegrated Sefiroth.

[2] In mitigation, the reader should bear in mind that the whole Kabbalah is used as a frame-work for the exposition of mysteries latent in Holy Writ. Therefore, however they pictorialize the forces of evil, the Kabbalists are always controlled by the monotheism of the Scriptures. May it also be suggested that few Kabbalists work out the metaphysical assumptions of their work, which is largely homiletical discourse, and demonstrations, from the Bible, of the need for purity, and of methods of attaining it.

.

Land of Israel: the Land has many places, none so Holy as Jerusalem: Jerusalem has Holy places, none so Holy as the Temple: and in the Temple, nothing is so Holy as the Holy of Holies. The year has 365 days, none so Holy as the Day of Atonement. The world has 70 languages, none so Holy as Hebrew: Hebrew has many Holy words, none so Holy as those pronounced by the High Priest on the Day of Atonement. At that moment, and in that place, there must be no lack of concentration, no impurity of thought. Why then, asks the Tsaddik, does not every Jew, on every day, in every place, at every moment, think of himself as if he were the High Priest pronouncing the Sacred Name in the Holy of Holies on the Day of Atonement?

That is Chassidic thought, in the Luria tradition.[1] The metaphysician will observe that it comes dangerously near to Pantheism. The lawyer will find it difficult to accept an equation of all things in the scale of importance. That is why mystical trends, lofty anti-nomianism, and theories such as the Pelagian, in which the "good will" is more important than the act, tend to be resisted by orthodoxy.

From the Rabbinic standpoint, however, the pure stream of mystery is an enrichment of tradition. Indeed, the list of great Kabbalist authorities includes the names of great Halachists, from Nachmanides to Caro and Elijah of Vilna. But the "magical" trend has been a cause of great discord. Superstition, the lore of evil eyes and enchantments, is against the best Jewish teaching. At all periods the graves of the wise have been regarded by the wishful as sources of benediction and healing. But the Misnaggidic Rabbis (literally: "in opposition") have been angered by the claims of magical cures by the living. Tsaddikim have even claimed

[1] Modern Chassidism is a movement inaugurated many years after Luria; but his influence is strong in it. So East European Chassidim use Sephardic orders of prayer because Luria used that liturgy and annotated it.

to be able to make contact with evil, and emerge unscathed. Moreover, the centuries between Spain and our own day have seen, among other schismatic occurrences, the appearances of pseudo-Messiahs. Such a one as Molcho, or Shabbetai Zevi, was, genuinely, or in fraud, able to make great use of mystery pronouncements, and mysterious ceremonials: strange blessings, and even stranger promises.

That pseudo-Messiahs caused civil strife among the Jews is history. The intellectual cleavages were deeper. So that when that keen analyst of texts (and editor of the Prayer-Book) Jacob Ashkenazi (known as Emden) decided to wage a cruel campaign against that much greater man—Jonathan Eybeschütz (Der Präger)—accusing him of Shabbataian sympathies, he found it all too easy to equip himself with quotations from the cryptic pronouncements of one who was a leading Kabbalist.

Kabbalah has also been in the background of the dissensions between orthodox Jewry and the Chassidic movement, which was founded by the Baal Shem, or BESHT,[1] (Israel of Miedzyboz) in the eighteenth century. This sect (Essene to the orthodox Pharisee) was in the nature of a reaction against the Rabbinic obsession with severe Talmudic methods of thought: was a plea for emotion in religion: was an ecstatic prayer movement, in a religion which has so often valued learning above prayer.[2]

[1] This is an acronym of BAAL SHEM TOV—Master of the Good Name. *Inter alia*, the title is due to the belief that he was qualified to use Holy Names.

[2] Let it be clearly understood that, though I have described Chassidism as a Jewish Counter-Reformation, there is no issue of doctrine to cause conflict between Chassid and Misnaggid (lit. opponent). Trouble between the two "attitudes" is traceable to the fact that Chassidic Rabbis tended to become dynastically-minded and arbitrary in their pronouncements in non-legal contexts. But the Misnaggid of today admires the Chassidim. A beautiful example of their emotionalism is illustrated in a "Rebbe's" statement of the difference between Tisha

The Chassidic belief in the virtues of Concentration in Prayer (Kavanah) is good Rabbinic doctrine, but Kabbalah has added mystic overtones. Consequently, there emerged "Saintly men" (Tsaddikim): and these founded dynasties[1] and the dynastic is incompatible with the truly religious. Also there developed a fanaticism, which does the good and the harm in religious communities that Jingoism and Chauvinism achieve in politics.

Therefore there was great opposition among the severe jurists who defended the tradition of a paramount law—paramount to all persons. And no less than Elijah of Vilna, Halachist and Kabbalist himself, countenanced and authorized severe repressions against the new sectaries.

It may be added that, after some dynastic abuses had been exposed and extremism moderated, Chassidism settled into a strong and spiritual branch of Jewry. Many of the Tsaddikim have been profound scholars and thinkers, and more than nominally saintly in their lives: and their mysticism has been an enrichment of experience in a period when religious experience has been otherwise diminishing.

In fine, the Kabbalistic tradition—rather than the formal Kabbalah itself—has corrected any tendency to denude Judaism by logical analysis.

A religion cannot claim to be above logic. But in modern times philosophy has developed critical powers to such sharpness that the sceptic can cut away the bonds and supports of all intellectual assurance.

In the reaction against extreme scepticism, religious experience, like the empirical experiences of everyday life,

B'Av (Day of Mourning for the Temples) and Yom Kippur, the Day of Atonement. "On Tisha B'Av who can eat? On Yom Kippur, who wants to eat?"

[1] This is the consequence of the teaching of DOV (BÄR), the Great Maggid, pupil of the Baal Shem; and not of the teaching of the BESHT himself.

like the processes of ordinary causation, are forced into the category of unprovables. And so much is now in that category that the philosopher becomes convinced of the illegitimacy of Pyrrhonism, Laodiceanism, Humeism, and all the too easy doctrines of doubt.

To Maimonides and his contemporaries, thorough-going scepticism was not philosophically important. Since then, the Newtonian Age—with its atomistic conceptualism—has made attack, not on religion only, but on all the apparatus of knowledge. Therefore philosophers in modern times have only been occupied with religion as one department of the whole order of thought, an order defending itself against scepticism. In these times, it is understandable that Jewish rationalistic philosophers have been, for the most part, either learned exponents of Maimonides (as were Isserlein and Isserles) or else not philosophers of Judaism at all, but Jews who happen to be philosophers—or philosophers who happen to be Jews. Doubtless, the dissociation is incomplete, for Jewishness is rarely irrelevant. But such a philosopher as Spinoza, though he owed some inspiration to Maimonides, though, indeed, he started as an historically-minded analyst of Holy Writ, and though he speaks with a clarity and comprehensiveness worthy of his Jewish background, works so objectively in the general fields of metaphysics and epistemology that one cannot call him a Jewish philosopher.

And yet there is something Jewish about Spinoza's philosophy in the ingenuity of his synthesis. Faced with many problems, faced with all the difficulties that the Spanish thinkers had of harmonizing a logical world with an order of creation, of harmonizing a natural order with the special place of man: faced with the logical problems of the Attributes, and the difficulties of reconciling necessity and chance: and faced with the special epistemological problem, re-discovered in his age, of explaining how the mind of man works out, in its processes, truths that describe an external reality: faced with all these problems Spinoza attempted a remarkable solution. Let the whole order—the totality—be called God. Then God has two Attributes in which he can be revealed to us—the Attribute of Extension: i.e. the whole external world including our bodies: and the Attribute of Thought in which participate our knowing minds. The two orders are parallel—are aspects of the same being. Man, participating in God's thought, can look at his external self for what it is, a set of particles, in the order of Extension, viewed against a background of eternity.

That is one answer to the question. "What is man that thou shouldst remember him?"

The Spinozistic system is a wonderful approach for the philosophic mind. As a metaphysic it breaks under severe questioning. The self-conscious activity of the mind destroys the perfection of the parallelism: and there are other difficulties.[1]

From some Jewish points of view Spinozism is a form of Atheism. If Spinoza can be described as a "god-intoxicated man", his intoxication is with a spirit vastly different from the secret forces that possess the Chassidic Tsaddik in his meditations.

Spinoza becomes, then, a Jew who happens to be a non-Jewish philosopher. Yet in this respect, he only differs in degree from Moses Mendelssohn, whose introduction to philosophy was through Maimonides, but whose first

[1] From the days of his correspondent, Trendelenburg, Spinoza has been under criticism that has seemed unanswerable, but which does not deprive his way of thinking of its tremendous value. What survives is a large, impersonal outlook, which only the best philosophy achieves. As a matter of Jewish interest, it is perhaps worth mentioning that Jewish critics have done good work in this field. One of the most recent was the late Nahum Sokolow, so greatly distinguished in Jewish scholarship, Jewish literature, and Zionism.

considerable effort was a prize-winning essay on the Cartesian Theory of Knowledge, successful in competition with Immanuel Kant, and who later deduced the Immortality of the Soul on purely Platonic lines.

But Mendelssohn made considerable contributions to Judaism short of a satisfactory philosophy. Books like *Jerusalem* are general demonstrations that religion is logically possible (Judaism in particular) rather than constructive statements of a Jewish system. Mendelssohn's best contributions to Judaism are his translation of the Bible, the scholarly commentary (*BIUR*) which he organized, and to which he contributed: and not least, a wonderful personal example to a Jewry that was meeting the new European civilization. Not the least of Mendelssohn's gifts to Jewry is Lessing's *Nathan the Wise*.

Following Mendelssohn, the bulk of Jewish philosophic thought has been expressed in the valuable, but uncreative, literature of Apologetics.[1] Be it added that the Philosophy of Religion in general has become the study of Religions as forms of experience rather than of any questions that vex the religious heart.[2]

After the Spanish philosophers, then, the choice is between

---

[1] In this I would include the considerable work of Hermann Cohen, author of *Religion der Vernunft*.

[2] This seems to be the correct account of the thought of the great scholar, Martin Buber, whose concept of an I-Thou relationship is a valuable description of religious experience. (Jewish blessings commence in the second person.) But his metaphysical writings do not leave it clear whether his Deity subsists beyond the ALS OB.

Worth mentioning of nineteenth-century thinkers, are Friedlander, Jacobson and Holdheim, exponents of reform: and their great opponent Samson Raphael Hirsch. These were not concerned primarily with philosophizing in their works, but were concerned with the relative importances of the factors in traditional Judaism, the language, the ritual, the metaphysical beliefs (if any) and the land. In effect, they were historians of the group, asking where the group had arrived. Reform is

Spinoza and Kabbalah: Spinoza ingeniously using a conception of world substance (which he need not have called God—the word in his mouth is a "homonym") in order to solve a problem of cognition: and the Kabbalists, defying strict logic and, with it, the advance of verbal scepticism.

Two forces these, not so remote from each other in the ultimate (for from mysticism of one type to mysticism of another is an easy transition): but between them exorcizing, as it were, philosophic questioning from Judaism.

In the present world the debt of religion is more to Kabbalah than to strict metaphysics.

The present metaphysical position is that we find ourselves working in a world of words, examining the legitimacy of the words—as it happens, in other words!

In all languages God is a word. But does the existence of the word prove anything? To say, with the author of the Parmenides and Theaetetus, that a concept must be subsistent if the word exists, is no longer acceptable. That is, after all, an application of the ontological argument: that what must be, therefore, is. Nor is an argument from causation acceptable, because there are other theories to account for facts which used to be evidences of Design.[1] But Spiritual experience—awareness of good and evil, awareness of something in the nature of Redemption—this is at least as good a reply to the sceptic against Religion as Dr. Johnson ever made to Berkeley. (And on that no one has ever improved!)

on the whole directed against the "national" function: though some distinguish between historical "nationality" and political "nationhood". As for the religion, their work is what the modern German theologians would call *Entmythologisierung*, i.e. the rationalization of the Scriptures with more violence than the Spanish schools could command. On the whole a manifestation of the German rather than the Jewish mind.

[1] For a statement, by a great publicist, of the arguments, see the Prefaces of Bernard Shaw—to *Androcles and the Lion, Back to Methuselah* etc.—in which he discusses "Paley's Watch".

Theoretically it is possible to draw up a language—a dialect of Russian, for example—in which the word "God" does not exist. Suffice it here to say that such a language will not be Hebrew. For Hebrew enshrines experiences, which in the parts, and in the aggregate, do much to establish the abiding presence of an unseen power that makes for righteousness.[1] [2] [3]

[1] Having made it clear that philosophers who are Jews are not, by that token, exponents of the Jewish Mind, I would yet refer to the brilliant Bergson, whose *Élan Vital*, is, however, too impersonal to be divine. I would also direct special attention to the late Samuel Alexander, whose system, monistic and realistic, is of great value, and is made more interesting by his conception of Deity as something evolving in space-time—a level to be achieved. According to Alexander we have an urge to seek Divinity as an aspiration higher in the plane of Being than the affection with which an animal turns to his master. Apparently, space-time is so creative that the higher forces, to contact with which we aspire, are for ever becoming real. At this stage the master of clarity becomes mystical. But the work (*Space-Time and Deity*) is one of the great philosophical efforts of this century.

[2] I cannot conclude this chapter without observing that I have not treated, because I do not regard, the Marxist system as a philosophy. There is, in it, however, a conception of a "general" and loose determinism, which is not entirely irrelevant. As to Marx's references to Jewry, these are on the whole "negative".

[3] By way of transition to the next chapter, it may be useful to observe that no Jewish philosopher (proper) seeks to reduce the ethical position of man, or to alter the traditional Jewish conception of Right and Wrong; according to which Wrong, or Sin, is a voluntary and intentional act.

The Psalmist asks to be purified from hidden faults: and distinctions are drawn between offences and mistakes (BEMĀZID and BESHO-GEG). But wickedness could never be other than knowing, intentional, and voluntary. In this the Judaeo-Christian tradition differs from the Ancient Greek. Oedipus could not be a Jew.

CHAPTER SEVEN

JEWISH AND CHRISTIAN ETHICS

I. *The High Standards*

SAUL of Tarsus learned, at the feet of Gamaliel, that a
man should teach his son a craft.[1] That advice may have
been tendered to a nation whose agrarian life was constantly in danger, and whose citizens could quickly be made
into nomads by the vicissitudes of politics. Since then, many
generations of Jewish artisans, fiddlers, hawkers, scribes,
writers, jewellers, and traders generally in "portable
property", men living by wits and skill, have made the
advice seem prophetic.

It can also be interpreted, as the later Rabbis treated it,
as a warning against the hieratic perils of priesthood and the
law: as an attempt to preserve the law against professionalism: so that a man need not make the law into "an axe
to delve with". It is also a warning, which has never lost

---

[1] Rabban Gamaliel I (grandson of Hillel: and fl. first century B.C.E. to
first century C.E.) is referred to. His descendant, Gamaliel, the son of
Rabbi Judah, is reported in Aboth II as saying that Torah without
work is futile. This could be quoted from the older Gamaliel. There
are also Talmudic dicta that a father is reprehensible who does not
teach his son a craft. It is also held desirable to find him a wife. The
plan of life laid down in Avoth is: five years of age, Torah; ten, Mishna;
thirteen, Responsibility; fifteen, Talmud; eighteen, Marriage; twenty,
Work.

its urgency, especially for Jews, against the dangers of intellectualism.

For history has made the Jews, with or without the approval of the best of them, into the intellectuals of the world. No realm of thought exists which is not full of their works. In emancipation, intellectual activity is a manifestation of their freedom, and they rejoice in it. They ride the chariots of literacy and language. In the confines of the ghetto, in the straits of poverty, learning is an escape. And Jewish society, striving for wealth in order to bribe its persecutors into apathy (and incidentally provoking them), has also striven to make its Rabbis and men of learning into an intellectual aristocracy.[1] Therefore in every generation, and in every ghetto, the successful merchant has sought to make his sons into scholars, his daughters into the wives of scholars. So that the cynic can say that the sons of the prophets have become the sons-in-law of the profit-makers.

In reality there is something human and good in the symbiosis of the materially successful Jew and the poor scholar. It suggests that effort to raise the level of life which takes place on the Sabbath. Then the Jew, with all his faults, seems to become more human, less conscious of struggle and bitterness. Having been for six days, as Heine puts it, *"ein hund mit hündischen gedanken"*, he becomes a human being. That difference between Sabbath and the week is a symbol of the spirituality which is latent in Jewish life and which the workaday world submerges.[2]

From the standpoint of Jewish society it is arguable that, from Yavneh onwards, intellectualism has been the pre-

[1] That, indeed, was the status claimed by the Pharisees in their campaign against the King-Priest dynasties.

[2] The thought is implicit in the Kiddush, and almost expressed in the Havdalah, where it is said that: "He distinguishes between light and dark, between Israel and the nations, between Sabbath and weekday".

server and the salvation of the group. But, as well as a great blessing, intellectualism can be a great curse. So it had been in the second Kingdom—that paradise of intriguers and informers. And so it was under many other authorities. So it is whenever responsibility is borne by those whose intellect has developed out of proportion to their moral sense and their humanity. So it is, particularly, when men endowed with intellectual capacity are forced (as in every period thousands of Jews have been) to struggle with their minds in fields which are not intellectual fields: to struggle for the physical well-being of themselves and their families: to struggle in order to fulfil those ambitions whose patterns in the outside world have appealed to them. Then, instead of the custodians of the mind, they become experts in the work of the brain—and that is an altogether lower level of experience.

The Jew of brain, rather than of mind, has been treated as the villain (not merely victim) of modern Europe. He comes from the "small-town" with wits sharpened by learning, or by the sharp thinking of the communities that value learning; sharpened further by need and energy. He struggles without restraint, even without humour; for restraint and humour can only develop easily in happy surroundings—in emancipation, or in the (rare) acceptance of the spiritual life.[1]

The shrewdness and crudeness of these brains, desperately

[1] Humour is found among Jews, and is in evidence among Rabbis and Jewish writers. But more frequent among the Jews is wit, which is a weapon of defence and of aggression. Intellect, however, is capable of irony without bitterness. In judging Jews, in this connexion, it is important to remember that there is education in humour: and that many Jews come from areas where life is hard and competition keen, and the people amongst whom they grew up were mentally unyielding and ungenerous. Let it be added that a habit system in the nature of acquisitiveness (becoming greed) is cognate to humourlessness. See p. 376 infra, et seq.

directed to profit-making and becoming too good at it, and too enthusiastic, are often alleged to be causes of justifications of anti-Semitism. That is not true. The anti-Semite, in the spirit of the hater, hates virtues not vices. If he envies the success of others, he envies the result rather than despises the means. But the unhappy consequence that matters is the effect on the spirit of the Jew and on his world. Learning from the Gentile the ways of commerce, he "betters the instruction". Learning the fierce games of materialism, he brings added skill to the play. Learning a cynical hedonism, he becomes a greater hedonist. Then he creates, with Gentile material, such golden calves as abound in the hills of Hollywood, and with them corrupts his corrupter. Therewith he does not cause anti-Semitism. Indeed the wealth of the Jew well spent, and his strength well exercised, have protected the ghetto walls of Spain, France, England, Russia, all the countries of the Western world. But these forces also help to maintain in being a world of materialists who, at any moment, can revert to the savagery which lies so little below the skin surface of the European.

If this were all, it would be enough. A subtler danger to the Jewish spirit (and with it the world of culture) is from the good Jewish student. The temptation to the spirit of the modern scholar with the mental equipment of Maimonides is to make the Jewish value into "an axe to delve with" and Science an end in itself. Parents who loved the dedication of the son to Torah love now his devotion to Science (also "for its own sake", and not merely as a trade). In that order of intellectual activity the danger is of a scepticism, an ethical neutrality, a godlessness, a loss of humanity; or of a superficial sentimentality, which is equally dangerous to the human spirit.

In Biblical terms, the brain (in the Bible called the Heart)[1]

[1] The brain as an organ of intellection is known to the Rabbis, many of whom were expert in Greek medicine.

can lead its possessor into idolatry. In Talmudic terms, these ways of thought make a man responsible for the destruction of his own spirit. In modern terms, they generate cynicism and materialism. Jewish ethics, at all periods, and however differently stated, is concerned to guard the human being against a selfishness, a narrowness of sympathy, a hardness, that Jews have always known to be the moral dangers of their over-intellectual race.

Two men were honoured by the Rabbis, if no third. One was the ordinary citizen, the Baal Habayith, the pious head of his household: and the other was the scholar acquiring learning for its own sake. In a happy society these two preserved a moral balance and ensured the continuance of the righteous life.[1] But that harmony was hard to maintain. The student isolates himself from the ordinary, and the ordinary sinks into the ignorant. Chover,[2] associate of the learned, stands in contrast, and hostility, to the Am-Haaretz the ignoramus. Neither of these is the proper custodian of the ethical system, because, in different ways, both these types, however fortified with honesty, can fail in the apprehension of the spiritual, fail in the perception of the good human values.

The Rabbis knew the faults of the ignoramus: that he is not to be trusted with the confidence of the spiritual man. The latter he regards, at the outset, almost superstitiously, as a "golden vessel". But once he sees that he is only a man, he devalues him to the value of earthenware. The ignoramus

---

[1] The saying that Rabbi Judah honoured the rich may be criticism: or may be a description of his magnanimity. There is a Jewish tradition that the poor man (like the blind) is comparable to the dead. ONI CHOSHUV KEMAYTH. Since CHOSHUV ("is reckoned") also means "worthy", punsters have said: "The worthy poor man is as good as dead". A more cynical, Talmudic, utterance is that "Silver purifies Bastards".

[2] A technical term among the Pharisees, and still used to denote the student of Rabbinics.

cannot be a saintly man.[1] Some would even deny him the Kingdom of Heaven.

But in those days, as now, the ignorant among the Jews bore clever children, as the learned bore unruly ones. There were foxes sons of lions, as well as lions sons of foxes. "Vinegar, son of wine" is a Talmudic epithet which suggests that intellectual aristocracy is not invariably a transmitted quality. Yichus[2] becomes corrupt in careerism, and maintains no advantage over CHUTZPAH. Very modern sounding (and rich in irony) is the Talmudic opinion of careerists. "Do not appoint a warden for your congregation, unless he has a bunch of snakes hanging behind him. Then, if his conceit rises, you can say to him: 'Look behind you'." (T.B. Yoma 22b.) That teaching might have been uttered in any modern, semi-emancipated, community: and has been fulfilled in many of those seething melting-pots in which the scum rises to the surface.

The only career that is relatively safe against the stigma of "careerism" is the study of the Torah. Even if one starts it not for its own sake, eventually the study will be continued for its own sake. So it is said in a well-known Mishna.[3] The same thought was uttered by a Chassidic Rabbi of the nineteenth century. When it was questioned whether Tsaddikim (Holy Men), whose title had become hereditary, could be genuinely religious, he replied: "Ask the tight-

---

[1] (Avoth). This saying is, however, susceptible to another translation, viz. that the saintly man cannot be ignorant. Observe, also (from the same source, Avoth) the compensating dictum addressed by Chanina ben Dotha to the learned. "If his good works do not exceed his cleverness, his cleverness will not prevail".

[2] Literally "connexion": a word used to connote "good family".

[3] There is another Talmudic text to the effect that a person who studies etc. not for the sake of the task itself had better not been born. But this clearly refers to purposive materialistic exploitation, unaccompanied by any regard for the subject-matter.

rope walker whether he is really doing what he seems to do, or whether he is only pretending".[1]

Nevertheless, the Rabbis knew the dangers of professional intellect, and warned against it, as we have seen. Moreover, the bulk of Jewish ethics is calculated to keep the clever man from the selfishness—or the dangers of self-centredness—that can accompany intellectual activity.

The devotee of the law must be humble like Moses. That pride goes before a fall was a platitude of Biblical thought. The Rabbis gave to the decencies of theory a practical application. It was wrong to scoff at the less learned. That was "laughing at the poor". On the same principle, one does not display "fringes" in a graveyard; the dead cannot fulfil that ritual.

Tact was valued highly. No mention of rope in the house of the hanged.[2] When Rab Jochanan threw in the teeth of Resh Lakish a reference to his past—"He is a robber,[3] therefore he knows the details of arms"—he was considered to have done a great wrong, and was not forgiven.[4]

Because of the proneness of man to wrong, he must be always repentant. "Repent one day before your death". As the day of death is never known— is always tomorrow— it follows that every day is a day of Repentance. Moreover, Repentance, in Jewish theory, is not verbal only—not an

[1] More convincing answers as provided by their acceptance of martyrdom in the Second World War.

[2] To this day, the pronouncing Rabbi says: "not KOSHER": and refrains from saying "unclean" (TRAYF, etc.).

[3] There are two theories of Resh Lakish's past. Consistently with this Talmudic text, he was a brigand in early life. According to Graetz and Weiss he was a student who became, under pressure of need, an arena performer—a gladiator. It may well be that such performers were suspect of brigandry.

[4] The Almighty, Himself, is said to have been criticized by the Angels for involving the Patriarchs in rebukes uttered through Isaiah—against a dictum in the Book of Proverbs.

empty expression of Regret. Repentance is TESHUVAH
—Returning (from bad ways into good ways). It is something that cannot be fulfilled by lip-service.

The underlying principle common to Biblical, and all
Rabbinic, thought is charity. Charity is, perhaps, the most
developed abstract idea in the concrete Bible. Many words
indicate its varieties,[1] for charity, for the Jews, covers a wide
range and has many subtleties.

Charity is, *inter alia*, something that differentiates righteousness from legal justice. The good Jew must not stand
upon his literal rights: especially if there is open the criticism
that he has taken advantage of a workman, or someone who
was driven into a hard bargain.[2] By the same token (and this
law is unique among all codes) the Judge must not give
preference to the poor man because he is poor; but must
apply the law and the equity relevant to the case. To the
facts of the case the poverty of the litigant may be relevant.
But the judgement must not be determined by a sentiment:
otherwise the work of the Judge is self-indulgence.

Rights, however, must be tolerantly asserted. The Jew is
distinguished from the son of Noah, who takes life for
defaults of infinitesimal value. In contrast the Jew abhors
the taking of life even justly: and the capital law of
the Jews was so hedged round with restrictions as to be
impracticable.[3]

---

[1] For a parallel reason, there are also many words to describe the
varieties of the poor. Dal, Evion, Oni, Rosh, etc. More modern is
Kabtsan (from an origin suggesting "scrounger"). There are also many
words to denote sin: and a large number to denote the varieties of fool.

[2] There is a law abrogating bargains which caused an undue enrichment, and which would be valid on the Roman, and modern, principle
caveat emptor. But let it not be supposed that Jewish ethics are im-
measurably in advance of the Gentile (who gets his Ethics from Judaism, of course). Jews held slaves in the days of slavery. In U.S.A.
they were to be found on both sides of the famous campaign.

[3] Some allowance must be made, from this judgement, in the light of

Away from the tribunal, and where the law imposed no express duties, the ethical precepts of the Rabbis were entirely charitable. It is significant that the Hebrew word that is used to mean Justice (TZEDAKAH) is the accepted word, to this day, for Charity. Charity is legally right, in all its many manifestations.

the fact that the Talmudic authorities speak from times considerably later than any period when the Sanhedrins functioned autonomously.

According to Talmudic accounts of Sanhedrin practice, a criminal could not be sentenced to death unless his crime was witnessed by two witnesses (later attesting together) and unless his act followed HATH-ROAH—a warning. Evidently this made the death penalty a rarity. But murderers etc. against whom the evidence and formalities were inadequate (an instance given is the man standing by the body with the dripping knife in his hand) were kept in captivity and given food and drink calculated to cause fatal distensions.

There is some reason to believe that Sanhedrins were not squeamish. We learn that Simeon ben Shotach, the Pharisee brother-in-law of King Alexander Jannaeus, hanged eighty harlots (possibly "witches"), and that another Rabbi dissected some hanged harlots and counted their anatomical constituents (according to the analyses of that period), finding 251. (A dissected male showed 248.)

Maimonides makes it clear that Jewish tradition does not hold the life of the wicked sacrosanct. On the other hand, when a Rabbi is quoted as saying that you may take an Am-Haaretz (probably meaning what we call a Sadducee) and gut him like a fish, even on a Yom Kippur which falls on the Sabbath, the comment of Lazarus is probably correct: that this is Talmudic rhodomontade. (Cf. Rabbi Akiva's statement: "When I was an Am-Haaretz (Sadducee?) I would take a Rabbi and bite him as if I were an ass. An ass, not a dog, because the teeth of an ass break bones".)

Of Bible times, we have seen that the commentators treat the Bible characters as peaceful and long suffering. But nothing can conceal that there were capital penalties, possibly castration (KORUTH?), and great slaughters in war. The last can be extenuated as part of a struggle for survival. A learned writer (Ben-Zvi) has suggested that the wrath against Amalek was due to the fact that the Amalekites were cognate Hyksos, escaping also from Egypt, competing bitterly for what oases the wilderness afforded, and aiming at Canaan.

273

The aged must be respected: and a man that has lost his mental powers must still sit in the seat of honour. Rabbi José, who suffered amnesia, used to say that he valued the Festival of Pentecost—the Festival of the giving of the Law—for, in connection with that day, we are told that not only the new tablets of the law, but the old broken tablets, were carried in the Ark.[1] Similarly, if a person had lived delicately, and then had fallen into poverty, the charity extended to him must be calculated to restore to him something of the comfort to which he had been accustomed. (If he was used to riding on a horse, a horse should be provided for him.) From Bible text, and simple exegesis, we know that the poor must be treated with compassion: the workman must not be kept waiting for his wages, or deprived of his perquisites: the gleaner must not be made to suffer through over-enthusiastic harvesting.

This is Biblical law. But through Talmudic, and all later, times the accepted principles of charity expanded, did not diminish. Not without significance is the word PARNASS. This (the lay leader of the community) is *Pronoos*, the Provider. His colleagues are GABBAI and GIZBOR, collectors—*inter alia* of Charity. In medieval communities they organized two funds and modes of distribution: the KUPPAH or Charity box, out of which every Friday the needy were paid sufficient for the requirements of the Sabbath and the following week: also the TAMCHUI, a provision of food and money for the itinerant poor. Never, be it added, did the existence of these funds relieve the individual from his own personal duty to give charity when required, KEMATNATH YODO, to the full extent of his capacity to give.

But charity does not stop at alms giving. The weak must

---

[1] According to other traditions another Ark. Rabbi José said: "If not for this day how many Josés would there be in the market place".

be helped. Children treated kindly.[1] The imbecile and the idiot must be protected: the sick visited. Animals must be well treated. The castration of animals was forbidden. They must also be fed. Rabbi Ishmael used to feed his camel before he took food for himself.[2] Neither man nor beast should be overburdened: the old and the learned should not be allowed to carry loads. One's own body should not be unworthily used. The extreme of delicacy is reached in the modern (seventeenth-century) code of duties. If a man puts on his left shoe first, he must fasten the right one first, because it is wrong to show preference for one part of the body over another.[3]

It is clear from these things that the Rabbis used keen intellect—the fine discrimination of their casuistry—in order to prescribe the refinements of generosity. The ethical case is a particular case; exceptional: the ethical rule must, therefore, be a subtle one.

They were opposed to all Oneia—all undue advantage—and were sharp to see its possibilities. To do a favour was a Mitzvah (a commandment—in later usage, the fulfilment of a commandment). To benefit from having done the favour was improper. The Jewish prohibition of interest is one single case—and a very strict case—of this general principle: and, independently, a law against cruelty.

Therefore there is a great tragic irony in the history of compulsion of circumstances, and the explicit commands of overlords and feudal princes, which combined to make

[1] The Biblical evidence is of a severe patriarchalism in which the rebellious son was a social problem. The severe treatment of children, counselled in Proverbs, is not Jewish tradition. If Jews, in some environments, treat women or children badly, it will be found that the practice is that of the land where they are living.

[2] It is reported in Baba Mezia (85a) that Rabbi Judah suffered for ten years because he had failed to save a kid escaping from the slaughter.

[3] This is, incidentally, a good example of the subtle intellectualism in which the Jews have been trained.

Jews at one period into Publicans (Tax Farmers) and at other times into usurers.[1] Even the dramatist who started to exploit a stage Jew, and found himself crucifying a human being, failed fully to appreciate (what was seen by the simple woman quoted by Heine) that the story of the Merchant is a tragedy: that "the poor man had been wronged".

Certainly the cruel usurer exists, among Jews as among Gentiles, but he exists in utter antagonism to every Jewish tradition. The un-Jewishness of the practice is recognized among traditionalist Jews, even though the usurer follows orthodox Jewish ritual in his daily life. When Shakespeare described Shylock as a Synagogue frequenter, he was writing only too truly. What he did not know was that the Synagogue would not value him. For that matter, Justification by Ritual is not a Jewish monopoly. Religions which have any reality must be judged by their high standards, not by the low levels, not even by the average, of conduct.

Exploitation of all sorts is against Jewish ethics: even the exploitation of an enemy. Certainly the Bible records horrible atrocities: but those are directed to the enemy of the nation, the enemy that threatens the group survival. The individual enemy must not be ill-treated. His animal must be rescued. The Rabbis go further. If you have a choice between helping a friend in trouble, and helping an enemy, you must help the enemy first; because only that is true

[1] One of the occasions of compulsion was a Papal Bull (of 1119 C.E.) which declared moneylending to be illegal for Christians. This, like the canon law, seems to have been based on a misreading of Luke VI.35. Eventually the Lombards found ways of evading the canon law. But the Bishops and Princes forced finance upon the Jews. Of Talmudic times, an amusing story (T.B.B.M. 84b) is told about a Rabbi who advised a Roman officer how to recognize thieves. (Men half asleep sitting in an inn.) The officer said: "You who can read, carry out the instructions", and forced him to act as an informer. This caused the Rabbi great distress of mind, from which he never recovered.

disinterestedness: an obedience to the categorical imperative "be righteous".[1]

Apart from the duty not to injure one's enemy, it is also laid down (in Scripture) that his downfall must not be the subject of rejoicing. The Hallel, say the Rabbis, must not be recited on the later days of the Passover, because God does not rejoice in the death of the Egyptians, who were, after all, His creatures.

From the scope of all principles of charity and forbearance, the alien, the non-Jew, is not excluded. The duty of the Jew is to pray for the welfare of the state in which he lives. He must be kind to the Gentiles, and cause them to praise the Jewish God. From the Rabbinic standpoint to rob or deceive a Gentile is exactly equivalent to robbing or deceiving a Jew. (It is said that one who deceives a Gentile will end by deceiving a Jew.) One must not treat badly even a hostile heathen. One must not hate.[2]

That one must not hate, that one must receive the whole world favourably: these express a positive attitude to life which the intellectual understands, but which the intellectual also finds it hard to adopt. The countryman is better able to contemplate life without hostility than is the townsman: but he is less likely to have achieved sufficient knowledge of the ways of the world to enable him to understand people: less likely to have achieved mental freedom from the difficulties of day to day. The irony of Jewish ethics is

[1] Not all Jewish ethical pronouncements, it should be added, are so Kantian in their implications. In some instances the formal Good was held good, even if the motive was "interested".

Let it be borne in mind that many dicta of fanciful altruism, whether in Talmud, New Testament, or later ethical writings, can legitimately be held suspect as utterances of pedantry or charlatanry.

[2] The Biblical battles, in which, and after which, enemies were slaughtered, express the needs of war: express a group attempt to eradicate the sources of evil. But the individual, if he hates, must hate evil as such, separating, if possible, the other from the evil in him.

that simple hearts can obey them: only sophisticated minds
be sure of their truth. And so outside Jewry: such a thinker
as Tolstoy achieved the recognition of the artist's need
for a love of life and of all that is living, but in his own life
he was unable to express the thought in action. Similarly,
Jewish and Christian education teaches these things, and
people learn them in words. But there are few who can
behave always so that a doctrine of love is manifest in
their deeds.

It must be clear, from any statement of Jewish precepts,
that there is no essential difference between them and the
ethical teachings attributed to Jesus. The ethical doctrines
of the Pharisee Rabbis and those of the Essene (who was
an extremist Pharisee) have everything in common, including the adventitious quality that they are the objects
of popular disobedience.

The fundamental distinction between Judaism and Christianity is that the Jew is pledged to the Second Commandment.[1] This is a theological or metaphysical difference,[2]
though it may lead to ethical consequences. Alone among
Western religions Judaism does not set its faith in a man.
Moses sinned and died. The law given through Moses was
the law of God, not the Mosaic law. The Jewish law, then,
is capable of an objectivity and a universality which the
creeds of Jesus and Mohammed—even the creeds bound up
with the personalities of Buddha and Confucius—cannot
perfectly achieve.[3]

[1] Jesus never quotes the first four Commandments as they are stated
in Exodus and Deuteronomy.

[2] The Christian theologians, who regard the Old Testament as *Pros-
toa* to the New, fail to recognize that the only valid difference between the two literatures is one of metaphysics rather than of ethics.

[3] It should be noted that the Jews have no traditional hostility to
Jesus, but rather a reticence about him. His name is not mentioned
because of the claim to Divinity, and because of the terrible associations
that the Church militant has driven into the Jewish consciousness. He is

As to principles of conduct, there is such an identity of thought between Jesus and the Jewish Essenes, at least, that

sometimes referred to as Joshua Pantera—on the basis of a story that he was born to a Roman soldier. (Pantera is a corruption of the Greek word for shield.) But this is not Jewish teaching. The Talmud makes reference to him (That Man) as suffering in Purgatory in circumstances unconjured by Dante, and from there uttering words in favour of his people (Gittin, 57—omitted in some editions of the Talmud). A collection of Talmudic passages censored by the Papacy, and later published under the title Chesronoth HaShass, includes many strange and crude items, which probably, for the most part, were not intended to refer to Jesus, but have been thought by ignorant Jews and Gentiles to do so. Certainly they lack all value as history of the man or the period.

A Jewish scholar, Dr. Joseph Klausner, has written what is probably the best account of the life and times of Jesus that has ever been penned. Klausner praises him for his skill in the Jewish art of parable. Indeed he ingeniously interprets "a man having authority" (an unlikely epithet) to "a man of parables" (reading Hebrew MŌSHOL instead of MŌSHOL).

That same Dr. Klausner has demonstrated that an account of Joshua ben Perachya's anathematizing of a pupil named YISHU, for being sensual, is a late, and therefore worthless, Amoraic (because Aramaic) gloss on one obscure BARAITHA. The Hebrew substance that is left after analysis—that Joshua ben Perachya pushed YISHU away with both hands—is too cryptic to be of value.

From difficult material such as this, Jewish medieval writers produced collections of stories calculated to devalue the Nazarene. A better historical approach is one suggested in the modern story, Procurator of Judaea, which reduces the whole narrative to an episode unimportant and unnoticed at the time when it took place.

That the Jews crucified Jesus is a false accusation which has exposed millions of Jews to the most un-Christian violence. But it is historically interesting in that here is one case—one of far too many—in which Jews have allowed Gentile forces to intercede in their domestic affairs, and take action against the leaders of unpopular—however harmless—groups. So Chassidim have suffered at all periods.

In this book, incidentally, I treat Jesus analogously to a Chassid, though it is not clear that he was officially a member of that party or sect. But much of his behaviour, e.g. his celibacy and his views on divorce, suggest that he was a sectary of that type.

ignorance of it is almost ununderstandable. Allowing for the human fact that familial hates are the keenest, it would yet be incredible to an objective observer that for centuries the leaders of Christianity found, in their belief in the superiority of their doctrine of love, justification for causing the repeated decimation of Jewish populations by the acceptors of the Gospel.

The principle that Jesus emphasized in his Judaism (for, of all Christians, Jesus himself was a Jew) is the precept: love thy neighbour as thyself. This is Old Testament doctrine. Some of his thought is inconsistent with this precept. There is evidence in Jesus' teaching of a monasticism, an asceticism, which the modern psychologist would describe as ungenerous or inhuman. A good Jew may sell his goods and give the proceeds to the poor, but he does not abandon his family in order to follow a spiritual leader. Nor did Jewish Priests, nor Jewish Rabbis, live as anchorites. "Increase and multiply" is Torah. Nor was it necessary for men to be childless in order to become Fathers of the Jewish Church.

A modern Jewish philosophical essayist (Asher Ginzberg), who was educated in the ways of Peshat, has emphasized that the Jew is told to love his neighbour *as* himself—not more than he loves himself; and argues that only that way can a universal, objective, system of law and ethics be achieved. To attempt to love the neighbour more than oneself is to make ethics a subjective fantasy.[1]

---

[1] One ingenious comment on Veohavto lerayacho komocho is that, in the sense of "as yourself", komocho is not as direct as keatsmecho. The argument is that the text means "love him as [you want him to love] yourself".

Interesting, too, is a distinction, observed by Nachmanides, and developed by the nineteenth century philosophic commentator, Samson Raphael Hirsch. He points out that "love thy neighbour" (LERAYACHO) is expressed with the dative: "love thy God" is expressed with the accusative (ET HASHEM). Therefore "be loving *towards* your neighbour". He may be unamiable. But be ready with a kind attitude.

Perhaps the issue is verbal. Perhaps love is impossible without self-oblivion; or to love a neighbour as oneself may even be the psychological maximum—and the neighbour, in the same creed, asks for less. But if the practical question is put: "What precept of Jesus puts a higher interpretation on the doctrine of love than do the Rabbis?", the answer can confidently be given that there is none: that there is no ethical teaching of Jesus (good or bad) which is not a statement, or an echo, of some Rabbinic tradition.[1]

It has been argued, against this thesis, that when Hillel was asked to state the Jewish law in one sentence, he said, "What is hateful to thee, do not do to another", whereas Jesus said, "Do unto others what you would have others do unto you". Perhaps this distinction, too, is verbal. But, lest anything turn upon the antithesis, let it be made clear that Hillel—a lawyer, living in days when people were beginning to distinguish between law and ethics—was stating the law.[2] Ethical law, unlike abstract Ethics, cannot

[1] This was demonstrated in detail by Rabbi Maseh of Moscow to Leo Nikolaevitch Tolstoy. A modern scholar, Dr. Daube, has worked out, in his Jordan lectures, a most impressive set of analogies between the thought, style, and language of the N.T. and the Rabbinic idiom and thought of the period. He goes far (giving scope to the "Maggid Manqué" that is in so many Jews) when he suggests that the Rabbis contemplated a virgin birth for Moses. Incidentally, many N.T. phrases are also Talmudic, e.g. "Remove the beam from thine own eye" (Baba Bathra), and "pass through the eye of a needle". "The eye of a needle" (KUPPAH DE MACHTEH) was the name of a pass near Jerusalem. The Talmudic expression is: "bring an elephant through the eye of a needle!"

[2] T.B. Shabbos 31a. Hillel's epigrammatic statement, given in answer to a challenge (to state the essence of the law while standing on one leg), is a very subtle one. "What is hateful to thee" connotes not only positive malpractice, but all failure to express a high standard. E.g. In the light of dicta of Hillel in Avoth, it would be an unpleasant thing not to co-operate with the community, not to be charitable (in all senses of the word), not to value learning, etc. Applying similar reasoning to the

lay down a principle of complete self-abnegation. The law lays down duties calculated to harmonize the life of a community, and to prevent the social and economic interests of individual persons from clashing in violence. Hillel may, then, have been stating the ethical minimum desiderendum, because he was stating the legal normal; and, that, a higher standard than Ulpian's statement, *sic utere tuo ut alienum non laedas*.[1] But inside the Jewish law we find recurring the doctrine that the Jew must not stand upon the letter; that he must do more than his duty. The Jewish law recognizes that the duty of man is ethical—not merely legal. "Righteousness, righteousness shalt thou pursue", just as earthly honour must not be pursued. In the detailed statement of duty in particular situations the Rabbis are not less advanced than Jesus in generosity, in submissiveness, in self-abnegations, in all the varieties of altruism.

"Thy friend has called thee an ass: lower thy back to be loaded."[2] Help your enemy rather than your friend, so that you shall surely be acting righteously. This has already been quoted: and there is no dearth of available examples to show that the Gospels hold no monopoly in doctrines of altruism.

On the other hand, as Ginzberg has pointed out, so great

New Testament dictum, it is surely reasonable to suppose that Jesus had in mind Righteousness, rather than exceptional altruism, as the conduct that one expects from a fellow man. Against the historical background, it seems that the Pharisee and the Chassid were uttering identical thoughts.

[1] The effect of which has been much mitigated by interpretation of the notion of injury. In the same way that Ulpian's dictum has been "strictly" interpreted by lawyers, so some of the Jewish lawyers tried to give a specific, relatively narrow, reference to "love thy neighbour as thyself". For example, they grounded in it the duty to bury the dead (even the executed dead) decently.

[2] (A "popular saying" quoted in B.K. 92a). This has been interpreted, by some scholars, as meaning that a man should accept the confident assertions of his fellows: "If they say he is drunk, he must go to bed".

an altruist as Akiva—a man who sacrificed his own life for the community in circumstances that called for great heroism—would not approve of an unworldly, excessively unselfish, interpretation of the verse "thou shalt love thy neighbour as thyself". If two men are alone in a desert, and one has enough water to enable him to escape from the desert, but not enough for two, Ben Petura thought that they should share it and die. Akiva held that one should use it and live.[1] "Your brother shall live with you"—not die with you, not live in preference to you.[2] Akiva realized that a system of ethics must also be a system of life. The Jew is required to be merciful: "merciful son of the merciful": and RACHMONOH—merciful—is a name given to the Torah (and to the Divine Spirit). But mercy is not the tolerance of evil, or a refusal to terminate, if necessary, the lives of evil people. Did Jesus think otherwise? If Jesus really departs from Akiva's Judaism[3], then he only does so in so far as he moves into an ascetic, mystical, other-worldism. This is not un-Jewish in the sense that it breaks Jewish law. But it is not the best Jewish tradition. Nor, be it suggested, is it the practical tradition of active Christianity. Thus, against the invasion of enemies, Jews and Christians fight. Even the "passive resistance" of the Hindu falls short of complete surrender to the forces of wickedness. When trials are held of wicked men, of men who murdered six million, no Christian or Jew who values civilization can afford to speak of forbearance. That there are men who do so is equivalent to the statement that, as there are villains, so there are idiocies that encourage villainies. Very apt is the

---

[1] The third possibility—give the water to the other—does not solve the problem, because the other lives according to the same ethics.

[2] But a Jew must refuse to kill another, even to save his own life. "Is his blood different in quality from yours?" asked Rovo when the question was put to him.

[3] I.e. the long accepted standards: stated later by Akiva.

Rabbinic epigram: those who start by being compassionate to the cruel, end by being cruel to the compassionate.

Without cynicism it may be said that Jewish tradition, in so far as it departs from Christian altruism (which few Christians practise), is a tradition of realism and common sense. Altruism, when it is not charlatanry, can be something so vague that in it valuations are lost. To love everybody is to love nobody. Not to hate may be psychologically desirable: but indignation, and the recognition of evil for what it is, must be expressed in the mind of anyone who values the Right and the Good. If, in modern times, Jewish psychologists, by confusing causes with their effects, have contributed to the belief that no one is really bad, and if Jewish publicists (many of them "tough merchants" in their ordinary lives) proclaim doctrines of pacifism and forgiveness, they are not—with their "economism" and "psychologism"—contributing much positive guidance to a world in which the troops of Midian prowl endlessly. They are departing from the best Jewish tradition, in the degree that they are departing from the realistic. If their claim is to that development of Judaism which Jesus expresses, they are carrying further than the Nazarene the practice of "turning the other cheek". Not in this way are money-changers driven from the Temple. Not in this way is the world rescued from Amalek.

In contrast, the Jewish tradition, and much Christian tradition, is realistic and wise even while it directs the mind away from the obsessions of reality: away from bitterness and hate, to acceptance and affection. Thus the prayer that was added to the Amidah runs as follows, "And to the Defamers let there be no hope: and let all the *wickedness* be immediately lost." This prayer refrains from bitter malediction against those who deserve it. But that leaves us far from loving them. The hateful conduct, at least, is to be hated. Perhaps the essence of the matter is that the notion of love is in danger of being cheapened by a verbal process of inflation.

The Jewish tradition is a generous law-abidingness, with an emphasis on the values of the mind. Within Judaism there have been many manifestations of mysticism and ecstasy: but movements so inspired have not lasted as long as the main Rabbinic tradition. That tradition is realistic, urbane, domestic, sober.[1]

If it be said that, in the Jewish theocratic system, children are overvalued[2] and women undervalued, let it be observed that in that respect Judaism is far from inferior to orthodox Christianity: which is, in those matters, a reversion to Judaism as it was before Hillel: even to Sadduceanism.[3]

Certainly the traditional law allows the Jewish woman less initiative than it allows to the male. But in Rabbinic times

---

[1] Self-controlled, rather than ascetic. (Asceticism is frequently a confession of weakness.)

The Jews are traditionally sober in the specific context of drinking and eating: excesses in these are un-Jewish excesses. "Economy for the belly: luxury for the back." (Ostentation rather than gluttony—if you must have a vice!) As for wine, the Jew is not forbidden to drink, but there seems to be a tradition of moderation. If, on Purim, a Jew is allowed to get so drunk as not to be able to distinguish between "Blessed be Mordekhai" and "Cursed be Haman", it must be pointed out that that is no very great confusion! That may be the subtle point of the instruction. (It is also remarkable that BARUKH MORDEKHAI is numerically equivalent to ARUR HOMON!)

[2] A favourite theme of Jewish homilists is that the Law was given, not because of the Patriarchs, not because of Priests, Levites, or People, or Moses himself, but because of the children. There is some elaborate Midrash to this effect.

[3] This is an instance of a philosophic phenomenon: that, in extremes Essene and Sadducee become nearer to each other than Essene and Pharisee.

One of the consequences of the ascetical standpoint of Jesus is his strange attitude to women, which has the consequence that Pharisaic divorce law moved more quickly (though not far) towards the emancipation of women than did Christianity.

we know that women were treated with very great respect. "His home, that means his wife" is well-known doctrine. But, though her advice might be taken her voice should not be heard. ("A voice in woman is an immodesty".) It must be admitted that the woman was not an equal.[1] To have a daughter was to be unfortunate. Bar Kapporah says that the world must contain tanners as well as spice-vendors: but who would be a tanner? To avoid the danger of any claim of female equality, it is advised that a man should "go down a step and take a wife". Nor is her education encouraged. "Who teaches his daughter Torah teaches her nonsense", says R. Eliezer, and the comment is that it would make her cunning rather than wise. But, for all those denigrations, she was valued, protected. The school of Hillel, while not giving women the initiative in Divorce, made it possible for the Rabbis to compel the husband to divorce an unhappy wife. After the Exile, Jewish life became practically monogamous: and, in Europe, that tendency was turned into law by the pronouncement of Rabbenu Gershom. But, this being said, it must be added that Jewry is very imitative of Gentile life. "*Wie es Christelt sich, so es Judelt sich.*" The Sheitel, the hideous wig with which Ashkenazic Jewish married women are accustomed to hide their hair, is a product of medieval convent Christianity (and of village caution), not of traditional Judaism; one of the effects on Judaism of medieval example and oppression.

Nevertheless, it would be no service to Jewry to pretend (as many apologists do) that the Jewish woman enjoys a position in life consistent with the full value of her personality. If now she enjoys power and influence, this fact is due to the spirit of the age, not to halachic tradition. By halachic

[1] Her very marriage took place under these strange auspices: that she should be married on a Wednesday, because the Sanhedrin was available on Thursdays, to hear any complaint that the husband might bring. (T.B. Ket. 2.)

tradition, men thank the Lord that He "did not make them women (or slaves, or idolators)". (Women, if they pray, thank the Lord for making them "according to His will".) Woman is deprived of many privileges, which are the Jewish duties. Woman is exempt from most of the ritual laws: has few duties except the domestic.[1] The Jewish woman's place, consequently, has been the place that was

[1] Of positive duties she has three: lighting the Sabbath candles, separating a portion of the Challah, and maintaining her menstrual cleanliness by bathing. A Mishna says that failure to fulfil these duties is a cause of death in childbirth. Other laws that she obeys—the observance of Sabbath, etc.—are stateable as prohibitions rather than positive duties (not to work, not to kindle fire, etc.). As to positive duties, in a Sugya in Kiddushin the principle is laid down that woman is exempt from all duties for which a time is set. This distinction is a hard one and it is not clear why women pray. Being, presumably, preoccupied with children and husband, she is not obliged to don fringes or Tefillin, although the time for this MITSVAH can be a period of six hours or more. When one bears in mind that she must observe Sabbath and Festivals (including Fasts), that she must light the candles, separate the dough, go to ritual baths, it seems that the principle of "set time" is an unrealistic test. This formula, it is submitted here, is nothing more than a rationalization. One legal doctrine that is relevant, but not exhaustive, is that, in the interpretation of the Bible, what positive obligation is laid down in the masculine does not bind the feminine. Unlike the British Statute of Interpretations the Jewish rule is that (except where the context determines otherwise) masculine does not include feminine. That rule, qualified by the postulate that the prohibitions—Thou Shalt not—do bind women (so that they must keep—i.e. not break—the Sabbath), affords an explanation of the exoneration of Jewish females from many duties (such as the laying of Tefillin) stated in the masculine. That these were never extended to the female is consistent with her inferiority of status. Of the Sabbath it was suggested that the two precepts, "observe" and "remember", (Ex. and Deut.), were uttered in one utterance precisely so that all aspects of the Sabbath, as if rendered in prohibitory form, shall bind women. (This is, incidentally, a real example of legal purpose in speculative exegesis.) Very interesting is the rule, stated in Shulkhan Arukh, that a woman *can* be called to the Reading of the Law: but that her modesty must prevent her from complying.

proper to woman at a level of civilization where she was not regarded as a companion to man in a spiritual sense.[1] The growth of a romantic conception of womanhood, and later the recognition of her equality, when all other statuses were being equalized, these belong to a late European history which is not reflected in Halacha. The normal of Jewish life, as of many old orders, was for long ages, the prepared Shidduch,[2] in which children were not coerced, but were apt to yield to parental wishes. The criterion was social dignity. This tradition produces a multitude of happy unions. But in such a tradition claims to freedom (and separate estate) are not conceived.

Granted that there have been eminent Jewish women. Seven prophetesses to rank with forty-eight prophets.[3] Evidently, in Bible times, a woman was more than a chattel. God tells Abraham to hearken to Sarah. We know also that the Kings treated their women courteously. ESHETH CHAYIL—the wife of character—is an ornament to her husband. If a man finds such a one, he finds something good (Proverbs: passim). Deborah and Chuldah (The Bee and the Polecat) are figures inconsistent with a life in which women were enslaved. There were Jewish heroines; a Jewish Queen. In Hellenic times, the figure of Imma Shalom

[1] It is doubtful whether the Scriptor, who describes a wife as "a helpmate over against him" contemplated the egalitarian and humorous interpretations that have been put on these words.

Even in Classical Greece, although we hear of Hetaerae (mistress companions) the writings (e.g. Plato's *Symposium*) indicate that men found their companionship with men. Hence Hellenic homosexuality.

[2] God is described as a selector of pairs.

[3] *See* Megillah 15. The list includes Hannah. She said: "My horn is exalted". Say the Rabbis, "My horn, not my cruse": Saul and Jehu (cruse-anointed) did not prevail: David (horn-anointed) prevailed. The implication of this Drash is that prophecy entailed foresight: which is not the case. Incidentally, the Targum to Samuel, attributed to Jonathan ben Uzziel, interpolates in the text a list of Hannah's visions as she prayed: visions extending to the triumph of the Hashmoneans.

suggests the social recognition of the wives of the great. In various ghettoes, when men dedicated themselves to scholarship, women were breadwinners, carrying on great commercial undertakings. The Diary of Glückel of Hamelin, one of the earliest examples of Yiddish literature, tells of the active life of a widow in commerce. Be it added that Glückel of Hamelin is of a most familiar Jewish type.

But if one regards the legal position—which, admittedly, need not accurately mirror the social position—the status of woman was a restricted one: and, in the narrow communities that lived within the ritual, woman's life was menial. An occasional daughter of a Rabbi, or a social potentate, received more education than merely learning to read the prayer-book (in the sense of learning to pronounce the prayers). But of the women of the masses J. L. Gordon has written:

"Childbearer, born to feed and cherish,
  To bake and cook, and quickly perish."[1]

Let it be observed, that though Maimonides holds the Hebrew language to be a very pure one, lacking in words to describe the gross, yet the Hebrew word for female is a crude one; and the crudeness is not mitigated by the fact that the word for male is cognate to an Arabic crudity.

The Jews compensate for this suggestion of contempt by setting high standards of continence for the male.[2] But the

[1] Ninth and tenth lines of KOTZO SHEL YOD.

[2] There is some worldly Talmudic advice to men oppressed by the "evil spirit": that they should dress in black, and go to a place where nobody knows them . . . etc. But in the best Rabbinic opinion, intercourse, which must only be conducted in complete darkness, *is* for progeny only. The student should compare the story of the Rabbi to whom nudes were "white geese" (Ber. 20) with the story in Avodah Zorah (17), about the sensualist R. Eliezer ben Dordia and the harlot of the cities of the West. (Also there are commentators who make Rahab "provisioner", not "harlot".)

laws of personal status still derive from an age of polygamy. That the female line is legally very important is a consequence of other considerations. Women's rights, on the other hand, are stated as protections to persons who require protection. Here, as the Yiddish has it, the dog lies buried.

Certainly, a Kethubah was invented to protect the woman's dowry if she were arbitrarily divorced. The dominant feature, however, is that the male (who was strongly advised to marry, for "it is not good to live alone") possessed the right of arbitrary divorcement even though these laws were articulated at a time when Gentile women (as we infer from Mark X.12) enjoyed some initiative. The Rabbis could not alter the Pentateuchal statement of the male privilege. The plain text of the Pentateuch suggests that there should be good reason, and Beth Shammai so maintained. But the "progressive" Hillelites made divorce depend on nothing more than male taste. Yet they did not approve. This disapproval is expressed in a Peshat by Jesus (Matt. XIX.8) who points out that Moses only *permitted* divorce because of the hardness of men's hearts. He did not command the giving of the Bill. And there are many similar Rabbinic utterances.[1] That Jewish righteousness was ever-present to protect against abuse is obvious: and we are told that tears flowed from the altar when a marriage was broken. But the fundamental proposition remains to this day undisturbed, that in matrimony there are male rights and no female initiative. In consequence of, or consistently with, this truth, we find that the widow who must submit to

[1] There is an amusing story, in the Midrash to Canticles, about the effort made by Simeon ben Yochai to save a marriage. The Rabbi said: "You married at a feast: part at a feast".When the man was drunk, he said to his wife: "Take the best thing in the house and go back to your father." When the man was asleep, she had him carried to her father's house. There was no divorce.

Levirate exoneration is at the mercy of a man, who may well make extortionate demands in consideration of his complying with the ritual. Not, evidently, if he is a good Jew: but a system of law should be adequate to protect the law-abider against the lawless exploiters of legality.[1] Even greater difficulty (because here human agencies are not available to be influenced) occurs in the case of the Aguna, or grass-widow, who can get no release, because there is no presumption of death available. In her favour the rules of evidence are relaxed: so that she can rely on one witness, or on hearsay, or on the honest statement of a Gentile. But, short of this proof of death, she cannot ask the Court to grant her release "as if" her husband were dead. The laws against adultery are too stern to allow even the remote possibility of adultery to be countenanced. In any event, she has no initiative for such a divorce proceeding as might solve her problem.[2]

Many mitigations of the legal problems of women have been made: from the doctrine of the "iron sheep"[3] to the

[1] Whenever there was any Jewish autonomy (i.e. any place in which the Rabbi had resources of enforcement) it was held right to compel cruel husbands to grant divorce, even, with the aid of violence. Maimonides asks: how can a fiat so given be valid, since the consent was not real? and replies that every Jew, in his heart of hearts, wishes to do right; but that a "fatty degeneration" impedes the expression of that desire. This is cured by the discipline. (This authority is of a Rabbi whose personal decisions were much invoked in social problems. I would add that Maimonides' explanation is a dangerous one if isolated from its context.)

[2] A well-known device was the "conditional divorce". A husband departing on a hazardous journey left behind him an instrument operating as divorce if he had not returned by a given date. American Rabbis have recently, and ingeniously, formulated a Kethubah (marriage contract) containing undertakings for later release in stated circumstances. So far this has not been accepted by the authorities of orthodoxy.

[3] *Inter alia*, the re-marrying widow's "separate estate". (The marrying

anathema by Rabbenu Gershom (1000 C.E.) who forbade polygamy in Europe for one thousand years. But no fundamental alteration of Halachic status is possible, because Halacha is held by the majority to be unchangeable, given even a Sanhedrin:[1] and would be held unalterable, even by a Sanhedrin, if explicit Holy Writ were in question.[2]

That Judaism is not worse in its consideration of women than is Christianity, is, from the Jewish point of view, no answer. That proposition is, however, relevant in a comparison between Christian and Jewish ethics. As between Old Testament and New, the New Testament restates Old Testament with some added Rabbinic Peshat.

From the standpoint of sexual morality, the New Testament is Rabbinic. That the lusts of the heart are worse than the acts of the body is a Talmudic platitude, notwithstanding that to lawyers only an intention actualized in the physical can be civilly punishable.

In this aspect, as in others, the New Testament is not new. In the general field we may hold it evident that Jewish ethics and the ethics of Jesus can only be distinguished by an elaborate casuistry. The common factor is that they are ethics, and, like all ethics that call for moral effort, are disobeyed. By modern definition ethics are sanctionless: and maiden had none.) Tson Barzel may well be a corruption of some Greek expression, such as Xun parazelo ("with (the duty of) care").

[1] There have been synods of Rabbis since the Destruction: but no Jewishly convened Sanhedrins. When Napoleon summoned a Sanhedrin, he asked them questions relating only to the relation between Jews and the civil order—i.e. between the laws of God and of Caesar. A great scholar, Sinzheim, presided: and their answers were Halachically sound.

[2] As it is e.g. in the case of Levirate obligation. This is the law that a widow who has born no children must be wed by the brother of the deceased spouse: or that the two persons should perform the ceremony of CHALITSA—Repudiation. Apart from this, a widow must not marry a brother-in-law. In Rabbinical practice even the childless widow must not: so that Chalitsa is always the only course.

in society there is a tendency—a sort of social entropy—by which the higher standards are lowered, and only the lower standards obeyed. In the course of centuries the Judaeo-Christian values have permeated into the social structure so that the average of conduct is slightly raised above crude conflict. But this average civilization is skin-deep: and does not survive such an emergence of psychological forces as we have seen in our own self-consciously psychological age. Then there is reversion to savagery. Then the Crucifix becomes the tree with a golden bough. Then the pagan gods flutter out from the amber of Christian festivals, and find their worshippers in the centres of hedonism. Then, from the Teutonic forest, fire music: and maniacal hordes from beyond the borders of lunacy descend on the evening lands.

Granted that there are forces that resist this reversion to type, yet the strongest of them is the sanction of law and order: the political sanction. Law: not ethics. Ethics only saves the city if there is a quorum of righteous men. Ethics is that which, being sanctionless, need not be obeyed. What are Jewish ethics and what are Christian ethics, when the individual seeks his own good to "the limit of the gates of Hell," or the gates of prisons?

This phenomenon is not new. In Bible times, in the days of established theocracy, and in Hellenistic times, it was commonplace that men stood on the letter of the law: obeyed a ritual and broke every high precept. So it was, as we learn, from the Rabbis and from New Testament alike, in the days that preceded the destruction. The nation was without moral fibre. One reason (if this was not a result rather than a cause) was the absence of that tenuous but vital function in social life which is moral authority.

Moral authority the Jews have only accepted and respected in the days of pressure. Fighting Maccabeans commanded it: but not their successful progeny. So, in times of massacre, Jews have looked to spiritual leaders. On that principle, the orthodox life—and a high moral life—was characteristic of the Russo-Polish ghetto: while emancipated Germany, before its reversion to savagery, encouraged a lax moral life, with legalism, and hedonism, and only ritual conformity to tradition.[1]

For long periods the Christians were more fortunate than the Jews in this: that a powerful priesthood preserved a religion which included some ethics within the scope of discipline. Eventually that religion disintegrated into ritualism and hierocracy, and lost its hold. Judaism was preserved from that complete ethical nihilism because of external pressure, and because the world of Jewry is a small one: and because, further, Judaism has always developed too much of ethical conduct in its practice to be able ever to sink into empty ritualism.

Judaism as an ethical continuum has shown this superiority over Christianity: that charity and domestic ideals have never vanished from Jewry. The poor have not ceased, and almsgiving has not ceased: nor a certain sentiment which even the ruffian among Jews can feel towards his kindred. Only very emancipated, or very desperate, Jewish groups contain many informers,[2] or contain any significant number

[1] That the Rabbis of old—like the Rabbis now—had no illusions about the moral quality of their congregations, and knew their envies and their greeds, is strangely evidenced by the belief (which still survives) in the activity and efficacy of "the evil eye". The great Amora Rav attributed 99 per cent of deaths to the Evil eye (Yerushalmi: Shabbos XIV.14) only descendants of Joseph are immune from it. (This by reason of a curious rendering of Genesis L.22).

[2] From Pentateuch onwards, the informer is the arch-villain of Jewry, and the type of villain that communities under pressure can produce. When the secular authority compelled a Rabbi to search out thieves he condemned himself, and was condemned by others. Yet Jewish history includes many names of traitors of this type, from Dathan and Abiram to such a one as Pfefferkorn, a renegade Jew against whose defamations the scholar priest Reuchlin so magnificently defended the Jews. Medieval England produced at least one example. In modern times, there

of such as do not value their kith and kin more than they do their Gentile environment, with the opportunities it affords for enrichment or escape.[1] The normal of Jewish conduct is cohesion. Even in the absence of leaders with moral authority (and Jews do not easily accept authority[2]) a sense of propriety seems to determine the average of conduct.

Being intellectuals in tendency, the Jews do not respect authority unless it be very commanding: and Jewish intellectuals have often failed to be sufficiently strong, or magnanimous, to command authority, or encourage respect for authority. Even when there have been Councils to organize Jewish life under pressure (as the famous Council of Four Lands) their authority had been weakened by faction. Jewish polemics are notorious for their bitterness.[3] Not only

has been treason enough when the Jews were surrounded by Nazis or Totalitarian Communists. There are lands now, not only in East Europe, where "informing" is regarded as a civic duty: and there are Jews, godless or merely wicked, who are ready to perform this "duty" and reap the reward.

Traditionally, the Jews condemn the Delator as the worst of criminals. But we know that, even at respectable levels, there has been a lamentable tendency among Jews to involve secular powers in their own doctrinal conflicts. I have suggested that the story of Jesus is one simple instance of this. The quarrels between Misnaggidim and Chassidim afford more recent, less spectacular, but quite comparable, examples.

[1] Of course in this, as in any traditionalist group, there occur psychological rebels. The Rabbis knew well the MUMAR LEHACHISS: the spiteful disobeyer. Today these are "ideologically" disguised—"rationalized".

[2] As we have seen, they either plunge into an acceptance (Ama Pezizah) or resist it stubbornly (Am Kesheh oref—stiffnecked people).

[3] As was mentioned above, to their great shame, they too frequently invoke Gentile interference. As recently as 1888, a Haskalah group called upon the Russian educational authorities to enforce their rules and compel the Yeshivoth to purvey some secular learning. In the result, Volozhyn was closed for fifteen years. It was reopened in 1903, and carried on in its traditional way with the mediation of that salutary degree of corruption which mitigates the harshness of most dictatorships.

every pseudo-Messiah, but every new genuine ethical movement, has led to strife. Typical is the Teutonic fury with
which Jacob Ashkenazi (known as Emden) pursued the
great Eybeschütz. So, it may be felt, the priests would have
pursued Jesus, had he been milder in his conduct and
utterances than he was.

These manifestations illustrate the difficulty of establishing an authority for sanctionless ethics in a non-political
group. Let it not be claimed that Jews have lived up to their
ethics. But a "remnant has survived". Jewish ethical practices have been saved from extinction by their integration
with a deeply felt religion. Religions die harder than ethical
systems. This particular religion dies the harder because
so many of its adherents have been killed in obeying it.
Other churches, being triumphant, have not prevailed.

2. *Jewry and the New Order*

We have seen that, notwithstanding the similarity of ethical
doctrine between Christianity and Judaism, yet there are
traditions among the Christians which make for Jew-hate.
This suggests two questions—which recent history heavily
underscores—first, as to whether that new alleged substitute for religion, that new ideology which is called Socialism, is theoretically in ethical conflict with Judaism: secondly
whether apart from doctrine, the citizens of a world that
has "turned to the left" will find in their hearts more or less
reason to hate the Jews. Will they possibly rationalize an
old hatred by using the Jew as a symbol of the hated "right"
just as, in the earlier days of Socialism, the hooligans of
"convention" were told that foreign Jews acted as the
agents of anarchistic or communistic revolution?

On the plane of social ethical thinking, it is necessary to
correct a possible error of perspective on the part of those
who only know Jewry in the lands of the West. These may

have observed that in Holland, England, France and the United States, the story of the growth of toleration is part of the history of the achievement of individual freedom among the peoples. The Jew in these realms owes his emancipation to the same forces that made it possible for a Protestant to live happily among Catholics, for a Catholic to live happily among Protestants. In the heyday of radical liberalism, in a period of some two centuries, which granted the individual large margins of privacy in which he could be immune from the control of political authority or from any coercive sanction, in that age and that atmosphere, the Dutchman, Briton, Frenchman or American could adhere to the Jewish persuasion without incurring any greater disadvantage than an inability to occupy the Lord Chancellorship of the United Kingdom.

This degree of emancipation having been achieved in lands where Jews were few, Jewishness—adherence to Jewry—became regarded as the religious conduct of individuals: respectable, but made rather exacting for its adherents by strict endogamy and by special dietary laws.[1] A favourable feature of this attitude to Jews was, and is, the accepted implication that anti-Semitism is deplorable as an interference with the privacies of life: with personal religion in particular. If this conception of Jewry engendered the complete truth, then it could be expected that Jewry, always allied to radical liberalism, would have much to fear from collectivism: and would be opposed to any movement which claimed authority over private domains, which classified society into groups rather than individual persons, which evidently could discriminate against individuals, and could charge social aggregates with vicarious responsibilities.

If that analysis were a complete account of Jewry (or of

[1] Shakespeare was aware of the same difficulties: and puts into the mouth of Shylock the argument that these are no proper cause for hate.

Socialism) then it would be surprising indeed to find so many Jews in the van of Socialism, even with allowance made for all the temptations of apostasy.

In factual reality, however, any analysis of Jewry made in the light of Western conditions must be an incomplete one. (Just as, be it added, any analysis would be incomplete which omitted to account for the Western phase of Jewish development.) In the quantitive history of Jewry the Western groups of emancipates occupy only a small measure of space-time. Over two millennia much Jewish life has been group life. In East Europe there were, until recently, Jewish "masses". At this moment of time the Jew in Russia carries on his passport the marking "Yevrei" (Jew) in the space allocated to the description of the holder's nationality. But this is not a peculiar manifestation of the present Russian régime. So it was under the Alexanders and Nicholases of the Romanoff dynasty. So it was in Central Europe of the Hapsburg and Hohenzollern. So it was in the Papal States and the Catholic lands. The purpose of the marking may be assumed to be the classification of alien types in the body politic: has, indeed, always been a hostile purpose. But it corresponded to, may, indeed, have caused, the reality of a group life such as were the ghettoes in which the Jewish masses lived or were incarcerated.[1]

In this group life some degree of individualism has flourished, in so far as the Jewish religion holds the individual to be the unit of ethical responsibility and religious activity. But that degree of individualism is quite compatible with a sense of social responsibility: with a sense of duty towards the group. We have seen that charity in Jewry is an individual virtue socially organized. (The Jew will not agree with Shaw

[1] The Russian rationalization (which I have heard accepted by distinguished Jews) is that the Soviet is a *Nationalitäten-Staat*. Where, then, is Jewish territory? Surely not in Birobidjan. That is too far beyond Sambatyon.

that charity is an evil, removing duties from the State, which should bear them.) Any political development, then, which treats the unit of politics as the group, rather than the individual, is not, by reason of the communal emphasis, inappropriate to Jewry. The Jews of Bible times were community conscious: and for most of the Diaspora, the Jewish Kahal was at least as communistic, in the unpolitical sense, as any of the Communes known to the Middle Ages. If, then, the Western Jew looks upon himself as a stem of the Jewish stock, he cannot say that, as Jew, he is committed to antagonism towards the forces that make for collectivist life. He will not, perhaps, be impressed by the fact of Jewishness in the teutonically systematic Marx, in the attractive intellectual adventurer Lassalle, in the enthusiast that was Rosa Luxemburg. But he will not reject their teachings merely because those theorists made little of the individual. There are sufficient teachings in Jewish ethics, and in the writings of the Jewish philosophers, to make acceptable the belief that the Jewish group matters more than the Jewish individual—if, indeed, the two can be separated.

On one issue only, though it may turn out to be the main one, do the traditions of Jewish culture, including the Jewish religion, conflict with the tradition of Socialism in any of its degrees. The Jew who participates in Jewish culture must fall short of complete, dedicated, materialism; and will not be able to take seriously the metaphorical claim of any materialistic, or metaphorically idealistic, theory to constitute a religion. Except for that claim, which is implicit in the attitude of its adherents rather than explicit in doctrine or dogma, Socialism, including that degree of it which is Communism, makes no claim to human obedience which is not acceptable to anyone whose life is determined by Jewish ethical ultimates. But when that tacit but blasphemous claim is made, then there is conflict: not merely doctrinal, not merely dogmatic: but in the circumstance that if people allow themselves (as most of the dwellers in the modern world do) to accept, as objects of adoration and occasions of enthusiasm, those economic and political considerations that are not the proper objects of worship, then not Jewry or Judaism is hostile to Socialism, but Socialism itself engenders the forces that are hostile to humanity and hostile to its own highest aims. If it then appears that Socialism is compatible with the continuance in the world of anti-Semitism (and it is), the spiritual attitude that makes this possible will consist in the identification of ethical ends with material purposes, so as to give validity to the basest and most inveterate human hates and jealousies. This will constitute one more piece of evidence for the established truth that, whether inside Judaism or outside it, the worship of the gods of gold and silver is conduct that endangers Jewish survival.[1]

Not Judaism as a religion, but the existence of Jews in the world in the traditional role of objects of hostility, is calculated to remind a world which has irreversibly turned Socialistic of its human, ethical, spiritual problems. Of these problems Socialism militant was acutely aware; of these Socialism triumphant, dynamic, and aggressive, is in danger of becoming completely oblivious.

[1] Karl Marx, from good Jewish family, was assimilationist and apostate in the manner of his fellow-Rhinelander, Heinrich Heine. Marx's pronouncements on Jews amount to a condemnation of them to complete assimilation. In an essay that he wrote in reply to Bauer, Marx treats the Jews as no longer religious or racially significant but only as artificially created economic group, which would disappear in world emancipation. This somewhat bitter utterance is, of course, consistent with his materialism, and his theory that Religion is an opiate exploited by the exploiters of labour. The early Marxists were, in consequence, indifferent to the Jews. Later they saw anti-Semitism as a bad reactionary "opiate". More profoundly, Bebel pronounced that "Anti-Semitism is the Socialism of the blockhead". In modern Socialism, less apt to ignore existing differences, we find the Jewish Arbeiter Bund preserving a social Jewish reality, with Yiddish as its language.

Doctrinally there need be no conflict. If Welfare States are being established, who shall welcome them more enthusiastically than those who think in terms of "bread for the poor", "housing the strangers", "visiting the sick", "supporting the fallen", and all the other Jewish charities? Charity is one of "those things on which the world is based".[1] Moreover, since it is accepted Jewish teaching that, short of murder, blasphemy and sexual abominations, the Jew must obey loyally the laws of the State in which he finds himself, it is impossible for a Jew to oppose the processes of political collectivism on Jewish grounds. These laws, as it happens, are not different from most of the laws of the so-called Christian States (recognized as such by International Law) which tend to embody an ethical minimum that is Biblically derived. We have seen that the Bible itself contemplates a Socialistic society; a limited agrarian Socialism of the type that was known to the world before industrialism made possible the large increases of population and the economics of crowding. It was Christianity which carried the Jewish belief in individual responsibility to the extreme of individualistic atomism: and Christianity forced individualism (as a formula of defence) upon the Jews, the best of whom have always regulated their personal freedom in the traditions of a humane ethical system. Individualism gave opportunity to the Jews to develop their abilities to the betterment of themselves and the societies in which they lived. Individualism saved the Jews in so far as it mitigated the one permanent collectivist Gentile demand, which is for Jewish blood: and turned it into a disseminated aggregate of rationalized hatreds directed against individuals. This, *ex hypothesi*, concedes to other individuals, against whom there is no charge, the right to survive. That concession has been called tolerance. The Jew, when he thinks, must realize that in any notion of

---

[1] The others are "learning", and "service" in the ritual sense (Avoth).

tolerance there is implicit the allegation against him of a vague guilt. He, however, has been forced to tolerate tolerance until the spirit of the age, turning collectivist, abolished tolerance, and vested him once more with collective reponsibility for the fact that any individual member of his group, or his group itself, happens to be disliked.

When Socialistic theory developed it found creative inspiration in Jewish tradition and in individual Jews. Individual Jews, in the main, have always tended to humanity: in the crucial economic relationships of master and servant, of creditor and debtor: also in their predisposition to charity.

Among the Jews, moreover, there has always been a great leavening of intellect, even among those who escape from Talmudics. Jewish intellectuals are always receptive, often creative, and their representatives are always present in the van of any social or scientific advance. So Jews became leaders of Socialistic thought: and Jewish enthusiasm has inspired generations of intellectuals with a devotion to Socialistic ideals. This, even when the translation of those ideals into practice has been to the detriment of some other Jews; whose wealth has been protective of Jewry (because of the venality, corruption and materialism of those who are the enemy).

To this should be added the reflection that Jewish "progressiveness" is in part due to the fact that the Jews are always among the oppressed: and, as in Tsarist Russia, are likely to be the literate element among the oppressed. So Jews were among the leaders of more than one Revolution. And what they learned in the literature and propaganda of those days they applied creatively when they sought escape from the exile. When the history of Socialism comes to be rewritten, it may be recorded as a remarkable fact, that only in one environment was there achieved the full Socialist principle: "From each according to his powers: to each according to his needs". That environment is the Zionist KIBBUTS, the success of which, though limited, is among the most instructive of political economic studies. That, however, in the land of ideals.

Until the rise of Nazism (and even after) Jews have succeeded in avoiding the identification of the Jewish position with that of any given political party. But their intellectualism has been easy prey to the recruiters of the parties of progress.

When the materialism of the nineteenth century expressed itself in ambitious theories such as the Marxian, Jewish intellect, and the Jewish taste for monistic world theories, were part of the inspiration. When in the twentieth century Socialism became at once the manifestation of, and the prophylactic against, the harder psychological materialism of an enlarged *bourgeoisie*, the Jewish understanding of hardship made the Jews receptive of the new development. Even alongside the crudest of class-war-makers and nationalists, Jews continued to march in the triumphal processions: but in the Jewish homes there was a corrective to this enthusiasm. Adversity has given the Jews many things, most of them bad: but among them it has equipped the group with a point of view which is sharp, sensitive, sympathetic and critical. The Jew is barometer and weather-cock of all the moods and drifts of the human spirit. Fifteen hundred years ago the Jews (in North Africa) found the Vandals kinder than the Romans: later, in Spain, they found the "cruel" Moors less harsh than the Christians they had supplanted. In this century, when the superficial doctrine of self-determination became the rage in international politics it was the Jew who could ask himself whether Roumania or Poland was going to be an ornament to the world of new, free, entities. When the Austrian Empire was broken up, it was the Jew who could remember that, for all the feudal arrogance of Hapsburg aristocracy, that Empire had been relatively humane.[1] Similarly, when the masses of many nations went Socialist, and their leaders claimed that the advent of the new Society was the end of terrors and oppressions, the Jew could ask himself whether a pogromist ceased to be a pogromist merely because he got a living wage, or because his Government had changed. Indeed only the Jew is qualified to bear witness to the degree in which revolutionary nations preserve the vices of their *anciens régimes*.

Theoretically, in a world completely internationalized, with all its parts co-operating according to an economic theory of plenty and not of scarcity, the conditions in which people live should be so good that men could not easily be exacerbated into violences: nor would they, in repose, cherish the arbitrary hatreds, and desires to oppress and be cruel, that are normal in a society where people live pessimistically and miserably, without hope and without belief. Theoretically, moreover, there is no insurmountable obstacle to keep humanity from entering on to those fertile pastures where nation does not make war upon nation, and where agriculture flourishes with the aid of the converted implements of war. But the Jew, to whom these ideals are not strange, and who is sufficiently endowed with faith to be capable of believing in their ultimate fulfilment, has also reason to believe that the best logical constructions, the greatest galleons of human aspiration, can founder on the rocks of human intransigence. Two thousand five hundred years ago, Isaiah said of Jews themselves, "I hoped to produce good grapes, but there were only bad grapes". Two millennia and more have taught the Jew the difference between lip-service and the devotion of the heart, between logic and psychology, between reason and behaviour. He has been taught to recognize that saintliness itself can spring

[1] There had been Jewish officers in the Austrian Army. Incidentally the Jews are quite capable of—indeed tend to—a loyalty to the land in which they live that amounts to Jingoism.

from sources of human cruelty which saintly teaching will not completely sublimate. Therefore the wise among the Jews could know half a century ago, what the intervening years have proved, that prosperity is compatible with arrogance, as well as contentment: that education is compatible with moral ignorance: that political progress (so-called) is compatible with the degeneration of civilization and the return of a more fierce barbarity.

What the Jew sees is what the idealist himself should see. Is it not, indeed, one of the Alexandrian Jewish traditions (and European Gentile practices) that the blood of Gog and Magog shall be spilt until the world becomes disgusted with its own blood-thirstiness? But the Jew cannot rejoice in the bloodshed that heralds the Messiah—for it is the Jew himself who embodies, in the modern world, the archetypal hate-object on which the inveterate blood-lust seeks to be sated. His existence shows, or should show, to the Socialist idealist that, in that order whose potential he is harnessing to his ideals, are latent forces so base that they will ultimately destroy whatever harmony he is creating. Thus we have seen that a Socialistically conceived anti-Semitism is something more massive, more destructive, and more cruel than any previous manifestation: that its impersonality lends to it a horror beside which pales the worst excess of personal hatred. We have also seen that Hitlerian anti-Semitism differed from the traditional precisely in the higher degree of its modern Socialistic organization. The Socialism of the blockhead turned maniac.

Another fact made clear in the same age is that the poor and the primitive are less dangerous than the well-equipped and the sophisticated. To the Jew this is, unhappily, more than a lesson. To the Gentile idealist it should constitute a demonstration of the exact nature of the forces which he is endeavouring to control and direct. His raw material is not a primeval horde of unsophisticated savages mysteriously animated by desires for well-being; which, when satisfied, render them civilized. He is dealing with the modern resultant of an over-developed social organization. His raw material is a *bourgeoisie*, ill-bred and materialistic: in some contexts demoralized by the inexorable processes that are its liquidation: but in all contexts avaricious beyond the economic, and desperate for self-assertion. This changing, bubbling, boiling, *bourgeoisie* is the raw material of Socialist enterprise. These are the aspirants to the fields of plenty, or the importunates of the bread and the circuses. Possibly, in favourable conditions, those forces can be canalized into the ideal directions. Equally those forces are capable of determining the form which their society shall take. We have seen in our generation that a Socialistic society, given the appropriately corrupt leadership, can translate itself into the mode of exploitation which is Nazism or Fascism. In political theory the process is easy. The social purpose is directed by the social administration.[1] There is no guarantee that the administrative technique will express in itself those aspects of the social purpose which are the humane ones. In the graph of political Socialism an idealized Communism may be the horizontal axis; but the vertical axis is Fascism[2].

Of this thwarting of society by its own forces any exhibition of public cruelty is evidence. The exemplar is anti-Semitism. Consequently the Jew, however spiritually animated to Socialistic sympathy, must remain with the melancholy knowledge that he is the crucial experiment (once again *experimentum crucis!*) in which this order will

[1] Or personnel of government. The factor of redemption is their corruptibility.

[2] The word is used here as a pejorative, because of its association with a militaristic gangsterism. There is a conceivable stage of political development, however, at which the so-called Fascist Dictator is temporarily necessary. Jews in backward lands have been loyal to such Dictators: at times with other reason than the simple duty of law-abidingness.

find the truth about itself. In the less happy lands (not necessarily impoverished lands) these experiments have been performed with terrible facts emerging. Whether any land can pass through the psychological stresses of growing collectivism without experiencing demonstrations of cruelty on conventional hate-objects is a question which only Jewish experience will convincingly answer.

To speak only of what has recently happened, East Europe between two Wars afforded striking examples of the rationalization into Socialist forms of an inveterate anti-Semitism. It was the trend to collectivism that made possible the modern statement of the so-called Jewish problem. According to the liberal categories of political thinking, there is no Jewish problem. Either a citizen is a good citizen or a bad citizen. If he is a bad citizen the laws should be adequate to prevent his badness from being deleterious to the community. Those laws would be enforced against him personally on account of his misdeeds; and against him alone. There fore (to cite a well-known example) there was no theoretical justification for the treatment of three million Polish Jews as a peculiar entity. They were three million citizens, each man to be judged on his merits. It was a Polish leadership, absorbing the spirit of modern collectivism, and learning from early German theory, that defined the Jews of Poland as a Minority. They signed treaties pledging themselves not to ill-treat this Minority. When the desire to ill-treat developed, Socialistic self-consciousness should have inhibited the tendency. But the resources of anti-Semitism are infinite; and the Jew is always made to suffer from quite contradictory accusations. The Polish technique is illuminating. The attack was not on a Minority. The attack was on an aggregate of individuals. If it happened that a majority of Jews were dealing in salt, for example, the Polish Government could declare salt a State monopoly, and thereby deprive them of their livelihood. That, they argued plausibly, was not anti-Semitism, but Socialist economics. It was just unfortunate that the sufferers were mainly Jews.[1]

Perhaps the same line of thought may help to explain how a certain Georgian succeeded in liquidating all his old comrades—and they nearly all proved to be Jews. His successors have admitted his crimes: but history has yet to pronounce upon the Russian *bourgeois* intelligences who guide the proletariat in their blind wanderings.

Germany, with Teutonic insolence, was more direct than the cunning Slav. That is not to say more honest: because not one German of normal intelligence really believed the excuses—the less than excuses, the less than ideology— under cover of which they enriched themselves by plundering some half a million Jewish citizens. (Nor were they later sincere believers in the German *Übermensch* when they undertook mass murder.) But again the collectivist technique was evident. That technique seemed, for a time, to the Jew-disliking peoples of the West, to be giving to German anti-Semitism the respectability of a political economic programme. Only years later, when, in East Europe, the blood-lust of maniacs was evidently being satiated in the alternating frenzies of victory and defeat, only then did the Socialist West realize that there was a limit to what could be explained away as a social economic programme. And at that point Socialistic thinking found itself

[1] It is arguable that some of the support for the not unreasonable Moneylending Acts and Hire Purchase Acts in modern British legislation came, not only from those who wished to mitigate some abuses, but from many who were aware that many Jews were involved in these commerces.

In the case of East Europe, however, the exposure of the falsity of the pretence is seen when attention is drawn to the *Numerus Clausus*. This, the arbitrary limitation of the number of Jews that would be admitted to gymnasia and universities, could only be discrimination against a group: penalizing individual applicants who had the intellectual qualifications for entry, on the grounds that other Jews were present.

unable to think of six million murdered persons as six million individuals. So they "classified" them as an ill-treated minority; which at all times was less important than any single Western soldier who happened to be ill-treated otherwise than according to the customs of war.

The Socialists of the West argue that the generations can accept no responsibility for what they regard as the unfortunate outcome of economic pressure.[1] Had the Polish or the German workmen been well paid, they say, these things would never have happened. That confusion of thinking needs no exposure. And the "psychology" is cretinous. Sufficient hardness and cruelty are to be found well above the lowest levels of the struggle for subsistence. Nor are the cries of the poor as bitter as the pride and the jealousy of him that has enough and wants more. The latter is the one to be feared. There has been Jew-hate in prosperity. There has been sympathy in adversity (as in the Warsaw ghetto). Just as economics can offer no explanation of the survival of Jewish orthodoxy among the Jewish poor, so economics offers no formula for the explanation of "rich" cruelty and "poor" kindness. These are psychological, not logical. So is anti-Semitism, under whatever rationalization it may hide itself: and its cruelties vary with the ferocity and discipline of individuals and nations.

Certainly in an economically satisfactory world mobs are harder to exhort to violence. But the lust for military glory can do it, given the proper traditions. So can an appropriately stated religion.[2] Nor does it follow, on the other hand, from

---

[1] It is a paradox in Western Socialism that the leaders deny vicarious responsibility in the group, yet act on all the other principles of collective liability.

[2] An interesting comparison is with "witch-hunting" in past centuries. There were religious reasons: there were also economic advantages to be gained; but the common denominator of the cases was cruelty.

poverty, that people need behave like beasts. How incalculable is the play of social forces has been made clear in the most "civilized" (at the same time highly materialistic) countries of the West. In some places it may require an economic motive to activate general hate into expression. But the reaction is never a simple one, from simple economic needs. Not poverty, not misery, may recently have been suffered: but the kind of pressure that is felt by a proud *bourgeoisie* fighting desperately for its status. And by Western *bourgeoisie* is meant the whole population of any Western land: because the modern aristocrat thinks in terms of *bourgeois* pleasures: and the Western working man will never acknowledge himself, except for political purposes, to be lower than the Upper Middle Class.[1]

The liquidation of a *bourgeoisie* would, by itself, not be the generating factor of anti-Semitism. It required ideas, as well as ill-feelings and needs, to inspire the subtleties of, say, the British Aliens Act, just as it required ideas to create the Polish salt monopoly. But the world is not lacking in these ideas. Moreover, they are not less prevalent now, in the parties that are the parties of progress, than they ever were in the parties of reaction. Those were pledged, in the main, to individualism, and had to resurrect an aristocratic Patriarchalism, and military Jingoism, in order to protect working men against alien immigrants. The new order faces the future with fewer academic difficulties. Psycho-

---

[1] Allowance must be made for the "continental" pride in low status. *Ich bin ein Arbeiter!* Psychologically this, too, is *bourgeois* thinking. An interesting reflection on the events of this century is that *bourgeois*, which literally means "urbane" or "civilized", has either shown itself uncivilized, or else altered the meaning of such words as "urbanity" and "civilization". To the Jew—"civilized", "bourgeois" in the good sense—this makes tragic irony. Particularly affecting is the role of the *bourgeois* "student" type; whether hooligan *freibürger*, or political agitator. This notion of the role of student is strange to the "pupil of the wise".

logical forces are here, as facts; to be deplored, but not to be denied. If they want anti-Semitism they have it.

Socialist parties throughout Europe do not acknowledge the right of the Jewish problem to exist. That may be one way of saying that they do not like the subject-matter of the problem. It is noteworthy in Socialist history that it was a Socialist (a very distinguished Socialist) who found sufficient sympathy with the oppressed Arab nomads to justify him in creating the maximum number of difficulties for the Zionist "Capitalists": even though the Zionist Capitalists were living communally according to the best ideas of Robert Owen, and the Arabs were slave-trading and lending money at exorbitant rates of interest. The fall of Sidney Webb to the level of the Passfield paper, was, for many, Miltonic tragedy. Nor has economics ever been so unenlightened as when the MacDonald formula of "economic absorptive capacity" was applied to the land of miracles. But the psychological truth was revealed some twenty years later, when a class-fighter demonstrated that the traditions of the Street Arab were more potent influences than the needs of the self-sufficient Bedouin. The later events revived the memory that among Western statesmen only a Socialist Prime Minister of Great Britain had refrained from any word, even of lip-service, in the world protest against the Hitlerian pogroms.[1]

These thoughts and these memories do not amount to a Jewish refutation of, or repudiation of, Socialism. Only they make it evident that ideals and ideologies are inadequate substitutes, in the human spirit, for the kindnesses that spring from the heart and are fostered by good traditions, by a good religion. We live, in this century, in a world of verbal expression: of ideology, of propaganda. These

[1] An interesting appendix is the hostile pronouncement of Mr. Gaitskell anent Sinai. This when an Arab-liking British orientalist had finally achieved an "enlightened self-interest" in Israel.

achieve nothing except the evasion of rights and the con-
cealment of wrongs. Just as, among religions, the lip-server
betrays the faith, so, even in political ideals, the lip-server
helps to preserve the cruelties which the idealist would
exorcize. In this confusion the Jew does not claim that his
path is the only path, nor attempt to direct others. He
recognizes that Balaam, too, is a prophet, even if his ass
speaks better wisdom. At the time of writing more than
one Balak is meditating upon the reluctant blessings of
Balaam. It is unprofitable to speculate on the outcome of
their deliberations.

3. *Gentile Problem*

"Why do the Heathen rage?" The Jewish reader can find
an answer in the second half of the verse: "Because the
nations imagine a vain thing". But their imaginings are,
unhappily, at least as important as the writing that one
foolish king saw on the wall.[1] They portend not only
terrors for the Jew, but horrors for the Gentile: the tearing
apart of the Kingdom of civilization by cruelties and all the
savageries known to psychology.

History is not an empty continuum. Just as the time-space
of physics was pictured, by a Jew, as a container whose
shape is moulded by what it accidentally contains, so those
principles, "political" or "economic", which historians
isolate as the frame of history cannot accommodate, in
adequately patterned periods and phases, the irrational, or
even the economic-national, movements of mankind. The
framework is shaped, or distorted, by psychological

---

[1] There is historical symbolism in the Rabbinic description of Aha-
suerus as MELEKH TIPESH (Idiot King). Many of the epidemics of
anti-Semitism were organized by cunning self-seekers, of the Haman
type, and "sold", as the Americans have it, to the weak, or the mad,
rulers of particular lands. The later Romanoffs hardly need mentioning.

idiosyncrasies in groups, even in individuals. So history is not pure, but impure. It happens that anti-Semitism is one of the impurities: and not the least important constituent in any account of European events. Nor is this said in the context of the last generation only. Anti-Semitism may well be the factor which accounts for the disappearance of Spain from world power: when the Dons refused to behave like Jews, and develop their great resources in trade; but were content to leave to more tolerant lands the scientific treatment of gold as a base metal.[1]

In our time we have seen at least one political force generated by Jew-hate and doomed to self-destruction. Surely, then, it is worth reflecting on this mania or this melancholy.

The apologists, including Jews who are unable to face the frightening reality of irrational evil, refer, in their speech and writings, to a Jewish problem. By this they seem to connote the inherence in Gentile communities of groups of people who between them have social difficulties of adjustment to the Gentile pattern. These include a different religion from the Gentile: some different customs, e.g. a distaste for certain foods; also a certain crude vivacity, an appearance of foreignness—enhanced in the West by the beardedness of the elderly orthodox—and in no country a completely similar appearance to the autochthonous. (If an individual Jew looks British or French or German that is an occurrence attributed to Jewish deceit.)

The Jewish conduct that is complained of—and for the most part their conduct is less complained of than their existence—is not in breach of any criminal law of any civilized, or even savage, system. Even if it is true that there have been Jewish moneylenders (created originally by, and

[1] There is some irony in the probability that Columbus was a Marrano Jew. Christopher is clearly a Christian name: Columbus (Dove) is typically Jewish. (It survives in Polish-Jewish Golombek.)

for the convenience of, Christian princes) and even if it be true (as it is not) that the Jews crucified Jesus, or that Jews have been known to have horns, or tails, or a bad odour, or a thirst for the blood of young Christians, those charges do not seem to justify pogrom against masses of Jews, of whom many must be innocent. Indeed, the variety of the charges, and their strangeness, and the fact that many Jews have been massacred because Christian priests pretended to be anxious to save Jewish souls, seems to prove that there is not any definite reason, at the level of intelligent thought, that can be invoked to justify that hatred of Jews without which epidemic massacre, endemic hostility, and permanent patronizing distaste, would not be possible. So far from Jews drinking the blood of Gentile babes, it has always seemed that Gentiles can easily acquire a thirst for Jewish blood.[1]

The truth is that the Jewish problem is a Gentile problem. The desire to oppress a relatively defenceless person or group, to whom the same oppressor has already done injury, constitutes the psychological fact of sadism, which

[1] This thought was uttered by Counsel for the Defence in the Beylis case—one of the notorious Blood Libel causes. Of "religious" anti-Semitism it is important to observe that some medievals were influenced by superstition and ignorance, rather than by blood-lust. But sadism is inseparable from the story as it is inseparable from the story of witch-hunting. Some great Christians were friendly to, and appreciative of, the Jews. Aquinas opposed forced conversions. Duns Scotus, on the other hand, advocated them. Ironically, this schoolman owed much of his philosophy to a Jew—Ibn Gabirol, whom he knew as Avicebron, and thought to be an Arab. Interesting is the manic-depressive Martin Luther, who started his career as a friend of the Jews, whose learning he appreciated. Later, perhaps because of his association with the Princes, or because he was disappointed in his hope of gaining Jewish converts to his form of Christianity, he became a bitter enemy. Of the anti-Litherans Roman Catholicism has become more humane than its leaders were at the Eve of St. Bartholomew. Yet Reinach records that, as recently as 1904, the ill-treatment of heretics etc. was "understood". But the years from 1939 changed all that.

is known to be deep rooted in many personalities. The Rabbis said that God sent a brazen insect to gnaw at the brain of Titus. But what they conceived to be the retribution was the vice. Modern psychology classifies better. Sadism is the common factor that explains many hates at many times: explains the Hep Hep[1] of the triumphant Roman legionary, the blood-lust of the savage crusader, urged on by the distorted minds of thwarted and scheming priests: it explains the mob fury to which oppressed masses can give vent when their attention is directed to a helpless object: explains also the logic of the German political thinkers who taught to the Tsars of Russia the political value of pogrom as a safety valve: and it explains in our own day the new nationalistic anti-Semitism which takes the vicarious liability of Jews for granted—and rationalizes its hate, the bitter gall of discontented paranoiacs, into theories of race and group, *untermensch* and *übermensch*.[2]

In the days of individualism, the rationalistic days of nineteenth-century England that were earlier described, every anti-Semite sought to give a reason for his Jew-hate. To the rich, the rich Jews were unscrupulous rivals: and, to rich and poor, the poor Jew was the raw material of nihilist conspiracy. Some said that they were unsocial: they would

[1] An acronym: Hierosolyma (Jerusalem) est perdita.

[2] Although anti-Semitism is very old, as we have seen, the word seems to be new. It appears, as a technical term, in the German literature of about 1888—the beginning of the period of "theoretical anti-Semitism", that attack on the "Talmud Jude" as the enemy of the State, which culminated in the criminal works of Rosenberg and Streicher. It is an interesting fact, showing the degrees of Anti-Semitism, that while Bismarck was in power, this theoretical movement was weak in Germany; and only used for export—to Tsarist Russia.

Of degrees of anti-Semitism, at a lower level, we find that English anti-Semites such as Belloc and Chesterton (village idiot among village atheists) changed their attitude when Hitlerism became strong, and they protested vehemently against his cruelties.

not eat with, or intermarry with, Gentiles. Others complained that they mixed too freely. And so to each his reason—or his taste. It was always clear that envy and jealousy were factors. Not Jewish vices are causes of anti-Semitism, but Jewish virtues. Half a century ago Dr. Max Nordau stated the truth: "Pretexts change, but the hatred remains. The Jews are not hated because they have evil qualities. Evil qualities are sought for in them because they are hated". This century has been less squeamish. This century has demonstrated, if it was not already clear, that the sadist knows himself to be rationalizing nothing other than a deep seated hatred for hatred's sake.[1] The nineteenth century was an abnormal century in its enlightenment. Therefore its oppressors sought reasons. The twentieth century is again continuous with the savage days of the Roman Empire, and of the Holy Roman Empire. The fine reasoning of the nineteenth century is an intellectual oasis in a spiritual desert.

The continuum is human psychology: and this age said Hail Psychology, and rejoiced in its own viciousness, while the forces of greed and crazy ambition sent a generation of jack-booted ruffians on a goose-step to glory.

There is no common factor in anti-Semitism except hate in the hater, and the Jew as object. It was a phenomenon before the existence of Christianity, when Manetho, in over-civilized Egypt, resented the prosperity and culture of the Jews of Alexandria, and wrote that they were Ass worshippers: when the Greek Apion promulgated the first

---

[1] This sadism is also clear in some of the manifestations of colour prejudice. Without condonation of the latter, the two hostilities should be distinguished. There are persons who, for some reason or other, *fear* the coloured individual, or the coloured groups. Nobody of culture has seriously suggested that Jews are to be feared in any comparable way. (incidentally there are coloured Jews; African groups, e.g. as well as individuals through exogamy. Recently, a coloured singer, finding life insufficiently difficult, embraced Judaism.)

recorded Blood-Accusation, to which Joseph the Cohen (Josephus) replied.

Religion, being then an active political principle, was the medium of anti-Semitic expression in the Middle Ages— and is still not free from the taint. But modern adversity has provided the Jews with strange bed-fellows; Roman Catholics and Protestants who have suffered at the hands of Totalitarian powers.

The period of Individualism produced individual Jew-haters. But then, at least, it was understood to be wrong to condemn a group for faults attributed (by way of excuse) to members of a group. Nationalism and Socialism, the two new forces that came out of the nineteenth century to con-quer the twentieth, know no compunction against penal-izing the sons for the faults of the fathers, the members of the group for the group as a whole. Earlier centuries (and through different processes the nineteenth) had forced Jews into large groups. The philosophy of the twentieth century found an easy formula for the liquidation of unwanted groups. The social-national purpose required it. Political philosophy, in this way, rationalized the develop-ment in this century of group violence, mass hysteria, and all the phenomena of a period which is only accurately describable by the competent psychiatrist. In this connexion Jews may find a bitter irony. A Jewish rationalist (Marx) helped to create a mass outlook, in which a Jewish psy-chologist (Freud) was to analyse some of the bestial forces that could express themselves in it.

But in whatever political or philosophic frame anti-Semitism be set, the technique of the anti-Semite is recog-nizable: because it is the technique of the bully. Is the Jew a successful merchant, he is fraudulent. If he is not a successful merchant he is a potential revolutionary. Is the Jew loud, then a menace—if quiet, a coward. It may be pointed out to the anti-Semite that so many Jews (out of proportion to their numbers in various lands) have fought for the countries of their adoption that there is a high statistical possibility that the Unknown Soldier is a Jew. But the anti-Semite ignores Jewish patriotism unless he can restate it as careerism. He seeks rather for Jewish deserters and shirkers, most of whom learned their devices from the kind of person who becomes an anti-Semite. These may steal horses—but the Jew must not look over a fence.

There is available always, be it remembered, in every description of human beings a field, or scope, for valuation. The facts are ethically ambiguous. The judge of character construes them "for favour" or "for disfavour". One man is loud: another (or the same seen by another person) has a fine personality. One is wisely cautious, the other a coward. One vivacious, the other ostentatious: one witty, the other insolent. The same facts in each: the interpretation different. From these possibilities of interpretation the Jew suffers, because the external judgement will tend to "disfavour".[1]

The state of mind that matters is the mind of the judge. If he is a person with a positive ethical attitude, acceptive of the world, loving his fellow men, then he will be just to the Jew. If not, he will disguise as impartiality his own bitterness, and pronounce, not without the aid of untruths, a reasoned condemnation.[2]

[1] I owe it to the memory of the late Harold Morris, M.P. (later Lord Morris) to relate the following irony. Morris had sacrificed two careers in order to volunteer as a private soldier in two world wars. From each war he emerged with the rank of Lieutenant-Colonel. When he was elected to Parliament in 1945, a back-bencher, who did not know him to be a Jew, remarked to him: "These Jewish members. They haven't got the British tradition".

Three years later the valid criticism that could be made of the Jewish members was that they had no loyalty to Jewish tradition. Was the back-bencher right in a wrong way?

[2] On Gentiles who are not Jew-haters—and of course there are

Set in its true perspective as a Gentile ailment, as the permanent impossibility of controlling the bitterness or savagery that lies beneath the thin skin of civilization, anti-Semitism is evidently an important historic fact, and cannot be disregarded in the account of the life of any European period, or of any European group. It has already been suggested that a test of a civilization may well be: how did it treat the Jews? And that question is a valuable corrective to a history of glorious Lionhearts and saintly Innocents.

In our own day anti-Semitism has been a factor in world politics on the grand scale. Because of chronic, if mild, Jew-hate, endemic in the western nations, a cruel and rapacious tyrant was able to achieve strength and assert it. He was only attacking Jews. He was only despoiling those who probably (in popular opinion) deserved to be despoiled. The West was morally unable to summon indignation against this Jew-baiting eccentric. The power in the East—a Georgian from a race of pogromists, and who had gloriously rid himself of a Jewish rival—did not take seriously the synthesis of Communist and Jew in the German vocabulary of abuse. Communism, said the Russian rationalist, was indifferent to the internal affairs of Capitalist nations; and the Jewish communists and communist Jews were the private concern of whomsoever owned them.[1]

When this was the attitude of the great powers, how could smaller nations, such as chronically feudal, priest-ridden,

myriads—the Russian writer Pasternak—a Jew whose Jewish feeling was barely concealed by his Marxist condemnations of this "senile" survival—shrewdly observed that opposition to anti-Semitism comes mostly from the head—not from the heart.

[1] The "official" attitude of the Soviet to foreign communists was expressed, by a Party official to the author, this way: "They may or may not be good for England, or France, where they live. They do not concern us. To us, foreign pro-communism is equivalent to anti-communism".

Poland, the land of Chmielnicki, or anti-Semitic Roumania, that comic opera land of the Iron Guard, or France,
in which the anti-Dreyfusard has never lost his audience
or abated his vocabulary: how could these appreciate the
realities of the savagery that was to overwhelm them? They
had too much in common with the new despots. All anti-
Semites together!

Let it not be supposed that all anti-Semitism is the same.
It varies more than Jews vary. It varies with national
temperament, with individualism and Socialism, with
religion and nationalism.[1] In modern times the Jew has been

[1] The differences in national tradition are striking. In England there
would be no "political" opposition to a Jew as Prime Minister; but the
social forces do not lend themselves to the emergence of such a phenomenon.

In France, on the other hand, there have been at least three distinguished Jewish Prime Ministers: and they have been politically attacked
as Jews. Léon Blum, in particular, was the focus of all the anti-Dreyfusard artillery. He was even credited with German origin and a German
name. This he refuted more completely than Hitler ever refuted the
suggestion that the Schickelgrübers were renegade Jews!

Germany, in its civilized moments, has been more comparable to
Britain. Jews do emerge, but rarely to the political heights. In thinking
upon Jewish Ministers of the Crown, the British Jew has to value an
unfortunate Prime Minister, because, at least, he was loyal to a Jewish
colleague. Hostile social forces are not lacking in this field. The distinction between the two lands (Britain and Germany) is that Britain
has nothing of the *furor teutonicus*.

The point of the comparison between the three lands is the observation that official anti-Semitism can be less of a barrier to Jewish careers
than the resistance which takes the form of collective dislike: if only
because to one "programme" there is always counter-programme.
And, happily, there are always Zolas. In contrast, it is interesting to
observe that, in more backward lands, where the struggle for survival
matters more than social forms, Jews—particularly Jews with little
cultural background, but abundant Jewish energy—have achieved the
high places more easily. So Monash became an Australian general. So
Sachs, a South African trade union leader. Roy Welensky became the
head of an African Federation. In America, where the politics are old

driven into townships. Therefore, at the hands of peasants
and proletariat, the Jew suffers as a *bourgeois*. In general,
history had made the Jew into the *bourgeois par excellence*.
In *bourgeois* lands, such as England, France and Germany,
where the proletariat has absorbed all the *bourgeois* standards
and ideals, and aspires to *bourgeois* prosperity, then the
attitude ranges from envy of Jewish success to a benevolent
contempt among the relatively successful.[1] The modern
charge of Plutocracy is the vice which would-be plutocrats
hurl at those they envy or hate. In the Rabbinic phrase
"they abuse with their own abuses". This hostility is not to
be dismissed with an epigram: for we have seen that when
a *bourgeois* revolution is organized, its violences, and its
wickedness, can exceed the worst of peasant pogroms: is
more systematic and characterized by an evil cynical cold-
blooded fury, of which peasants and physical workers are
less capable than the more neurotic clerks and shopkeepers
of the European towns.

And it varies with nations, and with periods in the history
of each nation. Feudal Norman England, into which the
Jew came as the King's Jew, whose oath was valid against
nine Gentile oaths, eventually produced a Jew-hate similar

and the economy new, Jews in the political high places were as rare as
Booker Washington. (England received from there the great lawyer
Benjamin, once high in the Confederacy.) In the economic sphere, the
evolution has been rapid, may one say respectfully, from Hyman
Kaplan to Henry Kaiser. The achievement of status by Jews in the New
World economy is strangely reminiscent of the successes of characters
like Ginzberg in the backwoods of Tsarist Russia. *Absit omen.* Present
auspices are much more favourable.

[1] Relevant is a remark by Oom Paul Kruger, who, when he was
reminded that the Jews had been called "salt of the earth", replied that he
was satisfied with very little salt. Interesting, too, is the attitude, already
mentioned, of Bismarck. This creator of German nationalism was a
Junker who despised Jews, but he would not allow the passing of laws
to exclude Russo-Polish Jewish immigrants from Germany. He said
that, against Socialism, anti-Semitism was the wrong flea-powder.

to that which overcame the Jews in nineteenth-century Feudal East Europe. It began with a blood libel, and ended with a blood bath.

In post-Reformation England, it seemed that the Jews, holding, as they do, the faith and morals that Milton held, had found, among his spiritual followers, the exponents of an elective affinity. That was true, and happily, has remained a valid description of events. But centuries of experience have demonstrated that even a liberal Protestant tradition is not adequate as a fence to prevent the incursion here of manias from beyond the borders of melancholy. Only it can be said that in very civilized England (where *bourgeois* still means civilized, and civilized still means humane), enlightenment ultimately survived, as the *Aufklärung* tradition of Germany did not survive, the surge of the new Mongolism—the psychological barbary—that swept the twentieth century.

In modern Europe, a Britain impoverished by war, falling back on the strength of its workers, having lost the labour of millions, a Britain with its back to the economic wall, was able miraculously to preserve its tradition of civilization. But anti-Semitism, very mildly endemic, had already spread at the turn of the century, when an Aliens Act effectively closed the doors of refuge to the victims of pogrom. Later there were some sporadic flares of the epidemic type. The latest began with a Jew joke (let them not try to be at the head of the queue): and ended with nothing worse than a hymn of hate. It did not become worse, because the Jews were saved by a display of resolution and strength in what was then a British Protectorate, at the mercy of office proconsuls who believed in dividing and ruling, in "making a desert and calling it peace".[1]

Then the sportsmanship of Britain, the tolerance that

[1] That British officials were animated by anti-Semitism is recognized in the Peel and the Singleton reports.

comes from centuries of triumph, was adequate to the recognition of courageous opposition. And by that time, perhaps, Britain could be said to have recovered, after the catharsis of war, from the moral apathy that had brought the Europe of the 1930s to ruin.

The history of the partnership between Britain and the Jews of the world, in the land that is now the State of Israel, is the most idealistic and romantic effort in politics since Bulan converted his Khazars to Judaism.

The inspiration and the background is the Zionism that emerged from the crowded ghettoes of nineteenth-century Russia. The Rabbis said that God prepares a remedy before inflicting a disease. Zionism came as rather a late remedy in two thousand years of persecution, but it came in time to alleviate some of the worst evils of our age. It could not come earlier, without some violent intervention of new forces into the course of history. Only the late nineteenth century found available large Jewish masses grouped together with a sense of solidarity and a grasp of the realities of secular civilization: only the nineteenth century found great Jewish wealth available, and that when Palestine was no longer the treasured possession of some dominant power. Only the nineteenth century had produced a science capable of making fertile the waste places. Zionism came when Jewish "life had said 'it's late' ":[1] but came as so clear an improvement on other-worldism, Messianism and pseudo-Messianism, and came when the escapes of the world were so rapidly closing, that it seized the imagination of Jewry and received the support of all the resources of poor and rich alike.[2]

[1] I adopt the words of an English poet who was a Jew (Humbert Wolfe).

[2] The sacrifices of the poor among the Jews, for Zionism, as for religion, are something of a refutation of any materialist theory of Jewry or of history.

In recent years events in Palestine, later Israel, have loomed large on the world stage: and have been treated as politics: and explained, as historians love to explain politics, in economic terms: in terms of oil and the like. In a longer perspective, the movements are better stated in terms of the ebb and flow of Jew-hate. It starts with British philo-Semitism, of which this nation can be proud even though there were practical considerations in what was done. During the First World War a British statesman who loved the Bible conceived the idea of making the Holy Land available to Jews under British auspices: and, with an almost Jewish ingenuity, used this idea in order to induce the support of Jews to a cause in which pogromist Russia was an embarrassing ally. With Zion as consideration, David Lloyd George bought American Jewry.[1]

Subsequent events are recent history. Whatever awards and dispossessions had been made in peace treaties, the Jews could not be allowed, by the impartial minds of a small-minded bureaucracy, to benefit even at the speculative expense of Arabs who had no claim. So the West discovered in the background of the text a latent—an invisible—ambiguity. The statesman Churchill, remembered for many things, will be remembered in Jewish history as the author of a Peshat. "A national home in Palestine." "That means", says the exegetist, "not a home which is Palestine, or in the form of Palestine, but 'in': that means 'in a part of it'." The leading Jewish Zionists, being mostly men who had forsaken Rabbinics for the sciences, were unequal to this. So was created, *ex nihilo*, Trans-Jordania, to accommodate a non-existent nation. Inside Palestine the Mandate,

---

[1] Romantic writers of the future may well describe "the miracle of the oranges", by which Weizmann, experimenting in Manchester, was able to find for Britain a source of an essential ingredient in explosives. Asked what he wanted in return, he requested Palestine for the Jews. Hence the orange-groves.

of which the preamble was the Balfour Declaration, was interpreted by the officials in the spirit of Pilpul. A clause declaring the national home to be without prejudice to the civil rights of existing groups was held not to refer to any groups that then existed, but to any group that might ever exist: and the civil rights were to include a political claim to the ownership of the whole country. In this way an Arab problem was created to cope with the Jewish problem; to cope with the possibility that the despised Jew might achieve something of dignity or prestige.

It is a feature of anti-Semitism that it corrupts the Jew at times, as well as the Gentile. A Jewish High Commissioner (an ex-English political functionary, appointed in the spirit of generosity that created the Mandate) found it necessary to indulge Arabs in order to demonstrate his impartiality.

Thereafter a long series of Arab raids, during each of which the Mandatory Power disarmed both sides. That may appear to a lawyer to be a bad "preference" in favour of the uncatchable raiding Bedouin. In a comparable legal situation, a temporary friend of Britain, President Roosevelt, caused to be repealed a Neutrality Act that favoured land powers at the expense of sea powers. Because of that Britain survived. The Jews in Palestine were the victims of an unrepealed neutrality: but nobody removed the injustice. Even that same Roosevelt was later to aggravate the Jewish plight by statesmanlike promises to Arab and Jew alike, with a "neutral" impartiality.

A series of Royal Commissions and international inquiries investigated carefully the affairs of Palestine: but nobody diagnosed, as the main cause of trouble (although it was mentioned by the tribunals) the permanent implacable anti-Semitism of the majority of the Gentiles who controlled its destiny. As it was in Europe, so it was there. The problem was eventually partially solved by violence, which was brought about by the conduct of a Socialist leader in Britain, who demonstrated many things. He demonstrated, first, that the working man in power is as unlikely to be friendly to Jews as a capitalist group in power: secondly, that the intellectuals among Socialists are not, because intellectual, free from hate. (Indeed, as we have seen, ethics are largely an effort to correct the moral limitations of the intellectual.) Thirdly, that the Jews could be driven to revolt, and successful revolt: finally, that the enemy of the Jew is not the desert Arab, but the street Arab.

To the efforts of an anti-Semite, then, is partly due the existence of the State of Israel, and it has survived the "non-belligerence" of a world that favours her enemies.

But in the history of Jewry this is only one instance of the realization of a familiar causal sequence. Anti-Semitism is a force that has preserved Jewry throughout the centuries for better or for worse.

On the Talmudic principle (of Beth Shammai) that it is better not to be born than to be born, it may be suggested that Jewry had better perished. And so Marx held. But if there is a value in Jewry, then it can be argued that a hostility which prevented emancipation kept in being something that has enriched the world: kept in being a cultural and moral system which is among the best products of human suffering and endeavour. Nor is it likely that the State of Israel, grounded as it is in that spirit, will ever emancipate Jewry out of existence. Weltschmerz will survive there, and the sense of an exiled spirit. And those feelings, inadequate to prevent the partition, or cantonization, of a small country, are strong enough to prevent its Balkanization.

On the group in Exile, in the past and present, anti-Semitism leaves psychological effects, good as well as bad.

It gives to the Jew a sensitivity and a "judgement". We have seen that the Jew who reads history and studies politics is in a position to correct the conventional valuations by asking the questions already mentioned: how did they, or how do they, treat their Jews?

By that acid test many a pretentious claim is dissipated. Certainly no claim to Idealism or Objectivity can survive a diagnosis that reveals a spirit permeated with hate.

Anti-Semitism has, it may be said without paradox, been disastrous to the Gentile world as well as to the Jewish individual: but, for it, the survival of Jewry, and the emergence of Israel, are compensations on the large scale of history. Yet, at any moment, hatred, as Tolstoy has it, smells of death. If there is a Jewish odour, it is a scent of the moral corruption that can attach to the victim of hate, as well as to the hater.[1]

4. *The Jewish "Jewish Problem"*

Psychologically, Jew-hate breeds an antibody which is the Jewish obsession. Few Jews are without this. Indeed it is a factor that suggests a definition: Jewry is not a race, or religion, but an obsession—an anxiety neurosis. Few Jews are strong-minded enough to be able to hear criticism of a particular Jew, or Jews in general, without sensing (unfortunately, so often rightly) the undercurrent of contempt, distaste, hostility. Even if a Shylock existed, a Jew could not allow himself to judge him. And from this sensitivity develops the hardness of the reverse case: where Jews with responsibility—proconsuls in Palestine, judges in America—have been suspect of trying to show their impartiality at the

[1] To those who feel that Jewish Separatism is bad, or anachronistic, let it be mentioned that Shakespeare, giving a stage Jew to his groundlings, yet makes it clear that "not eating together" is a poor excuse for hostility. As for intermarriage, it should be clear that Jewish Separatism is not "segregation". The Jew illustrates the belief that world-unity and social unity are not the obliteration of differences, but their preservation in harmony. Jewish endogamy is part of the discipline that makes Jewish life into a reality that is worth preserving.

expense of their fellow Jews. Even, they may have been trying to convince themselves.

Jewishness, in consequence, is a sensitivity.[1] To call a Jew a dirty Jew is vulgar abuse. To call a Jew a Jew suggests, to the lawyer, a slander, even if the words be literally true, because it carries an innuendo.

Among the Jews in relative emancipation there is to be observed a great range of mental-emotional types all reacting individually to a hostility that they feel around them. These types must be seen, in depth, in time, in the framework of history, because the immediate environment cannot account for them.

A character in Sholom Aleichem says: Unser Jüden seinen a miyusser Chevra. (Our Jews are an unpleasant lot.) Whether they live inside, or outside, some Pale of Settlement, such as the Tsars created, they are condemned to all the psychological dangers of prisoners. Unless they are free-developing minds, they are small-minded. If not actually in ghetto, they are in klein-städtel. Many, far too many, Jewish groups are, in this way, Cranfords. Here they hate each other. Dedicated, theoretically, to love of their fellow-men, they do not succeed in liking them. Some Jews dislike their neighbours the more precisely because they are Jews, making the disliker aware of his own frustrations, and jealous lest others are less frustrated. Here is Jewish anti-Semitism; and the terrible thought that Jewish anti-Semitism is the only kind that can be justified.

Here, in every klein-städtel—and it may be as large as

---

[1] Sartre, interestingly, describes the Jew as "resolutely taking on the nature of being a Jew. That is the permanent alienation of his being." From the standpoint of those who regard the essence of man as something manifest at the level of consciousness, and not below it, the word should be "articulation" rather than "alienation". Sartre may, some day, discover the "existentially" satisfactory Jew among future generations of Sabras. But this is unlikely.

London or New York—we find a range of psychological types. Most understandable of them is the suspicious, untrusting, ghetto Jew, determined that his life is to be spent in mitigating all contact with the Gentile. Usually this type is orthodox, deriving from lands of oppression, whose parents heard the terrifying approach of the Cossacks, or who himself heard the tread of Storm Troops. His life is made so narrow by resentment and fear, so pedantic and exacting, that we find his children escaping into the un-Jewish, often enough finding that there is no future outside, as there was none within.

In this setting, at an intellectual level, there can take place in any student the recapitulation of such a life as that lived over a century ago by Solomon Maimon, who escaped from narrow orthodoxy to become a good philosopher, but could not find a congenial life among the emancipated Germans that he despised. A better fate is that of the Jew who escapes from the Synagogue into the prize-ring. He commands the respect of kings and princes.

The oppressed Jew, however, is not the saddest type. More pitiable specimens exist in emancipation. These are, to adapt again the phrase of Smolenskin, "wanderers in the pathways of life". They do not know what they are, Jewish or British, Jewish or American: nor what their purpose should be.

They are in a moral transition which knows no definite loyalty. Mendelssohn has been quoted as saying that he would die a Jew, his grandson a Gentile: but he could not forecast the religion in which his son would end his days. In our time the fact of conversion is a rarity, because now religion is not held so important: nor is Christianity a disguise, when the satyrs start their tragic goat song. But the position that Mendelssohn described as his son's position is achieved in millions of individuals in semi-, or complete, emancipation.

They do not know whether or not to distinguish between Jews and Gentiles. Among both the placid and acrimonious there are types who feel some solidarity, and hate the idea of prosecuting, or oppressively pursuing, a fellow Jew, however badly the latter may be in default. Others say that the proper behaviour is to pursue the Jew as a Gentile would pursue a Gentile: and they do so: and they feel proud of doing justice, as witnesses, or as Counsel, or as Judges in the prosecution of Jews.

Yet they are suspect, these grandchildren of the ghetto. Are they not expressing a sadism, a perversion, which is due to the thwarting effect of their Jewishness, under the pressure of an environment? an environment which threatens to thwart their ambitions unless they adapt themselves to it.

The range of psychological varieties is immense. But the matter may be summed up in the proposition that not the least of evils wrought by anti-Semitism is the creation of the Jewish anti-Semite: the one who hates his fellow Jews in his anxiety to think himself different from them.

It was said of the Jews in Egypt, that they were saved because they did not change their names or their language, and did not inform against each other. That was among the slaves. It is not clear that the fish eaters who complained in the desert had been exponents of loyalty. Applying that thought to what Sholom Aleichem called "the land of fried fish", we may suggest that, as in Goshen then, so in Goshen now, there are many amongst whom no degree of cohesion has been maintained.

In the Western lands, where the Jews are at the moment completely emancipated, except from the social preferences that are shown against them, this social distaste generates what may be a beneficent defensive solidarity among the self-conscious Jews. Hence a certain freemasonry.[1]

---

[1] In France Freemasonry proper has been coupled with Judaism, or "international Jewry", as a subversive factor in world politics. This is

Jewry, in its strong centres, is capable of carrying out a policy of "Protection" or "Preference" in the economic sense. Not very thoroughly, because there are so many Jews who will concede nothing to sentiment, will only sell in the best market and buy in the best market. To these such a boycott as was made against Nazi Germany was too great a sacrifice. Again, the Jew is sufficiently cunning to see the dangers of Jewish co-operation. Or he may be of the type that has contempt for the too familiar (those with whom he is compelled to live), and feels more important, and better satisfied, when he deals with the stranger.[1] And, if he has secrets to hide, he prefers to trust those not too near to him, because, among the Jews, he thinks (as did the Rabbis of whose work he is ignorant) that "your friend has a friend, and your friend's friend has a friend".

At all phases of Jewish history there have been Jews who escaped from their own feeling of inferiority by preferring the society of Gentiles. Also, as we have seen, there have been too many cases where Jewish groups have called in Gentile forces against each other.

Nevertheless, Jewish cohesion has made possible some degree of protection against enemies: and, in freer circumstances, has made possible great Jewish successes in the Arts and Sciences and in Commerce—to a lesser degree only in Politics.

the nonsense of the "hidden hand", of the Protocols of Zion (a German production this). But that Jewry is made into something similar to Freemasonry, without its mysteries, is true. Even those Jews who are not very proud of their Jewishness are capable of taking advantage of it.

[1] Rufus Isaacs, a fairly ignorant man in the Jewish context, but who developed a Jewish heart, seems to say that, generally, Jews want Jewish Solicitors and Gentile Counsel. (They like to honour the Gentile.) But that in his case, they engaged a Christian Solicitor, because he was honest, and (himself) a Jewish Counsel because he was clever. He says, amusingly, that they were wrong in both respects.

But a more important fact in Jewish life is that Jewry, because of its problems, makes itself into a career. In any all but emancipated Jewish society the Jew, from early life, is encouraged to take part in the discussion of Jewish problems. This is an education in itself, of a type which only minorities enjoy. In the present century Zionism has been education and career. The young Jew, enthusiastic by temperament, has been acceptive of, and fluent in, its exposition. Many of them have made great sacrifices to spread the teaching. Those who have not, but who have attained success in other walks of life, find themselves invited to lead such a movement as this: and they do so because it is glamorous: and the ignorant think that these ornaments of commerce and the professions are very generous in giving leadership to the benighted ghetto men who have worked in the movement all their lives.

However, as the Talmud has it: "To one it is a gain, and to the other no loss: and that is the way of the world".

The fact is that Jews do make Jewry and Judaism "an axe to delve with". Some are compelled to, because it is the only way in which they can pursue scholarship. In the old days the Jew turned Christian in order to study. Today he turns Jew. The Minister of Religion at least achieves an education of sorts in Hebraica and Judaica. A less praiseworthy specimen is one type of "voluntary" worker, who pursues honour, and (against the experience of the Wisdom) finds that it sometimes fails to elude him. He achieves a career open to the talents—of gold and silver. His name is on donation lists: and he becomes the warden of Synagogues because he has the kind of background that the Rabbis knew was proper to that office.

Perhaps the phenomena of "Jewish professional" and "professional Jew" should not be harshly judged. They live among their redeemers. Of the humbler voluntary workers, who work without honour, and of the charitable who give charity anonymously,[1] or without seeking recognition or praise, these are the salt of the earth, and they express in their lives the ethics of Judaism: which is to love others.

For the Jew who ventures into public life, there is abundant difficulty. The difficulty is logically the same as that which occurs in private life—the acceptance of the gifts of the Greeks. Thus, can a Jew join a good club, which, to his knowledge, excludes Jews in general? Can he accept favours from an anti-Semite, who claims him as "one of my best friends"? What applies to private life, applies to politics. Only he is at ease in politics who is quite self-seeking, without irrelevant forethought or afterthought. He follows the party line, even when the "party" is organizing pogrom. And he has ready his answer: "let me strengthen myself in their councils, and I shall be better able to be of service to the Jews than if I make gestures of protest or revolt". To which the sophisticated may reply "*Credat Judaeus Apella non Ego*". Yet there are ghetto Jews who, being intelligent and unsuspicious, accept these rationalizations.[2]

But if a Jew, in his attitude to public affairs, seeks to follow a Jewish line, he will experience hostility: and also will find himself faced with great intellectual problems. Whom shall he prefer: for example, the Pakistani who showed the British Foreign Office how to behave, and is yet an adherent of the "Arab League": or the Hindu whose vote in the councils of the nations has favoured both the friends of Jewry and its enemies? Was Smuts his friend, Zionist and illiberal—or Malan—illiberal in the extreme, yet friendly to the State of Israel? Do we value Zionists who arm

---

[1] These days there may be ulterior motive even for this.

[2] In their support be cited the case of Josephus, who, at the time of the fall of Yodfat, the Zealot stronghold, used his mathematical ability so as to escape from a suicide pact. Each was to kill the next but one, and the last survivor to kill himself. Josephus contrived to be last, and decided against gestures. Nor did history lose by this!

Amalek? Do we value Jewish philanthropists, or campaigners for liberty, who have no good word for Zion? Always the friend has a friend who is not our friend! That we must accept the faults of our friends is normal humanity. That we must close our eyes to their unfortunate associations can be an unhappy Jewish necessity.

The story is related of a Batlon (an Idler) in an Eastern Synagogue, who was told of a great earthquake in Japan. He said: "I only want to know one thing. Is it good or bad for the Jews?"

As was the earthquake, so are the international, and even national, upheavals—very hard to assess in the light of a Jewish point of view. Yet the Jew, as he encounters hostilities, does become able to see through the appearances to the realities of human nature. This may leave him wandering in scepticism, but it may also enable him to point a moral. That he also uses it "to adorn a tale" is the story of the Jewish artist, which is another chapter.

One fact that emerges clearly, however, is that whatever psychological position is adopted by the Jew, whatever psychological escape he finds, any pretence of non-Jewishness is doomed to failure.

The Jewish disguise is very easily penetrated by the anti-Semite. Indeed he finds crypto-Jews where there are none.[1] In biological theory there is no reason why an assimilant to any group should be rejected, since no stock in Europe is pure unless it be the Jewish. Also there is no reason, in Jewish law, or Gentile law, why the Jew should not be more royalist than the king. Many Jews assume royalism, or reaction, as it were defensively.

Yet in that role the Jew is suspect, of Jew and Gentile alike. Few Jews have achieved, in any land, an estate that lasts for generations. The Jews that financed the Trans-

[1] The late Lord Simon was, quite wrongly, thought to be a Jew: but only by those who disliked him, and by a few "optimistic" Jews.

Siberian Railway received the ephemeral honours of a defunct autocracy. The Jews who have built commercial empires in this century have seen some of them vanish.

There is a story that a Jew (Saul Wahl[1] Katsenellenbogen) was King of Poland for twenty-four hours, in order to solve the problem of a disputed succession by using a power of appointment. In that time (a night in 1588) he enacted a law making it a capital offence to kill a Jew. The subsequent history of Poland demonstrates that, not only the Royalist Jew, but the Jew as King, has had very little influence on the destiny of his fellow Jews and the conduct of their oppressors. The Jews fought loyally for their Polish masters (the feudal lords) against the invading Cossack. For that they were massacred by Poles and Cossacks together, when the war was over. They provided the truce.

In the main, however, the Jew has invested his hopes with the rebel. Many factors contribute to his radicalism. Apart from the fact that his own culture gives him an approach to progress, we find that, in modern times, history has classified the Jews with that generally progressive class which is *bourgeoisie*. A rare century of enlightenment further brought it about that the Jew was morally bound to be a liberal: for liberalism in Europe gave to Jews the civic rights that they had not enjoyed before.

Intellectually, too, because intellect is a stimulus to progress, it might be expected that the Jews should find themselves in the rank and file, if not in the van, of all progressive movements. Jews played their part in Socialism wherever Socialism was the part of enlightenment. The names of Marx and Lassalle and Luxemburg are only the names of leaders. Jewish workers there were plenty. For a century, moreover, Jewish thought let itself be

[1] Wahl is probably a corruption of the Polish Wloch (Italian). His father was Rabbi Meir of Padua (an ancestor of this author's).

impregnated by Socialism: and some of those teachings are effective in practical Zionism.

But the golden gossamers of nineteenth-century Idealism were blown quickly to shreds by the industrial and political winds that blew round the turn of the century. In the twentieth century, the luxury of the over-productive times has gone. The lean years, the wars and the locusts, came. In this new atmosphere liberalism (as theory and as reality) seems to be doomed. There is no nutrition for any idea that is not an economic idea or a psychological indulgence. The economic ideas that were latent in liberalism are said, by the exponents of the New Order, to have amounted to an illusion of uneconomic ethics. It is said that they were only appropriate to a growing world, not to a contracting one. One pronouncement of Marxism makes a perpetual threat to come true in this century: that politics is class struggle. It is remarkable that that old Jew, who spent his creative years in the British Museum, was never associated with the dreams of Socialism, only with its bitter practicalities. In this period that we are living through now the Jew finds it hard to align himself with the party of progress, because, if he has eyes, he can see that this is not Idealism against Realism: but that two sets of royalists are fighting now for their "royalties". The Jew is no favourite with either group: and he has seen the cloven hoof in both.

The Jew, as Jew, then, has no guidance in modern politics. A friend of progress by birth, he has unfortunately outlived the best of progress. Many of his kindred died in its collapse.

Economically it seems that this century liquidated the *bourgeoisie* and with it the resources of Jewish existence. But life is subtler than that. The captured *bourgeoisie* conquers its conquerors. The capitalist meets his worker on common *bourgeois* ground. They are all salaried now. In the Western lands the worker wants no other grounds in which to flourish. All he wants is the relative independence and leisure that he thinks the middle class enjoyed. In consequence of this, and of the mass production of what were once luxuries, the Western industrial world continues middle class in its tastes, even though the strains and stresses of life are nearer to the surface, and the psychological average is neurosis.

In this world the Jew, as *bourgeois*, tries to live urbanely. The atmosphere is not as friendly to him as it was when to be *bourgeois* was an achievement of value, when the rich condescended and the proletariat showed respect.

In the *bourgeois* world of now, the teeth and claws of humanity are not so well concealed. Hatred is easy, and anyone who can reasonably be hated becomes the scapegoat of the psychologically frustrated. We have seen in this century that, when *bourgeoisie* becomes bitter, pogrom is possible such as priests and peasants never conceived.

Adaptive of the habits of the land, the Jews too easily behave as *bourgeois*. Blessed by Balaam, they move from the tents of (wandering) Jacob into the more luxurious "habitations of Israel". The unethical among them acquire *bourgeois* vices.[1] If the Jew appears as a criminal, he is likely to be involved in the kind of law-breaking which traders are involved in: the receiving of stolen goods: smuggling: breach of market laws. (There is, be it noted, something impersonal, something unviolent, something of mental in this type of criminality.) The anti-Semite, who, as already shown, hates the Jews for their virtues, not for their vices, finds in these things an excuse: and does not take into account their relative degree of freedom from crimes of passion and violence: and does not accept any statistics that show the high degree of Jewish correctitude in commerce.

---

[1] In wilder places and periods, there have been Jewish criminals practising the crimes of the environment; horse-thieving in the Ukraine, for example: and some gangsterism in U.S.A. In the world of commerce, the temptations extend to more, and gentler, persons.

Indeed, it has been said that the Jew succeeds because his word is his bond. That gave him wealth in the backward lands, as well as in the advanced. But one Jewish villain is more valuable to the enemy than many righteous.

This truth, however, does not justify the self-righteous, small-minded, Jewish communal sadist in oppressing the wrongdoers. "There, but for the grace of God, goes Cohen": and the tolerant may add: why should a group not be allowed its ration of criminals?

From these realities self-righteousness, and sycophancy to the Gentile, are no escape. Nor is the adoption of any political party, in the present generation, of value. The Jew, as we have seen, has been used by Feudal lords and then ill-treated. What Feudal lords can do, Party Officials can do better.[1] And worst of all errors is the self-induced amaurosis which refuses to see anti-Semitism when it is present.

"My name is Cohen—I have enemies—I do not confuse anti-Cohenism with anti-Semitism."

To that the answer is easy. "Yes. You, Cohen, may be a bad man who is entitled to his enemies on his demerits: but would you have those enemies, or have achieved those demerits, if your name was Smith?"

A conclusive word was said by an old Jewish orator whose son had changed an impossible foreign name (Rumyanek) into an unmistakably English one. Through doing that he was not recognized as a Jewish hero when he won the Military Cross. The father observed: that the son was entitled to change his name, but should have changed it to Cohen.

In that story lies a lesson for all the aspirants among the Jews who aim at Cabinet office, among Socialists and Conservatives, but cannot actually afford to buy it with hard cash.

---

[1] An authority of Tannaitic times warns men against the friendship of courtiers etc. (Avoth).

More pathetic is the case of any young Jew who throws himself with the enthusiasm of a fiery race into the good causes of the Gentile: and fails to understand why his voice seems to carry no conviction to his hearers. So often he himself can see no reason for the scepticism of his audience. When he finds out, he will not be any happier: but if he is a true Jew, by the standards, he will not hate anybody because the world has rejected him.[1]

[1] All the above, all the "ethics of the klein-städtel", fall back in perspective when the fore-ground is occupied by the events recounted in the recent Eichmann trial. In that story of years of planned massacre what gleams in the dark scene is the unselfish devotion of Jewish parents to children, children to parents: and of leaders to their communities. Among the leaders, few, if any, manifested any desire to gain safety through their powers or privileges. The Rabbi of Czernowitz would not save his life by playing informer, even as to the location of the synagogue ornaments or the community's wealth. That example is one of innumerable nobilities.

A melancholy thought is that many great lives could have been saved by a strong declaration of Reprisals, on the part of the Allies. Twenty years previously, Trotsky had saved many Jewish lives from the Ukrainian pogromist Psetlura, by promising to exact life for life. Although many Gentile authorities made great efforts in the Hitler years, the ultimate sanction was not invoked against the Amalekite.

CHAPTER EIGHT

ON SEVERAL THRESHOLDS

1. *Go with Elijah*

"ET thy standard on a high hill", demanded Isaiah: and the Jews have responded. But down in the vale of tears how have they conformed to their own standards? In an age when averages tend to replace standards the question is a pertinent one. But in a practical, though ill-defined, way the Jewish thinkers have always been aware that ideals may be held in theory without being maintained in practice: that the same group that is dedicated to virtue possesses vices. "Come and hear."

A legend is written of Joshua ben Levi—the choice of person is significant because this Rabbi was famous for kindness and integrity—that he travelled with Elijah in the world of men and was vastly perplexed by the prophet's extraordinary reactions to apparent human merits and perversities. Thus when they came to a certain township and received no offers of hospitality at the local Synagogue, Elijah said to the people: "may all of you become leaders of the congregation". At another place, where the Synagogue folk were most hospitable, Elijah said to them: "may one of you become leader of the congregation". The heart of Rabbi Joshua, we may infer from his question, was, for all his skill in Halacha, so simple that he could not understand why Elijah had pronounced a greater blessing upon the unfriendly than upon the warm-hearted!

Elijah, be it remembered, is traditionally the practical angel, remaining shrewd and percipient after his ascension as he was in dealing with the court of Ahab. He knew the mentalities of those that skip on divers thresholds. A modern interpretation of Joshua ben Levi's dream-experience would be that an idealist was being made aware (in glimpses) of elements of reality which disrupt the harmonious thinking of the unsophisticated heart. He was learning that the world of ethical doctrines is one world: that the world of empirical psychology, of individual behaviour, is another. Let this be true of humanity in general: then, in Rabbinic phrase, "of Jewry—how much more so!"

If, then, through the time-space of Jewry, any simple-hearted adherent of our beautiful ethics could travel with Elijah, when he goes searching, possibly, for the thirty-six anonymous good men who in each generation support the world order (and not merely deciding how much wine should be drunk at Passover[1]), he would find, in every corner of every sector of the continuum, some demonstration of the difficulty of judging Jews by their outward appearances and external conduct: and greater difficulty in awarding praises and blames.

"Leaders of the people by their counsel, and by their knowledge of learning meet for the people, wise and eloquent in their instructions. . . . Rich men furnished with ability, living peaceably in their habitations." Ben Sirach (evidently thinking in terms of Rabbis and Baalé Batim) showed his awareness of the difficulties of assessment when

---

[1] It is left to Elijah to determine whether four glasses should be drunk, because of four words of redemption; or five, because a fifth word can be included. The fifth glass at Passover awaits his decision. It is also possible that this glass corresponds to Elijah's chair at circumcisions.

he linked these two classes of men with "such as found out musical tunes and recited verses in writing": and so made the valuation a matter of taste.

Ben Sirach wrote at a culture-period: and to those who write in culture-periods some correction of perspective is necessary. There have been phases, too many phases, of Jewry in which the reality was not the individual but the huddled mass. In the settlements of the various Pales, whether Moorish, Teutonic, or Slav, the leaders of Jewry—one need not consider schemers and traitors—were carrying such a burden that they may be unreservedly praised. At the other pole, or when external pressure is not oppressive, Jewry itself has been notorious for its recalcitrance, its lack of respect for its leaders. In turn, the leader is suspect that his apparent spirituality, his energetic effort, his handsome show of philanthropy, are insincere.

Does one find a purveyor of charitable gifts, or one who seems to serve the congregation faithfully? Perhaps this is a seeker after honour? Or a superstitious layer-up of treasure in heaven by way of investment? That difficulty of assessment is inherent in any judgement of conduct, because, as the English lawyers put it: "the devil knoweth not the heart of man". The Rabbinic reaction is to judge "for favour": and this is supported by the optimistic proposition that one who pursues learning or good works with ulterior motive, will ultimately pursue them for their own sakes. (The same is only too true of those who follow base trades as means to an end.) But who shall say, reviewing the history of Jewry, what persons and which leaders have been unselfish and dedicated? Whether one is considering the career children of the aristocratic Hashmoneans, or the aristocrats of various European societies who have "dedicated" themselves to their ancient people, or even Rabbis asserting personal authority, is one not driven to questioning; so as to ask: is it not, possibly, the case that the honour that came by accident became later an object of pursuit for its own sake?

Do we seek some mark of apparently unrewarded conformity? Seek, let us say, those "who call the Sabbath pleasant".[1] Certainly there have been groups and times and places such that the visitor to them might feel himself to be Eldad the Danite on the banks of Sambatyon. But he could equally find himself on the banks of a quiescent mill-stream where the Jewish mill-owner releases his Jewish workmen for the Sabbath, but pays them less than they really earn in exchange for the concession. On such economic advantages sweat-shops have been founded. From this strong meat a sweet emerges: the fact that masses of Jews, ignorant and learned alike, have always made economic sacrifices for religious tradition. Surely when Marx dismissed religion as "an opium for the masses", distributed by exploiters, he was forgetting his own origins in a group which, in its Dietary Laws and its Festivals, to name but two features, has lived a history against the determination of economics.[2]

But would a celestial viewer condemn as un-Jewish those who make money on the Sabbath and give large amounts to charity? Present of harlot and sale of dog! The position of Jewry has never been so stable that that doctrine could be extended to exclude the benefits of all aid from all tainted sources. No false sense of righteousness has place amongst those who say in their liturgy: we and our fathers have

[1] To those who know the "Yom Kippur Jew", and such as buy new clothes for Festivals, let it be explained that the most important of Jewish Festivals (judged by the sanctions) is the Sabbath. Although Yom Kippur is called "Sabbath of Sabbaths", legally it amounts to a duty no higher, and its enforcement is less severe. (This is, incidentally, a good example of how Halacha complicates apparently simple Biblical text.)

[2] This observation is not refuted by the fact that some classes of Jews make profit out of Jewish ritual requirements. The majority does not.

sinned. Nor, for that matter, has the death sentence for breach of the Sabbath ever been carried out since the days of Moses and Joshua. The Sabbath is a ritual and a moral value. It may chance to be observed out of laziness: and people may happen to feel driven to break it under economic pressure, or through temptation. Someone may keep it whose life in the rest of the week is deplorable, as when Shylock goes to synagogue. Some may break it whose general lives are morally praiseworthy. Like all formalities, like all rituals, it cannot constitute a criterion. A condition, perhaps, of the average good Jewish life: even a purifier of life, in some degree; but after that no guarantee of morality.

There are, among the conforming Jews, as among the Christians, two orders of the apparently religious: those whose life is permeated by religion: and those who use the ritual as an escape, or as the purchasing of a pardon or indulgence. If there is a third class, a class of morally schizoid, who can be devout in ritual and let that exhaust all their spirituality, while behaving in other ways immorally and wickedly, it is less likely to be found in Judaism than in other religions; because Judaism has implications, if only social implications, that make the laws and customs into a way of life: and those implications are commonly felt.

When full allowance is made for all the swindler-philanthropists, it must be said that Israel Zangwill undoubtedly wrought injustice to Jewry in that savage poem wherein he projects his own unfaith, and the bitter dissatisfaction of his own unintegrated genius, into an accusation of hypocrisy on the part of the custodians of righteousness.

"Hear O Israel, Jehovah, the Lord our God, is one
But we, Jehovah his people, are dual and so undone."

If the indictment were limited to the bitter paradoxes of

Jewish history and Jewish psychology, it would be supportable.

Certainly we have seen the contrast:

"Slaves in eternal Egypt, baking their strawless bricks
    At ease in successive Zions, prating their politics,
    Rotting in sunlit Rumania, pigging in Russian pale,
    Driving in Park, Bois and Prater clinging to fashion's
    tail."

Those vicissitudes and their moral consequences are part of a familiar tragic history. But the poet goes further:

"Pious fanatical zealots, throttled in Talmud coil,
    Impious lecherous sceptics, cynical stalkers of spoil."

What he has been interpreted as saying is that Jewry has lost its moral battle: that the "duality", from being a doubting and an anxiety and a desire for escape, has changed into a complete hypocrisy. That there are Jewish hypocrites let no one deny. But the attribution to Jewry of hypocrisy as a characteristic cannot be honestly made by any one who has insight into Jewish life and the Jewish spirit. In this judgement the Jewish tradition "for favour" should not be abandoned because the Jews happen to be the objects of inquiry.

"Her ways are pleasant ways: and all her paths are perfect." That claim is still valid for any Jew—or Christian, or even Idolater—who follows the true path of his faith. But, at the lower level, does a formal conformity to a ritual constitute a good thing in itself, or help to constitute the nature of a good man?

One aspect of the truth of the matter emerges from the thought of Maimonides, when he says that the sacrifices were a good thing in the age when they were practised. He goes on to say, in effect, that ritual, at all periods, is arbitrary yet a good thing.[1] Certainly religion is a discipline, and

[1] This is thinking adopted by Mendelssohn. But the followers of the

The Jewish Mind

a help to morality. Perhaps they claim too much for it who argue that without religion, without, that is to say, the adoration of something beyond us, there would be no ground for morality. If morality is sanctionless (as by one definition it is) then one can conceive of a moral atheist. The better ethical argument for religion is that some discipline which is compatible with humanity can constitute a thread of moral fibre. There need be no "double-think" even on the part of the "Yom Kippur Jew". If the universe is more than atoms and the void, this communion must have some value. The Synagogue is more than one of Butler's "musical banks". Even the hypocrite pretending to be better than he is, and the sinner who knows that he is a sinner (to distinguish the arrogant heretic), may be feeling the necessity for some allegiance, for some obedience at some time, to justify his way of life.[1]

But the threads contributing to moral fibre may be very thin ones. "Some things hang by hairs." Even a remembrance of the beard of a beloved grandparent. Your Jew under investigation may be irreligious: may be an escaper from conformity: yet contrives to be conscious of his Jewishness even in relation to what he disregards—in the "shool he stays away from". Such a one, consciously or unconsciously, preserves an allegiance to the Jewish group

latter have interpreted his teaching as justifying the disregard of inconvenient ritual laws.

[1] I do not refer to the complete "actor" of religion, who does not believe at all: but does his lip-service for gain. As to the general condemnation of hypocrisy, let it be remembered that tact and a sense of shame are regarded as virtues. The Jew is forbidden to "make white the face of his companion in public". A poor man should be helped to keep up appearances. Distinctions are drawn between disobedience BEPARHESIA and BESETHER (between public and private: impudent and shamefaced). Although this is not an ultimate distinction, its existence shows that some value can be attached to the sense of shame, however that be engendered. For the rest, it can be said of life under the Talith, as someone said of life in evening dress, that it makes for equality.

346

as a social entity. We have seen that this group life is more than conformity to religion. Somehow a Jewish loyalty, without noticeable religious conformity, but without cynical disregard of the institutions, carries with it the decent traditions of the Jewish good life. Herein we may find a factor that has made for the success of the Jewish national movement. It has been said that when Zionism flowered, it was as if a remedy had been created in advance of the ills. Be it added: not only the ills of persecution, but the ills of emancipation. To the Jew who has been sceptical of the value of his ancient ritual, this old way of life became suddenly significant as an expression of social reality: as the spiritual badge of the partisans of a long-suppressed national effort. Conversely, the national effort took inspiration from the desire of the lover of tradition to follow his path in freedom. Therefore now, even in a political phase, Zionism seems to preserve values that prevent the Jewish State from equation with the barren political entities that are labelled Levantine or Balkan.

Nevertheless, at all levels, the preservation of standards is a contingent event: especially at times when standards tend to be replaced by averages. Whether in the religious context, or in some unreligious group context, the value of Jewishness as a redemptive factor for the individual cannot be guaranteed. Not all the pillars of communities—religious, social, or political—are made of marble or ivory. Not all the membranes that act as irritant in the Gentile oyster turn into pearls.

It was an apostate, Disraeli, who boasted (with the pride that survives apostasy) that his ancestors were scholars at a time when the ancestors of the British were savages. Some such feeling preserves many Jews, including many crude and ignorant men, from sinking to the level of crass materialism to which otherwise they might sink. But the preservative is not a sure one. The children of the Sons of Light have been as capable of materialism as the children of those that walk in darkness. Indeed the psychology of reaction from discipline makes this all too probable. And what of those whose lives are totally unillumined?

> Slave of the wheel of labour, what to him
> Are Plato and the swing of Pleiades?

What, to some prize-fighting son of a tailor or fishmonger, are the experiences of Joshua ben Levi, the thoughts of Maimonides? Ask of the neat-dancing young sensualist why his pride of ancestry does not prevent him from behaving as a common drunkard or fornicator. He will tell you, in other words, that he has forgotten his lineage: that the bestiary of his heraldry is contained in a motor-catalogue. And "his talk is all on sin and harlotries". Miraculously, such a one may go to the aid of an old Jew whose beard is being pulled by hooligans. By way of paradox let it be remarked that, if serious harm to the Jewish group is in question, this is less likely to be forthcoming from the "wide boy" or the "low life" than from the Jewish intellectual who decides that Jewry is an obsolete nuisance, and writes words to that effect in the newspapers of such a town as Moscow.

In a world grown individualized—and it seems that a socialized world, with only economic allegiances, is more individualized than any—the moral assessment of Jews is harder than ever it was, because the measurements are made of individuals.

Nor is it easier to find psychological group factors from which one can judge the probabilities of ethical conduct in the individuals. Here perspective is essential. If one judges Jews, as too many do, by their average behaviour in some Western town community, the judgement is worthless. Can we draw inferences, from these commercials, which will be true statements to describe, say, the close-packed Chevroth of old Eastern Europe, whose ancient Synagogues

exuded from their walls the spirits of dead generations; or
in contrast, the lumpen-proletariat of pre-1939 Warsaw, or
the Chalutzim in Israel, or the horse-dealers of the Ukraine,
or the playpeople of Hollywood? Common factors, yes—if
only a taste for gefüllte fish. More important factors,
redeeming features, probably not.

The words of Heraclitus are applicable to the stream of
Jewry. This river is not the same in two places: it is not even
the same in one place. Is there, indeed, a river?

To choose one example. There is popular belief that the
Jews are not physically brave or bellicose. The Bible gives
no support to this tradition: but the story of Ben Lakish
illustrates the belief that the student disqualifies himself from
athletic performances. In those ghetto aggregates of studious
and commercial Jews, which were surrounded by robust
savage peasantry, the contrast was clear between the strength
of the spirit and the brute forces. There were strong Jews:
butchers, cobblers, water carriers: but these were not regarded as typical either by themselves or by the more
learned. That great humorist Abramovitch (Mendele
Mocher Seforim) describes a scene where he, a traveller in
prayer-books, got his wagon entangled with that of Alter
Yaknehaz, a fellow merchant of the same type. In this way
they made the track impassable. But robust mouzhiks came
and applied their shoulders to the wheels, while the two
Jews shouted "Heave, heave" to such good effect that the
impasse was cleared. Says Mendele: "After those efforts we
were quite exhausted". So the *Luftmensch* laughs at himself.
One has heard also, of the Jew who thought that a rifle was
"to shoot with, God forbid". In countries like Tsarist Russia,
which had known the licensed kidnapping which was the
law of Cantonists (operative for two generations after the
1820s), the Jews used great ingenuity to evade military service. Only sons were not called; so seven brothers could be
found bearing seven different surnames: "not by different

fathers, but by different registrars". Ugly situations were created, in which Jews kidnapped Jews, in order to save other Jews (or because they were paid to do so). The picture that emerges from this must be contrasted with the picture of life in West Europe, when the immigrants had settled happily and the grandchildren of Joseph knew not Pharaoh.

In two world wars the Jews of Western Europe and America, and a less oppressive Russia, were in the front ranks of volunteers: won Victoria Crosses (and Iron Crosses!), and constituted, particularly in the Second World War, a significant ally against the forces of evil: we now know, a forgotten ally. Ironically, the Soviet Government, for various reasons hostile to Jewry, has produced lists of Jewish "heroes of the Soviet Union". There is evidence of great deeds by all the varieties of Russian Jew, from Rabbi to collective farmer. We also know (as was said above) that the percentage of Jewish fighters was so high in each army, in proportion to the soldiery of the native populations, that a statistician could establish the probability that the Unknown Soldier was Jewish. That the Jewish soldier was an unknown soldier is a separate proposition.

Of the performances of Jewish fighters in the prize-ring and on the battleground there is no need here for a catalogue. Of the later fighting by the soldiers of Israel: "are they not written in the book of the Wars of the Lord?" Nor must we forget the great exploits of the heroic Trumpeldor, and his devoted band, who, fighting against the Turks in the days before the Mandate, achieved heroic sacrifice in circumstances reminiscent of Leonidas and his Spartans. Perhaps things are not as they were in the days of Ben Lakish. Modern life has demonstrated the possibility of combining physical prowess with mental dedication. Yet it can be written down as significant that at least one courageous leader of Jewish soldiery has preferred the life of an archaeologist. It is as if, having established their physical powers, they elect, out of preference, to remain the people of the Book.

Of the Book: the cynic will suggest "of the books". The enemies of the Jews, who have included forgers, swindlers, liars, perverts and all the forces of corruption, are expert at attributing vices to Jews: as if following the Talmudic dictum: that one abuses by attribution of one's own defects. Certainly there have been many Jewish frauds. Individualists, anxious to escape from a restrictive environment, anxious to do well for their families, anxious, be it shamefully said, to give gifts and think themselves charitable: or anxious for anxiety's sake, and, in many instances, anxious for the sweets of the illicit—these have used their brains, their ingenuity, to find quick ways to wealth. From the Orient they have learned hard bargaining: from the subtler Westerners they have learned the possibilities latent in Company Law and Bankruptcy. The list of the wicked could also include killers (there are a few): could include hooligans (there are more than a few): could include traffickers in drugs and prostitution (there have been some): but, in fact, as we have seen, the average Jewish criminal has tended to commercial fraud rather than to other types of villainy. It is doubtful whether their contribution, even to that section of the criminal calendar, is big in proportion to their relative numbers. Nor could they claim (even recently) original distinction in the fields of spectacular conversion. But clearly it is the normal expectation that *bourgeoisie* will commit *bourgeois* crimes, rather than the crimes of the hooligan, and rather than the perversions of the aristocratic sophisticate. To attempt to mitigate these things is an absurdity of apologetics. Unfortunately, the exaggeration is so easy that apologists have been tempted beyond their function, if not beyond their capacities.

One difficulty of assessment derives from this: that the

Jew demands to be judged by his high standards.[1] That he is
conscious of them: that the majority of the people are conscious of them: these are factors for favour. The enemy, of
course, envying Jewish virtues, will base his propaganda on
what he alleges to be Jewish vices. To the objective student
of the Jews it is not a question of compromising between
these two attitudes: but of recognizing that no group lives
a life on the high plane where it has set its standard. The Jews
do not achieve a life in which Jewish ethics completely
prevail. They do achieve a life in which there is very high
consciousness that these standards should prevail. If that is
true, then they are justified in protesting against the defect
of perspective that is manifest when people use the word
Jew as a pejorative, suggestive of fraud and extortion.

They are also justified, it seems, in uttering this thought
by way of reprisal: that, whatever they may have become,
the Jews have never become—perhaps, never been allowed
to become—completely decadent. At its Biblical heights, and
in destruction and despair, the spirit of Jewry was something dynamic—a rising glory brighter, even in obscurity,
than the sunset glory of Greece, forever declining. Jews
have trailed their golden clouds through the mire of
history, but the light lingers. Jews have vacillated, as did
Elijah's Jews, between divers thresholds. But, even in their
indecision and uncertainty, they have preserved an intense
moral vitality. Therefore, their marble has not been suffused
with the pallors of Ancient Greece: nor have their colours
faded as did the colours of the Renaissance. In this age
they have been decimated, but have not shared the acedia
of the overcivilized, that apathy in the leucocytes which
is the contemporary history of the other white races.

[1] Freud, in what is probably the worst of his works, an essay on
Moses, says, pertinently, that Moses induced in Israel a super-ego.
What greater gift could he give?

2. *Psychology in Goshen*

Above a world that has said "Hail psychology" the Jewish standard, "set", as Isaiah demanded, "on a high hill", continues to blazon allegiance to those achievable ideals, which human nature can, and should, but does not, achieve: to the "should be", not to the "is": to the super-ego rather than the id: to the order of intellect and disciplined emotion, not to the impulsive, the self-indulgent, the uncontrolled. Is that standard visible to the masses—to the fish-eaters of Goshen? Certainly they do not grow up now in the intellectual austerities of the Beth Midrash. What austerities they suffer are economic, or social-political. But in the vast majority of Jewish families, in every place and every generation, an influence moves over the inchoate lives of the forming young, directing them to what the Ashkenazi Jews call Edelkeit.[1] Even when (as often) the children do not speak the language of the immigrant parents, they inhale something of this savour, an extra spirituality in life, symbolized by the image of the "extra soul" which possesses the Jew on the Sabbath. Allowing for the incidence of moral defect among parents, and allowing for the tendencies that disrupt home life, one can still predicate of Jewish groups that they teach their children diligently—however vaguely—to serve something higher than the flesh.

It must be remembered that Judaism is not an ascetic religion. Certain Chassidic sects, at many periods, have tended that way; but the Chassidic "girdle" symbolizes nothing more than the duty of a Jew, for most of his life, to think of his higher nature, not of his baser instincts.

In very orthodox phases of Jewish life the long prayers, and the frequent fasts[2], create a disciplined, severe, character.

---

[1] Refinement—in a fuller sense than the German word normally bears.

[2] Many Jews still fast each Monday and Thursday, quite apart from the very many mourning fasts in the calendar.

The Jewish Mind

Not for relaxation, not for games were we sent into the world.[1] Something in the Jewish make-up, a liveliness, a vivacity, militates against this sternness. Sublimated, it expresses itself in the cleverness of "pieces of Torah". But for the most part, the Jews do not live lives of intellectual severity. Nevertheless they are very conscious that life is not to be wasted. That accounts, on occasion, for hardness. In general it creates in family life a feeling that the existence of this family, or this group, is for something better than self-indulgence.

From this standpoint Jewish life is good life. Not the fulfilment of any "mission"—but a good effort to conserve itself for what it is.[2] If Jews, nevertheless, sink to "low life", at least there is nothing in the intellectual background that tends to this: no belief in materialism, no encouragement to rapacity: only some psychological facts, as that the intellectual is not compact of pure intellect: that the leaven of intelligence can be a corrupting as well as a creative force: that to know good is not necessarily to do good: that the fall

[1] Even chess, the Jewish game *par excellence*, has not been approved by all authorities. Some medieval authorities make it a game for women, which they can play on the Sabbath. In the context this implies a poorer conception of female status than of the game.

We know that some Rabbis played chess. The father of the Jewish Pope is said to have recognized his son (Anacletus) by playing chess with him when (after connivance with a friendly Bishop) he led a delegation to the Papal Palace. Perhaps at that stage in the evolution of the game styles were more recognizable than they are now.

Moses Mendelssohn achieved his friendship with Lessing through chess. He it was who said: "Für eine Partie zu viel Ernst: für Ernst, zu viel Partie".

In very modern times the Rabbinic families of Chajes and Moheliver have had their chess prodigies.

It may be of further interest to record that the only Jew for whom the Soviet authorities ever specially provided Kosher meat is Grand-Master Reshevsky of U.S.A.

[2] As, appropriately, Spinoza has it: *conatus sui esse conservandi*.

of Lucifer is deeper than the fall of those who were never angels.

Evidently the Jew does not escape the always accidental, but mysteriously inevitable, process of deterioration that operates among humans of all creeds. Maimonides speculates that a youth brought up in isolation from the world would never learn obscenities from Holy Writ. Theoretically, a young Jew so lives. Yet he learns the obscenities. Consequently, the Jewish world is peopled, like the Christian world, with the coarse, the gross, the materialistic. The Jew protests that Jews are not really like that. The enemy points to the bad Jew and says: what is this? Hence apologetics, which are apt to lose themselves in unreality when the authors forget the Biblical commonplace: that the inclination of the heart of man is wicked from his youth. No one has proved that the Jewish heart is worse than that of others. There is some evidence that it operates less cruelly in the main.

Jewish values (of which learning, ritual, and custom are constant reminders) form a world like other sets of values: and perhaps this order of ideals permeates Jewish life more thoroughly than other sets of ideals suffuse other groups of lives. But, granted this "participation", yet the order of behaviour is a different order from the order of ethics. (Incidentally, some Jewish names are famous among the psychologists, who, in the last hundred years, have worked out the implications of the difference between what ought to be and what is.)

One factor, however, is "special", if not to Jews alone, then to all oppressed groups. They will add to inferiority complex an extra sensitivity, called, in the Jewish case, Weltschmerz. From this can develop certain defensive antagonisms, certain hostilities, even hatreds. Such was the bitterness of Simeon ben Yochai after thirteen years of hiding in a cave. Some of his utterances have been held against the Jews. Yet they are not typical. And hatred is rare. Moreover, if there is hatred it need not be specifically anti-Gentile: it may form itself, as we have seen, into obsessive attitudes towards other Jews.

Simple manifestations of whatever this feeling is are evident when Jews have grown up among, or are closely related to those who have grown up among, really hostile Gentiles. "The sword has no place on the altar." But the child of parents who have heard the shoutings of the Cossacks, and have fled from Pogrom, can too easily (especially if the parents are unsophisticated people) come to feel violently: can develop an anti-Gentilism. From this fixation, coarse developments are normal. The Yiddish language furnishes evidence of this. The good Jew, in a full sense of that expression, does not apply words like Shaygitz and Shiksa[1] to non-Jews. But the words are there: and a great majority of Jews do not know their languages sufficiently well to know that the words are offensive: even use them quite innocently, unaware that they are recording an unpleasant obsession that has grown into the thought of their group. They do not know, or do not act upon, the frequent Talmudic statement that the Gentile is the object, together with the Jew, of all the mercies and all the charities that make up human duty. The Jew who knows his Bible knows that God not only brought the Jews out of Egypt, but brought "the Philistines from Caphtor and the Aramaeans from Kir" (Amos IX.7). The Rabbis record (in a comment on Deut. XXXIII.2) that the law was offered to various nations, but that they refused it because they would not forswear killing, adultery, etc. according to the taste of each tribe. That story is told in sorrow, not in anger. "The Gentiles are

[1] Corruptions of SHEKETZ, fem. SHIKTZA—meaning "obscene thing". Also used are YAKEL, YAKELTE (from German Jokel). Some recent English litigation has brought into prominence the word YOK—short for the German Jokel. Many did not know it to be offensive.

for killing" has been mentioned as a Talmudic text, which the best authorities deplore as a corruption of "the Egyptians are for killing". That text, incidentally, has cost more Jewish lives than Gentile ones. In a long history of ethical developments impeded by external pressures, there is quite a surprising unity of thought directed against any anti-Gentilism. It is against the learning that the other process—the psychological reaction as distinguished from the ethical tradition—expresses itself in the practice (not approved by the authorities) of ethical cynicism towards the non-Jew: as, for example, in the lending of money at interest to the Gentiles. If a Levitical text seems to justify this, let it be said that that text has been differently read in terms of a maturer morality.[1]

Let it not be thought that the Jew who contemns the Gentiles, or for that matter the Jew who does not contemn the Gentiles, is redeemed by some special loyalty to his own group, praiseworthy for its own sake. Among Heine's "dogs with doggy thoughts", it is not true to say that "dog does not eat dog". Jews have persecuted Jews enough: and rationalized, at times, their conduct by saying that in this way they keep the standards high. Certainly, against a background of civil authority, a Jew can find himself forced to use secular force against his brother, a criminal. Too often, however, the secular arm has been involved to settle domestic differences. Too often the attitude has been adopted that it is more dignified to ally oneself with the Gentile against

---

[1] Bible texts relating to Gentiles are not easily harmonized. But the general trend is to the recognition that they too, are the creatures of God. The Rabbis go further and say expressly: that "the righteous among the Gentiles inherit the world to come". There is also abundant Talmudic authority that no advantage should be taken of the Gentiles. If his goods are found they must be restored—even the goods of a pagan soldier. More than one Rabbi expresses the thought that the best words a Jew can hear are the words of a Gentile blessing the God of Israel.

the Jew. If, nevertheless, it remains true that Jews do support Jews, it must not be thought that the process is always easy, or in any sense universal. What does require to be said is that this solidarity never amounts to conspiracy against the non-Jews.[1]

Of the dangers to morality, not the least serious is the psychological treatment of the Gentile world as a pleasure-ground, as a place of escape. Time was when apostasy was a necessary condition (practical, if not theoretical) of secular education. So Heine, whose watch had "ticked in Hebrew", thought to find fulfilment in universities which did not admit Jews, and in a world of letters where objective thought seemed like an atmosphere of freedom—until he had breathed it deeply.

At a lower level, the Gentile female affords escape to the worldling whose home life is dully framed in monogamy, progeny and conventional respectability. The Jewish authorities are strong against harlotry. If some of them seem to allow concubinage, there is no general approval of this. But what traditional life, Jewish or otherwise, is strong in weapons of defence against the world, the flesh and the devil? This trinity is a greater danger to Jewry than ever was the Christian trinity. In modern times the forces of hedonism are strengthened by two centuries of that intellectual development which was Romance, and is now the Pleasure Principle. From the experiences of soul-mating, which come too easily to young intellectuals, and have been responsible for a percentage of exogamy, the way is easy to the free-life,

---

[1] It is laid down in Avoth and elsewhere, that a Jew must not "separate himself from the congregation". Although Judaism is a set of religious duties for each individual, they cannot be properly fulfilled by persons living in isolation from their fellows. The very prayers are communal. And the duties of charity, etc. imply a communal life. Therefore even the Jew who "loves his fellow men but cannot force himself to like them", must, in order to fulfil himself, associate with them.

which may be a euphemism for simple carnality. Jewish *bourgeois* organization, with its tradition of males dedicated to intellectual pursuits, has, perhaps, been sexually oppressive. The search for the well-endowed bride who can finance the unprofitable life of scholarship, is a process which causes many males and females to grow past maturity without fulfilment. Primroses were dangers to Jewry before Disraeli. And in the expanding life of the large industrial communities a recurrent force is the natural energy and initiative of the ignorant young, who have their share of imitativeness, and whose enthusiasm is too easily canalized into attractive channels. Hence the prevalence in Jewry of a being not unknown in Talmudic times, the polished "man of this world": equipped with the politeness which is the technique of all the commerces, the polish which is the pimp of prurience. So equipped, he pursues, to the limit of his earnings (for Jews are not miserly), "the harlot of the cities of the West".

Shakespeare has made a phrase which can be used to describe the special moral dangers that beset the Jew in emancipation. Shylock said: "I will better the instruction". Let Jews grow up among the tight-fisted hagglers of Slavlands, or Western peasant and small-town groups, and they will be meaner than the meanest. Show them an extravagant mode of life, and in that too they will show excess. "Oriental ostentation" is not a correct phrase for this. The factor is the enthusiasm and energy of people who are always, as it were, escaping into something, or somewhere, new. With this energetic spirit they conquer the new environment: and that, unhappily, conquers them.

Search not, then, for Jewish vices and virtues. If virtues are sought, at least we have established traditions which tend to the fostering of a good way of life. Whether many Jews follow that way is a more difficult question. Vices, however, they collect from all environments. At any moment of time it is reasonable to expect that the psychological problems of the general world are being experienced with special acuteness in some Jewish context. If there are barriers still standing to prevent the entropy of Jewish merits into mundane mediocrity, they are embodied in a religion which is not firmly held, and is the target of many revolutions; also in an intellectualism which has its own special defects, and has been weakened with many revaluations. But, strongest, perhaps, is a group consciousness, heightened by traditional hostilities, which are for ever being revealed in recurrent revelations.[1]

[1] In answer to the question, which is a Christian and Moslem as well as a Jewish question, whether the exponents of religion, the clergy or priesthood, or Rabbinate, exercises any influence on the morality of the group, let it be said that these functionaries can only exercise control, or exert influence, on those who listen to them, and to the limit of their own personal powers. The preacher who preaches about the desirability of attending places of worship is preaching to the absent, who do not hear him. But in orthodox communities, with congregations attendant on the Rabbi, great moral influence can be, and has been, exerted. Chassidism is one movement in which men of piety have strongly influenced the lives of their followers along good paths. Unhappily that degenerated into almost an idolatry of the Rabbi (Rebbe) or Tsaddik, as he was called. They looked to him for mystery rather than morality: snatched at particles of his food, so that they could absorb his virtues. Nevertheless, for all the temptations of obscurantism, and all the faults of dynastic tradition, the general influence was moral as well as pious. Piety can be, but is not easily, isolated from morality.

More expressly moral in its teaching is the MUSAR movement, associated with the great name of Rabbi Israel Lipkin, known as Salanter (from the place of his Rabbinate). Lipkin was aware that the Jews trading in the markets of Poland, Lithuania, and White Russia, were employing, in their commercial dealings, all the frauds and knaveries of the peasants with whom they were dealing. He insisted on the learning of morality. Just as, from learning the alphabet laboriously, one comes to read books fluently, so, he said, if one learns laboriously the small restraints of honesty in the most trivial situations, if one learns never to lie, never to overreach, whatever the temptation, and, particularly, if

3. *Axes for Delving*

It was a Jewish author—Israel Zangwill—who first presented to the public "an Irishman by birth and profession". Similar epithets have since been aimed at Roumanians, Poles, Albanians, Americans, and representatives, generally, of all oppressed, or impressive, groups. But they do not direct this sarcasm at Jews or Negroes: for some situations, however grotesque, do not stimulate laughter. Who wants to be a Jew? "By coercion you are in life" seems, at times, to apply specially to him. As an occupation Jewishness patently leaves everything else to be desired. Yet there are "professional" Jews; and it is the Jewish Chochmah writer who says: "He who seeks honour has honour run away from him." There is a sufficient history of Jewish assertiveness inside the group to make this an important Jewish thought. Certainly there have been times—most times—when to serve the community in any way was burdensome and unrewarding. A special prayer—so special that we retain it both in Hebrew and Aramaic—calls down the blessing of Heaven on those who work for the needs of the congregation faithfully. Certainly there have been times when to be a representative of Jewry to the outside world, or a leader of Jewry held responsible to the outside world, was (as Rabbi Joshua

one learns these things early in life, one comes to behave morally without effort, just as the scholar reads effortlessly.

In these teachings—and the same thought may be applied to the many works of Ethics in which Jewish literature abounds—Rabbi Lipkin was not adding to orthodox Judaism: but he was underscoring the dangers of thought of those who were content to be pious in the ritual sense and froward in the workaday world: or honest with Jews, and dishonest to non-Jews.

The Musarnik movement, with its special emphasis, eventually suffered the fate of sectary trends, became isolated and forgotten. But its founder's influence remains in the minds of all the exponents of Rabbinic orthodoxy.

found in Roman times) to be *caput lupinum*. This representative situation was even less pleasant than that of the early Burghers who came to the Lancastrian Parliaments like sheep to the shearing. But the universal evolution of representative government has opened, in all groups from African villages to American cities, careers attainable of the talents. As to the Jew, two centuries of access to the general, two centuries which have given almost complete emancipation, have offered acceptable opportunities to the Jewish talents: first, perhaps, to the talents of silver, which is said to purify bastards: and in the later phases to the golden talents—to the christomatous orators who spring in multitude from the stock of Isaiah.

Of what are we speaking? Of men who are Rabbis? "State" Rabbis, perhaps? Of men who are elected to Sejms as representatives of Jewry? Of men who are moneylenders, or shop stewards, or lawyers, and get themselves elected to the Parliaments of the nations, with or without a Jewish representative purpose? Of Public Relations Jews? Perhaps of all of these. The fact is that two centuries of emancipation and representationalism in public affairs, have also been two centuries of specialization, including specialization in religion and, if it be possible, in morality: at all events, in "leadership".

Jewish tradition, as we have seen, is differently grounded: anti-hieratic, anti-authoritarian, legalistic. What are now full-time occupations were never so regarded in most of the centuries of the Jewish past. The conductors of the religious services were laymen: and that is still good practice among the learned. The Baal Tefillah, who proclaimed the prayers, was never strictly necessary, and was lay. So the Baal Keriyah who "read" the portions: and (in very old days) the Meturgeman, who translated the reading into Aramaic. The Hebrew teacher was an ill-paid menial—always treated with the greatest respect. The Slaughterer, since the laws became complex and obscure, has been a part-time functionary of great learning and dignity.[1] The Mohel (Circumciser), another part-time functionary, was not, and is not, strictly necessary, since the obligation is on the male parent. That the latter does not usually perform the act himself is an accidental, and a humane, development. Chazanim, singers of the service, were always an unnecessary luxury, but popular in a people which has music in its soul. Yet for centuries the status of the Chazan (whose learning might be negligible in volume compared to his voice) was given the kind of pittance that fell to the strolling fiddlers, the KLEZMER[2] who performed at weddings. Be it remembered that the Middle Ages did not value the artist: and that music was not played in the Synagogue service after the fall of the Temple.[3]

The Preacher—Maggid—was also, in the last analysis, an entertainer. His treatment has varied with the culture and wealth of the various periods. But always his DROSHO, whether Hebrew or Jargon, whether homiletical MUSAR[4] or elaborate Halachic exposition, was a considerable

---

[1] Shechita, which has been stupidly (or wickedly) attacked as in-humane, is only validly criticizable for that the criterion of a correct slaughtering is stated in terms of medieval anatomy and physiology. But since, in fact, oesophagus and carotid must be severed with one incision, instantaneous death of the animal is assured.

[2] KLEI ZEMER—musical instruments.

[3] For some centuries now the paid Chazan has been normal, indeed essential: and the appointee frequently combines his work with Ritual Slaughter and Circumcision. Some relic of the traditional disregard for his personal value is expressed in the Yiddish saying that Chazanim are fools: and we are told that the letters of the title indicate this. Ch Z N being notarikon symbols (an acronym) of Chazanim seinen Narronim.

[4] Musar. Moral exhortation. At some levels Maggidim indulged in picturesque presentations of the sufferings of the wicked in Gehennom. Other discourses are of great beauty and subtlety.

intellectual and oratorical performance, and a source of great pleasure.[1] Yet nobody retained him.

Different in kind (but only little in degrees of emolument) was the Rabbi. He was an appointee at a very early stage in the history of the Diaspora. In Talmudic times we know that he could work as a craftsman, tailor, cobbler, and the like. In the Middle Ages he was medical man, or of independent means, or prosperously married. He was given perquisites, as at the fictitious sale of the leaven[2]; presents, at weddings, Bar Mitzvah celebrations, etc. Normally these would be administered for charity. Later, unhappily, they became essentials to his maintenance. But at all times the Rabbi was held to be above financial affairs. Some of the grimness, or the cynicism, of the lay attitude is reflected in the life story of the quite recent Rabbi Isaac Elchanan Spektor, held to be the greatest Talmudist of the late nineteenth century. He was paid by his congregation some five groschen per week (farthings according to the valuta of that time). When a larger community offered him twenty groschen, he had to be smuggled out of the "five groschen village" because the inhabitants esteemed him beyond money. Let it be added that the Russian Jewish villages knew the meaning of poverty.

The Rabbis enjoyed great prestige, subject only to these empirical limitations: that Jews are anti-authoritarian; that there can be rival Rabbis; that Jews may lose their orthodoxy. But at periods of religious fervour, and periods of external pressure, Rabbis led the communities and were revered by

[1] The pattern is a group of texts, from Pentateuch. Hagiographa, Talmud and/or Midrash; involving questions, but having no apparent connection. These the Maggid wove into a unity, conveying a moral lesson and a comfort.

[2] An artificial transaction in which one purports to sell to a Gentile, and later repurchase, those stocks of food, etc. that cannot be used at Passover, and, strictly speaking, should be "swept out" with all that is leavened.

them. In his KAHAL (or Kehilla) the Rabbi's word was law. When, as in two centuries (sixteenth–eighteenth), there was a Jewish Council of Four Lands (Poland, Lithuania and two provinces of Russia) Rabbis were included in, and presided over, the elected representatives. Also they constituted courts (original and appellate courts), and generally secured, by the rule of Rabbinic law, the discipline of a well-ordered community, that stood strong even through a period of wars and the bloody revolutions of the Pogromist Chmielnicki. In those and other periods, the Rabbi exercised, in the last resort, a power of anathema.[1] Its invocation would, of course, be a confession of weakness. That it was used against Spinoza is evidence of some moral weakness in Jewish Amsterdam in that age. But *in potentia* it sanctioned respect for the law and for the exponents of the law. The strongest support of the jurisdiction, however, lay in the great moral personalities who actually were Rabbis. There have been small Rabbis. There have been polemists: there have been impudent claimants to the title Gaon—a title that should be granted by educated consent to the outstanding luminaries of the law in any age. But the moral averages over two millennia have been high. In our day and age, when commercial interests can conflict with religion, when the purveying of food can involve licensing and the granting of certificates of Kashrut, it is obviously possible for Rabbis to be corrupt. In days when the standards of qualifications have been lowered from the high East European, either through Western needs, or through excess of humanity on the part of the great[2] it is possible for Rabbis to be little more than indifferent preachers and sorry publicists. And there are other modern developments to be considered. But when all that is said let it be recorded that, alone of intellectuals, Rabbis

[1] He never exercised it single-handed.

[2] Rabbi Isaac Elchanan Spektor was lenient in his awards because he was optimistic of the consequences of encouragement.

have inevitably been more than careerists. They seem, some-how, to reassert in their history a belief that it is better to be learned than to be ignorant. If this is snobbery, they redeem it.

They at least have lived lives that were unthinkable unless dedicated. Paradoxically the careerists of Jewry in most periods have been the lay: the Parnassim, the Gabbaim or Gizborim, appointed to collect the communal taxes and distribute the alms. These included plenty of men "with bunches of snakes hanging behind them". From these are recruited the honour-seekers: and they are always ready to recruit colleagues from the merely rich.

Traditionally they, too, have fine examples to follow. The Baal Habaith who devotes time to the service of the com-munity, and seeks no honour from it, is a character entitled to whatever rewards are granted for the survival of Jewry. But in modern days the Jewish leadership has suffered much from the absorption of secular thinking and the copying of Gentile behaviour.

In these days of specialization, the Rabbi, the Chazan, and Secretary, if not President, are together achieving function, vocation, status. They train for the jobs—and become professionals. The Germans invented the professional "Pradiger" who brooded in the pulpit on the mystery of the Akedah (Sacrifice of Isaac) as expressive of the highest cate-gories in the Hegelian classification of Religions. Western Jews following (but not listening) have evolved a species of "Minister" who, starting as modest substitute for Rabbi in a local Synagogue, is called Rabbi by the Gentiles (who know no subtleties) and then, by the equally ill-informed Jews, until inevitably, the title Rabbi becomes, in due course, debased coinage.

The resultant "personalities" range themselves alongside the lay "professionals", the lawyers and the politicians, who, in the course of their careers, claim to have suffered countless misfortunes through their dedication to the Jewish cause. This when they solicit Jewish votes and Jewish support. The suffering spirit is less evident when the Jewish Member of Parliament refuses to vote against his own (anti-Semitic) party. Below these high levels we find, also, an inveterate tendency among Jews to form committees and societies for philanthropic purposes. Almost they achieve parliaments of their own. In many cases these noble undertakings do good: always they afford to the loudest of their supporters the special pleasure that accrues to the "big noise".[1]

Perhaps it is a reasonable compensation for the losses that are incurred by many, because they are Jews, losses of opportunity, losses of the equities of life, that others profit in personal aggrandizement from the status of Jew. It happens that the one who loses is not the one that gains. What can be said in favour of the latter class is that not all of the careerists are undeserving of honour: that many in search of honour pay for it with the sweat of their brow. There is something to be written in the annals of humour about the ignoramus collecting for the Theological College. That he succeeds in establishing the foundation changes the nature of the irony. How Jewish careerism differs from other incidences can be expressed in the old formula. Some of them start an activity not for its own sake; they continue in it for its own sake. The Jew, in particular, not being really materialistic, tends to love his work for more than what he extracts from it. So the activities of ulterior motive come to be enjoyed as activities conscientiously pursued. When questions of prestige arise, cloven hooves emerge. But when the difficulties of the task are proper to the task, then great

---

[1] Talmudically "the small coin in the pitcher". "Cult of personality" is not new in Jewish history. It is interesting to note that Isaac Disraeli, father of Benjamin Disraeli, and author of *Curiosities of Literature*, used a quarrel with the wardens of his Synagogue as an occasion for apostasy.

367

efforts are made, and mountains are moved. Out of the depths of degradation and materialism that can be experienced in the ghetto, concerted social efforts, with rewards in personal acclamation, have drawn many spirits above the dross. Not all pure spirits—not all Neshama—but transmuting the "unclean bones" into a better personality. When they reflect, these honour-seekers, that they have done some good to Jewry, they will not always be aware that they have done a great service to themselves, apart from the recognition they have earned. When the history of our times comes to be written by the psychologists, they may find in ghetto-careerism one of the forces that made the State of Israel. Also they may recognize in the State of Israel a phenomenon that redeemed the "personalities" of the ghetto.

4. *The Literary Brood*

One career that has been open to Jewish talents for over a century is that of the secular writer—the belle-lettrist or novelist. Not only to Jews, but to the Western world in general, the eighteenth century gave new vehicles of communication: not the least important of which is the novel, or feuilleton, or romance, which, starting as story for the purposes of entertainment, becomes ideal experiment, becomes social survey, becomes psychological casebook. Here are children's night-candles which develop the glare of a volcano.[1] Admittedly there are many stories which are enjoyable narrative without ulterior motive. Indeed the ability to write narrative, as such, is essential in the writer's craft. But most of the novels that have mattered are tendentious in a good sense: are critical autobiographies in disguise: are satires or sarcasms: are modes of self-expression,

[1] I have reversed an epigram in which Kipling summed up the fate of *Gulliver's Travels*.

in which, explicitly or implicitly (the latter with the greater art) the writer sets forth his doubts, his despairs and his hopes.

In both Yiddish and Hebrew there has grown, in the modern period, a substantial literature in the form of fiction. To narrative in both languages there are, as we have seen, abundant antecedents. Glückel of Hamelin's Yiddish diaries are classical. Medieval Maase Bücher, though religious in content, are collections of religious stories well told—rather better than the Gesta Romanorum. Hebrew, apart from its Biblical masterpieces, and some of its more polished Midrashim, also has its travellers' tales from of old.

But the mature self-conscious Jewish fiction begins with Mapu: and Mapu, writing, early in the nineteenth century, in excellent Hebrew, set a standard, if not a style, for future generations. Mapu's explicit objective—criticism of Jewish life and institutions—has been, consciously or unconsciously, adopted by the majority of his successors.

From the standpoint of Jewish religion and group life, the Jewish novelists are, in the Hegelian phrase, "negative". Mapu's "Painted Popinjay" purports to be an exposure of hypocrisies.[1] He had many successors in this tradition: lesser men than himself. His earliest rival in quality must be looked for in the world of verse. Judah Loeb Gordon—a master of sarcasm—expressing his criticisms in polished couplets—is remembered particularly for his exposure of the legal disabilities of the Jewish woman, and the terrible personal consequences of some formal absurdities. As a poet he merits a wider fame.

Half a century after Mapu, a greater novelist, Peretz Smolenskin, carried on strongly the tradition of narrative that exposes the vices and hypocrisies of the contemporary Jewish life: and he was succeeded by another Peretz—Isaac Loeb Peretz—whose studies in Jewish life are somewhat less

[1] This is not an official translation of *Ayot Tsovuah*, but is, I think, correct.

astringent, and, formally, a more polished contribution to the aesthetic treasures of Israel.

In Smolenskin's work *Astray in the Ways of Life*, we find, for the first time in post-Biblical Jewish literature, the element of sexual iconoclasm. One episode in this episodic book is the discovery, made by the ingenuous youth, that the saintly man with whom he is travelling, and who has been very kind to him, is a libertine who uses the opportunities of the quasi-confessional available to the Tsaddik.

Among attacks on religion the exposure of saintly persons, as creatures vicious in their private lives, is terribly effective when spread among poor persons whose economic condition is always made harder by the requirements of the religion, and by communal charity demands.

I. L. Peretz is kinder to the professionals of religion: and one of his stories *Higher Than That* is a picture of a Tsaddik in the highest traditions of Chassidism.

But it may be compendiously said that the novelists attack religion, if only by emphasizing in their writings the demands of the world, and the fundamentals of human conduct, important for the religious and irreligious alike.

Their subject-matter is a ghetto, real and vital, but beginning to experience the strains and stresses of new pressures—the pressures of a quickening economy, and of quickening culture. As the darkness weighed solidly on Egypt, so a new enlightenment was weighing on Goshen—bearing down on the life of the orthodox enclaves. How will my son end? Peretz, in his study—*Four Wills*—describes, in turn, the pious studious elder, with a will phrased in homily, and characterized by philanthropy: his son, pious and respectable, but more worldly, and wealthier, leaving the will of a generous communal leader: succeeded in turn by a rich worldling: and, after his worldly testament, we read the suicide note of the blasé decadent.

Aware of the new culture, they still lived, these writers, in a world of Kahal, with Rabbis, Chazonim, Shochetim, Melammedim, Shadchanim. They have it in common that they are good at describing pleasant and unpleasant Jews. But they differ from all the European exploiters of the Jew in fiction, because they are able to describe him, adequately, in his spiritual, mental, social setting. Like the historians of the Jewish religion, they have the equipment of the believer who has ceased to believe. Into their Shylocks and their Fagins they have a deep insight because they know the true religious coefficient of their objects, and what they portray are, consequently, unpleasant characters of tragedy, not stock figures of farce.

Be it added that the Gentile is bound to fail as a portrayer of real Jews. Either he sees his objects as undesirable excrescences from a background into which they do not fit; or the author idealizes them as did George Eliot (that brilliant philo-Semite) when she presented the saintly Daniel Deronda: and as did Dickens, when, in order to atone for his picture of Fagin, he drew the even less convincing Mutual Friend.

Real Jews, be it emphasized, are not portrayed by the Gentile. The character in Galsworthy's *Loyalties* is a Jew of sorts—maybe a real existent—but, apart from his possible subscription to a West End Synagogue, not a contributor to Jewish life or culture.[1] What applies to the Gentile writer applies equally to any nominal Jew who sees the Jew, as it were, externally. Disraeli's *Alroy*[2] is, as a Jewish study—as well as aesthetically—worthless. When the better equipped Feuchtwanger gave to literature *Jew Süss*, he was describing a superficial type; but the essence of his work

[1] A more convincing presentation of the "link" Jew is to be found in Gilbert Frankau's *Outlier from the Tribe*. Frankau was, or had been, a Jew.

[2] David Alroy was a pseudo-Messiah in Saracen times; he is said to have been assassinated by his well-meaning father.

was the life of a Feudal Court with its Court Jews. History, this, and Jewish history in a sense.

Evidently, outside the ghetto the Jew is hard to describe, because outside the ghetto the writer has to search deeply, and call on the memories of sympathetic experience, to find the Jewishness of the character he portrays. As we shall see, there are Jewish writers—so far only in European languages —who being of "external" type themselves, describe persons who only reveal to the reader the externalia of Jewish appearance and Jewish name; but have no Jewish consciousness in the deeper sense.

Among the better equipped writers (of the Russo-Polish Pale) the Jew who describes Jews Jewishly at their lowest levels is Sholom Asch, one of the greatest of the Yiddish novelists. A product of an area—though not a family—in which life was hard and embittered, he could describe the pimps and pick-pockets of the Warsaw Ghetto as he had seen them. Mottke Ganov (*Mottke the Thief*) is a real Jew presented against a Jewish background. When Asch became ambitious, and painted on what he thought was a larger canvas, he succeeded as narrator and stylist—even, in *Three Cities*, as historian—but never recaptured the realism that could have made him into a Jewish Balzac.

Interesting in contrast to Asch is the more considerable, but less known, Singer, whose *Yoshe Kalb* (translated as *The Sinner*) is a perfect study in Chassidic life. In his work generally (*The Brothers Ashkenazi* has also been well translated) we see Jewish life through a more sympathetic medium. Singer is a greater writer than Asch, for the same reason that Tolstoy is greater than Dostoevski. His approach is more positive: undistorted by bitterness or cynicism. If acceptance is a form of distortion, at least it is the one that makes for high art. But even Singer, in his later work (*Eastward of Eden*), shows a certain consciousness that what he describes is passing.

Other great writers are also conscious of transience. The great Yiddish-Hebrew[1] humorist, Mendele, with the acceptiveness that characterizes real humour, yet conveys the sadness of more than ordinary Weltschmerz. People are going away.

Those successful playwrights, like Rappaport (Ansky), who portrayed real Jewish life to real Jewish audiences, also express from time to time this awareness of impermanence. Scepticism as to faith is there, and the knowledge of changing world conditions. It is not merely the temptations of the flesh drawing Frischman's Iluy (genius) "away from the path". Something of a more universal movement is developing. Over all of them hangs a cloud such as overhung the Jews in the desert: making them aware that they are in transition. In the minds of most of the Jewish writers this consciousness was turned bright by the pillar of fire which was rising Zionism. While Smolenskin was limning those *Astray in the Ways of Life*, Pinsker was writing *Auto-Emancipation*.

In languages other than Hebrew and Yiddish there is little original Jewish fiction that can be compared, without a sort of blasphemy, with the literature of Russo-Polish Jewry.

Israel Zangwill, a brilliant penman, living at the end of the nineteenth century, had before him a Jewry that was still rich in its own traditions. He, unhappily, was not well enough versed in the learning, and was, in sympathy, too alien from it, to do more than use it "as an axe for delving"—rather as the Jewish comedian has used the "stock" Jew.[2]

Of Golding, related to Zangwill as one who was too small for the Mantle of Elijah, suffice it to say that, after

---

[1] He translated his own works from Yiddish into a most rich and readable Hebrew.

[2] In contrast to *Children of the Ghetto*, Zangwill's *Dreamers of the Ghetto* is scholarly.

copying the first sentence of the *Children of the Ghetto* into *Magnolia Street*, he went on to describe the Jews of Manchester as might any Gentile citizen of that city who happened to be endowed with literary ability.

Magnolia Street—and Zangwill's *Fashion Street* for that matter—is a street. Anyone who tries to describe, in terms of streets, those whose home is in time, rather than space, is failing to describe Jewry. Yet here is a fact of life relevant to modern literature. There are Jewish streets in London, Paris and New York, which are describable—even if what is being described is not, in any deep sense, Jewish. The logical development of study of the "low life" Jew is achieved, and brilliantly achieved, in the novels of Weidman, describing an adventurer in the Jewish area of New York. "I can get it for you wholesale" is the slogan that expresses the "wide boy's" mentality. Needless to say, the mentality that it expresses corresponds to a very low order indeed of the Jewish Mind.

Thus, outside the Russian nineteenth century, the movement from Smolenskin to Asch is paralleled by the descent from Zangwill to the many pens that strive for pittances with Jewish material.

The lowness of the level is, in part, a consequence of the fact that most of those who write English fiction about Jews are not well equipped in any Jewish tradition, and are not aware, with concrete awareness, of the high standards— or, for that matter, of the low averages—in the mentalities of those that they describe. The best they can achieve—and this is not without literary value—is a nostalgia. British, American, and Canadian writers have expressed in stories and verses their sense of loss for a life that is passing away: the nostalgia that they have felt in their own homes. So they end with regrets for the books they could not read, for the thoughts that never succeeded in absorbing them.

But they share with greater ones a more fundamental

problem. What is the ultimate value of the content? In that word "content" lies perhaps the clue to the answer. Jewry, like the Jewish religion and the Jewish language, is something concrete. It is all too easy, along the lines of a Spengler-Toynbee dialectic, to think away the permanence of a nation with limited space, of a religion at the end of its time. But the Jews resist all dialectical patterns. In literature the truth becomes lost if the writers are not near enough to their subject, and the types that they study are not near enough to Jewish reality. Especially is this fact important in this century of scepticism. The writers, from Schnitzler to Miller, who search in vain for ultimate purpose in life, for a compensation for death, are not the holders of a tradition of values such as Jewish life can afford. So the Swann whom Proust projects into the unreality of the past, never had a Jewish past. Nor is there Jewish ballast in the Jew whom Joyce put on to the bark of Ulysses in order to journey his thought-land voyage. Nor is that Kafka fortified with Jewish thought or feeling, in its concrete reality, when he experiences the doubts and unrealities of the Castle of Faith. Too many Jews, too many Jewish writers, are, in some degree, heimatlos from a home that exists. Therefore over Jewish literature hangs the feeling that the Germans know as *Zwecklosigkeit*. To what purpose? The clear answer—suspect because it is clear—is that a worthwhile Jewish literature could be inspired by a religious impulse or could be inspired by a nationalist purpose. The former seems to be absent from writers. Only occasionally, in communities like New York, is it recaptured by writers in Yiddish: though let it be said that in the English writings of such as Wouk in U.S.A. there is discernible the possibility of future novel writing, in which some Jewish ethics will be a relatively stable framework, a framework that survives the questionings that are the novelist's theme. In more politically advanced England, Jewish playwrights, such as Wesker,

present Jews whose intellectual history is of tragic disappointment in Communism. Of the other Jewish purpose (the
Nationalist), this is too new, too nascent, for literary
conquest. Even in Israel, their best novels are historical
novels.[1] Of Jewish life, fully and truly lived in an environment which does not destroy it, one can only say that, if that
life obtains anywhere, it has not permeated fiction. The
epitaph to Jewish Diaspora fiction was, perhaps, best expressed by Herzl at the end of *Judenstaat*: "If you wish,
this is not a story".[2]

5. Jewish Laughter

If any type of writer is capable of presenting the blend of
idealism and reality which is Jewish life, that writer is the
mature humorist.

He is acceptive. He does not conceal nor excessively
denigrate. From Mendele Mocher Seforim, and Sholom
Aleichem, and Peretz and many others, there is a mass of

[1] There is, of course, valuable fiction expressing the religious life—
as, e.g. in the works of Agnon, who draws the Chassid sharply and
clearly.

Another field of fiction is that of children's books, in which war
stories (of the 1948 and other campaigns) are written rather Biblically,
and with "a moral".

[2] Let it be added that, at this moment of writing, there seems to be
stirring, at least in U.S.A., something of a positive spirit; something
that may give rise to literary work in which the Jewish background
is treated as permanent and valuable in itself. If this trend exists, it is
traceable to two things: to the world reaction against materialism,
and to the success of the Jewish State. As to the latter place, it is, of
course, too early to assess Israel literature. Most of it has so far been
written by those who come from Europe, and rejoice to express the
contrast between oppression and freedom. Some who wrote well
of Europe, write ununderstandingly of Israel. (E.g. Koestler, whose
best book is about Communism and whose worst book is about
Zionism.) For the rest, the generation of Sabras—Israel born (cacti)
—has not yet had time to judge or be judged.

work that speaks for itself as well as Jewry. But, for academic purposes, it is worth inquiring: what is the element that makes Jewish humour different from the humour of the other groups? Some examples may serve a useful purpose.

The story is told of the father of the celebrated intellectual misadventurist Solomon Maimon, that he was negotiating a betrothal for his brilliant son (then about thirteen years of age) and was asked how much NADAN (dowry) was required. He replied with a quotation from Canticles: "For a thousand to thee Solomon, and two hundred for the nurserymen of his fruit". The prospective MECHUTAN accordingly sent 1,200 golden roubles. But Solomon's father replied that he had wanted 300 for his own purposes: only he could not bring himself to misquote Holy Writ. It is in the true tradition that the other hundred was forthcoming.

If (and the hypothesis is a difficult one) there is such an element in culture as a specifically Jewish humour then that story of Maimon's father is an example of it. The story is humorous in that it contains a development in a human situation of the kind that stimulates laughter in the understanding spectator. It has this in common with other typically Jewish jokes that the movement is an intellectual one. For the rest there is the pleasant familiarity appeal, from an atmosphere of learning, to those who savour learning with full enjoyment.

But a story like this could possibly be told of learned medieval Christians playing intellectual games with their Vulgate. Erasmus and Rabelais played those games: and there is a suggestion of similar scholastic irony in the use that is made of literary quotations in the Platonic dialogues. Perhaps the proper statement is that Jews have indulged much in that intellectual humour: are journeymen (even masters) of intellectual fun, rather than monopolists of a special source of laughter.[1]

[1] Peculiarly Jewish, in content rather than form, will remain those

The Jewish Mind

In thinking of Jewish humour one must remember that the orthodox Jew in his ghetto, on the defensive against the enemy without and the sceptic within—and this state made the more depressing by his own hard struggle to survive—had little time, little desire, to appreciate the things of the ordinary world. "I have not sat in the seat of the scornful": because of the peril. That Jew found his pleasures, as it were, on the Sabbath: that is to say in the clever learning and the appealing homily: in the appreciation of wit and wisdom, not in the amusing mischances of the week-day world.[1]

The Jew in emancipation—particularly emancipation from the hard life of East Europe (or Western sweat-shops) —can laugh, and does so heartily. He is aware of the follies of the Goy—but even more keenly aware of the follies of the Jew. He has the worldly experience to see through the bluffer and the honour-seeker, unless their Western disguise is too impressive. But, even then, when he laughs it is at the cunning and cleverness in life rather than the stupidity. "Why did you change your name twice? From Zichlinsky to Wilberforce, and from that to Ferguson?" "Because when my name was Wilberforce, they asked me what it had been before; and I had to say Zichlinsky. Now if they

stories that are completely ununderstandable to persons without Jewish learning. E.g. jokes about the miracles that took place on Rosh Hashana —that Satan benefited from a miracle in that the Shofar is blown from the narrow end, etc. There is a great supply of these, and of stories of requests made to God by poor persons, illegitimates, and the like, and the clever replies that are made. A very simple and translatable piece of "learned cleverness" is the question why Adam did not eat of the Tree of Life first. The answer is that, until he had eaten of the tree of knowledge, he lacked the wisdom to do so.

[1] What would cause him to smile is such an explanation as accompanies that injunction: "Oppressed in his mind, let him work at the Torah". (T.B. Eruvin 54a.) It would be explained that a poor man's hut was very crowded; and he complained. So the Rabbi advised him to bring in the goat: later, when it was worse, to bring in the cow, etc. Afterwards when the man had got rid of them, he had plenty of space.

challenge me about my name I can say that it used to be Wilberforce.''[1]

For analytic purposes, compare the Jew who changed his religion twice—from Jew to Catholic, and then Catholic to Protestant. "It's a question of democracy. When I was a Jew, He could see me and I couldn't see Him—not equal. I went into the Catholic Church. There I could see Him and He couldn't see me—not equal. Now I'm a Protestant; I don't see Him: He doesn't see me. That's democracy."

The difference between the two stories is a degree of intellectual astringency. The only Jewish element in the second story is its intellectualism. The first story, however, has a background of Jewish social problems. Intellectual, too, if on a lower level, and Jewish in its setting. Yet can it be said to be a peculiar operation of the Jewish mind?

The difficulty in describing Jewish jokes is that many of the best of them could be translated into the idiom of other "eccentric" groups: of the Gaels of various species; of Gascons; of Saxons, etc.[2] "Tell me an oppressed minority joke" is a possible formula, and a jest in itself.

Jewish stories include the adventures of Chelmer Narronim. These simpletons were so anxious that the Shammos (Beadle) should not deface the pure white snow with his heavy feet, that they decided that four of the congregation

[1] An element of farce is introduced if the pronunciation of the W is appropriately voiced.

[2] There is, e.g. a Jewish story of an illiterate beadle, who (sacked on account of his ignorance) became rich. When asked what his lot would have been had he only been literate, he replied: A beadle in the United Synagogue. This has been made into an excellent short story, in an Anglican setting, by Somerset Maugham (*The Verger*). On the other hand, many Synagogue stories are too full of Jewish idiom and tradition, and too reliant on it, to be translatable in fact. In point are the jests about ignorant beadles. More sophisticated—but untranslatable—are jokes about the Pshettlach of Chassidic Rabbis. Easier are the stories about their "miracles" (holding back the Sabbath, etc.).

should carry him on his rounds. The reader will recognize the reasoning of the "Wise Men of Gotham".

Amusing Jewish songs such as "A Chazan for Shabbos"—in which cobbler, tailor, drover, and others, express their appreciation in their own idiom, could be translated into the idioms of Ireland or Wales, especially of those areas where the lower crafts are slightly contemned.

Similarly, "Mein Yiddishe Mamme" is "An Old-fashioned Lady" in Yiddish terms.

And so of many *bon mots*, sarcasms, etc. The atheistic, socialistic, Zionist leader is seen emerging from a Kosher restaurant. "Sh! I only had an egg." The Jewish content is richer than the egg. But the thing is still translatable into the story of a trade unionist emerging from the Ritz or Carlton: "I've only had beer."

Jokes based on mispronunciations, misunderstanding of words, malapropisms, are frequent: specially amusing to Jews, but not "logically" Jewish jokes.

Similarly there are abundant sarcasms, *bon mots*, and ironies, based on social, commercial, etc. situations. "He was not bankrupt but broke." "Oedipus complex—what nonsense—he's a good boy who loves his mother." Specially appealing is the comment of the merchant's mother on learning that her new acquaintance's son, a Rabbi, was earning less than £1,000 per annum. "It's no life for a Jewish boy."

In considering all these stories, it is hard to isolate the form from the content. Especially is it difficult to think away the pleasurable nostalgia which makes a Jew enjoy an accent, a malapropism, an idiom, a pshettel, an obstinacy. "You haven't asked how I am." "How are you?" "Don't ask." Any Jew who knows his Jews gets pleasure from the simple recognition of the mentality, whatever that is.

The topic, be it emphasized, is the Jewish joke: not the Jew-joke. But the latter warrants a digression. The Jew-joke, more properly the anti-Jewish joke, is comparable to the Scottish (or anti-Scottish), Irish (or anti-Irish) joke, and is only different in that it retains more venom. That it has been a source of profit to Jewish comedians is a melancholy mitigation of a mockery. Let it not be supposed that those jokers who mock the Jew are, to that extent, harmless. We have heard Jew-jokes from at least one unworthy representative of Christianity in this century; a pessimist whose existence was a justification of his pessimisn. Also, in an anti-Semitic moment, from one of the more optimistic of the world's statesmen. When the scholarly but unlamented Dean Inge spoke of American Jews in a favourable position for the "fleecing of the Gentiles", he was keeping alive a tradition of Jew-baiting not unknown to the Church. (Did they not in the eighteenth century appoint Jewish church-wardens in order to have them mulcted in penalties?) Speaking at a time when the dome of his cathedral (the spiritual home of so many worthier deans) was cracking, he strengthened thoughts that eventually led to danger of its destruction. When an English politician said: "Let them not try to get to the head of the queue" he added to the list of light-hearted blackguarding that Israel has had occasion to lament. In his reaction to Jew-jokes, the Jew is usually "humourless", for the good reason that the Jew-joke is either not a joke, or is a joke making possible a crueller conception of humour.

The Jew is, of course, particularly sensitive about cruelty. Jews of the old school do not "act the goat" (except in Purim Spiel). It is, indeed, from Jewish experience that we learn the etymological truth: that "caprice" derives from the same root as tragedy. The Jews have lived too long among "goat-players". Hence the apparent humourlessness of the immigrant.

When Bergson (Jew and philosopher) described laughter as a reaction due to a feeling of superiority to the situation, he contemplated that elements of hurt would terminate the laughter. Laugh at the man who skids on the banana skin because your reflexes make you feel relief that you were not so "mechanical" as to lose control of the physical situation. But when the victim proves to be injured other psychological factors supervene. Humour is not an isolable reaction. Humour is human. The Jew-joke, on the other hand, is sadism: is only describable as human, if a very crude definition of humanity be extrapolated. But it is sociologically important in the following sense: that, whereas many social movements begin and end with satire and irony—rather than with a sermon and song, as Brailsford has it—endemic anti-Semitism begins, continues, and does not end, with Jew-jokes. But how humourless can a Jew become? *Sufficit ad diem.* . . .

Of the Jewish jokes proper, many are, as was suggested above, jokes made more humorous than their content warrants (and the content can be very funny) by the circumstances of group eccentricity, and the sympathetic affection that this stimulates. So they could be Irish jokes, or the jokes of any minority, living its private life self-consciously. Only their idiom isolates them. But to say that is to say a lot. The Jewish idiom, whether it enters into the form of language, of gesture, or sing-song intonation, of funny appearance, or of recognized awkward situation, carries with it the element of laughter that is roused by the presentation of the dear familiar. So if one is told an elaborate account of why the rich man won't tell the time (because it might lead to the marriage of his daughter with a poor man who hasn't got a watch); or of the traveller who works out precisely the identity of the man opposite him, and when asked how he knows says: "It's obvious": or of the other traveller who calls the stranger a liar, "because he said he was going to Vilna—and he really is going to Vilna!" if one is told any of these anecdotes in Jewish phrase or setting, one recognizes the Jewishness of the story because of the familiar "style" that is presented. The fact that the stories could be translated into the idiom of other groups does not prevent them from being Jewish stories when they are about Jews and true to Jews.

In point are the many stories about the marriage-broker (Shadchan). He endeavours to persuade the simple youth of the merits of the bride. "But she is deaf." "Excellent! She can't hear scandal about you." "She has an impediment." "My dear sir, a wife who can't talk." "She can't see." "Do you want her to watch you?" "She's lame." "Can't run after you!" "She's not young." "So you'll be left to your own devices." "She has a hump." "My dear sir, can't a person have a defect? Do you expect perfection?" Again, the Jewish mother-in-law may differ little from other mothers-in-law; but her account of her daughter's lovely life with an indulgent husband, and her son's terrible life with an exacting wife (who really lives exactly as the daughter) is rejoiced in by Jews as true to a type they know, even though an intellectual can translate it all into Irish. Perhaps more exclusively Jewish is the study by an American Yiddish writer, of a widow, seeking a second husband—so good that my first husband will boast about him to his fellow Tsaddikim in Paradise. Stories of this type, at a lower level than the humour of Solomon Maimon's father, are describable as not necessarily Jewish. But they take place against a background familiar to Jews, and in well-told narrative (especially Yiddish narrative) there are overtones of sympathetic feeling, undertones of appreciative thought.

Very much appreciated—at times—is CHUTZPAH, an impudence without the wickedness that characterizes, *LEHAVDIL*, a claim by a barbarian to compensation for damage that he has wrought. Chutzpah is in the reply of the beggar who, being told: "You've been here an hour ago", shrugged and said, "They say that all the poor have the same face"! A stronger story is of the man who raised money when he said that he desperately needed medical aid. When it was discovered that he was really in good health, he protested: "My dear sir, would you really prefer me to be ill?" This Chutzpah differs from sheer impudence because there is an argument in it that appeals.

The common factor in Jewish humour is a measure of intellectual appreciation. This is heightened by the readiness of allusion on the Jewish tongue or the Jewish pen. When Sholom Aleichem describes, amusingly enough, the misery on the faces of the sheep owned by the poor crofter, he also records their bleat: MEH—MEH. He interprets: MEH ONU . . . MEH CHAYENU (what are we: what are our lives?) The quotation from the liturgy adds a delight for those familiar with it.

This suggests the reflection that much Jewish humour is almost inseparable from wit: is wit with sympathetic laughter, rather than derision. It is obvious that the people of Peshat are people apt in all the verbal felicities.

Wit is an intellectual operation—a clever revelation of implications or of relationships—which may even be incapable of stimulating laughter; or the laughter can be derisory. The rich ignoramus, sitting in the Synagogue next to the visiting Rabbi, tried to make conversation: "Why does it say 'Man and Beast will God preserve'? Why does Beast stand next to Man?" Said the Rabbi: "Ask the beadle". That is a verbal exploitation. (The verse has a meaning unguessed by the questioner.) One laughs at it. A more "situational" appreciation of ignorance is conjured by the story of the Yeshuvnik (Jew living in the wilds, and presumed to be very unlearned) who is celebrating the Passover Seder with the aid of a Machzor for the Day of Atonement. Consequently, instead of reciting a list of ten plagues, he reads an alphabetical list of sins (of which there are more than twenty). On being asked by his son: "Why so many plagues this year?" he meditates and suggests: "Probably because it's a Leap Year".

That story differs from the preceding as humour differs from wit—as a situational appreciation differs from a verbal or conceptual one. But in Jewish life this distinction is very hard to draw.

Among intellectuals particularly so. Thus, when Rabbi Loeb Shapero of Kovno wished to criticize the saintly Rabbi Israel Lipkin (Salanter) for founding a special Synagogue (a MUSARSTIEBEL) for the disciples in his moral movement, the critic quoted the Psalm (CXXXV.19): "House of Israel, Bless the Lord: House of Aaron, Bless the Lord: House of Levi, Bless the Lord: Ye that fear the Lord, Bless the Lord". Everyone has houses: but the text seems to tell us that those who fear the Lord do not require a special house. In that Pshettel (inspired, possibly, by the Midrash Rabbah) we have an exercise of wit which is also an ironical comment. The appreciation of it involves not only verbal appreciation, but that self-consciousness, and that knowledge of the subtleties of situation, and that modulation of seriousness, that go to make irony.

Irony we saw, too, in Mendele's account of his imbroglio with Yaknehaz. Irony is abundant even in that more boisterous humorist Sholom Aleichem,[1] when he pictures a dedicated ne'er-do-well explaining to a different type of unfortunate all the mysteries of the Stock Exchange, and the way to get rich there. Readers of Sholom Aleichem, being acquainted with the elaborate formulae of Hebrew letter-writing, find special pleasure in the writing of the speculator's spouse. "To the distinguished, pious, learned, wise, Menachem Mendel, may his candle burn . . . You idiot . . ." But Sholom Aleichem is more than a writer of farce. He recaptures in his work the irony that the Jew

[1] Mark Twain to Mendele's Dickens has been suggested—inexactly!

385

experiences when he is the victim of Gentile stupidity, especially the stupidity of not entirely vicious bureaucrats. In point is the brilliant story, *Shachmatist*, which relates how a cobbler's skill at chess gets him invited to see the Tsar: and the only way of conveying a Jew to Saint Petersburg was in a "chain-gang". The writer contrives a light-heartedness, as of those to whom worse things happen, equally arbitrarily: very much in the spirit of Gogol.

It may be suggested that writers like Abramovitch (Mendele) and Rabinovitch (Sholom Aleichem) were influenced by the Russian humorists; of whom it is said that they smile through unseen tears: to a lesser degree by Western examples—by Dickens, by Mark Twain. Perhaps it is also true to suggest that ghetto life, seen through Jewish spectacles only, was not congenial to easy laughter at situations. There were few situations to laugh at. The Middle Ages, says Zunz, did not close for the Jews until 1800. It may be added that their Middle Ages were also Dark Ages, and the Dark Ages did not terminate at 1800.

In the years since 1800, it may be true to say that Russian Jewry, inspired by Russian example, contrived to express something of the irony that is experienced by the strugglers, with more or less success, to live under a despotism, as fish may live among the nets. The interstices of escape are the corruptions, the human corruptions, of the bureaucracy. So there is plenty of laughter through the tears of Gogol and the sweat of Gorki. If Mendele and Sholom Aleichem have models and masters, they are probably in the tradition of Russian humour—which, happily, is not extinct even under the new, less corruptible, bureaucrats.[1]

So Sholom Aleichem's stories of the lazy train that foiled

[1] If Jewish humour owes something to the Russian, the debt is repaid—to America. Modern American humour makes use of Jewish idiom, words like Nebbich, Schlimmazol, Kibbitzer, etc., and Jewish sarcasm—"a politician, yet . . ." "need it like a hole in the head", etc. etc.

the pogromists, or of the youth who was dragged to enlist-
ment when he had already been rejected, these are experiences that would be understood—if sufficiently explained—
by the villagers who waited for Gogol's Revisor. This
section of literary humour is, however, a phenomenon that
is only possible when, through the darkness, chinks of light
are discernible and widening. In most of Jewish history the
darkness has been Egyptian. In a few centres there has been
light, and there laughter. But in the masses the atmosphere
has been such that the Jew could well be thought miserable
and humourless—people without laughter. That they had
some laughter is one of their many miracles.

Jewish life has, admittedly, been lived in environments
very different from those that the muses of play have created
in the present. There was a stern Psalmist who claimed that
he had never sat in the company of scoffers. There were
Rabbis who regarded playboys—dicers, pigeon-racers—
as untrustwothy in testimony.

But there is abundant evidence, from at least the periods
of relaxed pressure, that the Jews can laugh. The Talmud is
quite rich in ribaldry and the Rabelaisian.

Rabbi Ishmael ben Jose and Rabbi Eleazar ben Simeon
were so impressive in girth that when they stood in contact,
facing each other in conversation, a yoke of oxen could be
driven between them without touching them. A Roman
matron said to them, "Your children are not yours".
"Our wives", they replied, "are equally large." "That proves
what I say," she retorted. To which one of them answered,
"Love conquers the flesh." (T.B. Baba Mezia 84a.) It is a
far cry from Rabbi Ishmael ben Jose to Chaucer's plump
Wife of Bath displaying the sign *Amor vincit omnia*: but the
elements of humanity that make for laughter do not change
much in the generations.[1]

[1] It should be added that one of the editors of the Talmud inserts
an alternative tradition: that the Rabbis did not answer the Roman

There is something quite modernly sophisticated in the story (already mentioned) of the reception given in Tiberias to the visiting genius from Babylon. "The lion of Babylon is upon you", they said to the local disputant: but when the disputation had developed, one of the locals commented "This lion that you spoke about seems to have become a fox".

As they could exaggerate—and their accounts of the loves of Zimri show how they can exaggerate—so they could deflate exaggerations.

Reading between the lines of the Talmudim and Midrashim the student can suspect, without disrespect, that the stories of the Aggadists were being enjoyed as amusing narrative. How Solomon captured Asmodeus, with the aid of a formula, and harnessed him for the purposes of travel and culture: but found himself, when the formula had lost its efficacy, stranded in a distant desert: this must have stimulated to mirth the Rabbis who disliked Solomon. How that same Solomon tricked the hoopoe-bird by putting glass over its nest and causing it to drop the SHOMIR—the stone (or worm) which could penetrate all stones and metals —is at once a funny story and a neat account of how the king managed to build the altar without the use of axes.

In the course of centuries there has been abundance of Jewish wit: and much laughter—including some of the coarsest. The barnstormers aping Rabbis—reciting the

matron. It is also suggested, *contra*, that they were obliged to: but it is hard to see any reason other than the demands of pleasantry.

One is reminded of the conflict in Proverbs XXVI. vv.4 and 5. "Answer not a fool according to his folly, lest thou also be like unto him." "Answer a fool according to his folly, lest he be wise in his own eyes." Rabbinic exposition is that the second verse applies to doctrinal and religious matters, the first verse to the secular. Evidently the issue is the importance of the fool's error to himself and others.

Was it necessary for the Rabbis to rebut a jocular imputation on the legitimacy of their children? Probably the "necessity" was the "social", or the demand that any witticism makes upon the wit.

prayers for indelicate occasions—are the most ancient and most modern,[1] and coarsest, developments. So when, during the late days of the Mandate, a performer came on to the Israel stage praying, and, seeing a soldier, pronounced (from the liturgy) "behold our affliction", he was recapturing the spirit of people who found laughter even in their most solemn books and institutions.

That the Jews can laugh genuinely is to be expected from their mental richness. Laughter comes to the rich mind in relief and relaxation. The psychology of Jewish scholars was not appreciated by Thomas Carlyle—for all his scholarship—when he wrote (in his essay on Mohammed) of "that deadly terrible earnestness of the Jews", and opined that the Arabs added to it "something graceful and brilliant which is not Jewish". Carlyle's utterance could not have been made by any one familiar with Jewish literature, or with the vast Jewish contribution to Arab literature.

To those who read the Bible understandingly there is a happiness in it shining at times through the solemnity. Sarah laughs in her tent when she hears the angelic communication. Was that only mockery—the ridiculing of an impossibility? Or was it in the good Jewish tradition of Epithalamian rejoicing, witnessed by Jeremiah? the cries of joy hailing the bridal processions through the streets of Jerusalem. The same tradition is expressed, too celibately, in the Rabbinic rules for dancing in front of the bride, and medievally in BADCHANUS, the lore of the Wedding Jester with his extempore rhymes, riddles and rhodomontade.[2]

But the Bible story writers, being preoccupied with misfortune, had little incentive to laughter; little repose. They

[1] Purim Spieler are in an ancient tradition.

[2] Ingenious rhymes cause laughter to readers of Byron and Gilbert. Some Badchanus is of this type. At a higher level clever riddles are a feature of Jewish literature. The Ibn Ezras are responsible for many.

were not at ease in Zion: because the destiny of Zion has never been emancipated from anxiety.

If God "laughed at Egypt" (so Rashi translates the verse Exodus X.2) the laughter was scornful, was not sympathetic. And scornful is the jesting of Elijah: "Call him louder, perhaps he is on a journey". His enemy Ahab was also capable of a sort of humour when he said to his princely ally: "Let not the one who girds on his armour boast like the one who doffs it".

The Biblical occasions were not for irony. Not high in sophistication are the jests of the ruffian Samson—the Jewish Apollo.[1] His pranks are sadistic in a good cause. But when his real strength of character is invoked the irony is tragic. "Let my spirit perish with the Philistines." At that moment he is speaking across the ages and the sea for Aeschylus and Sophocles (and the English Milton) to hear.

Art has been called the laughter of the gods. But the forces of the spirit do not often inspire the art of laughter.

If Jews laugh and have laughed, it is because they are all too human, because they have been able to treat their Torah as not in heaven. When the Jewish humorist pictures his Jew praying along the wayside, addressing phrases from the Psalms by way of aside to his horse, he is demonstrating one of the secrets of salvation of the Jew, that they could take their solemnity into the heart of life, and treasure it without losing affection or respect. As a Chassidic Rabbi said of his noisy garrulous congregants: even on their most important commercial occasions they utter an occasional word of prayer.

---

[1] Samson is derived from SHEMESH, the sun. Delilah suggests "the night", cutting off the rays.

CHAPTER NINE

OF SOLUTION AND RESOLUTION

A T the time of this writing it seems that those who cried
out from the narrow places have been vouchsafed a
spacious reply. To some of the wanderers a destina-
tion: to those lacking purpose at least the consciousness
that they inhere in a life, not a mere "tale that is told".

Herzl called Palestine Altneuland: and in that expression
communicated that his dream was not the new "good idea"
of a European publicist. The question is not of Herzl's
theoretical antecedents, though, in Russia, modern Zionism
was growing more than a century ago. More important is it
to observe that the movement is not superimposed from
without, but canalizes and harmonizes many trends of
thought in a way typical of the Jewish Mind.

Zionism is deep-rooted in Jewish history: in a sense is the
essence of it. History, in fact, frustrated the idea, and made it
retreat into the Messianic imagery that moved in the deep
layers of Jewish memory. That it lived in more than empty
imaginings we know from such lives as that of Judah Halévy
who not only sang of Zion, but sacrificed his life in journey-
ing to it. Yet for centuries Zionism was in the category of
those verbal concepts which do not become practical until
history evolves practical conditions in which they can
translate themselves into action. As more than two millennia
separated a statement of Atomism from the marshalling of

atomic forces, so the Zionist aspiration could not be realized until the ages of transport and organization and money and political expression gave it a framework and a context. Then when the practical prospect dawned it was tragically natural that the Jew who prayed for Zion should say: "this is not it". Like love in the poem of the Anglo-Jewish poet already quoted, Zionism seemed to come "when life had said 'it's late' ".

Obviously Zionist activity on any significant scale could not take place until Jews were free to move: free, in the political, free in the economic, sense, free, psychologically, from the notion that life was a choice of ghettoes.[1] They had to be free, too, from the scholastic tradition that the Jews would never be farmers or shepherds again: that Resh Lakish could not leap back!

Of the events of Zionism too much is common history to require recapitulation. Of the Bilu and Lovers of Zion, and of the support they found in the imaginative French Rothschild, the evidences are to be found in settlements that are now centres of high civilization. That synthesis would perhaps make a proper conclusion to Isaac Peretz's sketch of the *Four Wills*. Zionism gave to the fourth generation something better than nirvana.

Zionism came to all levels of Jewry as a subject-matter of life. In the rich *bourgeois* centres, it eventually became a more satisfactory means of expression and path to honour than the organization of communal charity. Also it was the kind of cause to which those who espouse it for prestige find themselves becoming dedicated.

---

[1] Of what Palestine was like when its Jewish population consisted in those who had gone there to end their days, or to weep by the wailing wall, a good picture is available to English readers in Kinglake's *Eothen*, written over a century ago. One wonders what that slightly unfriendly man would have thought of modern Jerusalem where Jews live as well as pray.

Of Solution and Resolution

One of the marvels embodied in Zionism is precisely this: that through it the idealists of a new aspiration were able to harness the baser forces of the ghetto to their purposes. Zionism yoked the honour-seekers of the klein-städtel to a cause, and made them worthy of it.[1] And Jewry was fortunate at that time, for it was able to find great leaders to give example: men like Herzl, Nordau, Weizmann, Sokolow, and a host of not lesser orators, not lesser enthusiasts, who were able to kindle the rank and file with the belief that now was the time for more than parochial aims, for more than parochial efforts, for work as well as prayer, for generosity greater than charity.

In the person of Herzl Zionism was a triumph of modernity: a triumph of journalism, in an age which projects the publicist into statesmanship. Before the late nineteenth century it was unthinkable that anyone below the highest levels of diplomacy could approach such potentates as the Sultan of the Turkish Empire. But the nineteenth century

[1] The Jewish propaganda has been that Zionism was more than a Charity, was a duty. This is of publicistic value only. More serious for the Zionists were the opinions of the House of Lords that the Jewish National Fund was not a charity for tax purposes. It is of interest that one of the Law Lords then present was known to be unfriendly to Jewry. Apropos of this, let it be said that the Law Courts of England have been both friendly and unfriendly to the Jewish standpoint. Appellate Courts have rebuked judges for referring to Jews as if they were essentially cunning or bad citizens. On the other hand, Jews making wills insisting that their beneficiaries retain, or marry in, the Jewish faith, have been, on occasion, thwarted by judges who argued that the phrase was vague—although at least one jurist has repudiated this. On more than one occasion the British House of Lords has spoken well of Jewry; it has defended a poor Jew against an oppressive insurance Company (Glicksman's case). For the rest, since the J.N.F. decision, a different practice has resulted in Zionist funds being treated as charitable contributions. Let it be remembered, for favour, that the re-entry of Jewry to England was through the paths of judicial findings— English Halacha.

witnessed the travels of Moses Montefiore. The spirit of
that age—embodying itself in the powerful personality of
Theodor Herzl—proved itself strong enough to break
through the obscure portals of the Ottoman and make
claim to something that lay beyond. An even more important factor is the rise of Jews to significance in the life and
councils of the West. The story of Weizmann is of one who
saw the potentialities of English sympathy. In a coincidence
not far removed from miracle, this scientist of skill and
originality was able to render practical services to the land
that had won his affection. In return, his voice was listened
to with respect in the high councils.[1] It is too early to
decide whether the Anglophilism that this generated in him
was one of his trials or one of his errors. The rest of the
historic narrative is typical of the Jewish tragedy. A world
disaster, and the vastest pogrom in history, made Zionists of
those to whom the idea had been fanciful, if not ridiculous.
The force that sent the German *Kultur Jude* to work alongside the *schmutzige Ostjude*, whom he despised, was the most
violent pulsation of those permanent forces that repeatedly
make all Israel into comrades. It was as if, in return for the
work of the Jew Ehrlich, who cured one German disease,
a new German disease gave, at least to German Jewry, a new
Ehrlichkeit.

But the struggle for Zion having been won—or one stage
of victory gained—it remains to be said that the spiritual
problems of Jewry have not ceased. Weizmann declared (in

[1] Weizmann is a great name for too many reasons to allow of enu-
meration. One that is worth mentioning is that in 1904 he, against the
wish of Herzl, refused the offer of Uganda as a place for the Jews.
Although he was not himself orthodox, he was steeped in Jewish feeling.
The Jew from Pinsk knew the Jews better than did the Viennese
Kulturmensch.

An amusing footnote to this is that it was left to the proconsulate
of a Jew, named Cohen, for the affairs of innocent Uganda to be
thoroughly bedevilled.

effect) to the Peel Commission that, given a haven for Jews in Palestine, those who did not avail themselves of that shelter would be left with the melancholy prospect of inevitable liquidation. In the long reaches of history, this may be true (though small groups die hard!). In the present, Zion is what it has always been, a segment of the exile, a bastion of the exile: a strong fortress; but spiritually and materially continuous with the life of the overwhelming majority of Jewry in the outer world.

What we have here is a new (typically Jewish) synthesis, out of which have crystallized new problems—or old problems in a new form. This is not a land flowing with milk and honey. It is not a green pasture for the kindly shepherding of the spiritual. Its pathways are not yet peace —or perfection. Its roads ascend to Jerusalem, not like the palm-strewn paths of pilgrims, but like a mechanized army on the march. Over its streams Resh Lakish has to leap back from beside Rabbi Jochanan, and try to recapture his gladiatorial strength. In this land a Jew is generated whom the gentler spirits of the Exile may find too stern, and unyielding in endeavours that have not been conventional Jewish aims.

In this land are latent all the problems that are implied in the words "stiffnecked people". For here authority has to be exerted, as it was in the time of the Hashmoneans. That authority the Jew who is not in danger finds it hard to accept or trust.

We have it from the Rabbis that the "air of the land makes wise". We are told that the walls of Jerusalem are infinitely expansive, so that no pilgrim can ever say: the place is too small. Those statements are not supported by geographers. But there is this truth in them that the idealist in Jewry—and Jewry is rich in idealists—manifests a wisdom there, and expresses an acceptance. That fact is the secret of Israeli success. But what of the Erev Rav? the mixed mass that treks through the desert? Will they demand the fish they ate in England, or America, or places inferior to those? And what of the emancipated slaves? those who revolt against all *bourgeois* conventions, and justify a looseness of life by a glib use of the formulae of modern ideology. They are free citizens; and who can coerce them? Even in the higher strata, the forces that generate ideals do not last for ever. The Jew follows a leader who is Judas Maccabeus—but can too easily be persuaded that it is Jannaeus. A Western publicist (Harold Laski)[1]—declared that the Jew can play Trotsky to Lenin, but is not to be trusted with the leadership. Even though he confessed that that judgement was based upon a somewhat superficial assessment of Manchester Jewry, he was expressing, in his judgement, an unfortunately typical Jewish mistrust: a mistrust of Jew by Jew, which, however unjustified, remains a psychological fact. At the political level, the psychological conflicts are not made easier by that tradition in Zionism which periodically favours the new ally at the expense of the old. So the old Zionist accepted, in places of honour, old opponents who now took office in the Agency: and in turn the Agency accepted the blandishments of those that had been its opponents; and, in so doing, may well have slighted its own rank and file. That the un-Zionist Einstein could have been President of Israel is a strange comment on Jewish loyalties. That he did not accept the office is a tribute to his own personal greatness.

Psychologically akin to this valuing of outsiders is the fact that Jews, in this century as in previous centuries, are notoriously ungenerous to zealots, except in times of extreme peril. The great fighter and orator, Jabotinsky, died among the forgotten men: and *Real Politik* was cynical at the expense of terrorists, even when they were helping

[1] Who happens to have supervised the "education" of some of the present governors of Israel.

to establish the State. It may well be, however, that the moderation of the moderate counts, in the long run, for more than loyalty. Indeed, in the very long reaches of time, many who have failed to support the Zealots have proved better friends to the ultimate cause.

One problem inside Israel is that, without (as it is hoped) the urgencies of danger, and without the strong impulses of religion (for Zionist leadership is Secular Socialist), the morale, the discipline, the obedience must be maintained of masses educated in doubt and criticism. Here democracy reveals its quintessential difficulties. In that democracy a tradition requires to be wrought which shall make the citizens aware that their lives are part of something larger and more important than themselves. Jews have been capable of accepting such a tradition. They have also been capable of rejecting it. (That such rejection is not always mere intransigence is attested in the familiar utterance that every good Jew is a Revisionist at heart.)

Between the Jew outside Israel and the State itself other problems obtain. There are allies who want (not always for selfish reasons) a share in the councils. There are councillors who insist on shaping the destinies themselves. Both evidently right. But the conflict of rights can be as bitter as the conflict of wrongs. That the happy relationship of the two orders of Jewry is vital to Jewry must be emphasized now: because now, for the first time on a political scale, the citizen of any nation can find his local patriotism strained by his group devotion. If that strain exists, it should, at least, be spiritually justified.

That, in this situation, the material of conflict exists is an unhappy truth, not to be denied. And here, incidentally, apologetic is no more useful to Israel than it is to Jewry in general.

In Zion there are social cleavages; Jews who are Communists, Jews who are Socialists, Jews who are free-enterprisers.

Happily, the Jewish doctrine that "the hand of the worker is uppermost" can reconcile Jews to the demands of governing Socialists. (It is not an ethical equivalence.) More serious, perhaps, is the cleavage between Jews who are religious, and Jews who are irreligious.

The State of Israel, officially secular—if anything bound to the word "Jewish" can be secular—is in reality theocratically moulded: and, though its citizens include Christians and Moslems, the theocracy is of a Jewish species—expressed in Jewish forms.

The culture of the country is "on the Bible". The Sabbath and Festivals are official occasions. Jewish learning is of State concern. Yet much is done to cause, or enable, extremely orthodox Jews to revolt against what they hold to be blasphemy. The situation of the Jerusalemites who regard themselves as outside the State is not one that can be dismissed as the position of cranks or fanatics. As it was to Jeremiah, so it is to all Jews now, an important question: "What are they doing in the streets of Jerusalem?" If they are worshipping Apollo in some modern way, there is something understandable in the orthodox antagonism. If they are receiving, with favour, the trading emissaries of Amalek, antagonism without orthodoxy is also understandable.

The present position of Zion is not denigrated by the proposition that no one is at ease in it. Zion was never a place of ease. The need is for an ethos and a discipline expressive of all that is best in Jewish life, and capable of raising the morale of those who come to it, or look to it for inspiration. Such a place must be strong not weak: and capable of not surrendering to the doubter within, as it has not succumbed to the enemy without. Zion and Zionism, then, do not in themselves offer a solution. They constitute rather a Resolution. The moral resources that are needed to fulfil it are within the capacity of the Jewish Mind.

CHAPTER TEN

CODA TO THE JEWISH SYMPHONY

Now let the reader ask: after all these wanderings in the realms of gold, and base metal, have we discovered that there is a Jewish Mind? and do we know what contribution it can make to the common wealth of the modern world?

To the first question I do not know the answer. What seems to be proved is that Jews have always rejoiced in the things of the mind, and have organized their lives and their laws in many intellectual ways.

As to the second question, an answer is easier to frame. Although we have been concerned with Jewish thinking inside the Jewish circle, we have found that circle to be one of the spheres that harmonize the void.

Since the days when the great Amora Samuel declared that the ways of the stars were as clear to him as the ways of Nehardaa, the Jews have manifested a constant urge to creativity in all the orders of thought.

But what they specially contribute is, paradoxically, not some profound analysis, or some revolutionary scientific discovery. Rather is it in the nature of a homely, practical wisdom that warns intellect of its dangers. The Jew plunges into the delights of science for its own sake, as his ancestors plunged into the Torah. But if he retains something of the tradition of that Torah, he remembers that the teaching is inseparable from the ways of the world. He remembers that the learning of the Chover leads to righteousness: to kindness, charity, humanity. He remembers, that is to say, the truth that the activity of the mind is, properly, a spiritual activity; and that, in whatever doubts and confusions he may find himself involved in his quest for ultimates, he, the searcher, or researcher, is the custodian of some value whose nature is certain, even though its description is permanently uncertain.

If, then, the Jew—Israel Jew or Golus Jew—acting in science, or the Jew engaged in the work of a world that is increasingly organized according to the techniques of the physical sciences, retains some vestige of Jewish identity, whatever that is, he will, to that extent, be preserving his material order against the terrifying nothingness that would supervene in him if the spirit, and things spiritual, were to vanish from his picture of reality.

So long as the Jewish intellect remains in some sense Jewish, for so long we are assured that one spirit, at least, is moving in the void and giving it shape. And if the tradition goes on, we can also be sure that among human beings, there will always be some city of refuge for human feelings: some place where one can distinguish between sacred and profane, between good and evil, between the custodians of the "extra soul" and those miserable ones to whom any soul is a sorry illusion treasured by refugee exiles from some effete aristocracy.

INDEX

Index

Index

Index

406

Index

Index

Index

413

Index

Prophecy and Priesthood, 121
Prophet and Prophecy, 84n, 129, 171, 236n
Prophetesses, 288, 288n
Prophets, 59n, 70, 81, 88, 91, 92, 98n, 100n, 116, 116n, 119, 121, 123, 124, 147n, 170, 205, 288
Prophets, Minor, 170n
Proportional Representation, 179n
Prosbul, 126
Prose, 91, 96, 97, 98, 108
Prosperity, 305
Protestants, 297, 379
Protestantism, British, 13
"Protocols of Zion", 331n
Proust, 375
Provence, 218, 218n
Proverbs, Book of, 184, 202, 229n, 271n, 275n, 288
Providence, 186, 186n, 230, 245
Psalmist, 206
Psalms, 15, 61n, 63n, 77, 89, 92, 98, 100n
Pseudepigrapha, 218, 233n
Pseudo-Messiahs, 188n, 258, 296, 371n
Pshettel, 48n
Psychiatrist, 317
Psychology, 110, 254, 280, 284, 293, 295n, 304, 307, 309, 310, 310n, 311, 312, 314, 315, 316, 322, 327, 328, 330, 334, 336, 337, 348, 353, 354, 355, 358, 360, 368, 389, 396
Ptolemy, 218, 245
Pumpeditha, 128, 129, 223
Punishment, 229, 231, 236n, 239, 241n
Punning, homiletical, 48n
Purgatory, 279n
Purim, 285n
Puritans, 105
Pyrrhonism, 260
Pythagoras, 248
Pythagoreans, 81

Queen of Sheba, 28n

Rab José, 155
Rab Shesheth, 176
Rab Simlai, 234
Rabbenu, Isaiah, 116n
Rabbenu, Tam, 11n, 75, 156n, 228n
Rabbi, The, 71, 128, 143, 364, 365, 366
Rabbi, non-professional, 118n
Rabbinic, Greek, 148, 166
Rabbinism, 230
Rabbis, Modern Jewish, 132
Rabelais, 377
Rabinovitch, Rabbi, 154n

Rachel, 54, 54n, 95, 95n, 100n
Racine, 11
Rahab, 289n
Raphael, 81
Rappoport, 111, 227, 256, 373
Rashi, 15n, 40, 46, 46n, 50, 50n, 51, 51n, 52, 64, 75, 80, 84n, 99n, 112n, 156n, 390
Ratio decidendi, 150 et seq
Rationalism, 97, 191, 209
Rationalization of Scripture, 263n
Rav, 107
Reade, 110
Reading of the Law, 287n
Rebecca, 51n
Red Heifers, 120n
Red Sea (Reed Sea), 50, 55, 81, 102
Reductio ad Absurdum, 150, 150n
Refinement, 353
Reformation, The, 65, 179
Reform Movements, 60n, 195
Reinach, 248, 314n
Religion an Opiate, 300n
Rembrandt, 91
Remez, 61, 62n
"Remnant", 24, 296
Renaissance, 223, 352
Renan, 111n
Repentance, 173n, 243n, 271, 272
Repudiation, Levirate, 292n
Resh Lakish, 33, 33n, 47n, 109n, 233n, 271, 271n, 349, 350
Reshevsky, 354n
Reshut Harabbim ve Hayochid, 152
Responsibility, age of, 265n
Restoration, The, 13
Resurrection, 57, 139, 232, 236n
Retribution, 165, 222, 240
Return from exile, The, 124
Reuben, 91
Reubeni, 188n
Reuchlin, 294n
Revelation, 225, 226, 236n
Revolution, 302
Revolution, The French, 110
Revolutionaries, 187
Reward, 229, 231, 236n, 239, 240
Rhineland, 218
Richard I, 12, 23
Righteousness, 117n, 171, 183
Ritual, 137, 188, 198, 226, 227, 228, 228n, 256, 345
Ritualism, 294
Robles Case, 13n
Roman Catholics, 99n, 201
Roman Empire, 178
Roman law, 153 et seq

414

Index

Index

Validity, criterion of, 192
Vandals, 303
Vayikra Rabbah, 24n
Venice, 54n
Vespasian, 141
Vilna, 236n
Vindication, God's, of Right, 169n
Violin, 90n
Virgil, 95n
Virtues and Vices linked with senses, 214n
Vision of God, 203
Vocalization ("Pointing"), 153, 153n
Volozhyn, 295n
Volunteers, Jewish in War, 356
Vowel Forms, 251n
Vulgate, 90n, 377

Wailing Wall, 392n
Wandering Jews, 32n, 202
Wandering Spirits, 256
Warsaw, 349
Washington, Booker, 321n
Webb, Sidney, 311
Weidman, 374
Weiss, Rabbi, 145n, 147n, 271n
Weizmann, 324n, 394, 394n
Welensky, Roy, 320n
Welfare States, 301
Wellhausen, 95, 119, 122n
Weltschmerz, 113, 326, 355
Wesker, 375
Wesseley, 97
White, Bishop William, 114n
Widow, 291, 291n, 292n
Widow, childless, marriage of, 147n
Wigs, 198-9, 199n, 286
William, Saint, of Norwich, 22n, 88
Wine, red, abstention from, 193n
Wisdom Literature, 206, 218
Wit, 267n, 384
Witch-Hunting, 309n, 314n
Witches, 273n
Witness, false, 136, 137n, 161
Witnesses, 157, 158, 161, 162, 163, 164, 273n, 291. See also "Hazomo"

Wolfe, Humbert, 323n
Women, Duties of, 287, 287n
Women's Rights, 290
Women, treatment of, 275n, 285, 285n, 286, 287, 287n, 288, 289, 292
Word of God (logos), 219
Work, age to begin, 265n
Working man, Western, 310
World War, Second, 271n
Wouk, 375
Wyclif, 60

Yavneh, 71, 128, 135, 146n, 266
Yechiel, Asher ben, 135n
Yesh Aym le Mikra, 47
Yeshiva, 16, 86
Yetser Haro, 61, 217
Yiddish-land, 22, 24, 168
Yiddish language, 17, 23n, 24n, 40, 41, 60n, 91, 97, 105, 106n, 108n, 113n, 219, 289, 290, 300n, 369
Yitschaki, Rabbi Shlomo—see "Rashi"
York Massacre, 22

Zadok and Baithus, 139
Zadok High Priest, 133n
Zadokites, 133n
Zangwill, Israel, 100, 103n, 140n, 200, 249n, 344, 361, 373, 374
Zealots, 56, 58n, 94, 127, 333n
Zeitgeist, 247
Zelophehad, 131, 131n
Zemiroth, 107
Zephaniah, 170n
Zimri, 55, 56n, 127n, 388
Zionism, 21, 154n, 179n, 188, 195, 261n, 311, 323, 323n, 324, 332, 333, 336, 347, 373, 391, 392, 393
Zipporah, 55n, 121n
Zohar, 82, 208, 209, 213, 216, 229n, 251, 251n
Zola, 320n
Zoroastrians, 185, 256
Zunz, 111, 227

INDEX OF SCRIPTURE AND N.T. REFERENCES

INDEX OF REFERENCES TO TALMUD BABLI